D0984337

The Beat Generation

THE MAGILL BIBLIOGRAPHIES

The Beat Generation

A Bibliographical Teaching Guide

William Lawlor

Magill Bibliographies

The Scarecrow Press, Inc.
Lanham, Md., & London
and
Salem Press
Pasadena, Calif., & Englewood Cliffs, N.J.
1998

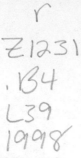

SCARECROW PRESS, INC.

Published in the United States of America
by Scarecrow Press, Inc.
4720 Boston Way
Lanham, Maryland 20706

4 Pleydell Gardens, Folkestone
Kent CT20 2DN, England

British Library Cataloguing in Publication Information Available

Library of Congress Cataloging-in-Publication Data

Lawlor, William, 1951–
    The beat generation / William Lawlor.
            p.   cm. — (Magill bibliographies)
    Includes index.
    ISBN 0-8108-3387-5 (acid-free paper)
    1. Beat generation—Bibliography. 2. American literature—20th
century—History and criticism—Bibliography. 3. American
literature—20th century—Bibliography. I. Title. II. Series.
    Z1231.B4L39   1998
[PS228.B6]
016.8109'11—dc21   98-3157
                                                              CIP

ISBN 0-8108-3387-5 (cloth : alk. paper)

for

Lillian Elizabeth Jeffs Lawlor

and

Edward James Lawlor

CONTENTS

ACKNOWLEDGMENTS

These persons have kindly and graciously given of their time to comment on the study and teaching of the Beats and to contribute to the gathering of information on the teaching of the Beats.

Kate Anderson, Albertson Learning Resources Center, Stevens Point, Wisconsin
Colleen Angel, Albertson Learning Resources Center, Stevens Point, Wisconsin
Gordon Ball, Virginia Military Institute
Marjorie Berlincourt, National Endowment for the Humanities
Ann Charters, University of Connecticut-Storrs
Barbara Cranford, sculptor and poet in Central Wisconsin
Richard Doxtator, Department of English, University of Wisconsin–Stevens Point
Dave Engel, Beat scholar, Rudolph, Wisconsin
Russ Haine, Beat scholar, Stevens Point, Wisconsin
Gary Handman, Media Center, University of California, Berkeley
Bobby Louise Hawkins, Naropa Institute
Hilary Holladay, University of Massachusetts–Lowell
Ron Janoff, New York University
Ronna C. Johnson, Tufts University
Robert Jordan, Northeast Louisiana University
Arthur and Kit Knight, Beat scholars, Petaluma, California
Jim Lawlor, Beat brother, Stevens Point, Wisconsin
David Meltzer, New College of California
Philip Milito, the Berg Collection, New York Public Library
Christine Neidleine, Albertson Learning Resources Center, Stevens Point, Wisconsin
Barb Paul, Albertson Learning Resources Center, Stevens Point, Wisconsin
Rodney Phillips, the Berg Collection, New York Public Library

Barbara Richards, Special Collections, Memorial Library, Madison, Wisconsin
Robin E. Rider, Special Collections, Memorial Library, Madison, Wisconsin
Mardee Rose, Department of English, University of Wisconsin – Stevens Point
Jill Rosenshield, Special Collections, Memorial Library, Madison, Wisconsin
Linette Schuler, Albertson Learning Resources Center, Stevens Point, Wisconsin
Rani Singh, Assistant to Allen Ginsberg and Bob Rosenthal
Michael Skau, University of Nebraska at Omaha
Jennie Skerl, West Chester University
A. J. Sobczak, Project Editor, Salem Press
Susan Sparapani, Albertson Learning Resources Center, Stevens Point, Wisconsin
Max Stewart, Department of English, University of Wisconsin – Stevens Point
John Tytell, Queens College – City University of New York
Anne Waldman, Naropa Institute
Regina Weinreich, School of Visual Arts
Sara Weisensel, Albertson Learning Resources Center, Stevens Point, Wisconsin

Chapter 1

APPROACHES TO TEACHING
THE LIVES AND LITERATURE
OF THE BEAT GENERATION

Telling the true story of the world in interior monolog
– Jack Kerouac

The Problem of Justification

Only emotion endures
– Ezra Pound

The teaching of the lives and literature of the Beat Generation presents challenges and delights to both instructors and students. Primary, secondary, and auxiliary materials are abundant and easily available, and a resurgence of interest is bringing more and more Beat texts to the university classroom. Despite these positive forces, a special responsibility to justify Beat studies exists, but that responsibility is being met and the Beats are gaining new prominence in the canon and the curriculum.

The responsibility to justify Beat literature is different from the responsibility to justify the study of other works. When one teaches Edmund Spenser's *The Faerie Queene*, John Milton's *Paradise Lost*, or John Bunyan's *The Pilgrim's Progress*, one is confident of the academy's approval, but feels a responsibility to justify the study of this literature to students. In laying out a pedagogy, an instructor

1

must give special attention to introductory material so that the scope and complexity of the works, the seemingly remote form, language, and theology, and the bewildering mass of scholarship do not present an intellectual challenge that, in the eyes of the uninitiated young scholar, is too burdensome to undertake.

In contrast, when one teaches the literature of the Beat Generation, one must justify the material not to students, who often are ready to celebrate Jack Kerouac, Allen Ginsberg, and William Burroughs, but to colleagues, academicians, and professionals, who in some cases doubt the validity and literary worth of *On the Road*, *Howl and Other Poems*, and *Naked Lunch*. Providing a rationale is appropriate standard procedure in proposing any university course, but for the instructor who intends to offer Beat studies, the responsibility to justify the material through bureaucratic channels represents a peculiar compromising of Beat values. In bringing the Beats to the curriculum, the individual instructor must serve as an informed and flexible mediator between a generation of students receptive to counterculture and a body of academicians judicious about maintaining rigor and discipline and sometimes skeptical about the Beats.

According to John Tytell, who has taught Beat literature since the 1960's at Queens College of the City University of New York, students enroll beyond targets for sustaining the classes whenever the courses are offered; nevertheless, in academic environments across the nation, occasional resistance to the offering of Beat studies exists. This mood is suggested by Dr. Marjorie Berlincourt of the National Endowment for the Humanities, who conducts workshops around the nation for potential candidates for NEH Fellowships: she advises that a fellowship proposal connected to Beat literature must make a special effort to justify the study of the Beats to reviewers who may not readily accept the Beats.

The doubting of the Beats, which ranges from skepticism to hostility to dismissal, survives in spite of unmistakable signs of the value and importance of Beat literature. The presentation of many prestigious awards to Beat writers, including the Pulitzer Prize and the National Book Award, marks the acceptance of the Beats in the established literary award structure. Indeed, Gary Snyder is and William Burroughs and Allen Ginsberg were members of the American Academy of Arts and Letters. In addition, though the Beat movement began as an American literary phenomenon, the ongoing international popularity of Ginsberg and Kerouac testifies to their worldwide importance, as is evident in cultural communities in Eastern Europe and Japan, where "Howl" and *On the Road* remain essential readings. Furthermore, if one considers the landmark decisions in censorship trials involving Beat literature, particularly the cases involving "Howl" and *Naked Lunch*, one can understand the impact the Beats have had on current possibilities in publications and communications. Influencing the counterculture of the 1960's and 1970's, the Beats contributed to the societal transformations in those years, which included movements against racism and in favor of peace.

While the study of the Beats during the 1970's shifted, to some degree, to courses in sociology and American studies, now the Beats are returning to academic courses in literature, making themselves part of the mainstream in literature, companions of Proust, Joyce, Pound, and Williams. Even if one considers only Jack Kerouac, whose works have sold millions of copies and remain available in current editions in twenty-five languages, one sees the undeniable influence of the Beats in literature today.

Although some obstacles persist in academic contexts, now that fifty years have passed since the first meetings of Kerouac, Ginsberg, and Burroughs near Columbia University, and now that more than twenty-five years have passed since the death of Jack Kerouac in St. Petersburg, Florida, course offerings in Beat literature have penetrated the curriculum from the New College of California to Southwest Missouri State University to the Virginia Military Institute. Publishers have responded with current editions of dozens of Beat texts; a second generation of Beat writers, many of them women, has written memoirs in counterpoint to familiar autobiographical novels by the Beats; anthologies, collections of letters, and journals have proliferated; and multimedia materials, including photos, audio tapes, video tapes, compact discs, and CD-ROMs, have become widely available. In May, 1994, New York University hosted an international conference on the Beat Generation, and in June of 1995 NYU held a conference on Jack Kerouac. At the University of Massachusetts – Lowell, Professor Hilary Holladay has established an annual Beat Literature Symposium. Obstacles to making the Beats a part of the curriculum may still exist in some quarters, but such impediments persist in spite of numerous openings and opportunities that have given the Beats a secure and expanding place in university studies.

The Selection of Primary Sources

Catch yourself thinking
– Allen Ginsberg

The choice of primary materials for a course focusing on the writers of the Beat Generation is difficult. The definition of "Beat" and the specification of who is legitimately Beat are annoying and stubborn issues. Indeed, some members of the Beat Generation went to their deaths battling these questions to the exclusion of the appreciation of their artistry. For some, Beat has a narrow meaning, refers to a limited time, and comprises only three or four principal participants; for others, Beat has vast implications, refers to an on-going and growing movement, and includes scores of writers, artists, and performers. Key studies of the Beats may be as succinct as John Tytell's *Naked Angels* or as broad as Ann Charters' encyclopedic edition *The Beats: Literary Bohemians in Postwar America*.

In selecting primary materials for a course on the Beats, one may emphasize the nucleus that John Tytell recommends, namely *On the Road*, "Howl," and *Naked Lunch*. Over thirty years of teaching, Tytell has often varied the contents of his course, but he maintains that these three works are the essential Beat documents. To this basic list, Ann Charters, a prolific scholar, bibliographer, editor, and photographer on Beat subjects, as well as a leader in teaching Beat literature, adds "Kaddish." Noting that one book is not really sufficient to reflect the style and themes of a principal author, she calls for William Burroughs' *Junky* to be paired with *Naked Lunch*, Jack Kerouac's *Visions of Cody* to be paired with *On the Road*, and Allen Ginsberg's "Kaddish" to be paired with "Howl."

Establishing the core of Kerouac, Ginsberg, and Burroughs is essential, and some professors, such as Gordon Ball, Jennie Skerl, Michael Skau, and James Jones, choose three titles from these principal authors, adding *Dharma Bums* by Kerouac, *Planet News* by Ginsberg, and *Nova Express* by Burroughs. In my own addressing of the three who are at the heart of the Beats, I choose *Junky* as an accessible first experience with Burroughs so that the resistance of *Naked Lunch* may be met with more confidence and background. I concur with the selection of "Howl" and "Kaddish," but I add "White Shroud," completing Ginsberg's lifelong artistic journey with his mother, Naomi. Finally, in the case of Kerouac, I link *Visions of*

Gerard and *On the Road*, exploring the loss of the brother in the first novel and then the search for the new brother in the second.

One can debate the choices for dealing with Kerouac, Burroughs, and Ginsberg, but to round out Beat studies, one is likely to select a key publication, *The Portable Beat Reader*, an anthology edited by Ann Charters. Though limited by the need to present snippets in many cases, Charters succeeds in compiling a diverse collection of poems, essays, prose, and criticism that effectively complements the choice of full-length pieces by principal figures. Without such a collection, the cost of buying separate editions quickly mounts, and broad coverage is elusive. One might turn to *The Postmoderns: The New American Poetry Revised*, edited by Donald Allen and George F. Butterick, which is an outstanding collection, but that volume focuses only on poetry, leaving essays, criticism, and prose fiction uncovered. Recently published anthologies include *Beat Voices: An Anthology of Beat Poetry*, edited by David Kherdian, and *The Beat Book: Poems and Fiction from the Beat Generation*, edited by Anne Waldman. These recent anthologies are not quite as broad in their selections as *The Portable Beat Reader*, but one must evaluate their contents to determine if they meet the needs of a particular course.

In making the selections that round out the study of the Beat Generation, the instructor must consider writers like Gregory Corso, Lawrence Ferlinghetti, Michael McClure, Kenneth Rexroth, Gary Snyder, Neal Cassady, Herbert Huncke, Philip Whalen, Bob Kaufman, Frank O'Hara, Lew Welch, Robert Creeley, Amiri Baraka, Ray Bremser, Bob Dylan, and Ed Sanders, among many others. One may incorporate writings of Carolyn Cassady, Joyce Johnson, Hettie Jones, and Diane DiPrima, whose nonfiction and memoirs create interesting correspondences with the autobiographical fiction of the Beat period. Other instructors enjoy following the influence of the Beats into the 1960's, 1970's, and 1980's, selecting texts by Richard Fariña, Richard Brautigan, Ken Kesey, and many others. In the end, as in the teaching of any literature course, the exclusions are the hardest decisions to make and justify.

Allen Ginsberg himself, who taught courses in Beat literature at Brooklyn College of the City University of New York, offers a list of incunabular texts. Instead of listing key novels and poems that contribute to a body of work that might be called Beat, Ginsberg cites various manuscripts, magazine articles, letters, and texts that account for the Beat movement "in the cradle." Ginsberg includes his own "A Definition of the Beat Generation," a series of manuscripts

that are part of *Friction*, a magazine prepared at the Naropa
Institute in Boulder, Colorado (a selection now included in *Beat
Culture and the New America 1950-1965*, published by the Whitney
Museum of American Art). The 1966 interview in *Paris Review* reveals Ginsberg's commentary and is also on the list. Kerouac's prose
pieces titled "Origins of the Beat Generation," "Essentials of
Spontaneous Prose," and "Belief and Technique for Modern Prose,"
as well as Kerouac's first novel, *The Town and the City*, and
Kerouac's letter to John Clellon Holmes dated June 24, 1952, are
also listed as sources for understanding the birth of the Beat movement, giving Kerouac five citations on a list that includes only eleven
selections. From *Jack's Book*, by Barry Gifford and Lawrence Lee,
Ginsberg recommends "The Duluoz Legend: Chronological
Bibliography" (333-334), which clarifies the ordering of works in the
legend of Kerouac's life, an ordering that may not otherwise be clear
because it does not correspond to dates of publication. In Herbert
Huncke's *That Evening Sun Turned Crimson*, Ginsberg cites pp. 11-
13 and pp. 38-40; in Neal Cassady's *The First Third*, Ginsberg
recommends pp. 47-67 and 70-77. William Burroughs' "Gave Proof
Through the Night," a 1938 manuscript subsequently adapted for
Nova Express (105-109), completes Ginsberg's list of materials especially related to the birth of Beatness.

Going beyond the limited incunabular material, Ginsberg has also
created "A Mini-Anthology of Poets & Texts Associated with Beat
and Open Form." The anthology is an informal photocopy assembly
of materials, now available in the library at Brooklyn College.
Apparently there are other photocopy collections that Ginsberg
assembled on a homemade basis and made available at the Brooklyn
College library. Beyond the familiar citations of Ginsberg himself,
Burroughs, and Kerouac, Ginsberg provides references to R. Blyth,
David Cope, Philip Lamantia, Richard Lattimore, Ezra Pound, Carl
Rakosi, Charles Reznikoff, Nanao Sakaki, John Wieners, Philip
Whalen, and William Carlos Williams. At this point, I think, the fo-
cus on the Beats is loosened in favor of apprehending a much
broader sense of literary history and the place of the Beats in that
literary history.

The Secondary Sources

Work from pithy middle eye out, swimming in language sea
– Jack Kerouac

The number of secondary sources on the Beats continues to grow, and to guarantee a base for research, the instructor should be sure that essential sources are available for students. The two-volume encyclopedia titled *The Beats: Literary Bohemians in Postwar America*, edited by Ann Charters, is indispensable. The volumes include biographical and critical material, as well as significant bibliographical guidance. For most students, this collection should be the first port of call. Photos, time lines, facsimiles, and other records give depth and breadth while entries for each author remain concise and lively. Thomas Parkinson's *A Casebook on the Beat* presents a worthy gathering of articles and gives students a chance to recognize the diversity in the critical response to the Beats. The casebook, like the encyclopedia, has the advantage of letting students defer searches in indexes so that time may be immediately spent on the sources. However, both the encyclopedia and the casebook are done so well that students will have both inspiration and direction to extend their investigations through the full scope of library resources. Other collections of articles, some of them more current than either the casebook or the encyclopedia, are Lee Bartlett, ed., *The Beats: Essays in Criticism*; A. Robert Lee, ed., *The Beat Generation Writers*; Scott Donaldson, ed., *"On the Road": Text and Criticism*; Lewis Hyde, ed., *On the Poetry of Allen Ginsberg*; and Jennie Skerl and Robin Lydenberg, eds., *William S. Burroughs at the Front: Critical Reception, 1959-1989*.

Certainly one must require the reading of John Tytell's *Naked Angels*, which is admirable for its erudition, brilliant interpretation, and brevity. Students may struggle to keep pace with Tytell's broad background, but the challenge inspires the seriousness that the literature ultimately requires.

The range of secondary sources on the Beats is constantly expanding, and John Tytell foresees numerous studies of the Beats emerging during the next twenty years. However, if a short list of essential secondary materials beyond those already mentioned must be conceived, it should include, according to Ann Charters, such studies as Michael McClure's *Scratching the Beat Surface*, John Maynard's *Venice West*, Tim Hunt's *Kerouac's Crooked Road*, Theodore

Roszak's *The Making of a Counter Culture*, Aram Saroyan's *Genesis Angels: The Saga of Lew Welch and the Beat Generation*, and David Meltzer's *The San Francisco Poets*.

Bibliographical sources on the Beats are also developing, and in addition to the bibliography presented in this volume, one may consult Charters' valuable list of sources in *The Portable Beat Reader*. Other bibliographies and checklists include Bill Morgan, *The Works of Allen Ginsberg 1941-1994*; Bill Morgan, *The Response to Allen Ginsberg 1926-1994: A Bibliography of Secondary Sources*, Michelle P. Kraus, *Allen Ginsberg: An Annotated Bibliography 1969-1977*; Michael B. Goodman with Lemuel B. Coley, *William S. Burroughs: A Reference Guide*; and Robert J. Milewski, *Jack Kerouac: An Annotated Bibliography of Secondary Sources 1944-1979*.

Approaches and Methods

*One perception must immediately
and directly lead to a further perception*
– Charles Olson

Approaches to the teaching of the Beats, like approaches to teaching any form of literature, are founded in traditional methods such as the lecture, the class discussion, and the seminar, but the opportunity to teach Beat literature also presents various possibilities not usually associated with other literary movements. For example, Ron Janoff, Ann Charters, John Tytell, and various others note that the Beats are the most photographed literati of all time. Beat literature, says Charters, is a spoken art, and documentation through film provides a retrievable record of the spontaneity and visual impression of the artists. Thus, the instructor of Beat literature can plan on using collections of photos available from Ann Charters, Fred McDarrah, and Allen Ginsberg. Almost every book on the Beats has a section of photos to help capture the visual appearance of the artists and to give an impression of the time period. Numerous videos feature biographical treatments of the Beats and provide an experience in hearing and seeing the Beats perform their material. Some films reveal the art of filmmaking by Beats, and some dramatize the lives and times of Beat authors. Of particular interest and usefulness is *Kerouac*, a film by John Antonelli that has been released several times under various titles. Recently Antonelli's film has become available at moderate cost in VHS video. A film titled *Burroughs: The Movie*, directed by Howard Brookner, is also available in video, and it effectively highlights Burroughs' life and work. Ginsberg appears in many films and videos: if time must be limited to half an hour, the video *A Moveable Feast: Profiles of Contemporary American Authors* by Atlas Video offers both an interview and selected readings; if up to two hours can be allocated, then *The American Poetry Review Presents Allen Ginsberg* offers a substantial sample of readings by Ginsberg. *The Life and Times of Allen Ginsberg* by Jerry Aronson is also a fine selection. All these materials are valuable supplements to courses on Beat literature, and the principal problem is the task of reviewing and selecting from the wide range of available materials.

Music, especially contemporary and popular music, is also tied to Beat writings, and a teacher can present the many available combined efforts of Beat writers and musicians, especially jazz musicians. In many cases, the soundtracks of celluloid and video materials highlight the music associated with the Beats, but one may also create an interdisciplinary approach, developing a unit on jazz, blues, and improvisation, following that unit with a study of the primary sources in literature, noting musical formats in the poetry and spontaneity as a creative method. In advanced studies, one may analyze musical styles of particular performers, including Charlie Parker, Miles Davis, John Coltrane, Thelonious Monk, Dizzy Gillespie, and others. A set of recordings *The Beat Generation* from Rhino Records offers numerous musical selections related to the Beats. On CD-ROM, musical selections are part of *A Jack Kerouac Romnibus* by Penguin Electronics and *The Beat Experience* by Voyager. Finding correspondences between music and the styles of prose and poetry by the Beats is rewarding for many students, but jazz is not to the taste of some students, so caution must temper the design of assignments.

Making use of a wealth of audio and visual resources, a colleague and I did a special multimedia presentation. Video monitors, overhead projections, music, and literary readings filled a small theater-in-the-round setting. We featured a video bibliography with images of book covers, bindings, and still photos from the books. Boom box jazz established background rhythms, and a trade-off of selected readings by me and my colleague provided live action. Such performances require extensive planning and some cooperation from an audio-visual team, but the results can make strong highlights for classes.

In her classes, Ann Charters has organized a dramatic re-creation of the legendary reading at the Six Gallery in San Francisco on Friday, October 7, 1955. This reading launched the Beats on the West Coast and, in the view of many, spurred the San Francisco Poetry Renaissance into full swing. For her class, Charters attempted to verify the precise list of contributions done that night by Kenneth Rexroth, Philip Lamantia, Michael McClure, Philip Whalen, Allen Ginsberg, and Gary Snyder. She sought to develop a cast of graduate students to play each part, and for her students the program was intended to create the vision, language, and mood of the Beats.

The possibilities for exploiting audio-visual materials are also well revealed in the work of Ron Janoff, who with his staff and co-chairs worked to organize the 1994 conference *The Beat Generation: Legacy and Celebration* at New York University. Professor Joy Gould Boyum served as curator for a film festival that gathered dozens of films and videos that showed the Beats at work as film-makers, presented documentaries of their lives and times, and revealed Hollywood's treatment of the Beats. The festival was enhanced by the appearance of filmmakers and Beat personalities, who offered their commentaries on the visual materials, the personalities featured in the films, and the processes involved in production. The NYU Beat Film Festival goes beyond what any instructor might hope to do in connection with a class, but the marathon length of the festival suggests how much an instructor has to choose from in deciding on a film or video rental for classroom use. While a course is in progress, a film series might well be established to offer films on a weekly basis. With the cooperation of media people at a university library, a selection of materials can be on hand for students to see individually and at their convenience through library resources.

If the teaching of the Beats crosses over to the area of creative writing, coffeehouse readings make strong supplements to class activities. A guest reader can form the base for the reading, and then an open reading can carry it further. If not carefully planned, the coffeehouse idea can degenerate into something rather tedious, but with some planning and some room for freedom and improvisation, the open reading can create a natural reflection of the spontaneity and performance art that were essential to Beat creativity.

Beyond the supplementing of Beat Studies with the many available films, videos, and sound recordings, some instructors have developed special methodologies that enhance classroom activity. At the Naropa Institute in Boulder, Colorado, Bobbie Louise Hawkins has created a spontaneous curriculum that in its concept echoes the technique of the writers her class analyzes. According to Hawkins, "There are times when what happens in class determines the assignment, supplanting what is in the syllabus." She warns that students who miss one of her classes must check on what happened in class so that they can be aware of revised assignments for classes still to come. This method may have some disadvantages and may lead to violations of university procedures with respect to catalog descriptions of courses, but the method may also have a special strength in seizing upon inspiration and moments of class excitement. A skilled instructor can steer between the unexpected and the required just as a Homeric poet can combine stock phrases and newly invented lines.

A special application of the Beats to the teaching of creative writing is part of Regina Weinreich's course "Experimental Writing," which she teaches at the School of Visual Arts in New York. Weinreich states that "writing is [her] focus, not 'beat'ness." She sees "the Beats as exemplars par excellence of Experimental Writing." Weinreich's class directs attention to linearity versus non-linearity, appropriation of stories, and invention of new versions of familiar stories. Her students reconsider established distinctions between fact and fiction, propaganda and literature. In teaching this kind of writing, Weinreich finds the writing of the Beats to be a valuable resource for discussion.

An even more specialized application of the Beats to teaching is shown in a design for a special-theme course prepared by Charles Brooks Dodson. In a presentation at the annual meeting of the College English Association in 1987, Dodson showed how literature can serve well to help nursing students comprehend emotions and attitudes as well as medical data in dealing with impairments. In the course design, William Burroughs' *Junky* is designated as a text revealing the human side of drug addiction and alcoholism.

Anne Tobias argues that Lawrence Ferlinghetti's poetry offers teachers an especially effective tool for testing. In "A Poet for Teachers and Students: Lawrence Ferlinghetti," an article originally published in *English in Texas*, Tobias argues that when testing students, teachers can create a valid instrument by providing material that is not familiar to students and not often reviewed in scholarly discussions. The students must read carefully and demonstrate self-reliance in forming their interpretations. Ferlinghetti's poetry, Tobias argues, meets these requirements and is accessible, thought provoking, and enjoyable. She finds that selections from Ferlinghetti serve well on tests and also work well when a teacher uses exams as a means for teaching.

Bob Jordan of Northeast Louisiana University wants students to appreciate that Beat writers were often social activists who had the conviction "to speak both for the truth and against injustice." Jordan requires students ."to send a one-page letter to the editor of a newspaper or magazine on a subject of political or social interest to them." To earn credit, they must submit the printed letter.

Another lively and surprising approach is the slogan method of Allen Ginsberg. Instead of the lectures, discussion, and student presentations that make up the ordinary class, Ginsberg provides numerous proverbs and concise words of wisdom. Like *Proverbs of Hell* by William Blake, Ginsberg's slogans abandon the rhetoric of the paragraph or essay to present pithy poetic truth, inspiration, and guidance. Ginsberg uses Kerouac's "List of Essentials," a thirty-item document under the rubric "Belief & Technique for Modern Prose." Phrases like "Be crazy dumbsaint of the mind" and "You're a genius all the time" sometimes create the literary mood of the Beats more than dozens of academic treatments of the subject. Similarly, "Mind Writing Slogans" such as "My writing is a picture of the mind moving" and "Notice what you notice" are the Beat literary counterpart to the current journalistic technique of reaching for a sound bite. These slogans and phrases do not constitute a course by themselves, but they can take strong advantage of the power of brevity and repetition in underpinning the study of various authors.

Thematic approaches to the study of the Beats can go in dozens of directions. Those interested in academic and intellectual freedom find rich material to review in the life stories of William Burroughs, Allen Ginsberg, and Michael McClure, whose works faced the intervention of the police and the censors but nevertheless found vindication in the courts. Those interested in the literature of the pending apocalypse may adopt the approach of David Meltzer, who teaches Beat literature under the course title "Bomb Culture." Those interested in philosophy and religious studies find much material to stimulate discussion of Christianity, Judaism, Buddhism, and other faiths. Those interested in gender and sexual preference discover an intricate web of human weaknesses and strengths. Ron Janoff suggests that the Beats provide a special opportunity for the investigation of travel writing, both as travel journals and as metaphor. Janoff sees the Beats as globetrotters venturing not only to every part of the United States but also to Mexico, Tangier, India, China, Eastern Europe, Italy, Japan, and dozens of other places. Finally, as Ann Charters notes, one may find "rich material to review in the *careers* of William Burroughs, Allen Ginsberg," and other Beats.

These thematic approaches are valuable, but one may also focus on the perception of the Beats in the general and literary communities and assess the place of the Beats in literary history. Ronna C. Johnson, who teaches "Writing in the 'Beat' Generation" at Tufts University, explains that her "course asks if the writers and texts [of the Beat Generation] constitute substantive departures from canonical nineteenth-century and late modernist literatures." In her class, she and her students examine "how cultural meanings given to the category 'Beat' function as strategies for the marginalization or dismissal of the writers of this era." With these considerations, Johnson makes her class take a comprehensive sweep, assessing not only the place of the Beats in literary history, but also the effects of gender, race, sexual orientation, and politics on the perception of the Beats.

In addition to the various approaches and topics already mentioned, analyses of spontaneous composition and its later descendant known as free writing may be undertaken. Discussions of autobiography and the picaresque novel cannot really be complete unless the Duluoz legend is reckoned with. Confessional writing, which is central to the spirit of twentieth-century literature, cannot be complete unless "Howl" and "Kaddish" have their places. The study of didactic and satiric literature is similarly incomplete unless *Naked Lunch* is read perceptively. Finally, the study of literary history itself, including the study of the ongoing revisions of literary history, must address the initial exclusion of the Beats and the subsequent reevaluation of their critical reputation.

Conclusion

And being old she put a skin/ on everything she said
–W. B. Yeats

The teaching of the Beats provides a special opportunity for professors to reach out to students. While Kerouac, Ginsberg, and Burroughs remain at the center of the Beat Generation, dozens of others stand out as predecessors, contemporaries, and descendants. The study of the Beats has led to a rich body of secondary material, a body that is steadily growing in depth and variety. Approaches to teaching the Beats, whether through the use of standard methods, deployment of media, or employment of methodologies and thematic unities unique to the Beats, gain strength as more and more instructors bring the Beats to the university curriculum and to the academic community as a whole. While doubt about the validity and worth of Beat literature may still exist in some academic and professional circles, that rejection contributes to the attractiveness of the Beats as representatives of the counterculture. In the end, the questioning of the Beats may be the key to their prominence.

Chapter 2

THE BEATS IN GENERAL

I won't promise
you'll never go hungry
or that you won't be sad
on this gutted
breaking
globe

but I can show you
baby
enough to love
to break your heart
forever.
         – Diane DiPrima

The Beat Generation inspires debate about which individuals merit status as Beat artists. As a reviewer, critic, or anthologist evaluates the Beat Generation, he or she makes decisions about which people are representative of Beat thinking and artistry and makes judgments about quality. Students can monitor how these evaluations and judgments have evolved with the passing decades.

Subjects for class consideration include the ways the definition of Beat originated and evolved. Differences of opinion about the meaning of "beat" should be analyzed and compared, and the ongoing reevaluation of the Beats over the course of half a century should be noticed. As one thinks of the Beats in general, one must go beyond literature into the areas of visual arts and music. Interdisciplinary analysis may go beyond the focus of most classes on Beat literature, but an awareness of a multiplicity of artists working in diverse forms is the key to the understanding of any single artistic endeavor and the reactions it inspires.

Bibliographies

The range of available bibliographical sources related to the Beat Generation is impressive. Any student who returns to the instructor with the complaint that no research material on the Beats can be found can be offered plenty of specific references. The bibliographies in Ann Charters' *The Beats: Literary Bohemians in Postwar America* are very useful, though the references may not include the most recent material. The list "Books for Further Reading" in Charters' *The Portable Beat Reader*, though not comprehensive, includes many essential sources and is current. Advanced students and researchers can check the list below for bibliographies that open the door to dozens of approaches to the lives and literature of the Beat Generation.

Akeroyd, Joanne Vinson. *Where Are Their Papers? A Union List Locating the Papers of Forty-Two Contemporary American Poets and Writers*. Storrs: University of Connecticut Library at Storrs, 1976.
   This slender volume is dated and not widely available, but for those interested in locating the papers and correspondence of numerous Beat authors, Akeroyd's work is helpful.

Beam, Joan. "American Social Attitudes and Popular Culture of the 1950's: A Selected Annotated Bibliography." *Reference Services Review* 17.3 (1989): 7-18. (ERIC # EJ401063)
   This article lists monographs on the Red Scare and Senator McCarthy, popular culture, Hollywood, and the Beat Generation.

Carney, Ray. "The Beat Movement in Film: A Comprehensive Screening List." *Beat Culture and the New America 1950-1965*. New York: Whitney Museum of American Art/Flammarion, 1995.

See 210-213 for the list. For Carney's "Escape Velocity: Notes on Beat Film," which is a companion essay for the screening list, see 168-208.

Charters, Ann. "Books for Further Reading." *The Portable Beat Reader*. New York: Viking Penguin, 1992. 623-631.
This list is not comprehensive, but it includes the essential works for understanding and interpreting the Beats.

Charters, Ann, ed. *The Beats: Literary Bohemians in Postwar America*. Detroit: Gale Research, 1983.
These two volumes of the *Dictionary of Literary Biography* (Volume 16, Parts I and II) feature numerous articles on the Beats, and each article has a worthwhile bibliography. Other materials include photos, time lines, and facsimiles of manuscripts. A list titled "Books for Further Reading" appears at the end of Part II and presents books to establish a general background on the Beats.

Charters, Ann, and Sam Charters. *Beat Beat Beat Beat Beat Beat Collection*.
This unpublished three-hundred-page inventory list for the collection of materials now held as part of the Berg Collection at the New York Public Library is a valuable bibliography on the Beats as well as a clear indication of the depth and range of Ann Charters' work with the Beats.

Cook, Ralph T. *The City Lights Pocket Poets Series: A Descriptive Bibliography*. La Jolla, CA: Laurence McGilvery, 1982.
The first forty of Ferlinghetti's series of tiny books of poetry is catalogued so that the reader who has not seen some of the volumes can get an idea of cover pages, publication data, and information about paper and binding.

Hickey, Morgen. *The Bohemian Register: An Annotated Bibliography of the Beat Literary Movement*. Metuchen, NJ: Scarecrow, 1990.
Hickey's work serves as an introduction to the Beat Literary Movement, dividing listings into "General Works and Critical Studies," "Collections and Anthologies," and "The Beats." Hickey provides a time line for the movement and presents biographical data for selected authors. The text features cross references and is compact.

Kherdian, David, ed. *Six Poets of the San Francisco Renaissance: Portraits and Checklists*. Morris, NY: Giligia Press, 1967.

This work serves as a reference for primary sources on Ferlinghetti, Snyder, Meltzer, Whalen, McClure, and Everson, including books, broadsides, items in periodicals and newspapers, recordings, items in anthologies, and tapes. The portraits of the authors capture a sense of daily life, and a photo of each writer is included.

Lepper, Gary M. *A Bibliographical Introduction to Seventy-Five American Authors*. Livermore, CA: Serendipity Books, 1976.

Lepper provides lists of titles and gives publication information, including the size of print runs, for many authors, among them Blackburn, Burroughs, Creeley, DiPrima, Duncan, Everson, Ferlinghetti, Lamantia, McClure, Mailer, Meltzer, O'Hara, Snyder, Whalen, and Wieners.

Meltzer, David. "List of Works by the Five Poets" and "Courses." *Golden Gate: Interviews with Five San Francisco Poets*. Revised edition. Ed. David Meltzer. Berkeley: Wingbow Press, 1976.

Since Meltzer interviews Rexroth, Everson, Ferlinghetti, Welch, and McClure, a list of original works by each author is featured. The interviews are filled with references to literary history, and Meltzer provides "Courses," which is a comprehensive reading list based on works referred to during the interviews. The interviews and "Courses" suggest the erudition of the Beats and indicate to students the necessity to be widely read.

Anthologies and Collections

Allen, Donald, ed. *The New American Poetry 1945-1960*. New York: Grove Press, 1960.

This classic anthology brings to light important poems from Ferlinghetti, Ginsberg, Corso, Kerouac, Olson, and Creeley. "Statements on Poetics" articulate the artistry of featured poets, and "Biographical Notes" provide glimpses of their lives.

Allen, Donald, and George F. Butterick, eds. *The Postmoderns: The New American Poetry Revised*. New York: Grove Press, 1982.

This anthology is an updating of the classic anthology listed above. The editors remark, "Of the thirty-four original poets, twenty-nine were retained, with nine new poets added." The added poets are intended to be representative of authors whose influence on literature became most important in the 1960's. The editors include biographical notes and bibliographies.

Allen, Donald, and Robert Creeley, eds. *New American Story*. New York: Grove Press, 1965.

Featured artists include Kerouac, Burroughs, LeRoi Jones, Creeley, and Michael Rumaker. Warren Tallman provides an introduction. Commentary from the authors is collected at the end of the anthology.

The American Literary Anthology/1: The First Annual Collection of the Best from the Literary Magazines. New York: Farrar Straus and Giroux, 1968.

Includes Coolidge, Dorn, Duncan, Jones, McClure, Olson, Wieners, Berrigan, Creeley, Ginsberg, McClure, and Sanders. The book was made possible by a $55,000 NEA grant.

Annis, Michael, ed. *Stileto, Volume One*. Kansas City, MO: Howling Dog Press, 1989.

This anthology anticipates the perception of the Beat movement as an interdisciplinary phenomenon. Included are short stories, poems, and art work, including pieces by Burroughs, DiPrima, and Waldman.

Baro, Gene, ed. *"Beat" Poets*. Dallas: Vista Books/Longacre Press, 1961.

Corso, Ferlinghetti, Ginsberg, Kerouac, McClure, and Wieners are included. Baro provides an introduction that comments on his perception of Beat identity.

_____. *Famous American Poems*. Dallas: Vista Books/Longacre Press, 1962.

This anthology highlights some of the authors who exerted an influence over writers during the emergence of the Beats following World War II. Selections from Emerson, Poe, and Whitman, among others, are presented.

Berg, Stephen, and Robert Mezey, eds. *Naked Poetry: Recent American Poetry in Open Forms*. Indianapolis: Bobbs-Merrill, 1969.
   As the work's subtitle indicates, the focus is on open forms, and some Beats find a place under such a heading. Rexroth, Patchen, Creeley, Ginsberg, and Snyder appear. A photo of each author is presented along with biographical information.

_____. *The New Naked Poetry: Recent American Poetry in Open Forms*. Indianapolis: Bobbs-Merrill, 1976.
   This volume is an enlargement and updating of the collection listed above and best serves as a companion to the first anthology. New selections from Ginsberg, O'Hara, Snyder, and Rexroth are featured along with biographies, photos, and "artistic statements."

The Black Mountain Review, Numbers 1-8. New York: AMS Press, 1968.
   Some of the Black Mountain poets had an influence on Beat writers, some of whom found expression in the issues of *Black Mountain Review*. Duncan, Olson, Burroughs, Selby, and Rumaker are included.

Brogran, James E., ed. *The American Search for Identity: A Reader*. New York: Harcourt Brace Jovanovich, 1972.
   This historical survey starting with Whitman proceeds through Kerouac, Ginsberg, Kesey, and Corso.

Charters, Ann, ed. *The Portable Beat Reader*. New York: Penguin, 1992.
   Charters' anthology is comprehensive and chronological, covering both poetry and prose, monitoring the development and changes in the Beat Literary Movement through the 1970's and 1980's. The introduction and headnotes give historical background and biographical information.

City Lights Journal, Numbers 1-2. Ed. Lawrence Ferlinghetti. Milwood, NY: Kraus Reprint, 1963-64.
   Ginsberg, Snyder, Sanders, Kerouac, Burroughs, Norse, McClure, Perkoff, Joans, Ferlinghetti, Doyle, Kandel, Neal Cassady, and O'Hara appear in a reprint that reveals Ferlinghetti's work as an editor.

Feldman, Gene, and Max Gartenberg, eds. *The Beat Generation and the Angry Young Men*. Secaucus, NJ: Citadel, 1958.

This text showcases representatives of the Beats in America and the Angry Young Men in Britain and features critical evaluations of the artists and movements. This work reveals an early stage in the history of the perception of the Beats.

_____. *Protest*. London: Souvenir Press, 1959.

The text includes selections from Holmes, Kerouac, Ginsberg, Mailer, Rexroth, and others, and the book serves as an example of how the Beats were perceived in the late 1950's.

Ferlinghetti, Lawrence, ed. *Beatitude Anthology*. San Francisco: City Lights, 1960.

A compilation, "not all on the Beat frequency," from the first sixteen issues of *Beatitude*.

Fisher, Stanley, ed. *Beat Coast East: An Anthology of Rebellion*. New York: Excelsior Press Publishers, 1960.

This small anthology offers a selection of short poems by Bremser, Orlovsky, Corso, Ginsberg, Kerouac, DiPrima, Jones, and Mailer. The work has interest as a collection published in 1960.

Frank, Robert, and Henry Sayre, eds. *The Line in Postmodern Poetry*. Champaign: University of Illinois Press, 1988.

The focus of this anthology is on the composition of the poetic line, and ten interpretations of the poetics of Beats such as Baraka, Creeley, Duncan, Ginsberg, Joans, Kaufman, Kyger, McClure, O'Hara, Olson, Rexroth, Snyder, and Whalen appear.

Girodias, Maurice, ed. *The Olympia Reader: Selections from the Traveller's Companions Series*. New York: Ballantine Books, 1965.

Includes Miller, Burroughs, and Corso.

Goodman, Paul, ed. *Seeds of Liberation*. New York: George Braziller, 1964.

DiPrima, Lipton, and Snyder are included in this large collection of topical materials first published in *Liberation*.

Hall, Donald, ed. *Contemporary American Poetry*. Baltimore: Penguin Books, 1962.

Includes Duncan, Creeley, and Snyder. Hall provides an introduction.

Harlan, Gerald W. *Many Californias: Literature from the Golden State*. Reno: University of Nevada Press, 1992.
Historical survey includes Everson, Ginsberg, Kerouac, Ferlinghetti, Rexroth, Duncan, Kaufman, Snyder, and Bukowski.

Harvey, Nick, ed. *Mark in Time: Portraits and Poetry/San Francisco*. San Francisco, CA: Glide Publications, 1971.
The emphasis in this collection is on broad coverage, as eighty poets appear, each allotted a poem and a photo. Meltzer, Snyder, McClure, Kaufman, Kyger, and many others are included.

Hoffman, Frederick J., ed. *Marginal Manners: The Variants of Bohemia*. New York: Row, Peterson and Company, 1962.
This anthology includes selections from Kerouac, Ginsberg, Corso, and Kaufman. The unifying theme for the anthology is an examination of the "marginal" figure in American society.

Honan, Park, ed. *The Beats: An Anthology of "Beat" Writing*. London: J. M. Dent, 1987.
This anthology includes poetry, prose, commentary, biographical notes, and a selected bibliography. Poets include Ginsberg, Corso, Ferlinghetti, Snyder, Lamantia, Kupferberg, Stern, Propper, and Jones. Prose is represented in the work of Ginsberg, Kerouac, Burroughs, Holmes, and Krim. Commentary and criticism are offered by Holmes, Diana Trilling, Ginsberg, Honan, Rexroth, Podhoretz, and Johnson.

Hoover, Paul, ed. *Postmodern American Poetry: A Norton Anthology*. New York: Norton, 1994.
Selected authors include Olson, Duncan, Ferlinghetti, Bukowski, MacLow, Kerouac, Whalen, Spicer, O'Hara, Ginsberg, Creeley, Blackburn, Eigner, Corso, Snyder, McClure, Baraka, DiPrima, and Wieners. Hoover: Postmodernism "is the most encompassing term for the variety of experimental practice since World War II, one that ranges from the oral poetics of Beat and performance poetries to the more 'writerly' work of the New York School and language poetry." Hoover's introduction offers commentary on the Beats.

Horemans, Rudi, ed. *Beat Indeed!* Antwerp, Belgium: EXA, 1985.

This anthology features articles, essays, and literary works by Montgomery, Nicosia, Carolyn Cassady, and Ann Charters, who discuss Kerouac, Holmes, Burroughs, DiPrima, and Ferlinghetti.

James, Laurence, ed. *Electric Underground: A City Lights Reader.* London: New English Library, 1973.

Ginsberg, Corso, Kerouac, Ferlinghetti, Neal Cassady, McClure, Mailer, Lamantia, Burroughs, and Snyder are featured in a sampling of the best of City Lights. The influence of several French authors is also recognized.

Jones, LeRoi, ed. *The Moderns: An Anthology of New Writing in America.* New York: Corinth Books, 1963.

The selections are short stories and essays on writing. Beats are represented by Creeley, Kerouac, Burroughs, and DiPrima as writers of the short story. Rumaker, Creeley, Kerouac, and Burroughs discuss writing. Biographical data are listed.

Kherdian, David, ed. *Beat Voices: An Anthology of Beat Poetry.* New York: Henry Holt, 1995.

The subtitle sets a focus on poetry, and most of the collection is poetry, but some prose by Kerouac and Bukowski appears. The selections are organized under the headings "East Coast," "On the Road," and "West Coast" and reveal Kherdian's special connection to Beat culture.

_____. *Traveling America with Today's Poets.* New York: Macmillan, 1977.

This anthology is ordered according to the geography of the United States, weaving back and forth with poems about places done by artists often associated with cities and states. Includes O'Hara, Whalen, Snyder, Bukowski, and Blackburn.

_____. *Visions of America by the Poets of Our Time.* New York: Macmillan, 1973.

An anthology of writers who are indebted to Whitman and William Carlos Williams, based on themes of "Growing up/In America/and Its Cities." Illustrated by Nonny Hogrogian. Welch, Kerouac, Snyder, Jones, and Corso are included.

Knight, Arthur Winfield, and Glee Knight, eds. *unspeakable visions of the individual* (1.1). California, PA: unspeakable visions of the individual, 1971.
This volume initiates a series that collects diverse materials by and about the Beats, including work by Kerouac, Ginsberg, Ferlinghetti, and Mailer. This first volume, although it is dedicated to Kerouac, is a journal of creative writing that does not include writings by Beat authors.

_____. *unspeakable visions of the individual* (1.2). California, PA: unspeakable visions of the individual, 1971.
This issue includes the poems "Rimbaud" by Jack Kerouac and "Friday the Thirteenth" by Allen Ginsberg.

_____. *unspeakable visions of the individual* (1.3). California, PA: unspeakable visions of the individual, 1971.
This issue includes "Mother Light Mantra" by Ferlinghetti and "Husbands" by Norman Mailer.

_____. *unspeakable visions of the individual* (2.1). California, PA: unspeakable visions of the individual, 1972.
The connection to the Beats here emerges from letters between Seymour Krim and Sidney Bernard.

_____. *unspeakable visions of the individual* (2.2). California, PA: unspeakable visions of the individual, 1972.
A Breakable Bird by Erje Ayden fills the issue.

_____. *unspeakable visions of the individual* (2.3). California, PA: unspeakable visions of the individual, 1972.
This "Tuvoti" edition is devoted to Henry Miller.

_____. *unspeakable visions of the individual* (3.1/2). California, PA: unspeakable visions of the individual, 1973.
This issue features various materials by and about Huncke. John Tytell interviews Huncke. There are letters to and from Holmes and a comment on Huncke's book by Allen Ginsberg.

_____. *unspeakable visions of the individual* (3.3). California, PA: unspeakable visions of the individual, 1973.
This issue features collages by Charles Plymell.

_____. *The Beat Book*. California, PA: unspeakable visions of the individual, 1974.

This issue is volume 4 and is the only issue for the year. Diverse materials include photos, drawings, reviews, interviews, poems, and prose by and about a wide range of authors.

Knight, Arthur Winfield, and Kit Knight, eds. *The Beat Diary*. California, PA: unspeakable visions of the individual, 1977.

This issue is volume 5. Burroughs, Whalen, and Snyder are interviewed. Selections include Corso, DiPrima, Ginsberg, McClure, Norse, Solomon, Ferlinghetti, Holmes, Kerouac, and Orlovsky.

_____. "Neal in Court." California, PA: unspeakable visions of the individual, 1977.

This broadside is volume 6 in the series and presents "Neal in Court," a poem by Jack Kerouac, with a drawing of Kerouac by Carolyn Cassady.

_____. *The Bowling Green Poems*. California, PA: unspeakable visions of the individual, 1977.

This little book is a collection of poems by John Clellon Holmes and is offered as volume 7 in the series.

_____. *The Beat Journey*. California, PA: unspeakable visions of the individual, 1978.

This item is volume 8 in a series. Writers included are Kerouac, Holmes, Whalen, Burroughs, and Corso; there are drawings by Kerouac and Corso; interviews with Ginsberg, McClure, and Holmes appear; and a selection of photos by Fred McDarrah is included.

_____. "Alchemical Poem." California, PA: unspeakable visions of the individual, 1979.

This broadside is volume 9 in the series and features a poem and drawing by Corso.

_____. *unspeakable visions of the individual* (10). California, PA: unspeakable visions of the individual, 1980.

This tenth-anniversary issue includes letters by Kerouac, a selection from Huncke's *Guilty of Everything*, an interview with Jan Kerouac by Gerald Nicosia, photos of the San Francisco scene by Larry Keenan, Jr., letters between Holmes and Ginsberg, an interview of Amiri Baraka by Debra L. Edwards, and poems by Whalen, Kerouac, Joanna McClure, and Bonnie Bremser. Also included are prose by Carolyn Cassady and drawings by Kerouac.

_____. *Visitor: Jack Kerouac in Old Saybrook*. California, PA: unspeakable visions of the individual, 1981.
This memoir by John Clellon Holmes is volume 11 in the series.

_____. *The Beats*. New Sharon, PA: Rat and Mole Press, 1981.
Stony Hills 10 (1981) is this special issue dedicated to the Beats with the Knights as guest editors. This tabloid features reviews of various Beat publications. Contributors include John Tytell, John Clellon Holmes, Ann Charters, Gerald Nicosia, Charles Jarvis, A. D. Winans, Ted Joans, Jim Burns, Joy Walsh, and Dennis McNally. Poems by Kerouac and Corso are also featured.

_____. *Beat Angels*. California, PA: unspeakable visions of the individual, 1982.
This volume is number 12 in a series. Photos of Kerouac and Ted Joans. Interviews with Duncan, DeLattre, and Ted Joans. A variety of other writings is also included.

_____. *Jack Kerouac: Dear Carolyn: Letters to Carolyn Cassady*. California, PA: unspeakable visions of the individual, 1983.
This volume is number 13 in a series. Kerouac's letters to Carolyn Cassady reveal a wide range of personal feelings and preferences.

_____. *The Beat Road*. California, PA: unspeakable visions of the individual, 1984.
Number 14 of a series. Correspondence, poems, and prose by Kerouac, Holmes, Corso, and Ginsberg. An interview with Diane DiPrima is also present.

_____. *unspeakable visions of the individual* (15). California, PA: unspeakable visions of the individual, 1985.
This color poster of Kerouac is the final publication in a series.

_____. *The Beat Vision*. New York: Paragon, 1987.
Arthur Winfield Knight: This book "contains what we believe to be the 'best' work published by us in the last decade and a half; we have also included some previously unpublished photographs."

_____. *Kerouac and the Beats: A Primary Source Book*. New York: Paragon, 1988.

John Tytell is the author of the foreword. Interviews with Burroughs, Whalen, Kerouac, Holmes, McClure and Ginsberg accompany letters and essays. Most of the correspondence is by Kerouac, and commentaries on the Beat scene are provided by Carolyn Cassady, Huncke, and Frankie Edith Kerouac Parker.

Knight, Brenda, ed. *The Women of the Beat Generation*. Berkeley, CA: Conari Press, 1996.

The lives and literature of forty Beat women, including Elise Cowen, Diane DiPrima, Hettie Jones, Joan Burroughs, Jan Kerouac, Jane Bowles, Carolyn Cassady, and ruth weiss. Photos. Foreword by Anne Waldman. Afterword by Ann Charters. Knight: "The women in this anthology were talented rebels with enough courage and creative spirit to turn their backs on 'the good life' the fifties promised and forge their way to San Francisco and Greenwich Village." See the companion audio tape listed in the section on audiovisual materials on the Beats in general.

Koch, Kenneth, and Kate Farrell, eds. *Sleeping on the Wing: An Anthology of Modern Poetry: Poetry with Essays on Reading and Writing*. New York: Random House, 1981.

An anthology starting from Whitman, going on to include Ginsberg, O'Hara, Snyder, and Jones. Includes "A Note for Teachers."

Krim, Seymour, ed. *The Beats*. Greenwich, CT: Fawcett, 1960.

This early anthology should be compared to Elias Wilentz, ed., *The Beat Scene*. Krim's anthology includes Holmes, "The Philosophy of the Beat Generation"; selections from Kerouac's *Visions of Cody*; selections from Corso, Krim, DiPrima, Brossard, Ray Bremser, Burroughs, Lamantia, Ginsberg, Micheline, Mailer, Joans, and Ferlinghetti.

Landesman, Jay, ed. *Neurotica*. New York: Jay Landesman, 1981.

John Clellon Holmes provides an introduction for this collection of the nine volumes of the magazine originally published by Landesman. The magazine was an early proving ground for Patchen, Holmes, and Ginsberg, and the magazine itself offers a visual impression of the developing Beat mood of the times.

Lowenfels, Walter, ed. *Poets of Today: A New American Anthology*.
New York: International Publishers, 1964.
Includes Bukowski, Corso, Dylan, Ferlinghetti, Ginsberg, LeRoi
Jones, McClure, and Snyder.

McDarrah, Fred W. *Kerouac and Friends*. New York: William Morrow, 1985.
A broad perspective on the Beat Generation is presented in this
collection of writings, photographs, and satire. Holmes, Lipton,
Rexroth, Krim, Kerouac, and Ferlinghetti are featured.

Morris, Tina, and David Cunliffe, eds. *Thunderbolts of Peace and
Liberation*. Blackburn, Lancashire, England: BB Books, 1967.
Contributors to this anthology include DiPrima, Eigner, Ferlinghetti, Kandel, Kupferberg, and Snyder. An opening invocation,
which lists the names of the contributors as subscribers to the invocation, declares, "May my poetry become that therapy which annihi-
lates hangups. May my words consume the planet with compassion.
May this book slaughter the forces of evil."

Peace, Warren, ed. *Readings on the Beat Generation*. San Francisco:
The Peace Press, 1992.
This limited edition is a collection of articles about the Beats
which originally appeared in standard magazines such as *Harper's
Magazine* and *Commentary* and less familiar ones such as *Scamp*,
The Dude, and *Rogue*. Many photos, cartoons, and jokes. A non-
circulating copy is at the Bancroft Library in Berkeley. The
collection originally came with a packet of "peace seeds," but that has
disappeared. A phonographic recording titled *Millions of Images* is
kept separately as phonodisc 729.

Rosenthal, M. L., ed. *The New Modern Poetry: British and American
Poetry Since World War II*. New York: Macmillan, 1967.
Contributors include Everson, Blackburn, Creeley, Ferlinghetti,
Ginsberg, LeRoi Jones, Rexroth, and Snyder. While this anthology
ranges far beyond the Beats, Rosenthal accounts for the feelings of
many Beat writers when he says, "The memories of the last war, with
its genocide and mass bombings and finally the Bomb, have branded
themselves deep within the psyche of this age."

Schuyler, James, and Charles North, eds. *Broadway 2: A Poets and Painters Anthology*. New York: Hanging Loose Press, 1989.
Drawings and sketches accompany the work of poets, including Ginsberg, Creeley, and Waldman.

Seaver, Richard, Terry Southern, and Alexander Trocchi, eds. *Writers in Revolt: An Anthology*. New York: Frederick Fell, 1963.
Editors: "[I]f ever the artist is to be truly free, his public must shed its apathy, its own ambivalence." This volume centers on the theme of revolt and includes Ginsberg, Artaud, Celine, Henry Miller, Genet, Selby, and Burroughs.

Tonkinson, Carole, ed. *Big Sky Mind: Buddhism and the Beat Generation*. New York: Riverhead Books, 1995.
This collection features selections from Kerouac, Ginsberg, DiPrima, Norse, Snyder, Whalen, Kyger, Welch, Kandel, Kaufman, Burroughs, Ferlinghetti, McClure, Rexroth, and Waldman. An editor's preface, an introduction by Stephen Prothero, and generous headnotes make this text a valuable source for understanding the connection between Buddhism and the Beats. A section of photos is included.

Topp, Mike, ed. *Evergreen Review Reader 1957-1966*. New York: Blue Moon Books, 1993.
This volume selects materials from the magazine originally edited by Barney Rossett, with associate editors Dick Seaver, Fred Jordan, and Donald Allen. The volume presents a year-by-year selection of publications in the magazine. In the introduction, Ken Jordan writes, "The second issue was a landmark. A banner across the cover declared 'San Francisco Scene,' and inside held the first work by the new Beat writers—including Lawrence Ferlinghetti, Gary Snyder, Michael McClure, Philip Whalen, Jack Kerouac (before the publication of *On the Road*), and Allen Ginsberg." Compare a previous and larger volume: Barney Rossett, ed., *Evergreen Review Reader 1957-1967* (New York: Castle Books, 1968). This volume, though it has no introduction and does not specify decades in the table of contents, is twice as long.

Vendler, Helen, ed. *The Harvard Book of Contemporary American Poetry*. Cambridge, MA: Harvard Belknap, 1985.

An anthology including Ginsberg, O'Hara, and Snyder among other contemporary writers. Brief introduction. Short biographies.

Waldman, Anne, ed. *The Beat Book: Poems and Fiction from the Beat Generation*. Boston: Shambhala, 1996.

This collection features both poetry and prose and includes a foreword by Allen Ginsberg. Key selections from the Beats are present as well as a list of Beat places.

Wholly Communion. London: Lorrimer Films, 1965.

This book published selections from the International Poetry Reading at the Royal Albert Hall in London on June 11, 1965. Ginsberg, Ferlinghetti, and Corso contribute. A film by Peter Whitehead documents the reading, and photos in the book give impressions of the film.

Wilentz, Elias, ed. *The Beat Scene*. New York: Corinth, 1960.

This classic anthology combines black-and-white photos by Fred McDarrah with short selections from many artists, including Ginsberg, Ferlinghetti, Krim, O'Hara, Joans, Corso, Orlovsky, Kupferberg, DiPrima, Bremser, and Creeley. Wilentz: "Without presuming to be all-inclusive, the attempt here is to show the new young literary world of New York's Greenwich Village–its writers, its parties, its readings, its *scene*."

Wolf, Daniel, and Edwin Fancher, eds. *The Village Voice Reader: A Mixed Bag from the Greenwich Village Newspaper*. New York: Doubleday, 1962.

The reader gets an impression of the *Village Voice* and topics it covered prior to 1962. Ginsberg, Corso, Rexroth, Kerouac, Krim, and Mailer participate in the debate on the Beat Generation. See "'Witless Madcaps' Come Home to Roost" by Dan Balaban, "Jack Kerouac: Back to the Village–but Still on the Road" by Jerry Tallmer, "Allen Ginsberg: Here to Save Us, but Not Sure from What" by Marc D. Schleifer, a letter from Corso, five columns by Norman Mailer, a review of Mailer's *The Deer Park* by Robert Lindner, "The Press of Freedom: From Riches to Rags" by Niccolo Tucci, "The Chronic Footnote Writer" by John Wilcock, "Jack Kerouac: Off the Road, Into the Vanguard, and Out" by Howard Smith, "The Beat Debated–Is It or Is It Not?" by Marc D. Schleifer, "Politics and 'the Beat': Youth 'Disaffiliated' from a Phony World" by David

McReynolds, "This Hip Historian Knows a Man's Pad Is His Castle" by Suzanne Kiplinger, "I Was a Teen-Age Fascist" by Adam Margoshes, "New Girl in Town" and "The Blind-Date Bit" by John Wilcock, "Beat Generation? Dead As Davy Crockett Caps, Says Rexroth, Passing Through" by Kenneth Rexroth, a review of Kerouac's *The Dharma Bums* by Allen Ginsberg, "Saloon Society" by Bill Manville, and "The Hipster General Strike" by David McReynolds.

Books About the Beats in General

Aldridge, John W. *After the Lost Generation: A Critical Study of the Writers of Two Wars*. New York: McGraw-Hill, 1951.
Aldridge compares writers in the wake of each world war and establishes a background analysis for the arrival of the Beats.

Allan, Blaine. *The New American Cinema and the Beat Generation, 1956-1960*. Ann Arbor: University Microfilms International, 1985.
A dissertation on a topic not discussed as commonly as the texts. University Microfilms order no. 8423199.

Allen, Donald, and Warren Tallman, eds. *The Poetics of the New American Poetry*. New York: Grove Press, 1973.
The editors gather poetic statements that range back to Whitman and include others who predate the Beats, but the main focus is on the writers of the 1950's and 1960's and how they comment on the nature and genesis of their work.

Allsop, Kenneth. *The Angry Decade: A Survey of the Cultural Revolt of the Nineteen-Fifties*. London: John Goodchild, 1985.
According to Allsop, the French Outsider, the British "delinks," and the Beats have "a similar international pattern perceptible: that of the social dissentient who is searching for moral coherence and religious belief." This item is a reprint of a 1958 edition done by Peter Owen, Ltd.

Bartlett, Jeffrey. *One Vast Page*. Berkeley, CA: Provine Press, 1991.
Harold Norse: "Bartlett evokes the turbulent Beat era and personalizes it with vivid, accurate portrayals of Kerouac, Burroughs, Ginsberg, Genet, and Mailer."

Bartlett, Lee, ed. *The Beats: Essays in Criticism*. Jefferson, NC: Mc-
Farland, 1981.
Bartlett gathers from previously published material a set of four-
teen essays that provide useful information for student projects. The
essays focus on Burroughs, Ginsberg, Kerouac, Snyder, Corso,
Whalen, Kaufman, McClure, and Ferlinghetti. A perspective on the
Beat Generation is included, along with bibliographies on the Beats
in general and ten Beat authors. Holmes' essay "Unscrewing the
Locks: The Beat Poets" opens the collection.

The Beat Journals: Volume One. Warwickshire, England: The Beat
Scene Press, 1995.
This volume collects essays and interviews previously published in
Kevin Ring's *Beat Scene*.

Beat Talk. Tulsa, OK: The Studio Press, 1960.
This tiny book is a dictionary for Beat vocabulary. Illustrated with
small amusing drawings.

Breslow, Paul. *The Support of Mysteries: A Look at the Literary
Prophets of the Beat Middle Class*. New York: Perth Pamphlets,
1960.
Breslow: "It is the argument here that it is [the middle class pub-
lic] to which the term 'beat' is most appropriately applied, that most
of us in the moderately educated middle class are beatniks and that
in the contemporary cesspool of American political life the beat
middle class is unpleasantly confined to a petty and confusing con-
solation for its social anxieties in a search for an undefinable, unsatisfying, irrelevant, mystical salvation." According to Breslow, the
"literary favorites" of the "beat middle class" are James Gould
Cozzens, J. D. Salinger, and Jack Kerouac.

Carr, Roy, and B. Case and F. Dellar. *The Hip: Hipsters, Jazz and the
Beat Generation*. London: Faber, 1986.
A chapter "Nighthawks" (102-107) combines images of book covers and album covers with photos of the Beats, but the discussion is
brief. As a whole, this book serves as a source for impressions of
musicians who developed bop and jazz.

Cassady, Carolyn. *Heart Beat: My Life with Jack and Neal*. Berkeley,
CA: Creative Arts, 1976.

This memoir was expanded, improved and later published as *Off the Road: My Years with Cassady, Kerouac, and Ginsberg* (New York: Viking Penguin, 1991).

Charters, Sam. *Some Poems/Poets: Studies in American Underground Poetry Since 1945*. Kensington, CA: Oycz, 1972.
Charters offers personal perspectives on Olson, Snyder, Everson, Ginsberg, Ferlinghetti, Duncan, Welch, and Creeley. Photos are included.

Cherkovski, Neeli. *Whitman's Wild Children*. Venice, CA: Lapis Press, 1988.
Chapters on Bukowski, Wieners, Broughton, Lamantia, Kaufman, Ginsberg, Everson, Corso, Norse, and Ferlinghetti.

Clark, Tom. *The Great Naropa Poetry Wars*. Santa Barbara, CA: Cadmus, 1980.
Clark describes "*L'affaire Merwin*," an incident involving poet W. S. Merwin, his friend Dana Naone, and Chogyam Trungpa at a retreat led by Trungpa, the founder of the Naropa Institute. Clark reports on the aftermath of the incident, including efforts to publish information and other efforts to suppress details. The story of the forced nudity of Merwin and his friend "became a hot gossip item on the coast-to-coast literary scene." Clark appends "a copious collection of germane documents."

Cook, Bruce. *The Beat Generation*. New York: Scribners, 1971; New York: Quill, 1994.
Written in the period following the death of Kerouac, this book describes the movement as a whole, discusses major and minor figures, and analyzes the transition to the Hippie movement.

Davidson, Michael. *The San Francisco Renaissance: Poetics and Community at Mid-Century*. New York: Cambridge University Press, 1989.
Essays focusing on Snyder, Whalen, Duncan, and Spicer. Davidson: "[R]ather than attempt to unify all of the communities of the San Francisco literary community under one heading, I would see them representing a necessary diversity and pluralism in a time of globalized ideologies."

Duberman, Martin. *Black Mountain: An Exploration in Community.*
New York: Dutton, 1972.

Duberman provides a history of Black Mountain College and its
famous community of artists 1933-1956, including Creeley, Rice,
Duncan, Rumaker, Wieners, Williams, and Olson. Duberman: "a
book about the impact of Black Mountain on *me*."

Ehrlich, J. W., ed. *Howl of the Censor: Lawrence Ferlinghetti, Defendant.* San Carlos, CA: Nourse, 1961.

A lawyer from the *Howl and Other Poems* obscenity trial, in
which Ferlinghetti, the book's publisher, faced prosecution, evaluates
obscenity and censorship in America. Includes a full transcript of the
trial.

Faas, Ekbert, ed. *Towards a New American Poetics: Essays and Interviews.* Santa Rosa, CA: Black Sparrow Press, 1979.

Faas provides interviews and essays on Olson, Duncan, Snyder,
Creeley, Bly, and Ginsberg.

Ferlinghetti, Lawrence, and Nancy Joyce Peters. *Literary San Francisco.* New York: Harper and Row, 1980.

Literary history of the city by the bay.

Foster, Edward Halsey. *Understanding the Beats.* Columbia: University of South Carolina Press, 1992.

Chapters on Kerouac, Ginsberg, Burroughs, and Corso. Foster:
"Beat poetry and fiction were rooted in hip culture, but they also
drew from literary traditions which encouraged personal and spontaneous styles."

French, Warren. *The San Francisco Poetry Renaissance.* Boston:
Twayne, 1991.

French: "This is not another book about the misadventures of
Burroughs, Ginsberg, and Kerouac in New York in the 1940s, as a
springboard for the beatnik antics of the 1950s. This book . . . seeks
to provide a comprehensive portrayal of the beats' contribution to
post-World War II American literature."

Géfin, Laszlo. *Ideogram: History of a Poetic Method.* Austin: University of Texas Press, 1982.

Géfin traces a "succession of poets" beginning with "Pound (or Fenollosa and Pound) through Williams, Zukofsky, and the objectivists to Olson, and from them to Duncan, Creeley, Ginsberg, and Snyder," who "have produced discrete poetics that in themselves are coherent wholes in which the juxtapositional-ideogrammic method has become fully integrated."

Gold, Herbert. *Bohemia: Where Art, Angst, Love, and Strong Coffee Meet*. New York: Simon and Schuster, 1993.
Gold: "'North Beach,' 'Bohemian,' 'beatnik,' 'hippie,' 'New Wave' are not substitutes for real life but metaphors of reality." This memoir also ranges into Paris, Israel, and Greenwich Village, commenting saucily on the evolution of life outside the margins.

_____. *Traveling San Francisco*. New York: Little Brown and Company, 1990.
A memoir about San Francisco, referring occasionally to the Beats and their legacy in the city.

Gruen, John. *The New Bohemia*. New York: a capella press, 1990.
This discussion of arts in the East Village in the 1960's includes many photos by Fred McDarrah.

Halberstam, David. *The Fifties*. New York: Villard Books, 1993.
Halberstam provides a historical context as he recounts the activities of the Beats.

Herron, Don. *The Literary World of San Francisco and Its Environs*. Ed. Nancy Peters. San Francisco: City Lights, 1985.
Herron: "*The Literary World of San Francisco* gives you the addresses, and maps out areas easily toured on foot." Within a general picture of the literary community, the text gives background on various Beats, including Kerouac, Ginsberg, Ferlinghetti, and Henry Miller.

Holmes, John Clellon. *Nothing More to Declare*. New York: Dutton, 1967.
A collection of Holmes' articles on the Beats, including "This Is the Beat Generation," "The Philosophy of the Beat Generation," and "The Game of the Name."

_____. *Passionate Opinions: The Cultural Essays*. Fayetteville: University of Arkansas Press, 1988.

This collection of essays often focuses on the Beats and includes "The Name of the Game," "This Is the Beat Generation," "The Philosophy of the Beat Generation," and "The Game of the Name." Also included: "Broken Places: Existential Aspects of the Novel," "The Golden Age of Jazz," "The Beat Poets: A Primer" and introductions originally written for *Go, The Horn* and *Get Home Free*.

_____. *Representative Men: The Biographical Essays*. Fayetteville: University of Arkansas Press, 1988.

Essays on Jay Landesman, Allen Ginsberg, Jack Kerouac, and Neal Cassady.

Hornick, Lita. *The Green Fuse*. New York: Giorno Poetry Systems, 1989.

Autobiography of a philanthropic woman supportive of the efforts of the Beats.

_____. *Night Flight*. New York: The Kulchur Foundation, 1982.

Essays on writers, including Berrigan, Wieners, and Kerouac (poems). Material on Giorno Poetry Systems and the Jack Kerouac School of Disembodied Poetics.

Huncke, Herbert. *The Evening Sun Turned Crimson*. Cherry Valley, NY: Cherry Valley Editions, 1980.

This frank autobiography relates Huncke's friendships and relationships in short chapters. Two chapters are devoted to William Burroughs. The life of drug use and subsequent incarceration and hospitalization is also covered.

_____. *Guilty of Everything*. New York: Hanuman Books, 1987.

William Burroughs: "This book is not just the story of a thief and drug addict. It covers a whole section of recent history seen through the writer's association with a number of key figures: Dr. Kinsey, Allen Ginsberg, Jack Kerouac, Neal Cassady, Gregory Corso, [and] Alex Trocchi."

Investigative Poetry Group. *The Party: A Chronological Perspective on a Confrontation at a Buddhist Seminary*. Woodstock, NY: Poetry, Crime and Culture Press, 1977.

Under the direction of Ed Sanders, a class at Naropa Institute investigated "the stripping incident at Snowmass, Colorado," otherwise referred to as the "Merwin-Naone-Trungpa matter." This volume collects comments, interviews, responses to questions, and other materials in order to create a clear record of what occurred.

Jacobs, Paul, and Saul Landau. *The New Radicals: A Report with Documents*. New York: Vintage Books, 1966.
This study of "The Movement," whose particpants "seek to find a new politics and a new ideology that will permit them to link existential humanism with morally acceptable modes of achieving radical social change."

Kerrigan, Michael. *Bluff Your Way in Literature*. London: Ravette Ltd., 1987.
How to give the appearance of a well-read person. Some reference to the Beats.

Kherdian, David. *Six San Francisco Poets*. Fresno: Giligia Press, 1969.
Ferlinghetti, Snyder, Whalen, Meltzer, McClure, and Brother Antoninus are each assigned a chapter in this personalized account of the San Francisco scene.

Larsen, Carl, and James Singer. *The Beat Generation Cook Book*. New York: Seven Poets Press, 1961.
Humorous pamphlet with illustrations by D. G. Christian. The editors describe "the favorite dishes of real honest-to-Zen members of the brotherhood."

Lauridsen, Inger Thorup, and Per Dalgard. *The Beat Generation and the Russian New Wave*. Ann Arbor: Ardis, 1990.
The Beat Generation and the Russian New Wave "emerged independently, . . . did not influence each other, and yet . . . exhibited many similarities." This volume features interviews with Ginsberg, Snyder, McClure, and Ferlinghetti in addition to interviews with comparable Russian writers.

Lee, A. Robert, ed. *The Beat Generation Writers*. London: Pluto Press, 1996.

This is an anthology of articles and essays about Ginsberg, Kerouac, Corso, Ferlinghetti, Burroughs, Holmes, Cassady, Jones/Baraka, Joans, Kaufman, and women of the Beat Generation. The essays offer the perspectives of British critics.

Lhamon, W. T. *Deliberate Speed: The Origins of a Cultural Style in the American 1950's.* Washington, DC: Smithsonian Institution Press, 1990.
Lhamon: "The focus here is on the fifties, particularly the middle of that decade, because then all the elements of American contemporary culture were in the pot, swapping around and affecting each other." Numerous brief references to Ginsberg, Kerouac, and the Beats.

Lipton, Lawrence. *The Erotic Revolution: An Affirmative View of the New Morality.* Los Angeles: Sherbourne Press, 1965.
Brief references to Beat writers, with an appendix on Reich.

_____. *The Holy Barbarians.* New York: Messner, 1959.
An early study described as "the first complete and unbiased survey of the beat generation and its role in our society." See an excerpt in Thomas Parkinson, ed., *A Casebook on the Beat* (New York: Crowell, 1961): 291-309.

McClure, Michael. *Lighting the Corners: On Art, Nature, and the Visionary: Essays and Interviews.* Ed. Lee Bartlett. Albuquerque: University of New Mexico College of Arts and Sciences, 1993.
Selected materials, some previously unpublished, from throughout McClure's career. Comments on Dylan, Duncan, Spicer, Ginsberg, Creeley, Snyder, and others.

_____. *Scratching the Beat Surface.* San Francisco: North Point Press, 1982.
McClure "reviews his own career and the contributions of his contemporaries over the past three decades, including poems by Hart Crane, Charles Olson, Allen Ginsberg, Robert Creeley, Jack Kerouac, Gary Snyder, Philip Whalen, and others."

McDarrah, Fred W., and Patrick McDarrah. *The Greenwich Village Guide.* Chicago: a capella books, 1992.

A visitor's guide to Greenwich Village, with maps, photos, and background information. A few brief references to the Beats, including small photos of Ginsberg, Kerouac, and DiPrima by Fred McDarrah.

McNally, Dennis. *Desolate Angel: Jack Kerouac, the Beat Generation, and America*. New York: Random House, 1979.
McNally "traces Kerouac's frenzied, difficult, and intense life." This book was reprinted in paperback by McGraw-Hill in 1980.

Maynard, John. *Venice West: The Beat Generation in Southern California*. New Brunswick, NJ: Rutgers University Press, 1991.
History of the West Coast Beats, including Rexroth, Perkoff, and Lipton. Maynard: "*Venice West* takes the form of a collective biography, with the narrative intentionally written, for the most part, as if nothing similar had ever happened before. . . . The significance of Venice West lies less in its artistic achievements – although there were quite a few – than in the audacity of its people trying to live for art *and nothing else* in a city that adored, and still adores, its status as the world's biggest, gaudiest, and wildest symbol of material success."

Meltzer, David. *The San Francisco Poets*. New York: Ballantine Books, 1971.
Meltzer interviews Rexroth, Everson, Ferlinghetti, Welch, and McClure. This book was later reproduced under the title *Golden Gate: Interviews with Five San Francisco Poets* (Berkeley, CA: Wingbow Press, 1976). The earlier volume includes an interview with Richard Brautigan.

Montgomery, John. *Kerouac West Coast: A Bohemian Pilot's Detailed Navigational Instructions*. Palo Alto, CA: Fels and Firn Press, 1976.
This pamphlet analyzes Kerouac's connection to artists on the West Coast of the United States.

Morgan, Bill. *The Beat Generation in New York: A Walking Tour of Jack Kerouac's City*. San Francisco: City Lights, 1997.
Maps and subway information are included in eight walking tours.

Morrison, Blake. *The Movement: English Poetry and Fiction of the
   1950's*. New York: Oxford University Press, 1980.
   Morrison: "I have tried to rescue the term 'Movement' and to
show that it stands not for what is peripheral and debilitating in
[writers such as Donald Davie, Thom Gunn, Kingsley Amis, Iris
Murdoch, and John Wain] but for what is central and enriching."

Nutall, Jeff. *Bomb Culture*. New York: Delacorte Press, 1968.
   Nutall: "The people who had passed puberty at the time of the
bomb found that they were incapable of conceiving of life *without* a
future." Making a strong contrast, Nutall observes, "The people who
had not reached puberty at the time of the bomb were incapable of
conceiving of life *with* a future." Nutall refers briefly to Burroughs,
Ginsberg, Kerouac, and other Beats.

Ossman, David. *The Sullen Art: Interviews by David Ossman with
   Modern American Poets*. New York: Corinth Books, 1963.
   Interviews with Rexroth, Carroll, Blackburn, Rothenberg, Kelly,
Bly, Logan, Sorrentino, Creeley, Merwin, Levertov, Jones, Dorn, and
Ginsberg. Selected interviews from radio programs 1960-1961.

Ostergard, Geoffrey. *Latter-Day Anarchism: The Politics of the
   American Beat Generation*. Ahmedabad, India: Harold Laski
   Institute of Political Science, 1964.
   Ostergard: "Beat politics . . . is the politics of the non-political.
The hipster believes that what holds the world of squares together is
the Social Lie."

Parkinson, Thomas, ed. *A Casebook on the Beat*. New York: Crow-
   ell, 1961.
   Selections from Ginsberg, Kerouac, Corso, Burroughs, Fer-
linghetti, Snyder, Whalen, McClure, and Wieners. Criticism by
Rexroth, Sisk, Podhoretz, Van Ghent, Tallman, Miller, O'Neil, Gold,
Ciardi, Gaiser, Parkinson, and Lipton.

Parry, Albert. *Garrets and Pretenders: A History of Bohemianism in
   America*. Mineola, NY: Dover Publications, 1960.
   Originally published in 1933, Parry's book surveys bohemianism.
The Dover edition includes addenda on Greenwich Village and the
Beats. Harry T. Moore contributes the chapter "Enter Beatniks: The

Bohème of 1960," which is a skeptical review of the Beats, including photos and a cartoon. See 376-395.

Phillips, Lisa, ed. *Beat Culture and the New America: 1950-1965.* New York: Whitney Museum of American Art/Flammarion, 1995.
Maurice Berger, Ray Carncy, Maria Damon, Allen Ginsberg, John G. Hanhardt, Glenn O'Brien, Mona Lisa Saloy, Edward Sanders, Rebecca Solnit, and Steven Watson contribute to this volume of essays and photos related to the exhibit at the Whitney Museum.

Plimpton, George, ed. *Poets at Work: "The Paris Review" Interviews.* New York: Penguin, 1989.
Tom Clark interviews Allen Ginsberg: 187-228.

Rexroth, Kenneth. *The Alternative Society: Essays from the Other World.* New York: Herder and Herder, 1970.
Fifteen essays, including an opening piece "Disengagement: The Art of the Beat Generation."

_____. *American Poetry in the Twentieth Century.* New York: Herder, 1971.
An opinionated survey of twentieth-century poetry, beginning with the basis of its tradition in the nineteenth century and proceeding to the Beats, particularly in San Francisco.

Rigney, Francis J., and L. Douglas Smith. *The Real Bohemia: A Sociological and Psychological Study of the "Beats."* New York: Basic Books, 1961.
The authors present their findings based on tests administered to fifty-one people from the San Francisco Grant Avenue Bohemian Colony.

Roszak, Theodore. *The Making of a Counter Culture.* New York: Doubleday, 1969.
Chapters on various artists, including Ginsberg, Watts, and Leary. Roszak: "[T]he counter culture, far more than merely 'meriting' attention, desperately requires it, since I am at a loss to know where, besides among those of these dissenting young people and their heirs of the next few generations, the radical discontent and innovation

can be found that might transform this disoriented civilization of ours into something a human being can identify as home."

Roy, Gregor. *Beat Literature*. New York: Thor Publications, 1966.
Monarch Notes on the Beats! "This guide is intended to supplement and enhance, and is not a substitute for, the original work of art." Discussion of the definition of Beatness, the tradition of rebellion, and the history of Bohemianism.

Saroyan, Aram. *Genesis Angels: The Saga of Lew Welch and the Beat Generation*. New York: William Morrow, 1979.
This biographical study of Welch becomes a general study of the Beat Generation as the companions and associates of Welch are dealt with.

Schock, Jim. *Life Is a Lousy Drag*. San Francisco: Unicorn Publishing, 1958.
A "roasting" of the Beats and their lifestyle through the development of a caricature. Drawings by Trubee Campbell.

Schumacher, Michael. *Dharma Lion: A Critical Biography of Allen Ginsberg*. New York: St. Martin's, 1992.
This biography of Ginsberg is thorough and clear, offering insightful examination of the life and writings of Ginsberg, and providing a detailed sense of the Beat Generation as a whole.

Silverman, Herschel. *High on the Beats*. Brooklyn, NY: Pinched Nerve Press, 1992.
The owner of a candy store in Bayonne, New Jersey, writes about his enthusiasm for the Beats, especially Allen Ginsberg, who corresponded with Silverman.

Stephenson, Gregory. *The Daybreak Boys: Essays on the Literature of the Beat Generation*. Carbondale: Southern Illinois University Press, 1990.
Essays on Kerouac, Ginsberg, Burroughs, Corso, Holmes, McClure, Fariña, Ferlinghetti, and Neal Cassady.

Sterrit, David John. *Mad to Be Saved: The Beats, the Fifties, and Film*. Carbondale: Southern Illinois University Press, 1997.
Sterrit explores the presence of Beats in film.

Taylor, John Russell. *Anger and After: A Guide to the New British Drama.* London: Methuen, 1962.
A study of drama in Britain emerging in the 1950's.

Tytell, John. *The Living Theater: Art, Exile, and Outrage.* New York: Grove, 1995.
New York Times: "Mr. Tytell . . . focuses mainly on the dynamics between [Julian] Beck and Ms. [Judith] Malina, with long accounts of their personal and sexual activities, as well as a pop history filled with a Who's Who of painters, writers, and actors."

_____. *Naked Angels.* New York: Grove Weidenfeld, 1976.
The classic biographical and critical study of the Beats, with principal focus on Burroughs, Ginsberg, and Kerouac. Tytell: "Once the Beats were a few Lears raging in the storm, obscured by the vastness of the system. Their transformation of literary form and the informing power of what they had to say aroused mounting interest. A growing audience responded to their expression of libertarian values while recognizing them as prophets of the future."

Vidal, Gore. *Palimpsest.* New York: Penguin Books, 1995.
This memoir includes references to Ginsberg, Kerouac, Burroughs, and Bowles. The chapter "Now You Owe Me a Dollar" serves as a running commentary on the Beats, but in particular describes the sexual relationship of Vidal and Kerouac.

Watson, Steven. *The Birth of the Beat Generation: Visionaries, Rebels, and Hipsters, 1944-1960.* New York: Pantheon Books, 1995.
The life, times, and literature of the Beat Generation, with accompanying maps, photos, and a chronology.

Watts, Alan. *Beat Zen, Square Zen, and Zen.* San Francisco: City Lights, 1959.
Watts: "Beat Zen . . . ranges from a use of Zen to justify sheer caprice in art, literature, and life to a very forceful social criticism and 'digging of the universe' such as one may find in the poetry of Ginsberg and Snyder, and, rather unevenly, in Kerouac." See this item in Charters, ed., *The Portable Beat Reader* (New York: Viking Penguin, 1992).

Weinberg, Jeffrey H., ed. *Writers Outside the Margin*. Sudbury, MA: Water Row, 1986.

Essays, poems, drawings, and memoirs by or about Jack Micheline, Gregory Corso, William Burroughs, Jack Kerouac, Neal Cassady, and Allen Ginsberg.

Wilcox, Fred. *Chasing Shadows: Memoirs of a Sixties Survivor*. Sag Harbor, NY: Permanent Press, 1996.

Wilcox: "For so many years I hid in the closet, not wanting people to know that I had been 'observed and evaluated' on psychiatric wards, that I was given electro-shock treatments, that I was an alcoholic, that I once cut my wrists, that the army didn't want me, nor I them, that I am, and always will be, 'an ex-mental patient.'"

Wilson, Colin. *The Outsider*. Boston: Houghton Mifflin, 1956.

A study of the figure of the outsider in literature.

Yapp, Nick. *Bluff Your Way in Poetry*. West Sussex, England: Ravette Books, Ltd., 1989.

How to give the appearance of someone familiar with poetry. See a comment on Ginsberg: 57.

Zaranka, William, ed. *Literature in Briefs*. Cambridge/Watertown, MA: Apple-wood Books, 1983.

Parodies of famous works. See Craig Weeden's "A Pizza Joint in Cranston," a parody of Ginsberg's "A Supermarket in California."

Sections or Chapters

Allen, Walter. *The Modern Novel*. New York: Dutton, 1965.

Allen: "Kerouac and the rest belong to sociology rather than to literature." Short commentary.

Allsop, Kenneth. *Hard Travelin'*. London: Pimlico, 1983. 427-428.

Brief reference to Kerouac. In this extensive study of migrants and people of the road, no special appreciation of the Beats emerges.

Armour, Richard. *American Lit Relit: A Short History of American Literature for Long-Suffering Students*. New York: McGraw-Hill, 1964. 159.

Ironic subtitle: "A short history of American Literature for long-suffering students, for teachers who manage to keep one chapter ahead of the class, and for all those who, no longer being in school, can happily sink back into illiteracy." Fleeting reference to Kerouac and Ginsberg.

Ashton, Dore. *The New York School: A Cultural Reckoning*. New York: Viking, 1973. 225-229.

Ashton's book focuses on the legendary New York School of painters and briefly refers to the connection to Ginsberg, Kerouac, and the Beats.

Austen, Roger. *Playing the Game: The Homosexual Novel in America*. New York: Bobbs-Merrill, 1977. 184-187.

See a section titled "The Gay Beats: Cats at Play in the Closet."

Balaban, Dan. "Witless Madcaps." *The Village Voice Reader*. Ed. Daniel Wolf. New York: Grove Press, 1963. 31-32.

Balaban relates a conversation with Corso, Kerouac, and Ginsberg in New York. The trio was ending a three-year period in San Francisco and moving on to Tangier.

Berthoff, Warner. *A Literature Without Qualities: American Writing Since 1945*. Berkeley: University of California Press, 1979.

A general view of American literature 1945-1975. Some mention of Kerouac, Burroughs, Ginsberg, O'Hara, and Kesey. Extended discussion of Henry Miller and his *Tropic of Cancer*.

Bold, Alan, and Robert Giddings. *True Characters: Real People in Fiction*. Essex, England: Longman, 1984.

"This dictionary has been designed to reveal the facts of life that lurk behind the business of fiction. Some of the most celebrated characters and incidents in literature are modeled on actual originals and events." Short entry on Cassady.

Bradshaw, Steve. *Cafe Society: Bohemian Life from Swift to Bob Dylan*. New York: Weidenfeld and Nicolson, 1978.

This historical review of cafés and their patrons includes a chapter "Neon, Jukes, Heavenly Blue" that refers to the San Remo, where "a clientele of potheads, Negroes, socialist sailors, and Communists, who mixed with the future avant-garde like Allen Ginsberg, or Julian Beck and Judith Malina, who would found the Living Theatre." A section of reproductions of paintings gives an idea of café life since the eighteenth century.

Broyard, Anatole. *Kafka Was the Rage: A Greenwich Village Memoir*. New York: Carol Southern Books, 1993.
    The author describes life in Greenwich Village 1946-1947. Mention of meetings and relationships with authors and artists.

Bryant, Jeffrey H. *The Open Decision: The Contemporary American Novel and Its Intellectual Background*. New York: The Free Press, 1970. 199-228.
    A discussion of Kerouac, Holmes, Brossard, and Burroughs. For Bryant, the spontaneity of the Beats is their means of surviving repression.

Burgess, Anthony. *The Novel Now: A Guide to Contemporary Fiction*. New York: Norton, 1967.
    Burgess comments on Bowles, Kerouac, Burroughs, and Mailer, but his discussion encompasses many writers since World War II.

Butterick, George F. "Periodicals of the Beat Generation." *The Beats: Literary Bohemians in Postwar America*. Ed. Ann Charters. Detroit: Gale Research, 1983. 651-688.
    A comprehensive listing of "periodicals inspired by the Beat Generation," followed by photos of the covers of the magazines.

Cándida Smith, Richard. "After the War or Before: Kenneth Rexroth Confronts History," "The Beat Phenomenon: Masculine Paths of Maturation," and "Gary Snyder on the Responsibilities of Utopia: Expanding the Boundaries of Domesticity." *Utopia and Dissent: Art, Poetry, and Politics in California*. Berkeley, CA: University of California Press, 1995. 36-66, 145-171, 372-399.
    The author explores the pre-WWII bohemian culture in California to discover an important source for the emerging counterculture of the 1950's and 1960's. Chapters include references to Rexroth, Kerouac, Ginsberg, Snyder, and Duncan.

Couch, William T., ed. *Collier's Encyclopedia 1958 Year Book: An Encyclopedic Supplement and Review of National and International Events of 1958.* New York: P. F. Collier and Son, 1959. 699-700.

An article on Kerouac as one of the year's personalities notes publication of *The Subterraneans* and *The Dharma Bums* following the best-seller *On the Road,* but says the latest books are "somewhat less frenetic."

_____. *Collier's Encyclopedia 1960 Year Book: An Encyclopedic Supplement and Review of National and International Events of 1959.* New York: P. F. Collier and Son, 1960. 40-41.

Beats are called "Beatniks" by John Albot Clark. Their poetry has "dubious value" but they are breathing life into poetry and forcing other "better poets" to reexamine themselves. Notice is given to the publication of Lipton's *The Holy Barbarians* and Rexroth's *Bird in the Bush,* which is "refreshingly annoying."

Dane, Robert, ed. *Against the Grain: Interviews with Maverick American Publishers.* Iowa City: University of Iowa Press, 1986. 1-41, 87-112.

Interviews with Ferlinghetti and James Laughlin.

Dickey, James. *Babel to Byzantium: Poets and Poetry Now.* New York: Farrar, Straus and Giroux, 1968.

Dickey offers short essays to express his reactions to Allen Ginsberg, Kenneth Patchen, Brother Antoninus, Charles Olson, and Robert Duncan, among many other poets.

Dodge, John V., and Howard E. Kasch, eds. *Britannica Book of the Year 1960: A Record of the March of Events of 1959.* Chicago: Encyclopedia Britannica, Inc., 1960. 42.

The author sees the "serious new Bohemians, the 'beatniks,' occupied with reading their deliberately undisciplined, protesting verse." They "created more publicity than verse."

Donald, Miles. *The American Novel in the Twentieth Century.* New York: Barnes and Noble, 1978.

See chapter 3 for commentary on Burroughs and Kerouac.

Ebner, David Y. "Beats and Hippies: A Comparative Analysis."
Studies in the Sociology of Countercultures. Ed. Kenneth West-
hues. Toronto: McGraw-Hill, 1972.

Ebner: "[O]ne may often expect to find a retreatist movement as
the predecessor of a revolutionary one." In this scheme, the Beats
are "retreatists" while the Hippies are "revolutionary."

Edmiston, Susan, and Linda D. Cirino. *Literary New York: A History
and Guide.* Boston: Houghton Mifflin, 1976.

Authors: "We began with the simple motive of seeking out the
houses of writers who had lived in New York and the places they
wrote about." As the work progressed, the authors found it necessary
"to describe how writing developed in New York and suggest something of the city's character and style." Photos and descriptions of
Kerouac, Burroughs, Ginsberg, Corso, and LeRoi Jones.

Ehrenreich, Barbara. "The Beat Rebellion: Beyond Work and Marriage." *The Hearts of Men: American Dreams and the Flight from
Commitment.* Garden City, NY: Doubleday, 1983. 52-67.

Ehrenreich assesess the version of the Beats established in films
like *The Wild One* and *Cool Hand Luke* and in periodicals such as
Esquire, *Life*, and *Playboy*. She analyzes the transition into the Hippie movement.

Everson, William. "Dionysus and the Beat Generation." *Earth Poetry.*
Berkeley, CA: Oyez, 1980.

Everson: "It is the endeavor of the Beat Generation to fuse Eros
and Agape in a profane synthesis, but by settling for ecstasy at any
price, it roves restlessly from the delirium of sensational licentious-
ness to compulsive flights at the infinite through drugs or dithyram-
bic aestheticism." See this item reprinted in Lee Bartlett, ed., *The
Beats: Essays in Criticism* (Jefferson, NC: McFarland, 1981): 181-
186.

Feied, Frederick. *No Pie in the Sky: The Hobo as American Cultural
Hero in the Works of Jack London, John Dos Passos and Jack
Kerouac.* Secaucus, NJ: Citadel Press, 1964.

See chapter 3 for a discussion of Kerouac's *On the Road* and *The
Dharma Bums*.

Fiedler, Leslie. *Love and Death in the American Novel.* Rev. ed. New York: Stein and Day, 1966.
In the course of an extended analysis, Fiedler refers to Kerouac, Bowles, Burroughs, Kesey, and Mailer.

_____. *The Return of the Vanishing American.* New York: Stein and Day, 1968.
Fiedler develops his interpretation of the New West with references to Burroughs, Ginsberg, Creeley, Dorn, Kesey, Mailer, Snyder, and Watts.

_____. *Waiting for the End.* New York: Stein and Day, 1964.
Ginsberg, Kerouac, Burroughs – all passing references.

Fuller, Edmund. *Man in Modern Fiction: Some Minority Opinions on Contemporary American Writing.* New York: Random House, 1958.
Fuller expresses his objections to vulgarity and sex in Kerouac, Bowles, and Mailer.

Geismar, Maxwell David. *American Moderns: From Rebellion to Conformity.* New York: Hill and Wang, 1958. 171-179.
An attack on Mailer.

George, Paul S., and Jerold M. Starr. "Beat Politics: New Left and Hippie Beginnings in the Postwar Counterculture." *Cultural Politics: Radical Movements in Modern History.* Ed. Jerold M. Starr. New York: Praeger, 1985. 189-233.
This chapter is divided into short segments with subheadings. The authors trace the development of the Beat Generation and the evolution of the meaning of the term "beat" before proceeding to the political views of Ginsberg and Kerouac, especially in the 1960's. George and Starr: "As cultural radicals, Beats condemned power as inherently corrupting of the individual spirit. They were not interested in seizing the state to promote equality, especially if such a program required the bureaucratic regulation of social life. On the contrary, they were concerned with opposing the state in order to maximize individual liberty."

Gold, Herbert. "My Dinner with William S. Burroughs and the General's Daughter." *Bohemia: Digging the Roots of the Cool*. New York: Simon and Schuster Touchstone, 1994. 129-134.

Gold describes his meeting with Burroughs at the "Beat Hotel" in Paris while Burroughs was completing *Naked Lunch*. Reference also to brief meeting in Paris with Ginsberg and Corso, the "beat Shelley."

Goodman, Paul. *Growing Up Absurd*. New York: Vintage Books, 1960. 63-70, 123, 135, 156, 164-165, 170-190.

Goodman: "Beat literature and religion are ignorant and thin, yet they have two invaluable properties. First, they are grounded in the existing situation, whatever the situation, without moralistic or invidious judgment of it. . . . Their religion is unfeasible, for one cannot richly meet the glancing present, like Zen, without patriotic loyalty, long discipleship, and secure subsistence. Nevertheless, their writing has a pleasant bare surface, and it *is* experience."

Goodwin, Donald. *Alcohol and the Writer*. New York: Penguin, 1988.

The problem of alcohol and its peculiarly common connection to prominent American writers. No specific reference to the Beats is indexed, but the text might serve as background for an understanding of the problem of alcoholism in a writer like Kerouac.

Gunn, Drewey Wayne. *American and British Writers in Mexico 1556-1973*. Austin: University of Texas Press, 1974.

Features a chapter "The Beat Trail to Mexico." A study of biographical data and references to literature to account for Kerouac, Ginsberg, Burroughs, Corso, and Cassady in Mexico, starting in 1950.

Harrison, Gilbert A., ed. *The Critic as Artist: Essays on Books 1920-1970*. New York: Liveright, 1972. 351-357.

An attack on Burroughs' *Naked Lunch*.

Hassan, Ihab. *Contemporary American Literature, 1945-1972: An Introduction*. New York: Ungar, 1973.

In surveying literature since 1945, Hassan is receptive to numerous Beats.

_____. *Radical Innocence: Studies in the Contemporary American Novel*. Princeton, NJ: Princeton University Press, 1961.
Hassan offers some commentary on Mailer, Kerouac, and Bowles.

Hoffman, Daniel, ed. *Harvard Guide to Contemporary American Writing*. Cambridge, MA: Belknap Press of Harvard University, 1979.
Ten critics present essays on literature since 1945 and its social environment. In "Realists, Naturalists, and Novelists of Manners," Leo Braudy discusses Kerouac: 109-110. In "Poetry: Schools of Dissidents," Daniel Hoffman refers to writers associated with the Beats, including Rexroth, Ginsberg, Snyder, Olson, McClure, and Corso: 496-563.

Hoffman, Frederick John. *Modern Novel in America, 1900-1950*. Washington, DC: Regnery Gateway, 1951.
This general view of modern literature includes references to Kerouac and Mailer.

_____. *The Mortal No: Death and the Modern Imagination*. Princeton, NJ: Princeton University Press, 1964.
This broad view of death in modern literature includes references to Bowles, Burroughs, Ginsberg, Kerouac, Mailer, and Rexroth.

Holmes, John Clellon. "Unscrewing the Locks: The Beat Poets." *The Beats: Essays in Criticism*. Ed. Lee Bartlett. Jefferson, NC: McFarland, 1981. 5-13.
Holmes: "I take this movement to embrace all those writers who rejected the formalism, conservatism, and 'classicism' that Eliot's influence grafted on American writing."

Honan, Park. "A Beat Precursor: Nelson Algren." *The Beats*. Ed. Park Honan. London: J. M. Dent, 1987. 193-198.
Honan: "Algren's intention is . . . to show us how the world strikes the consciousness of one normal idiosyncratic man bent upon discovering why his own city is less than humane."

Howard, John R. *The Cutting Edge: Social Movements and Social Change in America*. New York: J. B. Lippincott, 1974. 183-185.

Howard examines the links among the Lost Generation, the Beat Generation, and the Hippies.

Howard, Richard. *Alone with America: Essays on the Art of Poetry in the United States Since 1950*. New York: Atheneum, 1969.
Howard's general approach finds room for essays on Corso, Creeley, Ginsberg, Snyder, and others.

Howe, Irving. *A World More Attractive: A View of Modern Literature and Politics*. New York: Horizon Press, 1963. 123-129.
A favorable reading of Mailer.

Jacoby, Russell. *The Last Intellectuals: American Culture in the Age of Academe*. New York: Basic Books, 1987.
The Beats "are more than a lesson in the risks of cultural forecasting. They are the last bohemians, and the first of the 1960's counter culturalists."

Jones, Granville H. "Jack Kerouac and the American Conscience." *Lectures on American Novelists*. Pittsburgh: Department of English, Carnegie Institute of Technology, 1963.
Jones: "Through autobiography, social criticism, and prophetic mysticism [Kerouac] speaks to America of the mid-twentieth century." Jones adds that Kerouac "sees America as a mighty land, but a land shackled by fear." Further, Jones says, "This is Kerouac's less-than-obvious message. Hope lies in the individual who believes, and acts on belief, in love." See this item in Scott Donaldson, ed., *"On the Road": Text and Criticism* (New York: Viking Critical Library, 1979): 485-503.

Kazin, Alfred. *Bright Book of Life: American Novelists and Storytellers from Hemingway to Mailer*. New York: Atlantic Monthly Press/Little Brown, 1973.
This broad interpretation of literature includes references to Mailer, Burroughs, Sanders, and Jones.

_____. *Contemporaries*. Boston: Little, Brown and Company, 1962.
An attack on Kerouac and the foolish Beats.

Kostelanetz, Richard. *Twenties in the Sixties: Previously Uncollected Critical Essays*. Westport, CT: Greenwood Press, 1979.

Kostelanetz includes references to Burroughs and Ginsberg in these essays.

Kowalewski, Michael. "Jack Kerouac and the Beats in San Francisco." *San Francisco in Fiction: Essays in a Regional Literature.* Eds. David Fine and Paul Skenazy. Albuquerque: University of New Mexico Press, 1995. 126-143.
   Author: "By examining images of the region that emerge from three works—his prose sketch 'The Railroad Earth' and his novels *On the Road* and *The Dharma Bums*—it becomes apparent that Kerouac's 'images' are often more auditory than visual."

Ludwig, Jack. *Recent American Novelists.* Minneapolis: University of Minnesota Press, 1962.
   Ludwig: "The Beat novel spangles a chintzy weave of souvenir strands." This work is University of Minnesota Pamphlets on American Writers No. 22.

McCarthy, Mary. *The Writing on the Wall and Other Literary Essays.* San Diego, CA: Harcourt Brace and World, 1970. 42-53.
   An insightful essay on William Burroughs' *Naked Lunch*.

McWilliams, Wilson Carey. "The Beats." *The California Dream.* Eds. Dennis Hale and Jonathan Eisen. New York: Macmillan, 1968.
   McWilliams: "The Beat Generation is refeshing because it opens a door: it is a negative 'cosmic meaning' in place of the 'best-of-possible-worlds' doctrine of official intellectuality." McWilliams adds, "Symbiotes the Beats are: they allow officialdom to define nature and the world, point out the shams and follies of the definition, and seek to betake themselves somewhere else."

Meine, Franklin J., and Ruth C. Hunt and W. Stewart Wallace, eds. *The American Peoples Encyclopedia Yearbook: Events and Personalities of 1959.* Chicago: Spencer Press, 1960. 810-811.
   In 1959, "in the popular mind *poet* and *beatnik* often seemed synonymous." The author adds, ". . . the beatniks' work was of questionable merit." Notice is given of City Lights, Grove Press, and New Directions for publication of Corso, Ginsberg, and others.

Miller, Richard. *Bohemia: The Protoculture Then and Now.* Chicago: Nelson-Hall, 1977. 227-232.

Miller: "[T]he Beat movement gave a center and a legitimacy to Wild West poetry, to the crude, rebel, democratic literature erected in defiance of the East Coast's polite tradition and effete literati."

Moore, Harry T., ed. *Contemporary American Novelists*. Carbondale: Southern Illinois University Press, 1964.
See essays on Mailer and Kerouac.

_____. "Enter Beatniks: The Bohème of 1960." *Garrets and Pretenders: A History of Bohemianism in America*. Ed. Albert Parry. New York: Dover, 1960. 376-395.
Negative assessment of the Beats and their art.

Myers, Jack, and David Wojahn, eds. *A Profile of Twentieth-Century American Poetry*. Carbondale: Southern Illinois University Press, 1991.
Selection of essays, some commenting on various Beats.

Newfield, Jack. "The Beat Generation and the Ungeneration." *A Prophetic Minority*. New York: New American Library, 1966. 35-48.
How does the generation coming of age in the 1950's compare with the Beat Generation? Some discussion of Kerouac, Ginsberg, and Burroughs.

Packard, William, ed. *The Craft of Poetry: Interviews from the New York Quarterly*. New York: Doubleday, 1974.
Blackburn, Ginsberg, Creeley, MacLow, and others – a total of seventeen interviews. The interviewing technique is designed to arrive at a discussion "of the artist's work and not the work itself. And [the interviewer attempts] . . . to restrict . . . questions to those which might occur to a practicing writer."

Parkinson, Thomas. "Phenomenon or Generation." *A Casebook on the Beat*. Ed. Thomas Parkinson. New York: Crowell, 1961. 276-290.
Parkinson: "The reception of the Beat writers, the extraordinary interest in the novels of Kerouac, Ginsberg's little pamphlet of poems, Ferlinghetti's *Coney Island of the Mind* (which has sold over 40,000 copies), the San Francisco issue of *Evergreen Review* (entering its seventh printing), and the publicity accorded the beat way of life

by national magazines – all this has passed into not only social history but also literary history."

Podhoretz, Norman. *Doings and Undoings: The Fifties and After in American Writing*. New York: Farrar, Straus, and Giroux, 1964.
See "The Know-Nothing Bohemians" and "Norman Mailer: Embattled Vision" in this collection.

_____. *Making It*. New York: Random House, 1967.
Podhoretz: "Did I really care whether or not a bunch of idiot kids thought *On the Road* was a great novel?"

Polsky, Ned. "The Village Beat Scene: Summer 1960." *Hustlers, Beats, and Others*. Garden City, NY: Anchor Books, 1969. 150-185.
Polsky generalizes about the Beats in the Village, providing his impressions of their attitudes, racial background, economic status, political views, sex lives, drug use, literacy, and taste in music. Polsky: "Most Beat literature is poor when it is not godawful."

Prescott, Orville. *In My Opinion: An Inquiry into the Contemporary Novel*. New York: Bobbs-Merrill, 1952.
In this general study, Bowles and Mailer are mentioned.

Rexroth, Kenneth. "The Commercialization of the Image of Revolt." *The Beats: Literary Bohemians in Postwar America* Ed. Ann Charters. Detroit: Gale Research, 1983. 643-650.
Rexroth: "[A]n awful lot of people are buying false merchandise, an awful lot of people are being deluded. They are thinking that they are reading somethinbg very much up-to-date, something very vital, something which is still a trenchant and meaningful indictment of society, and they're just reading cheap sensationalism."

_____. "Disengagement: The Art of the Beat Generation." *New World Writing* 11. New York: New American Library, 1957. 28-41.
This essay evaluates the avant-garde movement among painters, musicians, and literary artists. San Francisco is praised for "intense literary activity." Rexroth: "The avant-garde has not only not ceased to exist. It's jumping all over the place. Something's happening, man." See this item in Park Honan, ed., *The Beats* (London: J. M. Dent, 1987): 199-215. The piece is also reproduced in Thomas

Parkinson, ed., *A Casebook on the Beat* (New York: Crowell, 1961): 179-193. It also is included in Kenneth Rexroth, *The Alternative Society: Essays from the Other World* (New York: Herder and Herder, 1970): 1-16.

Rickett, Arthur. *Vagabond in Literature*. New York: Kennikat Press, 1968.
Rickett evaluates predecessors of the Beats, such as Thoreau, Whitman, and Baudelaire.

Ruas, Charles. *Conversations with American Writers*. New York: Knopf, 1985.
A 1975 roundtable discussion with Allen Ginsberg, Maurice Girodias, William S. Burroughs, and James Grauerholz. Focus on censorship and publication of material likely to arouse censors.

Sanders, Ed. *Tales of Beatnik Glory*. New York: Stonehill Publishing, 1975.
A stylized interpretation of the artistic scene in New York in the late 1950's and early 1960's.

Schleifer, Marc D. "The Beat Debated—Is It or Is It Not?" *The Village Voice Reader*. Ed. Daniel Wolf and Edwin Fancher. New York: Grove Press, 1963. 238-240.
An encapsulated version of Kerouac's definition of the Beats.

Server, Lee. "Paperback Beat." *Over My Dead Body: The Sensational Age of the American Paperback, 1945-1955*. San Francisco: Chronicle Books, 1994. 70-81.
Server: "For this volume I have gathered a sampling from the era of lurid softcover publishing, artifacts now highly prized by collectors and trading hundreds of times their original cost." A chapter on the Beats discusses their efforts to be published through Ace Books and Olympia Press. Includes large, full-color illustrations of original book covers.

Shepard, Sam. *Rolling Thunder Logbook*. New York: Viking, 1977.
Dylan and Ginsberg performed in the Rolling Thunder Revue, and Shepard recounts some of their performances.

Simpson, Louis. "The Eye Altering Alters All." *A Revolution in Taste: Studies of Dylan Thomas, Allen Ginsberg, Sylvia Plath, and Robert Lowell.* New York: Macmillan, 1978.
Simpson's chapter on Ginsberg serves as a compact critical biography and provides background on the genesis of the Beats in general.

Smith, John J., ed. *The Americana Annual 1959: An Encyclopedia of the Events of 1958.* New York: Americana Corporation, 1959. 34.
David Lloyd Stevenson cites a *New York Times* review (February 23, 1958), noting publication of *The Subterraneans* and *The Dharma Bums*. The first is "a monologue on the details of love-making" while the second is "the flirtation" of Beats with "Zen dharma, or 'truth.'"

_____. *The Americana Annual 1960: An Encyclopedia of the Events of 1959.* New York: Americana Corporation, 1960. 35-37.
Notice of publication of *Maggie Cassidy*, a "novel of adolescence." A story by Kerouac, the author notes, was in *Short Stories from the "Paris Review."* Photo from *Life* (September 21, 1959). Notice of Rexroth's *A Bird in the Bush*: Rexroth is a "middle-aged beatnik poet" and his book holds "18 impressionistic essays."

Solnit, Rebecca, ed. *Secret Exhibition: Six California Artists of the Cold War Era.* San Francisco: City Lights, 1990.
West Coast writers interact with avant-garde artists. Bill Berkson: Solnit "wants us to reconsider the importance of hybrid operations in visual art."

Solotaroff, Theodore. *The Red Hot Vacuum and Other Pieces on the Writing of the Sixties.* New York: Atheneum, 1970.
This volume collects previously published reviews, including selections on Henry Miller, Seymour Krim, William Burroughs, and Paul Bowles.

Stauffer, Donald Barlow. *A Short History of American Poetry.* New York: E. P. Dutton, 1974.
Predecessors of the Beats, such as Whitman, Pound, Eliot, Jeffers, and William Carlos Williams, are discussed, and in many cases, Stauffer turns to the Beats themselves: Corso, Ginsberg, Snyder, Olson, Creeley, Duncan, and Baraka.

Straumann, Heinrich. *American Literature in the Twentieth Century*.
    New York: Harper and Row, 1965. 80-82.
    The Beat movement was "just one of those revolts." Straumann
adds, "The Transcendentalists of the age of Emerson, the Muckrak-
ers at the beginning of this century, and the lost generation writers
are instances of corresponding movements." Straumann refers to
The Subterraneans as "a powerful and yet delicate presentation of the
changing moods of the young couple . . . a metaphor of the predica-
ment in which a great many of the younger generation of the Western World find themselves." This book was previously published by
Arrow Books in London in 1962.

Sutton, Walter. *American Free Verse: The Modern Revolution in Po-
    etry*. New York: New Directions, 1973.
    In this overview of free verse, see a section devoted to Creeley,
Duncan, Ferlinghetti, Ginsberg, Olson, Rexroth, and Snyder.

Tanner, Tony. *City of Words: American Fiction 1950-1970*. New
    York: Harper and Row, 1971.
    In this general study, some references are made to Burroughs and
Mailer.

Trilling, Diana. *Claremont Essays*. San Diego, CA: Harcourt, Brace
    and World, 1964.
    In this collection of previously published essays, see "The Moral
Radicalism of Norman Mailer."

Vendler, Helen. *Part of Nature, Part of Us: Modern American Poets*.
    Cambridge, MA: Harvard University Press, 1985.
    In this collection of previously published essays, see two selections
on Ginsberg and a separate piece on Frank O'Hara.

Von Hallberg, Robert. *American Poetry and Culture: 1945-1980*.
    Cambridge, MA: Harvard University Press, 1985.
    In this general study, the author includes references to Blackburn,
Crane, Duncan, Dylan, Ginsberg, Jones, O'Hara, Olson, Snyder,
Creeley, Ashbery, and Dorn.

Waldmeir, Joseph J., ed. *American Novels of the Second World War*.
    Hawthorn, NY: Mouton, 1969.

This general study focuses on works by or about those who have had experience on the battlefield. References to the works of Norman Mailer are included in the development of the theme.

_____. *Recent American Fiction: Some Critical Views*. Boston: Houghton Mifflin, 1963.
Includes Bernard Duffey, "The Three Worlds of Jack Kerouac," and Oliver Evans, "Paul Bowles and the 'Natural' Man." Duffey: "[T]he writer comes to a practical knowledge of himself as a writer about his experience and invites the reader to share in that particular and radical literary experience."

Widmer, Kingsley. "The Beat in the Rise of the Populist Culture." *The Fifties: Fiction, Poetry, Drama*. Ed. Warren French. Deland, FL: Everett Edwards, 1970. 155-173.
Widmer: "[T]he Beats helped regenerate the cultural rebellion and allied social dissidence which the hot-and-cold-war cultural nationalism of the preceding decade and a half had muted in literary and social awareness."

_____. *The Literary Rebel*. Carbondale: Southern Illinois University Press, 1965. 4-14, 143-153.
Widmer comments on the Beats as he discusses Biblical and Greco-Roman rebels. In addition, he questions the merit of Beat rebellion and sees the Beats as "mawkish, pathetic, fragmented, unrigorous, and not very defiant."

Articles About the Beats in General

Adams, J. D. "Speaking of Books." *New York Times Book Review* 18 May 1958: 2.
The writers of the Beat Generation might as well be called the "bleat" generation. The Beat writers are boring. They write nothing memorable.

"The Alluring Cupful." *Newsweek* 8 Oct. 1956: 86-88.
The article reviews the attraction of coffeehouses in eighteenth-century England, mentioning Samuel Johnson and John Dryden,

noting the rising popularity of coffeehouses in London and New York in 1956.

Aronowitz, Alfred G. "The Beat Generation." *New York Post* 9-22 Mar. 1959. 12-part series.
Interviews and discussion about the Beats from an early perspective.

_____. "The Yen for Zen." *Escapade* Oct. 1960: 50-52, 70.
Aronowitz: "The attraction of the Beat to Buddhism is probably as difficult to explain as Zen itself."

Baciu, Stefan. "Beatitude South of the Border: Latin America's Beat Generation." *Hispania* 49.4 (Dec. 1966): 733-739.
Baciu gives a brief survey of the special development of literary movements in Latin America akin to the Beat Generation, with reference to key authors and magazines in which they published.

Baker, George. "Avant-Garde at the Golden Gate." *Saturday Review* 3 Aug. 1957: 10.
Baker notices the avant garde in San Francisco, including Kerouac, Rexroth, Ginsberg, and *Evergreen Review*, and he is "glad to know."

"Bam; Roll on with Bam." *Time* 14 Sept. 1959: 28.
In language that mocks the Beats, this report describes the rise of literary activities in "Venice West."

"Bang Bong Bing." *Time* 7 Sept. 1959: 80.
Report on the successful sales of "beat blather" by Kerouac, Ginsberg, and Ferlinghetti. Corso's "Bomb" is quoted.

Baro, Gene. "Beatniks Then and Now." *Nation* 5 Sept. 1959: 115-117.
Review of Allen Churchill, *The Improper Bohemians*, and Lawrence Lipton, *The Holy Barbarians*. Baro: "Both [books] denigrate contemporary civilization and support promiscuous individual freedom at the expense of social regularity."

"Beat Mystics." *Time* 3 Feb. 1958: 56.
Mike Wallace, Kerouac, and Philip Lamantia talk about the religious ideas that underpin the thinking of the Beats.

"Beatnicks [sic] Just Sick Sick Sick." *Science Digest* July 1959: 25-26.

Report on the work of Dr. Francis Rigney, staff psychiatrist for the Veterans Administration Hospital in San Francisco, who after giving personality tests to about 150 persons, found "a wide spectrum of behavior – happy, sick, tragic, creative and just plain no-good."

Benedetto, Rosanne. "The Kerouac Symposium: An Afterword." *Soundings/East* (formerly *Gone Soft*) 2.2 (1979): 91-96.

Discussion of Ginsberg, Kerouac, and Corso.

"Big Day for Bards at Bay: Trial Over *Howl and Other Poems.*" *Life* 9 Sept. 1957: 105-108.

The trial of *Howl and Other Poems* provides an occasion for a photo essay. Samples of work from Ferlinghetti, Ginsberg, Rexroth, McClure, and Everson.

"The Blazing and the Beat." *Time* 24 Feb. 1958: 104.

Review of *The Subterraneans*, which "is about an oddball fringe of social misfits who conceive of themselves as 'urban Thoreaus' in an existential state of passive resistance to society."

Brady, Mildred Edie. "The New Cult of Sex and Anarchy." *Harper's Magazine* Apr. 1947: 312-322.

Brady: "[A]s you drive along the coast, up state highway number one, you can see, if you look for them, the shacks, even tents, where literary immigrants have already set up typewriters."

Breslin, James E. "The Beat Generation: A View from the Left." *Village Voice* 16 Apr. 1958: 3.

Report on socialist viewpoint about Kerouac and the Beats.

Burdick, Eugene. "The Innocent Nihilists Adrift in Squaresville." *The Reporter* 3 Apr. 1958: 30-33.

An analysis that proceeds from the assumption that "the vision [of the Beats] has suffocated." There is "something remarkably thin" about the Beat Generation.

Burns, Jim. "*Yugen.*" *Poetry Information* [London] 16 (Winter 1976-1977): 139-141.

Yugen, ed. LeRoi Jones, was definitively a Beat publication, providing a forum to a wide spectrum of Beat writers.

Butler, F. A. "On the Beat Nature of Beat." *American Scholar* 30 (Winter 1960-1961): 79-92.
Neither "Howl" nor *On the Road* is worthy of the time of intelligent and sensitive readers.

"Bye Bye Beatnik." *Newsweek* 1 July 1963: 65.
Newsweek reports on the marriage of Sally November and Gregory Corso as an end to the Beat era and a beginning of Corso's conformism.

"California: Heat on the Beatniks." *Newsweek* 17 Aug. 1959: 36.
A report on a controversy in Venice, California, about the influx of "shaggy, arts-dedicated beatniks," who are ruining the neighborhood. Photo of Lawrence Lipton at the Gas House.

Charters, Ann. "The Beats Go On." *San Francisco Chronicle* 26 Nov. 1995: 28.
The Beats, once perceived as a passing fad, endure as artists and legends. Their manuscripts are valuable, their publications sell, and they stir the hearts and minds of young and old.

Ciardi, John. "Book Burners and Sweet Sixteen." *Saturday Review* 27 June 1959: 22.
Ciardi may not admire the Beats, but he defends intellectual freedom.

_____. "Epitaph for the Dead Beats." *Saturday Review* 6 Feb. 1960: 11-13.
An early roasting of the Beats. See this item in Parkinson, *A Casebook on the Beat* (New York: Crowell, 1961): 257-265.

_____. "In Loving Memory of Myself." *Saturday Review* 25 July 1959: 22-23.
Review of *Maggie Cassidy*. Ciardi finds that the novel is "a badly mothy bit of juvenilia."

Coates, Robert M. "The Art Galleries: The 'Beat' Beat in Art." *The New Yorker* 2 Jan. 1960: 60-61.
Review of an exhibition at the Museum of Modern Art. Coates: "[T]races of the Beat philosophy . . . seem to be invading the plastic artists' point of view, too."

"The Coffeehouse Urn Runs Dry." *Business Week* 13 Aug. 1960: 83.
A report on the decline in the popularity of coffeehouses.

Cravens, Gwyneth. "Hitching Nowhere: The Aging Young Man on the Endless Road." *Harper's Magazine* Sept. 1972: 66-70.
The Beat figure on the highway is an unproductive fantasy.

Dardess, George. "The Delicate Dynamics of Friendship: A Reconsideration of Kerouac's *On the Road.*" *American Literature* 46.2 (May 1974): 200-206.
An open-minded reading of *On the Road* in the wake of various negative reactions. Dardess: "To have responsibility for your friend means not only providing him with companionship or with money, not only defending him before a jury of his peers; it means also – and painfully – maintaining a sense of how your friend sees himself apart from the way you see him. But, perhaps more painfully, it means maintaining a sense of how the friend sees *you* apart from the way you see yourself. Maintaining such difficult senses is an act of generosity few people care to perform unless they are in love."

Dempsey, David. "In Pursuit of 'Kicks.'" *New York Times Book Review* 8 Sept. 1957: 4.
Review of *On the Road*. Kerouac "throws his characters away," but "as a portrait of a disjointed segment of society acting out of its own neurotic necessity, *On the Road* is a stunning achievement."

Dickey, James. "From Babel to Byzantium." *Sewanee Review* 65 (Summer 1957): 508-530.
Dickey: "Ginsberg's writings are of the familiar our-love-against-their-machines-and-money variety, strongly akin to those of Henry Miller, Kenneth Patchen, and Kenneth Rexroth."

Dickey, R. P. "The New Genteel Tradition in American Poetry." *Sewanee Review* 82 (Fall 1974): 730-739.
An attack on selected contemporary poets, including Ginsberg, Bly, Snyder, and Creeley.

"The Disorganization Man." *Time* 9 June 1958: 98, 100, 102.
Review of Gene Feldman and Max Gartenberg, eds., *The Beat Generation and the Angry Young Men*. *Time* believes that this anthology reveals the weirdness of the Beats.

D'Orso, Michael. "Man Out of Time: Kerouac, Spengler, and the 'Faustian Soul.'" *Studies in American Fiction* 11.1 (Spring 1983): 19-30.

D'Orso: "Examining Kerouac's work through a Spenglerian perspective reveals Kerouac's intellectual struggle with the concepts of the breakdown of civilization and man's consequent loss of union with time, a struggle that was acted out by the characters he created."

"Eat to the Beats." *Time Out New York*, 8-15 Nov. 1995: 6-13.

Jean Nathan, Howard Halle, and Gia Kourlas discuss the Beats on the occasion of the exhibit at the Whitney Museum.

Eberhart, Richard. "West Coast Rhythms." *New York Times Book Review* 2 Sept. 1956: 7.

Survey of lively poetry events on the West Coast. Particular appreciation of Ginsberg's "Howl." Mention of Ferlinghetti, Whalen, and Snyder.

"80 Beatniks Protest." *New York Times* 13 June 1960: 32.

Protesters object to the closing of the Gaslight and the Bizarre.

"Endsville: Zen-Hur." *Time* 14 Dec. 1959: 66.

Description of the film *Pull My Daisy* by Robert Frank. *Time*: "The first pure Beat movie gives an authentic impression of beatnik habits and tastes."

Everson, William. "Dionysus and the Beat: Four Letters on the Archetype." *Sparrow* 63 (Dec. 1977).

Lee Bartlett received five letters from Everson between August 2 and August 8, 1975. The last four letters analyze the tension between Dionysian and Apollonian forces. The entire volume of *Sparrow* is dedicated to this material. See this material in Lee Bartlett, ed., *The Beats: Essays in Criticism* (Jefferson, NC: McFarland, 1981): 186-194.

"Every Man a Beatnik?" *Newsweek* 29 June 1959: 83.

Notes on a symposium held at Wagner College on Staten Island, including comments from Norman Mailer, Lionel Trilling, and Gregory Corso. Photo of Corso eating ice cream.

Fischer, J. "Editor's Easy Chair: Old Original Beatnik." *Harper's Magazine* Apr. 1959: 14-16.

Karl, a bartender referred to in this column, says, "So if these West Coast youngsters are half smart, they'll get out of the game while they're still ahead."

Fleischmann, Wolfgang B. "A Look at the Beat Generation Writers." *Carolina Quarterly* 11 (Spring 1959): 13-20.

Fleischmann codifies the Beats, placing Kerouac, Ginsberg, Everson, John Logan, Whalen, Ferlinghetti, Michael Rumaker, McClure, Lamantia, Duncan, and Josephine Miles into the groups "metaphysicals," "ultra-terrestials," and "experimentals."

_____. "Those 'Beat' Writers." *America* 26 Sept. 1959: 776.

The Beats are "a school of romantic experimentalists with a bent toward using the sordid contemporary scene as a theme for literary expression." Because of a "total lack of a premise, religious, philosophical, or political," the Beat Generation "will become a curiosity."

Fles, John. "The End of the Affair, or Beyond the Beat Generation." *Village Voice* 15 Dec. 1960: 4, 12.

Fles sees the Beat revolution coming to an end and wants the field to be cleared for new writers.

"Focus: The Beats." *American Book Review* 3.4 (May-June 1981): 7-14.

Gerald Nicosia reviews *The Beat Book*, eds. Arthur Winfield Knight and Glee Knight, *The Beat Diary*, eds. Arthur Winfield Knight and Kit Knight, *The Beat Journey*, eds. Arthur Winfield Knight and Kit Knight, and *the unspeakable visions of the individual*, eds. Arthur Winfield Knight and Kit Knight. John Tytell reviews William Burroughs, *Cities of the Red Night*. Ginsberg's preface to William Burroughs, *Letters to Allen Ginsberg 1953-1957* is reproduced. Arlene Stone reviews *Straight Hearts' Delight* by Ginsberg and Orlovsky. Arthur Winfield Knight reviews Ginsberg's *Composed on the Tongue*. Rochelle Ratner reviews *Skinny Dynamite* by Jack Micheline. Samuel Charters reviews *I Remain: The Letters of Lew Welch and the Correspondence of His Friends*, 2 volumes, ed. Donald Allen. Two reviews of Bob Kaufman, *The Ancient Rain* are included, one by Raymond Patterson and the other by Ken Kesey. Carl Solomon reviews Ed Sanders, *Fame and Love in New York*. William

Plummer contributes a review of Herbert Huncke, *The Evening Sun Turned Crimson*.

Gleason, Ralph. "Kerouac's Beat Generation." *Saturday Review* 11 Jan. 1958: 75.
   Gleason: "Kerouac is of a generation that willingly acknowledged jazz as its voice."

Glicksburg, Charles I. "The Rage of Repudiation: Polemic of the Beats." *Southwest Review* 45 (Autumn 1960): 338-344.
   Glicksburg: Ginsberg's "Howl" and Kerouac's *On the Road* are morally and artistically deficient. Holmes' *Go* reveals some talent, but as a whole the Beat Generation has very little literary or social merit.

Gold, Herbert. "Hip, Cool, Beat – and Frantic." *Nation* 16 Nov. 1957: 349-355.
   Writers like Ginsberg and Kerouac "are unauthentic exactly to the degree that they are literary."

_____. "How to Tell the Beatniks from the Hipsters." *The Noble Savage* 1 (Spring 1960): 132-139.
   Gold: "The hipster is a straw horse trying to be a dead horse; the beatnik is a horse that never was." The Beat is "the hipster parodied and packaged as a commercial product."

_____. "What It Is – Whence It Came." *Playboy* Feb. 1958: 20, 84-87.
   Gold: "Who is the hipster, what is it?" Gold concludes that the Beat Generation is an "unstable compound with an indefinite content." See this item reprinted in Seymour Krim, ed., *The Beats* (Greenwich, CT: Fawcett, 1960): 154-164. See this item also in Thomas Parkinson, ed., *A Casebook on the Beat* (New York: Crowell, 1961): 247-256. The article as a whole is "The Beat Mystique" and Gold's piece is one of three items under the heading. Another item is Sam Boal, "Cool Swinging in New York," which describes "an upper-class Beat party in New York": 21, 26, 50. The third item is Noel Clad, "A Frigid Frolic in Frisco," which describes "aspects of the new nihilism – frozen faced, far out, devoid of normal meanings": 21-22, 74-75.

Hall, Donald. "It's Not Bohemia or the Beard That Makes the Poem, It's the Poet." *The New York Times Book Review* 3 May 1959: 4.

Hall: "Neither bohemianism nor graduate school is going to make anyone a poet, nor will either prevent anyone from writing the best of which he is capable."

Halley, Peter. "Beat, Minimalism, New Wave, and Robert Smithson." *Arts Magazine* 55 (May 1981): 120-121.

Halley: "Robert Smithson's writings are a link between the Beat generation and the Minimalists, and between Minimalism and New Wave." Some reference to Ginsberg's 'Howl' and Burroughs' *Naked Lunch* and *The Soft Machine*.

Hamlin, Jesse. "The Art of Beat." *San Francisco Chronicle* 26 Nov. 1995: 31.

Hamlin identifies where Beat art may be seen in San Francisco.

_____. "Bebop–The Sound of the Beats." *San Francisco Chronicle* 26 Nov. 1995: 31.

A listing of available CD's that feature music by artists associated with Beat tastes, such as Charlie Parker, Dizzy Gillespie, and Thelonius Monk.

_____. "How Herb Caen Named a Generation." *San Francisco Chronicle* 26 Nov. 1995: 28.

An explanation of Caen's coining of the word "beatnik."

Harrington, Michael. "We Few, We Happy Few, We Bohemians." *Esquire* Aug 1972: 99-103, 162-164.

Some reference to Bob Dylan, Allen Ginsberg, and the Beats in a review of Bohemian haunts. Harrington: "I wonder if mass counter-culture may not be a reflection of the very hyped and videotaped world it professes to despise."

Harrison, Pat. "Who Really Gave Birth to the Beats?" *New York Magazine* 7 June 1976: 12-13.

Defense of David Kammerer.

Hills, Rust. "Introduction." *Esquire* Oct. 1979: 42-44.

Hills provides background on the Beats and Neal Cassady as he introduces Kesey's fictional memoir.

"Hipitaph." *Time* 10 Feb. 1961: 48.

The Beat Literary Movement, if it was a movement, "was one of the great stationary movements of all time." The article adds, "The beats are gone, man, gone," and coffeehouses and nightclubs are peopled by a new, clean-cut crowd.

Holmes, John Clellon. "The Philosophy of the Beat Generation." *Esquire* Feb. 1958: 35-38.

Holmes: The Beats' "real journey was inward; and if they seemed to trespass most boundaries, legal and moral, it was only in the hope of finding a belief on the other side." See this item reproduced in John Clellon Holmes, *Passionate Opinions* (Fayetteville: University of Arkansas Press, 1988): 65-77. See this item also in Park Honan, ed., *The Beats* (London: J. M. Dent, 1987): 145-158 or in *The Beats: Literary Bohemians in Postwar America*, ed. Ann Charters (Detroit: Gale Research, 1983): 631-636.

_____. "This Is the Beat Generation." *New York Times Magazine* 16 Nov. 1952: 10-22.

Holmes: Being Beat "means being undramatically pushed up against the wall of oneself." See this item reproduced in John Clellon Holmes, *Passionate Opinions* (Fayetteville: University of Arkansas Press, 1988): 57-64 or in *The Beats: Literary Bohemians in Postwar America*, ed. Ann Charters (Detroit: Gale Research, 1983): 629-631.

Hyams, Joe. "Good-by to the Beatniks!" *Boston Sunday Herald* 28 Sept. 1958, *This Week* sec.: 4-5, 33-34.

Who are the Beats and what threatens to adulterate the Beat spirit?

Hynes, S. "Beat and Angry." *Commonweal* 5 Sept. 1958: 559-561.

Hynes rejects the American Beats and England's Angry Young Men. *On the Road* and "Howl" fall into "self-alienation, self-pity, self-destruction, and windy confession."

Jacobs, Andrew. "Bohemian Rhapsody." *New York Times*, sec. 13: 4.

A return to Cafe Figaro, a former Beat haunt in Greenwich Village. Jacobs: "[G]one are the Figaro layabouts, the rebellious artists and the angry writers, many of whom also worked there. Sunday night belly-dancing has replaced poetry readings, and coffee refills are no longer free."

Jacobsen, Dan. "America's Angry Young Men." *Commentary* Dec. 1957: 475-479.

A selection of Beat writers published in *Evergreen Review* provokes Jacobson to doubt their literary merit.

Jones, LeRoi, David Fitelson, and Norman Podhoretz. "The Beat Generation." *Partisan Review* 25 (Summer 1958): 472-479.

An exchange of views on literature and the Beats following the publication of Podhoretz's attack in "The Know-Nothing Bohemians."

Kerouac, Jack. "Beatific: On the Origins of the Beat Generation." *Playboy* June 1959: 31-32, 42, 79.

Kerouac: "The word 'beat' originally meant poor, down and out, deadbeat, on the bum, sad, sleeping in subways. Now that the word is belonging officially, it is being made to stretch to include people who do not sleep in subways but have a certain new gesture, or attitude, which I can only describe as a new *more*." See this item in *Jack Kerouac, Good Blonde & Others*, ed. Donald Allen (San Francisco: Grey Fox Press, 1993): 55-65; Ann Charters, ed., *The Portable Jack Kerouac* (New York: Viking, 1995): 565-573; and Thomas Parkinson, ed., *A Casebook on the Beat* (New York: Crowell, 1961): 68-76.

_____. "Belief & Technique for Modern Prose." *Evergreen Review* 2.8 (Spring 1959): 57.

Kerouac provides a "List of Essentials" that suggestively stimulates a frame of mind for writing. See this item in Jack Kerouac, *Good Blonde & Others*, ed. Donald Allen (San Francisco: Grey Fox Press, 1993): 72-73; Ann Charters, ed., *The Portable Jack Kerouac* (New York: Viking, 1995): 483-484; and Thomas Parkinson, ed., *A Casebook on the Beat* (New York: Crowell, 1961): 67-68.

_____. "Essentials of Spontaneous Prose." *The Black Mountain Review* 7 (Autumn 1957): 226-228, 230-237.

Kerouac creates a glossary for his method, focusing on "Set-up," "Procedure," "Method," "Scoping," etc. See this item in Jack Kerouac, *Good Blonde & Others*, ed. Donald Allen (San Francisco: Grey Fox Press, 1993): 69-71. See this item in Ann Charters, ed., *The Portable Jack Kerouac* (New York: Viking, 1995): 484-485 and Thomas Parkinson, ed., *A Casebook on the Beat* (New York: Crowell, 1961): 65-67.

Killian, Michael. "The Beat Lives On." *Chicago Tribune* 7 Jan. 1996,
    sec. 7: 3.
    Another look at the Beats on the occasion of the exhibit at the
Whitney Museum in New York.

Klinger-Vartabedian, Laurel, and Robert A. Vartabedian. "Media
    and Discourse in the Twentieth-Century Coffeehouse Move-
    ment." ERIC # 332254.
    This study of coffeehouses in the 1950's credits the Beat Genera-
tion for starting a movement in which "social discourse" became "the
basis for social change." At first, the movement was founded on conversation and emphasized interpersonal relationships, but later the
media, especially television, drove the movement out of the coffeehouses. This study was originally a paper presented at the annual
meeting of the International Communication Association, May 23-
27, 1991.

Krim, Seymour. "A Hungry Mental Lion." *Evergreen Review* 4.11
    (Jan.-Feb. 1960): 178-185.
    Review of *Advertisements for Myself*. Krim: "Mailer is a serpentine
ten-headed unclassifiable writer."

Kupfer, David. "An Interview with Paul Krassner." *The Progressive*
    57.11 (Nov. 1993): 28.
    Krassner sees the counterculture as an ongoing process from the
Beats to the hippies to the yippies.

Lacayo, Richard. "If Everyone Is Hip, Is Anyone Hip?" *Time* 8 Aug.
    1994: 48-59.
    In this cover story, Lacayo searches for the meaning of "hip" and
argues, "In the course of four decades, the poses and postures of hip
have moved outward from the back rooms to the great plains of
America's cultural space." References to Kerouac, James Dean,
Miles Davis, Ginsberg, Huncke, and others.

Latham, Aaron. "The Columbia Murder That Gave Birth to the
    Beats." *New York Magazine* 19 Apr. 1976: 41-53.
    A discussion of the slaying of David Kammerer by Lucien Carr.
In the investigation of this slaying, Jack Kerouac became a material
witness, in part setting the stage for the association of the Beats with
criminal behavior. Robert J. Milewski, *Jack Kerouac: An Annotated*

Bibliography of Seconday Sources, 1944-1979 (Metuchen, NJ: Scarecrow Press, 1981), lists eight articles from the *New York Times* that report on the case: 17 Aug. 1944: "Columbia Student Kills Friend and Sinks Body in Hudson River": 1, 13; 17 Aug. 1944: "Kammerer's Parents Prominent": 13; 18 Aug. 1944: "Student Is Silent on Slaying Friend": 14; 25 Aug. 1944: "Student Is Indicted in 2nd Degree Murder": 15; 31 Aug. 1944: "Witness in Slaying Case Freed": 19; 16 Sept. 1944: "Guilty Plea Made by Carr in Slaying": 15; 7 Oct. 1944: "Student Slayer Sent to Reformatory": 15; 10 Oct. 1944: "Young Slayer Goes to Elmira": 38.

"Learning." *New Yorker* 1 July 1961: 19-21.
    Stanley Isaacs, a councilman in New York City, tours coffee-houses and night spots in Greenwich Village. Isaacs remarks, "There's *life* down here. That's what counts, isn't it?"

Leonard, G. B. "The Bored, the Bearded, and the Beat." *Look* 19 Aug. 1958: 64-68.
    Leonard: "Most of those who 'make the scene' are totally engaged in the personal drama of doing absolutely nothing." Photos by Cal Bernstein.

Leonard, John. "Epitaph for the Beat Generation." *National Review* 12 Sept. 1959: 331.
    The Beat Generation was "a panicked flight from reality." Real artists work individually.

"Life Line." *New Yorker* 6 Aug. 1960: 21-23.
    The Figaro, on Bleecker and Macdougal in Greenwich Village, is depicted as "an authentic old-fashioned bohemian place" and a "truer bohemia than Montparnasse of the late twenties."

"Life Line of the Beat Generation." *San Francisco Chronicle* 26 Nov. 1995: 29.
    A time line of Beat events 1943-1994.

"The Little Magazine in America: A Modern Documentary History." *Tri-Quarterly* 43 (Fall 1978).
    This issue is devoted to the modern little magazine. Articles include Seymour Krim, "A Backward Glance O'er Beatnik Roads"; Ted Wilentz and Bill Zavatsky, "Behind the Writer, Ahead of the

Reader: A Short History of Corinth Books"; Clayton Eshleman,
"Doing *Caterpillar*"; Richard Grossinger, "A History of *Io*"; Peter
Michelson, "On *Big Table, Chicago Review,* and *The Purple Sage*";
David Ossman, "LeRoi Jones: An Interview on *Yugen*"; and Cid
Corman, *"Origin."*

Lynch, Nancy. "The Square Root of Bohemia." *Mademoiselle* June
    1962: 84-87, 127-128, 137.
    Because of successful and creative management, the Figaro is a
popular coffeehouse in New York. Some people find it hip to work
at the Figaro as servers. However, the article develops into the concluding observation that "coffeehouses are being dwarfed by their
square roots."

McClure, Michael. "Sixty-six Things About the California Assem-
    blage Movement." *Artsweek* 12 Mar. 1982: 10-11.
    This numbered listing of observations on "Assemblage" refers to
artists such as Bruce Conner, Wallace Berman, George Herms, and
Jay DeFeo. See this essay in Michael McClure, *Lighting the Corners*
(Albuquerque: University of New Mexico College of Arts and Sciences, 1993): 181-190.

McFadden, J. P. "Howling in the Wilderness." *National Review* 12
    Sept. 1959: 338-339.
    McFadden: "The 'Beats' neither comprise nor even represent
their generation: they are but a handful who think society sick, and,
without seriously asking *why*, have withdrawn from it."

Mahoney, Stephen. "The Prevalence of Zen." *Nation* 1 Nov. 1958:
    311-315.
    Review of Kerouac, *The Dharma Bums,* and Alan Watts, *Nature,
Man, and Woman.* Mahoney: "Beat Zen . . . is screwball Wildwest."

Mailer, Norman. "The White Negro: Superficial Reflections on the
    Hipster." *Dissent* 4 (Summer 1957): 276-293.
    Mailer: "Like children, hipsters are fighting for the sweet, and
their language is a set of subtle indications of their success or failure
in the competition for pleasure." Reprinted as a pamphlet (San
Francisco: City Lights 1957). See also Ann Charters, ed., *The
Portable Beat Reader* (New York: Viking Penguin, 1992): 581-605.

"Manners and Morals: Fried Shoes." *Time* 9 Feb. 1959: 16.

In a mocking manner, *Time* reports on the appearance of Ginsberg, Corso, and Orlovsky in Chicago to promote *Big Table*.

Mashbeck, Joseph. "A Note on Surrealism and the Beat Generation." *Artforum* 15 (Apr. 1977): 58-59.

Mashbeck: "To suggest the continuity of a Surrealist tradition in Beat art and literature involves an irony like that of speaking of 'anarchist tradition.'"

Millstein, Gilbert. "Rent a Beatnik and Swing." *The New York Times Magazine* 17 Apr. 1960: 26, 28, 30.

An account of Fred McDarrah's rental service providing live beatniks for parties and other occasions.

Mitchner, Stuart. "Those Phony Beatniks." *Chicago Tribune* 8 Nov. 1959, magazine sec.: 47-49

The Beats have strayed from their original path.

Montgomery, John. "Report from the Beat Generation." *Library Journal* 84 (15 June 1959): 1999-2000.

Montgomery: "It is difficult to see ebbing tendencies as yet in this apparent pagan renaissance." Montgomery, who is depicted as Henry Morley in Kerouac's *The Dharma Bums*, wrote this article in response to a previous article by Basil Ross.

Moody, Howard R. "Reflections on the Beat Generation." *Religion in Life* 28 (Summer 1959): 426-432.

Beat writing is "loaded with Biblical allusions" and "there is great evidence of the Jewish and Christian roots of the beat writers."

Moore, Rosalie. "The Beat and the Unbeat." *Poetry* 93 (Nov. 1958): 107-116.

This review of four books includes comment on Ferlinghetti's *A Coney Island of the Mind*. Moore: "Ferlinghetti claims to write for the street, in the language of the street, yet you can hear on any street in the country language more beautifully and meaningfully and vigorously cadenced than his."

Morad, Jim. "The Coffee Houses of America." *Playboy* July 1959: 42-45.

Casino Alley, Cafe Bizarre, Coexistence Bagel Shop, and Venice West are revealed in a series of photos. Poems by Kerouac, Ginsberg, and Corso. A "Beat Playmate" appears on the following pages.

"Movement." *New Yorker* 16 Apr. 1960: 36-37.
Describes a party in honor of the publication of Seymour Krim, ed., *The Beats* (Greenwich, CT: Fawcett Books, 1960).

"New Test for Obscenity." *Nation* 9 Nov. 1957: 314.
Analysis of the decision by Judge Horn that Ginsberg's "Howl" is not obscene.

"Of Time and the Rebel." *Time* 5 Dec. 1960: 16-17.
A commentary on Norman Mailer's literary career with some reference to "The White Negro" and the Beats.

O'Neil, Paul. "The Only Rebellion Around." *Life* 30 Nov. 1959: 114-116, 119-120, 123-124, 126, 129-130.
O'Neil: "The poets, almost to a man, are individualistic and antisocial to the point of neuroticism." He adds, "The bulk of the Beat writers are undisciplined and slovenly amateurs."

Perlman, David. "How Captain Hanrahan Made 'Howl' a Bestseller." *Reporter* 12 Dec. 1957: 37-39.
A compact and engaging summary of the trial of Ferlinghetti over the publication and sale of Ginsberg's *Howl and Other Poems*.

Perry, Tony. "The Beats Are Cool – and Hot." *Los Angeles Times* 2 Aug. 1994, Part A: 1.
Perry: "The beats – once the consummate outsiders – are being embraced by the same Establishment players that shunned and mocked them: academia, the publishing world and the mass media."

Pinchbeck, Daniel. "Children of the Beats." *New York Times Magazine* 5 Nov. 1995: 38-43.
The son of Joyce Johnson discusses the children of famous Beat writers, and Barron Claiborn provides beautiful photos.

Pincus, Robert. "The Open Road of Risk: George Herms, Wallace Berman, the Beats and West Coast Visionary Poetics." *LAICA Journal* 4 (Fall 1982): 50-55.

Pincus finds that visual artists George Herms and Wallace Berman, like Beat Allen Ginsberg and Jack Kerouac, are inspired by the creativity and spontaneity of bebop jazz.

Podell, Albert N. "Censorship on the Campus: The Case of the *Chicago Review*." *San Francisco Review* 2 (Spring 1959): 71-89.

Podell narrates the events related to the censorship of *Chicago Review* by university authorities because of plans to include Beat authors and the initiation of *Big Table* as an alternative magazine without restrictions on its authors.

Podhoretz, Norman. "Howl of Protest in San Francisco." *New Republic* 16 Sept. 1957: 20.

Podhoretz: "[T]he San Francisco group is comprised of two or three good writers, a half dozen mediocre talents, and several worthless fellow travelers."

_____. "The Know-Nothing Bohemians." *Partisan Review* 25 (Spring 1958): 305-311; 313-316; 318.

Podhoretz: "[T]he spirit of hipsterism and the Beat Generation strikes me as the same spirit which animates the young savages in leather jackets who have been running amuck in the last few years with their switch-blades and zip guns." See this article reprinted in Thomas Parkinson, ed., *A Casebook on the Beat* (New York: Crowell, 1961): 201-212. It also appears in Park Honan, ed., *The Beats* (London: J. M. Dent, 1987): 216-229.

_____. "Where Is the Beat Generation Going?" *Esquire* Dec. 1958: 147-150.

Podhoretz: "The Beat Generation is a significant phenomenon . . . and it can't be disposed of by showing up its literary fakery."

"Politics: Beat in the Hip of Texas." *Life* 7 Mar. 1960: 48-51.

Two young political candidates in Fort Worth, Texas, adopt a Beat platform.

Pritchett, V. S. "The Beat Generation." *New Statesman* 23 Aug. 1958: 292, 294, 296.

Pritchett compares the Lost Generation with the Beat Generation and finds that the Beats are "purely American."

Rexroth, Kenneth. "Bearded Barbarians or Real Bards?" *The New York Times Book Review* 12 Feb. 1961: 1.
    Rexroth: "The poems written by these young poets . . . are fresher and more humane than the poetry of the preceding period."

_____. "Jazz Poetry." *Nation* 29 Mar. 1958: 282-283.
    Rexroth: In jazz poetry, the "voice is integrally wedded to the music and . . . is treated as another instrument with its own solos."

_____. "The New American Poets." *Harper's Magazine* June 1965: 65-71.
    Rexroth: "With the exception of the neo- and post-Beats of the unprintable school . . . the last five years of American poetry give the impression of being a little more at ease." Tired of the efforts by the Beats to promote themselves, Rexroth attacks the Beats for falling into "free verse doggerel full of dirty words."

_____. "Revolt: True and False." *Nation* 26 Apr. 1958: 378-379.
    Rexroth: "Who objects to what and why, and what is it that is wrong with what we used to call 'The System?'"

_____. "San Francisco's Mature Bohemians." *Nation* 23 Feb. 1957: 159-162.
    Rexroth sees the dominance of the Beats on the artistic scene in San Francisco, commenting on Henry Miller, Kerouac, Everson, Duncan, Ginsberg, Lamantia, Ferlinghetti, and McClure.

Robertson, David. "Real Matter, Spiritual Mountain: Gary Snyder and Jack Kerouac on Mount Tamalpais." *Western American Literature* 27.3 (Nov. 1992): 209-226.
    Robertson: "This article . . . consists of historical and photographic documentation plus my own imaginative response to [Kerouac's and Snyder's] journey and to the place where it occurred."

Rosenthal, M. L. "The Naked and the Clad." *Nation* 11 Oct. 1958: 214-215.
    This review focuses in part on Ferlinghetti, *A Coney Island of the Mind*. Rosenthal: "Apart from the 'Oral Messages,'" Ferlinghetti is "a deft, rapid-paced, whirling performer."

_____. "Poet of the New Violence." *Nation* 23 Feb. 1957: 162.
   Review of *Howl and Other Poems*. These poems contain "the fury of the soul-injured lover or child."

Roskolenko, Harry. "The Sounds of the Fury." *Prairie Schooner* 33.2 (Summer 1959): 148-153.
   Commenting on jazz poetry, especially as performed by Kenneth Rexroth and Lawrence Lipton, Roskolenko says, "All in all, it is a doubtful medium."

Ross, Basil. "California Young Writers, Angry and Otherwise." *Library Journal* 83.12 (15 June 1958): 1850-1854.
   Survey of the rising Beats, including Ginsberg, Kerouac, Everson, Ferlinghetti, and Duncan. Information about San Francisco, San Francisco State College, and other San Francisco writers. Photos.

Ross, Tim A. "Rise and Fall of the Beats." *Nation* 27 May 1961: 456-458.
   Compared to Robert McGrath, who ignored the draft board and made his protest meaningful by going to jail for a year, the Beats "seem rather unimportant." The Beats "are performing for a society which apparently likes to be told it is phony."

Ryan, Richard. "Of the Beat Generation and Us." *Catholic World* 187 (Aug. 1958): 343-348.
   The Beats are not new and unique, but represent a familiar human struggle.

Schleifer, Marc D. "Kenneth Patchen on the 'Brat' Generation." *The Village Voice* 18 Mar. 1959: 1, 7.
   Kenneth Patchen, quoted by Schleifer: "Actually, there's been very little real Poetry Jazz, just a lot of Johnny-come-latelies reading to a jazz background."

Scott, James F. "Beat Literature and the American Teen Cult." *American Quarterly* 14.2 Part 1 (Summer 1962): 150-160.
   "[T]he Beats have played perfectly the role of the adolescent delinquent who, despite his . . . omniscience, knows only enough about the adult world to sustain a boastful but shallow cynicism."

Shapiro, Karl. "Poets of the Silent Generation." *Prairie Schooner* 31.4
(Winter 1957): 298-299.
Shapiro: "The silent generation is as good a name as any. It is a
generation of poets who grew up amidst the intellectual wreckage of
the century."

_____. "Romanticism Comes Home." *Prairie Schooner* 31.3 (Fall
1957): 182-183.
Shapiro recognizes the talent of Kerouac, Ginsberg, Everson, and
Spicer and their revolt against the "Classicism" of Eliot, Pound,
Joyce, and others.

Sisk, John P. "Beatniks and Tradition." *Commonweal* 17 Apr. 1959:
75-77.
Sisk argues that the Beats "are in what may be called the subversive tradition in American literature." See this article in Thomas
Parkinson, ed., *A Casebook on the Beat* (New York: Crowell, 1961):
194-201.

Smith, W. R. "Hipcats to Hipsters." *New Republic* 21 Apr. 1959: 18-
20.
Ginsberg is an insubstantial imitator of black musicians.

"Squaresville U. S. A. Vs. Beatsville." *Life* 21 Sept. 1959: 31-37.
A contrast is drawn between Hutchinson, Kansas (Squaresville)
and the activities of the Beats, especially in Venice, California
(Beatsville).

Stack, Peter. "Ferlinghetti: Offbeat Beatnik." *San Francisco Chronicle* 26 Nov. 1995: 29.
Ferlinghetti comments on Beat history and ways in which Beat
spirit lives on today.

Stimpson, Catherine R. "The Beat Generation and the Trials of
Homosexual Liberation." *Salmagundi* 58/59 (Fall-Winter 1982-
1983): 373-392.
Stimpson: "The Beats . . . wrote about sex as inevitably as Shelley
did eternity. In letters, journals, memoirs, essays, fiction, and poetry,
they textualized the body–be it celibate, heterosexual, bisexual, or
homosexual."

"Symposium on the Beat Poets." *Wagner Literary Magazine* (Spring 1959): 2-31.

This periodical presents three student essays about the Beats and "Two Beat Poems" by a student. Also included are various short responses by famous writers to the Beats, including remarks by Marianne Moore, Paul Tillich, Dorothy Van Ghent, William Troy, Lord David Cecil, Robert Lowell, Daisy Aldan, George Barker, e. e. cummings, Norman Mailer, Sir Herbert Read, William Carlos Williams, Lionel Trilling, Carl Sandburg, and Philip Rhav. A reply from Corso, Orlovsky, and Ginsberg rounds out the discussion.

Tilling, Diana (Pseudonym). "The Other Night in Heaven." *The Fifties* 3 (1959): 54-56.

A parody (apparently written by Robert Bly) of the Diana Trilling article that attacked the Beats. See the parody in Lewis Hyde, ed., *On the Poetry of Allen Ginsberg* (Ann Arbor: University of Michigan Press, 1984): 75-77.

Treuhaft, Jessica Mitford. "The Indignant Generation." *Nation* 27 May 1961: 451-456.

Treuhaft: "While students are acutely aware of the difficulties confronting them, they also have a strong feeling of achievement; they have already had an impact on national life. They have seen both major political conventions give official praise and recognition to the Southern sit-ins. Their attack on the HUAC has had countrywide repercussions. Their walks for peace have been headlined in papers from coast to coast."

Trilling, Diana. "The Other Night at Columbia: A Report from the Academy." *Partisan Review* 26.2 (Spring 1959): 214-230.

Trilling: "Ginsberg at Columbia on Thursday night was not Ginsberg at Chicago – according to *Time*, at any rate – or Ginsberg at Hunter either, where Kerouac ran the show, and a dismal show it must have been, with Kerouac drinking on the platform and clapping James Wechsler's hat on his head in a grand parade of contempt – they were two of four panelists gathered to discusss 'Is there such a thing as a Beat Generation?' – and leading Ginsberg out from the wings like a circus donkey." See a selection in Lewis Hyde, ed., *On the Poetry of Allen Ginsberg* (Ann Arbor: University of Michigan Press, 1984): 56-74.

Tytell, John. "The Beat Generation and the Continuing American Revolution." *The American Scholar* 42.2 (Spring 1973): 308-317.

Tytell: "[T]he Beats proposed a creed of individuality and a commitment to the life of the spirit with a passion that recalls the struggles of the American transcendentalists–Emerson, Thoreau, and Whitman."

Van Den Haag, Ernest. "Conspicuous Consumption of Self." *National Review* 11 Apr. 1959: 656-658.

Being Beat is "an unsuccessful attempt to escape the routine of a meaningless life."

Van Ghent, Dorothy. "Comment." *Wagner Literary Magazine* (Spring 1959): 27-28.

Van Ghent: "In the Beat literature we are observing the development of an articulate myth of swift growth and in the very process of its formation." See this article in Thomas Parkinson, ed., *A Casebook on the Beat* (New York: Crowell, 1961): 213-214.

"'Village' Beatniks Heckle Firemen Closing Gaslight." *New York Times* 11 June 1960: 23.

Protesters express anger about the closing of the Gaslight cafe by the order of the Fire Department.

Wakefield, Dan. "Night Clubs." *Nation* 4 Jan. 1958: 19.

A negative review of Jack Kerouac's performance at the Village Vanguard. Preference for Richard Wilbur.

Whiting, Sam. "Ghosts of the Beat Generation Haunt North Beach." *San Francisco Chronicle* 26 Nov. 1995: 30.

This article and an accompanying map identify key locations in San Francisco that relate to Beat history.

_____. "Neo-Hipsters Keep the Beat in the Mission." *San Francisco Chronicle* 26 Nov. 1995: 30.

Contemporary San Francisco offers "plenty of public places to sit and smoke and drink and read and write and not spend money."

Wolfe, Bernard. "Angry at What?" *Nation* 1 Nov. 1958: 316-322.

The Beats call attention to sexuality but have no new or fresh ideas.

Audio-Visual Materials

Adler, Edward J. *Beat Art: Visual Works by and About the Beat Generation.* New York: 80 Washington Square East Galleries, 1994. An exhibition brochure.

The Atomic Café. Produced and directed by Kevin Rafferty, Jayne Loader, and Pierce Rafferty. Film now available in video. Black and white and color. Sound. Archive Project, Inc., 1982.
A study of the government's promotion of acceptance of atomic weaponry. Documentrary footage from the 1940's and 1950's includes training films and clips of musical hits.

The Bachelor Party. Delbert Man. Film. Black and white. Sound. 93 minutes. United Artists, 1957.
Reveals middle-class anxieties and fears through a Hollywood examination of a self-doubting "organization man." See Paddy Chayefsky, *The Bachelor Party: A Screenplay* (New York: New American Library, 1957).

Barfly. Produced by Barbet Schroeder, Fred Boos, and Tom Luddy. Directed by Barbet Schroeder. Starring Mickey Rourke, Alice Krige, and Faye Dunaway. Color. Film available in video. 100 minutes. Cannon Films, 1987.
Written by Charles Bukowski. Tape package: "[T]he noiresque comedy *Barfly* captures . . . giddy, gin-soaked attempts to make a go of life on the skids." *The Movie, "Barfly": An Original Screenplay by Charles Bukowski for a Film by Barbet Schroeder* (Santa Rosa, CA: Black Sparrow Press, 1987) is available for comparison with the film itself.

The Beat Experience. Video. 60 mins. New York: Red Hot Production, Whitney Museum of American Art, 1995.
Based on the exhibit on the Beats at the Whitney Museum, this tape offers documentation of the voices and film productions of Beat artists.

The Beat Experience. CD-ROM. South Burlington, VT: Voyager, 1996.

Voyager catalog: On this CD-ROM, the "portrait of the artists – writers, musicians, poets, filmmakers – who gave birth to this influential counterculture goes beyond the basic information about who the Beats were to explore sexuality, intoxication, and other relevant issues."

The Beat Generation. Charles Haas. Film. Black and white. Sound. 95 minutes. Albert Zugsmith, 1959.
   Louie Armstrong appears in this Hollywood impression that a beatnik is a rapist.

The Beat Generation. 3 CD's or 4 audio cassettes. Santa Monica, CA: Rhino Word Beat, 1992.
   A widely available collection of readings, interviews, programs, and selections that gives a broad perspective on the Beats, especially the music associated with the Beats. Tracks include Kerouac's "San Francisco Scene (The Beat Generation)," "October in the Railroad Earth," and the sound track of his appearance on the Steve Allen Show with readings from *On the Road* and *Visions of Cody*. An excerpt from Burroughs' *Naked Lunch* and Ginsberg's reading of "America" also appear. Featured musicians include the Gerry Mulligan Quartet; Dizzy Gillespie and His Orchestra; Charles Mingus; Slim Galliard & His Middle Europeans; Lambert, Hendricks & Ross; the David Amram Quintet; and the Charlie Parker Quartet. The liner notes include information on Beat history, numerous photos, a selection by Bob Dylan about the Beats, "Beatnik Jive: A Primer," and a survey about the Beats on film.

The Beat Generation: An American Dream. A film by Janet Forman. Color. Sound. 87 minutes. Sydney, Australia: Special Broadcasting Service, 1990.
   Provides social and intellectual background with archival footage of the Eisenhower era and interviews with Beat artists.

The Beat Generation: Legacy and Celebration. New York: New York University School of Education, Office of Program Development, 1994.
   Audio tapes of presentations given at the New York University conference *The Beat Generation: Legacy and Celebration* held in May, 1994.

The Beat Generation Map of America. Los Angeles: Aaron Blake
  Publishers, 1987.
  A large print of a scene depicting a Beat reading, with a key to
identify the participants. Maps of key locations where the Beats
flourished. Colorful display.

The Beats: An Existential Comedy. Directed by Philomene Long.
  Produced by J. D. Kugelman. Video. Sound. 41 minutes. New
  York: Cinema Guild/Raven Productions, no date.
  Television and film clips about the Beats, giving a humorous per-
spective on the West Coast Beats, especially in the era of Mc-
Carthyism.

Before Stonewall (The Making of a Gay and Lesbian Community).
  Film. Color. Sound. 87 minutes. Greta Schiller, Robert Rosenberg, and John Scagliotti, 1984.
  Bohemian life in San Francisco and New York, with treatment of
the establishment of the gay and lesbian community following riots
in response to a police raid on Stonewall Inn in 1969.

A Bucket of Blood. Roger Corman. Film available in video. Black
  and white. Sound. 66 minutes. American International Pictures,
  1984.
  Hollywood presents a waiter who poses as a beat sculptor but is
actually a serial killer. Originally produced in 1959.

Celebrating Bird!: The Triumph of Charlie Parker. Gary Giddins and
  Kendrick Simmons. Video. Black and white and color. Sound. 59
  minutes. Kultur Video, 1987.
  Emphasis on biography, but some scenes of performance.

Censorship and the Beats. Sound recording. Boulder, CO: Naropa
  Institute, 1982.
  Part of the discussion at the conference on Kerouac held at
Naropa in 1982. A non-circulating copy is available at the Bancroft
Library in Berkeley, and a non-circulating copy is also included at
the Berg Collection at the New York Public Library. The Naropa
Institute has a large inventory of tapes, including readings and lec-
tures. Many tapes include three readers doing full-length presenta-
tions of their works, and almost all Beat figures are represented. A
collection of tapes documenting the 1982 conference on Jack Ker-

ouac held at Naropa would benefit from some editing, but the tapes are a valuable collection of speeches and readings in Kerouac's honor.

Chapman, Harold. *The Beat Hotel*. Paris: Gris Banal, 1984.
A photographaphic memoir of "the now-famous Beat Hotel at 9 rue Git-le-Coeur in Paris." Burroughs says, "The hotel had no name, just a street number." Photos include Burroughs, Ginsberg, Orlovsky, Corso, and others at the hotel, where art flourished in Bohemian conditions.

Charters, Ann. *Beats and Company*. Garden City, NY: Doubleday, 1986.
Photos by Ann Charters in large format. Accompanying passages by Ann Charters make the photo collection an appealing introduction to the Beats.

_____. *Scenes Along the Road: Photographs of the Desolation Angels 1944-1960*. New York: Portents/Gotham Book Mart, 1970; San Francisco: City Lights, 1984.
Snapshots of the Beats in four chapters: "New York 1944-1954," "On the Road 1947-1956," "San Francisco and Berkeley 1954-1959," and "Mexico and Abroad 1951-1960." Comments on the snapshots by Ginsberg are included. Three poems by Ginsberg refer to persons in the snapshots: "Neal's Ashes," "Memory Gardens," and "In a Car."

Clemente, Francesco. *India*. Pasadena, CA: Twelvetrees Press, no date.
Poems by Wieners, Ginsberg, and others, with accompanying art by Clemente.

The Cry of Jazz. Ed Bland. Film. Black and white. Sound. 35 minutes. Grove Press Film Division, 1959.
Jazz, blackness, and the Beat interest in both.

Dorfman, Elsa. *Elsa's Handbook: A Woman's Photojournal*. Boston: David R. Godine, 1974.
Many photos of the Beats, mostly early 1970's.

Drugstore Cowboy. Directed by Gus Van Sant, Jr. Produced by Nick Wechsler and Karen Murphy. Starring Matt Dillon and Kelly

Lynch. Film available in video. 104 minutes. Avenue Pictures. International Video Entertainment, 1990.

Tape package: "This gripping film about a family of drug thieves is based on a novel by a convicted drug robber [Gus Van Sant], a man who knows his subject well." William S. Burroughs plays the drug-addict priest, Tom Murphy, but the role is a thin veil for Burroughs himself, who speaks of the rise of the international police state through hysteria about drugs.

Essential Alan Watts: Man in Nature, Work as Play. Video. Color. Sound. Produced by David Grieve and Henry Jacobs. New York: Mystic Fire Video, 1993.

Filmed talks from the early 1970's reveal the ties between the beats and zen.

Essential Alan Watts: On Meditation and Nothingness. Video. 50 minutes. New York: Mystic Fire Video, 1994.

Watts explains various methods of meditation and teaches how to sit, listen, and watch the breath and the thoughts as they arise in the mind.

Essential Alan Watts: Time and the More It Changes. Video. 50 minutes. New York: Mystic Fire Video, 1995.

Watts offers his views on time and change and shows how the past depends upon the present.

Essential Alan Watts: Zen and the Art of the Controlled Accident. Audiocassette. 2 tapes. 142 minutes. New York: Mystic Fire Video, 1994.

Watts discusses the spontaneous life and the state of "no-mind." Watts assesses the art of the controlled accident and the discovery of the spiritual in the ordinary.

Felver, Christopher. *Angels, Anarchists, and Gods.* Baton Rouge: Louisiana State University Press, 1996.

An oversize book featuring many photos of the Beats. Introduction by Douglas Brinkley. Foreword by Robert Creeley. Poem contributed by Gregory Corso.

_____. *The Poet Exposed: Portraits by Christopher Felver.* New York: Alfred Van Der Marck Editions, 1986.

Prologue by Gary Snyder. Foreword by Robert Creeley. Afterword by William E. Parker. Poems in the handwriting of the authors
set opposite black-and-white portraits. Beautiful procession. Extraordinary variety.

Ferlinghetti, Lawrence, and Nancy J. Peters. *Literary San Francisco:
A Pictorial History from Its Beginnings to the Present Day.* San
Francisco: City Lights and Harper and Row, 1978.
The Beats, their works, and their performances.

Fleischman, Christa. *Mark in Time: Portraits and Poetry.* San Francisco: Glide Publications, 1971.
Welch, Snyder, McClure, Schevill, Ferlinghetti, Kaufman,
Wieners, Ginsberg, Rexroth, Kyger, Parkinson, Brautigan. Beautiful
juxtapositions of black and white photos with poems by the photographed artists.

Frank, Robert. *The Americans.* New York: Grove, 1959; Washington, DC: Scalo Publishers, 1996.
Features an introduction by Jack Kerouac. Kerouac remarks,
"The humor, the sadness, the EVERYTHING-ness and American-
ness of these pictures!" This set of black and white photos was taken
by Robert Frank during 1955 and 1956 with the help of a grant from
the John Simon Guggenheim Foundation.

_____. *Moving Out.* Washington, DC: Scalo Publishers/National
Gallery of Art, 1994.
A survey of Frank's career, with a chapter on *Pull My Daisy.* Earl
A. Powell says in the introduction to the volume, "With these pre-
scient images Frank redefined the icons of America, noting that cars,
juke boxes, diners, gas stations, even the road itself formed a far
more truthful index of contemporary life than the majestic landscape
that had once symbolized the nation." This volume collects Frank's
extensive gifts of his work to the National Gallery. New York, Peru,
Spain, and England are displayed; photos from *The Americans* are
reproduced; photos of Kerouac, Ginsberg, Wieners, and Peter
Orlovsky appear; scenes from *Pull My Daisy* are featured.

_____. *Thank You.* Washington, DC: Scalo Publishers, 1996.
Features postcards sent to Frank, including items from Kerouac
and Ginsberg.

Fried Shoes, Cooked Diamonds: The Beats at Naropa. Costanzo Cal-
lione. Video. Color. Sound. 55 minutes. New York: Mystic Fire
Video, 1989.
Burroughs, Ginsberg, Corso, Anne Waldman, and Diane
DiPrima at Naropa in the early 1970's.

Gang of Souls. Maria Beatty. Video. Color. Sound. 60 minutes. New
York: Giorno Poetry Systems, 1990.
Burroughs, Ginsberg, Corso, DiPrima, and others appear.

Ghosts at No. 9. Anthony Balch. Film available in Video. No city or
production company listed, 1962.
Container description: "1962 film footage by Anthony Balch with
William Burroughs and Brion Gysin; soundtrack by William Burroughs; from the archives of Psychic TV."

Ginsberg, Allen. *Allen Ginsberg: Photographs.* Altadena, CA:
Twelvetrees Press, 1990.
Introduction by Corso. Afterword by Ginsberg. Oversize volume
featuring black and white photos of Ginsberg and his milieu from
the 1940's through the 1980's. Captions beneath the photos are
printed in Ginsberg's own hand, but are reproduced at the back of
the book in standard type. Bios of photo subjects are appended at
the back.

_____. *Snapshot Poetics: Allen Ginsberg's Photographic Memoir of the
Beat Era.* San Francisco: Chronicle Books, 1993.
A collection of black and white photos taken by Ginsberg during
the period 1953-1991. There is some repetition of photos from *Allen
Ginsberg: Photographs*, and this volume is slender and paperbound.
Ginsberg's captions appear in his hand and are set in type at the
back of the text. Bios of the subjects of the photos also appear at the
end. Ginsberg provides a discussion of his photos, his subjects, and
the people who influenced the way he thought about photos.

Glass, Philip. *Hydrogen Jukebox.* CD. New York: Elektra Nonesuch,
1994.
Libretto by Allen Ginsberg. Conducted by Martin Goldray. An
"opera" that includes excerpts from Ginsberg's poetry.

Graubart, Rose. *Portraits of Poets*. Martin, TN: Tennessee Poetry
    Press, 1970.
    Portrait drawings of various poets, including Ginsberg and Sny-
der.

Gruen, John. *The New Bohemia*. New York: a capella books, 1990.
    Fred W. McDarrah provides many photographs.

Hartweg, Norman. *Can You Pass the Acid Test?* San Francisco:
    Artrock, 1993.
    An intricate poster of blue lettering and drawings against a yellow
background with references to Burroughs, Ginsberg, and Neal Cassady and the Merry Pranksters.

Hairspray. Directed by John Waters. Produced by Robert Shave.
    New Line Cinema in association with Stanley F. Buchthal. Star-
    ring Sonny Bono, Ruth Brown, Debbie Harry, Ricki Lake, and
    Jerry Stiller. Film available in video. 92 minutes. RCA/Columbia
    Pictures Home Video, 1988.
    Set in 1962. A scene about one hour into the film shows Ricki
Lake, the hairspray heroine, accidentally wandering into a "Beat
pad," featuring a wild Beat painter (Ric Ocasek) and a "stoned chick"
who reads from "Howl."

Heart Beat. A film by John Byrum. Orion/Warner Brothers, 1979.
    The film promises a worthwhile performance with stars Sissy
Spacek, John Hurt, and Nick Nolte, but is a disappointment.

Heavy Petting. Produced and directed by Obie Benz. Video. Color.
    Sound. 75 minutes. Academy Entertainment, 1989.
    Provides social and intellectual background in a humorous vein by
presenting interviews with Ginsberg, Burroughs, and Judith Malina
about their sex lives in the 1950's. Numerous others are also included.

Hopper, Dennis. *Out of the Sixties*. 2nd edition. Pasadena, CA:
    Twelvetrees Press, 1988.
    A few photos of Ginsberg, Leary, McClure, and others. Some
material later was included at the exhibition at the Whitney Museum.

Howls, Raps, and Roars: Recordings from the San Francisco Poetry Renaissance. Produced by Bill Belmont. Four CD's. Berkeley: Fantasy, 1993.

A widely available collection of key materials. Includes Welch, Ginsberg, Whalen, McClure, Meltzer, Patchen, and others. For the liner notes, Ann Charters writes "Howls, Raps, and Roars: The Spoken Arts in San Francisco at Midcentury," in which she remarks, "*Howls, Raps, and Roars* captures the sound of San Francisco's literary explosion during one of the most tumultuous American cultural shifts in our century. The whirlwind that blew the poets' voices through the city in the 1950s and the 1960s swept their words into the ears of receptive listeners all over the country and out into the world."

A Jack Kerouac Romnibus. CD-ROM. New York: Penguin Electronics, 1995.

The CD-ROM provides extensive coverage of the life and times of Jack Kerouac and his milieu, mapping out connections between personalities. Emphasis on *The Dharma Bums*.

Jazz on a Summer's Day. Bert Stern. Film available in video. Color. Sound. 85 minutes. 1960. New York: New Yorker Video, 1987.

Documentary of the 1959 Newport Jazz Festival, including Louie Armstrong, Dinah Washington, and Gerry Mulligan.

Karel Appel. New York: Albeville Press, 1985.

Ginsberg essay on Appel: 247-248. Collaborations of Appel, Kerouac, and Ginsberg: 246, 248.

Kathy Acker. With Angela McRobbie. Video. Color. 40 minutes. Ho-Ho-Kus, NJ: The Roland Collection, 1995.

As Acker discusses post-structuralist and post-modern writing, including the cut-up method, she acknowledges the influence of Burroughs. This video is available from the Roland Collection, 22-D Hollywood Avenue, Ho-Ho-Kus, NJ 07423.

Knight, Brenda, ed. *Women of the Beat Generation: The Writers, Artists and Muses at the Heart of a Revolution.* Four cassettes. Six hours. San Bruno, CA: Audio Literature, 1996.

This is the audio companion to the anthology by the same editor. Includes Ann Charters, ruth weiss, Diane DiPrima, Hettie Jones,

Janine Pommy Vega, Lenore Kandel, Anne Waldman, Joyce John-son, Joanne Kyger, Joanna McClure, Eileen Kaufman, Mary Nor-bert Korte, and Brenda Knight (the editor). Material is usually read by the original artist. Biographical material is read by Debra Winger. Catalog description: "With less commercial success than the men but with no less power, the women of the Beat Generation . . . tell of their lives and work."

The Lectures: Volume One. Video. New York: Thin Air Video, 1994.
    Ginsberg, Baraka, Creeley, and Houston Baker lecture on poetry.

McDarrah, Fred W. *The Artist's World: In Pictures*. New York E. P. Dutton, 1961.
    Three hundred black and white photos document the life and work of painters known as the New York School. Scattered refer-ences to DiPrima, Ted Joans, and LeRoi Jones.

McDarrah, Fred, and Gloria McDarrah. *Beat Generation: Glory Days in Greenwich Village*. New York: Schirmer Books, 1996.
    An oversize collection of black and white photos, many of them classic photos of the Beats in performance. Though the subtitle indi-cates a focus on Greenwich Village, the book also has some images from San Francisco and Lowell. Includes bibliography, brief bio-graphical sketches, and index.

_____. *Kerouac and Friends: A Beat Generation Album*. New York: William Morrow, 1985.
    A collection of photos, writings, and excerpts that provides a rich and varied impression of the Beat period and the responses it pro-voked.

Malanga, Gerard. *Scopophilia: The Love of Looking*. New York: Al-fred Van Der Marck Editions, 1985.
    Foreword by Creeley. Afterword by the editor. Burroughs writes an essay: "Voyeurism as Appropriation Aesthetics": 11-19. Erotic photos.

The New York Beat Generation Show: Volume One: History and Overview: The Censorship Years. New York: Thin Air Video, 1995.

A tape of principal participants at the New York University program *The Beats: Legacy and Celebration*, including Ann Charters, Ginsberg, Michael McClure with Ray Manzarek, Micheline, Corso, Amram, Ferlinghetti, Waldman, Sanders, and Hunter S. Thompson.

The New York Beat Generation Show: Volume Two: Women and the Beats. New York: Thin Air Video, 1995.

Another tape of principal participants at the New York University program *The Beats: Legacy and Celebration*. Includes Anne Waldman, Joyce Johnson, Hettie Jones, Joanne Kyger, Jan Kerouac, Ann Charters, and Carolyn Cassady.

The New York Beat Generation Show: Volume Three: Music Moves the Spirit. New York: Thin Air Video, 1995.

A music video prepared from performances at the New York University program *The Beats: Legacy and Celebration*. Includes David Amram and his quartet, Allen Ginsberg, Ted Joans, Ray Manzarek and Michael McClure, and Terry Southern. Art D'Lugoff provides historical background on jazz and folk music.

Nowinski, Ira. *Cafe Society: Photographs and Poetry from San Francisco's North Beach*. San Francisco: Seefood Studios, 1978.

This collection of black and white photos sometimes set alongside poems by the artists in the pictures includes Ferlinghetti, Ginsberg, Corso, Micheline, and other artists. Neeli Cherkovski: "In the photos that make up *Cafe Society* [Nowinski] has chosen to focus on the habitues of those hangouts where he and his friends have cleared enough space in the mad/sad tangle of life in the seventies to find friendship-joy-creativity in neverending flow."

Oracle Rising. Parts One and Two. Produced and directed by Claire Burch. Video. Sponsored by Arts and Education Media. Regent Press, 1991-1992.

New York Times: "Here indeed is the old *Oracle* in all its Oriental opulence. Open any page and you are back on the streets of Haight-Ashbury in a time when that tiny urban spot was the Olympus of the newborn world." These comments are about the facsimile edition of *Oracle*, an underground newspaper from Haight-Ashbury that featured Leary, Ginsberg, Snyder, and many others. The video documents the facsimile reproduction of the magazine and reveals its colorful and elaborate design. Each part is about 28 minutes, and the two parts are on one video cassette.

Peggy Sue Got Married. Directed by Francis Coppola. Produced by Paul Gurian. Starring Kathleen Turner and Nicolas Cage. Film available in video. 104 minutes. Tri-Star Pictures, 1986.

Tape package: "A freak mishap sends [Peggy Sue] decades back in time, giving her the incredible power to change almost anything she wants and letting her create an entirely different future for herself." Lots of old cars, scenes of decades past. Some dialogue comparing Hemingway and Kerouac. Peggy Sue goes off with Michael Fitzsimmons, a "beatnik poet."

Percy, Ann, organizer. *Francesco Clemente: Three Worlds.* Philadelphia: Philadelphia Museum of Art, 1990. 111-128.

A section titled "New York" includes a few small photos by Ginsberg of Clemente, Creeley, and Corso.

Pivano, Fernanda. *C'Era Una Volta Un Beat: 10 anni di ricera alternativa.* Rome: Arcana Editrice, 1976.

The text is in Italian, but the black and white photos are numerous. Some photos show the Beats in Italy. Reproductions of correspondence.

Poetry in Motion. Ron Mann. Film available in video. Los Angeles: Voyager Press, 1985.

Performers include Snyder, Bukowski, Waldman, Baraka, Ginsberg, and Jim Carroll. The material in this video has now also been adapted for a CD-ROM by Voyager titled *Poetry in Motion I and II.* The CD-ROM permits the viewing of the artist in presentation simultaneously with the reading of the text.

Poets of the Cities New York and San Francisco 1950-1965. Dallas: E. P. Dutton, 1974.

An exhibition organized by the Dallas Museum of Fine Arts and Southern Methodist University under the direction of Neil A. Chassman, Chairman, Department of Art History. Creeley writes "On the Road: Notes on Artists and Poets 1950-1965": 56-63. Holmes writes "Unscrewing the Locks: The Beat Poets": 64-71. Photos and images of works of art, some to reappear at the Whitney exhibit.

Point of Order! Directed by Emile de Antonio and David Talbot. Film available in video. Black and white. Sound. 97 minutes. Emile de Antonio, 1964. Zenger Video, 1984.

Provides some social and intellectual background for the period by documenting the investigation of Senator Joseph McCarthy and his associates. Includes introduction by Paul Newman.

Pull My Daisy. Robert Frank. Film available in video. Black and white. Sound. 28 minutes. Houston, TX: Museum of Fine Arts, Houston, 1995.

Jack Kerouac narrates and Allen Ginsberg and Gregory Corso appear in a supposedly improvised 1959 work. The video is now available at moderate cost.

Rebel Without a Cause. Directed by Nicholas Ray. Film. Color. Sound. 111 minutes. Warner Brothers, 1955.

James Dean shapes perception of what beatness is about.

The Savage Eye. Joseph Strick, Ben Maddow and Sidney Meyers. Film. Black and White. Sound. 68 minutes. City Film Corporation, 1959.

An attack on the American emphasis on materialism in life.

Self-Portrait: Book People Picture Themselves: From the Collection of Burt Britton. New York: Random House, 1976.

Bowles, Burroughs, Holmes, Southern, Rumaker, Dawson, Creeley, Ginsberg, Waldman, Berrigan, Everson, Ferlinghetti, DiPrima, McClure, MacLow, Plymell, Orlovsky, Joans, Krim, and Thompson contribute hand-drawn self-portraits. Most are simple pencil figures.

Shadows. John Cassavetes. Film. Black and white. Sound. 87 minutes. Cassavetes/Cassel/Maurice McEndree, 1959.

Exploration of racial issues and the question of identity. Mingus and Shafi Hadi are featured on the soundtrack.

The Subterraneans. Ranald MacDougall. Film. Color. Sound. 89 minutes. Music by Gerry Mulligan. Carmen McRae and Shirley Mann. MGM, 1960.

Hollywood transformation of Kerouac's novel.

Too Late Blues. John Cassavetes. Film. Black and white. Sound. 103
   minutes. Paramount, 1961.
   The artistic individual, set in a jazz milieu, feels conflict with the
surrounding material world.

West Coast, Beat, and Beyond. Produced by Chris Felver. Video.
   Color. Sound. 58 mins. 1984. Sausalito, CA: Chris Felver, 1993.
   Features Ginsberg, Kerouac, Ferlinghetti, Kesey, and others.
Narrated by Gerald Nicosia.

Wholly Communion. Film. Black and white. Sound. Video VHS. 33
   minutes. 1966. New York: Contemporary Films/McGraw-Hill,
   1967.
   Ginsberg, Ferlinghetti, Corso, and others read at the Royal Albert Hall in 1965.

The Wild One. Laslo Benedek. Film. Black and white. Sound. 79
   minutes. Columbia Pictures, 1954.
   Marlon Brando displays the style and mannerisms that came to
be associated with the Beats.

Wilentz, Elias, ed. *The Beat Scene*. New York: Corinth Books, 1960.
   A classic collection of black and white photos by Fred McDarrah
blended with a variety of writings by Beats.

The World According to John Coltrane. Toby Byron and Robert
   Palmer. Video disc. Black and white and color. Sound. 59 min-
   utes. New York: BMG Video, 1991.
   Selections of Coltrane from television appearances.

Addresses on the Internet

LitKicks is a hypertext presentation that features plenty of information on the Beats, including text on Kerouac, Ginsberg, Burroughs, Cassady, Snyder, Ferlinghetti, Corso, and McClure. A tribute to Allen Ginsberg on the occasion of his death is also available,
as are segments on topics such as "The Beat Generation," "Beat
Connections in Rock Music," "Films About the Beats," "Buddhism:
The Beat Religion," and "Origin of the Term Beat." Bibliographies

on the Beats in general, Kerouac, Ginsberg, and Kesey are also featured. Levi Asher, the developer of this site, which has been on line since July 23, 1994, provides updates on news about the Beats, and speeds access to other sites on the web by providing connections. The address is **http://www.charm.net/~brooklyn/** and Levi Asher may be reached at **brooklyn@netcom.com**.

BEAT-L is a message center open to all people interested in the Beats. One may post a question or make a suggestion for discussion, and other subscribers to the list will post their answers. William Gargan of the Brooklyn College library is the founder of this site for communications, which often features news about beat writers and announcements about readings. To sign on to BEAT-L, one sends an e-mail to **listserv@cunyvm.bitnet** or **listserv@cunyvm.edu**, leaving the subject line blank. One then types in the message **subscribe Beat-L first name last name**. A reply will confirm the subscription and offer some tips on operation. One should be prepared to receive numerous messages, and if too many accumulate, one can discontinue the service by sending an e-mail to the same address with the message **signoff BEAT-L first name last name**.

One finds a listing of numerous Beat sites on the internet at **http:www.halcyon.com/colinp/beats.htm**, and with a click on any item on the list, one can go instantly to another Beat site without the bother of typing a long address.

An annotated list of media resources related to the Beats held at the University of California, Berkeley is at **http://www.lib.berkeley.edu/MRC/BeatGen.html**. Many videos and audios are listed, as well as some CD-ROM's.

A site devoted to the traveling exhibit "Beat Culture and the New America: 1950-1965," which appeared at the Whitney Museum in New York, the Walker Art Center in Minneapolis, and finally the DeYoung Museum in San Francisco, is available at **http:www.thinker.org/deyoung/exhibitions/beat/links.html**.

At **http://www.npg.si.edu/exh/rebels/index2.htm** one finds a site for "Rebel Painters and Poets of the 1950's," an exhibition done at the National Portrait Gallery in Washington, D. C. The site includes an essay by Steven Watson, Guest Curator for the exhibit.

At **http://www.clark.net/pub/cosmic/archives/95beats.html** one finds the Beats displayed on a roster as if they were baseball players. Photos accompany the text on each Beat artist.

At **www.kerouac.com**, one finds a bookstore's colorful display of books and other items related to Kerouac and the Beat Generation. At **http://waterrowbooks.com** the on-line catalog for Water Row Books, a dealer in Beat books and merchandise, can be found.

At **http://shell3.ba.best.com/~lcmag/** is a site devoted to women of the Beat Generation. The site is connected to *Left Coast Magazine*.

At **http://www.harbour.sfu.ca/~hayward/UnspeakableVisions/ TableOfContents.html** one finds a series of texts about the Beats and a bibliography.

Two chronological narratives, one on the Beats, the second on the Beats as covered on the internet (mostly *LitKicks*) is *Route 66 and the Beats*, which appears at **http:www.virgin.fr/virgin/html/us/ nostalgia/route66/beat_generation.html** or **http:www.virgin.fr/ virgin/html/us/nostalgia/route66/byte_generation.html**.

The *Addicted to Noise* piece at **http://www. addict.com/ATN/issues/1.05/Features/Beatnik_Books/** includes "Another Superficial Piece About 176 Beatnik Books," a sometimes venomous review of various titles associated with the Beats.

Andrew Phillips presents an essay on the Beats with links at **http://www.geocities.com/solto/studios/7667**.

Chapter 3

WILLIAM S. BURROUGHS (1914–1997)

My purpose in writing has always been to express human potentials and purposes relevant to the Space Age.
                                        – William S. Burroughs

Books by Burroughs

The writings of Burroughs prove attractive to some readers because of the fantasies described and the bizarre taste of some passages, but other readers find these passages vulgar and abhorrent and are put off by the lack of conventional narratives and character development. Ultimately the style of Burroughs must raise an important double question for students: What are the experimental writing methods of Burroughs, and to what degree does he use them successfully?

Junky serves as an effective opening assignment to Burroughs because the style and narrative are conventional, and the major themes of his work are foreshadowed. *The Yage Letters* also establishes a background for *Naked Lunch*, a required text for any course about the Beats. *Naked Lunch*, which abandons conventional narrative for the most part, is more accessible following the reading of *Junky* and *The Yage Letters*.

The enjoyment of these books can be enhanced through the playback of various recorded "routines" by Burroughs, whether on audio cassette, CD, or video. Burroughs' voice and delivery encourage a second effort at texts that may put off some readers at first.

Going beyond these materials by Burroughs may take a course on the Beats beyond the time available for Burroughs, but if Burroughs is the central focus of a course, the study of his sequence of trilogies may be in order. One may also want to give an example of Burroughs' current writing, such as *My Education*.

The Adding Machine: Collected Essays. London: John Calder, 1985.
These essays are numerous, diverse, and short. See 176-181 for "Remembering Jack Kerouac." Other pieces include "The Limits of Control," "Women: A Biological Mistake," and "My Experiences with Wilhelm Reich's Orgone Box." Published as *The Adding Machine: Selected Essays* (New York: Seaver-Holt, 1986). These volumes were preceded by *Essais, tome I*, published in Paris by Bourgois in 1981, and *Essais, tome II*, published in Paris by Bourgois in 1984.

Ah Pook Is Here and Other Texts. London: Calder, 1979; New York: Riverrun, 1982.
"Ah Pook Is Here" is a fantasy about controlling death; this volume reproduces "The Book of Breething" and "Electronic Revolution."

Ali's Smile. London: Unicorn, 1971.
Accompanying this short novel is a recording of Burroughs reading the text.

Blade Runner: A Movie. Berkeley, CA: Blue Wind, 1979.
This short novel is set in New York and satirizes healthcare.

The Book of Breething. Berkeley, CA: Blue Wind, 1975. 2nd edition. 1980.
Burroughs writes on how to avoid linguistic controls, and Robert F. Gale provides illustrations.

The Burroughs File. San Francisco: City Lights, 1984.
Anthology of diverse writings 1960-1976. Biographical information provided by James Grauerholz, Paul Bowles, and Alan Ansen. Samples of "cut-up" method. Contains full text of *White Subway*, *The Retreat Diaries*, and *Cobblestone Gardens*.

Cities of the Red Night. New York: Holt, Rinehart and Winston, 1981; New York: Owl-Holt, 1982.

Seymour Krim describes this novel as "the Wagneresque capper of the five or six homosexual planet-operas Burroughs has scripted since *Naked Lunch*." Michael B. Goodman perceives a "mordant satire of cultural aspirations, homosexual eroticism and political power." Burroughs declares that this work marks a departure from "verbal experiments" in an effort to write a "more or less straight narrative."

Cobblestone Gardens. Cherry Valley, NY: Cherry Valley Editions, 1976.
This work blends autobiographical fiction about Burroughs' youth and family in St. Louis with material drawn from *Naked Lunch* and *Wild Boys*.

Dead Fingers Talk. London: Calder/Olympia, 1963.
Steely Dan and Dr. Benway are among those who appear in short episodes unified through recurring phrases and references.

The Dead Star. San Francisco: Nova Broadcast Press, 1969.
This broadside folds out and features a "cut-up" on the death of Dutch Schultz.

Dr. Benway. Santa Barbara, CA: Bradford Morrow, 1979.
An alternate version of the famous passage from *Naked Lunch*. Burroughs provides a new introduction.

Early Routines. Santa Barbara, CA: Cadmus, 1971.
These routines are written in the style and spirit of *Naked Lunch*.

Electronic Revolution. Cambridge, England: Blackmoor Head, 1971.
Discourse on tape "cut-ups."

Exterminator! New York: Viking/Seaver, 1973; London: Calder and Boyers, 1975; New York: Penguin, 1979.
This work collects short pieces written between 1966 and 1973. The themes are typical of Burroughs.

Health Bulletin: APO-33, a Metabolic Regulator. New York: Fuck You Press, 1964.
This pamphlet, a "cut-up," focuses on apomorphine.

Interzone. New York: Viking Penguin, 1989.

Introduction by James Grauerholz. Selected writings from the 1950's, including Lee's journals.

Junkie [written under the pen name William Lee]. New York: Ace Books, 1953.

This version combined with *Narcotic Agent* by Maurice Helbrant to form one book. Later published as *Junky*, unabridged, with the author's true name (New York: Penguin, 1977). This narrative predates the style of *Naked Lunch* but anticipates the major themes in Burroughs, including the life of an addict.

The Last Words of Dutch Schultz: A Fiction in the Form of a Film Script. London: Cape Goliard, 1970; New York: Viking Seaver, 1975; New York: Seaver, 1987.

Photos accompany Burroughs' film script and present Burroughs' interpretation of Dutch Schultz.

My Education: A Book of Dreams. New York: Viking, 1995.

This volume collects many short pieces or episodes originally written on scraps of paper or index cards. The collection approximates a memoir.

The Naked Lunch. Paris: Olympia Press, 1959.

This text is the single work most often associated with Burroughs. Its revolutionary style sets the pattern for much of the author's later work, and the controversy about its contents makes *Naked Lunch* part of the history of the quest for literary freedom. Burroughs is ultimately a didactic author warning society about mind control. Later published in the United States as *Naked Lunch* (New York: Grove, 1962). Grove Press published a 1969 edition which includes an introduction titled "Deposition: Testimony Concerning a Sickness" and an appendix titled "Letters from a Master Addict to Dangerous Drugs."

Nova Express. New York: Grove, 1964; London: Jonathan Cape, 1966.

One may see a struggle between the Nova Mob and the Nova Police in opposing efforts to establish control, but this difficult-to-read text is really an anti-novel: an effort to write a novel without a narrative or thematic unities. This novel is included in *Three Novels* (New York: Grove Press, 1980).

The Place of Dead Roads. New York: Holt, Rinehart and Winston, 1983; New York: Holt, 1984; New York: Owl-Holt, 1985.

Burroughs sees this work as a sequel to *Cities of the Red Night*. Burroughs says that the conflict arises between those who see journeys into space as a means for survival and those who are unprepared and threatened by such journeys.

Port of Saints. London: Covent Garden, 1975; Berkeley, CA: Blue Wind, 1980.

This work, according to Burroughs, is part of a cycle that begins with *The Wild Boys* and *Exterminator!* and continues with *Ah Pook Is Here*.

Queer. New York: Viking Penguin, 1985.

Burroughs writes "to chronicle . . . carefully these extremely painful and unpleasant and lacerating memories." Set in Mexico City during the 1940's, *Queer* explores addiction and homosexual desire. Another edition was done in London by Pan Picador in 1986 and still another in New York by Penguin in 1987.

Roosevelt After Inauguration. New York: Fuck You Press, 1964.

This short satire was originally part of "In Search of Yage." A later publication (San Francisco: City Lights, 1979) adds three routines from the 1970's to the title piece, which was completed in 1953.

The Soft Machine. Paris: Olympia Press, 1961.

Like *The Ticket That Exploded* and *Nova Express*, *The Soft Machine* is a compilation based on materials left over from the composition of *Naked Lunch*. A revised edition was done in New York by Grove Press in 1966. A further revision was published in London by Calder and Boyers in 1968. *The Soft Machine* is included in *Three Novels* (New York: Grove Press, 1980).

The Ticket That Exploded. Paris: Olympia Press, 1962.

The Ticket That Exploded is a compilation based on materials left over from the composition of *Naked Lunch*. Jennie Skerl writes, "*The Ticket That Exploded* continues the basic montage collage form of *The Soft Machine*, but carries the experiment with cut-up and mythology much further." A revised edition was done in New York by Grove Press in 1967, and further revision is revealed in the edition published in London by Calder and Boyers in 1968. Another edition was done in New York by Grove Press in 1987.

Time. New York: C Press, 1965.
   This pamphlet features drawings by Brion Gysin and follows the "cut-up" method in mocking a famous weekly news magazine.

Tornado Alley. Cherry Valley, NY: Cherry Valley Editions, 1989.
   A series of short pieces displaying Burroughs in typical form.

Valentine's Day Reading. New York: American Theatre for Poets, 1965.
   This pamphlet features short pieces on Dutch Schultz and Bradly Martin.

The Western Lands. New York: Viking Penguin, 1987.
   The Western Lands concludes the trilogy begun with *Cities of the Red Night* and *The Place of Dead Roads.* Another edition was done in London by Pan Picador in 1988, and another was done in New York by Penguin in 1988.

Where Naked Troubadors Shoot Snotty Baboons. Northridge, CA: Lord John Press, 1979.
   This pamphlet reproduces a section from *Cities of the Red Night.*

The Wild Boys. New York: Grove Press, 1971; London: Calder and Boyers, 1972. Included in *Three Novels.* New York: Grove, 1980.
   Burroughs writes, "*The Wild Boys* could be considered a kind of homosexual *Peter Pan.*" He adds that he is "increasingly preoccupied by space travel and biological mutation as a prerequisite for space travel."

A William Burroughs Reader. Ed. John Calder. London: Pan Books, 1982.
   Calder includes excerpts from eight novels, an introduction to Burroughs' life and work, and a bibliography.

Works in Collaboration with Others

Brion Gysin Let the Mice In. With Brion Gysin and Ian Sommerville.
West Glover, VT: Something Else, 1973.
This collection gathers "cut-ups" by Burroughs, Brion Gysin, and
Ian Sommerville.

The Exterminator. With Brion Gysin. San Francisco: Auerhahn
Press/Dave Haselwood Books, 1960.
A collaborative "cut-up."

Mayfair Academy Series More or Less. With Roy Pennington.
Brighton, Sussex, England: Urgency Press Rip-Off, 1973.
This pamphlet features previously published fiction.

Minutes to Go. With Sinclair Beiles, Gregory Corso, and Brion
Gysin. Paris: Two Cities, 1960.
A collection of "cut-ups." Another edition was done in San
Francisco by Beach Books in 1964.

The Retreat Diaries. With Allen Ginsberg and James Grauerholz.
New York: City Moon, 1976.
Burroughs records dreams that he had during a retreat to a
Buddhist center in Vermont in 1975. Grauerholz records a dream he
had, and Ginsberg adds "A Dream of Tibet."

So Who Owns Death TV? With Claude Pélieu and Carl Weissner.
San Francisco: Beach Books, 1967.
This pamphlet is a "cut-up."

The Third Mind. With Brion Gysin. New York: Viking, 1978.
The Third Mind includes the critical article "23 Stitches Taken" by
Gérard-Georges Lemaire: 9-24. Another edition was published in
London by Calder in 1979, and another was done in New York by
Seaver in 1982. Originally published as *Oeuvre croisée*, trans. Gérard-
Georges Lemaire and C. Taylor (Paris: Flammarion, 1976).

White Subway. With Alan Ansen and Paul Bowles. London: Aloes,
1973.

This volume collects "cut-ups" previously published during the 1960's.

The Yage Letters. With Allen Ginsberg. San Francisco: City Lights, 1963.

The eleven letters from Burroughs to Ginsberg that make up the section titled "In Search of Yage" were written in 1953 and contribute to a trilogy in conjunction with *Junky* and *Queer*. *The Yage Letters* includes a letter from Ginsberg to Burroughs written in 1960 and Burroughs' reply of the same year. The text concludes with a short piece by Ginsberg titled "To Whom It May Concern" and a piece by Burroughs titled "I am Dying, Meester?" Skerl considers the first eleven letters a short epistolary novel and writes, "The mode of composition (actual letters, the collaborative editing and publication, and the inclusion of later material in 1963 are all typical of Burroughs's practice as a writer."

Correspondence

Harris, Oliver, ed. *The Letters of William S. Burroughs, 1945-1959*. New York: Viking, 1993.

Harris provides an introduction to this valuable selection of letters. The letters are mostly to Ginsberg, with some selections from letters to Kerouac and Paul Bowles.

Padgett, Ron, and Anne Waldman, eds. *Letters to Allen Ginsberg*, 1953-1957. New York: Full Court Press, 1982.

These letters reflect on Burroughs during his stay in Tangier, where he composed *Naked Lunch*. Burroughs contributes a preface and Ginsberg an introduction.

Publications in Periodicals

For a thorough listing of Burroughs' publications in periodicals, see Joe Maynard and Barry Miles, *William S. Burroughs: A Bibliography 1953–1973* (Charlottesville: University of Virginia, 1978).

"But Is All Back Seat of Dreaming." *Big Table* 1.4 (1960): 13-19.

Using an unusual sequence of words and strange punctuation, Burroughs offers a prefatory note to this selection: "'Back Seat of Dreaming' is part of my current novel. It is based on recent newspaper account of ?four young explorers? who died of thirst in Egypt desert."

"Censorship." *Transatlantic Review* 11 (Winter 1962): 5-11.

Burroughs: "In any form censorship presupposes the right of the government to decide what people will think, what thought material of word and image will be presented to their minds – I am precisely suggesting that the right to exercise such control is called in question."

"Coming of the Purple Better One." *Esquire* Nov. 1968: 89-91.

Burroughs provides a creative interpretation of the mood and spirit in Chicago during the Democratic National Convention of 1968.

"Comments on the Night Before Thinking." *Evergreen Review* 5.20 (Sept.-Oct. 1961): 31.

Burroughs: "Photo falling – Word falling – Break Through in Grey Room – Towers open fire."

"The Cut Up Method of Brion Gysin." *Yugen* 8 (1962): 31-33.

Burroughs explains Gysin's use of the cut-up.

"Day the Record Went Up." *Evergreen Review* 60 (Nov. 1968): 47-50, 76-77.

Editor's note: "The author of *Naked Lunch* offers a chilling picture of a time when mankind destroys itself by its consuming addiction – not to drugs – but to an overly righteous sense of the proprieties."

"Deposition: Testimony Concerning a Sickness." *Evergreen Review* 11 (Jan.-Feb. 1960): 15-23.

Burroughs: "Junk is the ideal product . . . the ultimate merchandise. No sales talk necessary. The client will crawl through a sewer and beg to buy." This article appears as an introduction to *Naked Lunch* (New York: Grove Press, 1962).

"From *Naked Lunch*." *Evergreen Review* 5.16 (1961): 18-31.
  "Doctor 'Fingers' Schafer, the Lobotomy Kid," presents his "Master Work: The Complete All American Deanxietized Man."

"In Quest of Yage." *Big Table* 1.2 (1959): 44-64.
  This selection anticipates *The Yage Letters* (San Francisco: City Lights, 1963).

"Kerouac." *Soft Need* 8 (1973): 17-21.
  Burroughs: "Kerouac was a writer. That is to say he *wrote*. Many people who call themselves writers and have their names on books are not writers and they do not write[,] the difference being a bull fighter who fights a bull is different from a bullshitter who makes passes with no bull there." See this essay published in a slightly modified form in "Remembering Jack Kerouac," *The Adding Machine* (London: John Calder, 1985): 176-181.

"Kicking Drugs: A Very Personal Story." *Harper's Magazine* July 1967: 39-42.
  Burroughs describes his life as a junky and criticizes foolishness in law enforcement and therapy. He advocates a cure via apomorphine.

"Last Words." *New Yorker* 18 Aug. 1997: 36-37.
  Ten short journal entries are presented here, covering the period May 3, 1997 through August 1, 1997. Topics of the entries cover the familiar span for Burroughs, including government, drugs, and literary figures. A photo by Robert Mapplethorpe is included.

"The Literary Techniques of Lady Sutton-Smith." *Times Literary Supplement* 6 Aug. 1964: 682-683.
  Lady Sutton-Smith, who inhabited a villa in Tangier, serves as a voice for describing literary methods associated with Burroughs.

"My Purpose Is to Write for the Space Age." *New York Times Book Review* 19 Feb. 1984: 9-10.
  Burroughs reviews the critical interpretations of his works. See this piece reprinted in *William S. Burroughs: At the Front*, eds. Jennie Skerl and Robin Lydenberg (Carbondale: Southern Illinois University Press, 1991): 265-268.

"Points of Distinction Between Sedative and Consciousness-Expanding Drugs." *Evergreen Review* 34 (Dec. 1964): 72-74.

Editor's note: "William S. Burroughs first delivered this essay as an address before the American Psychological Symposium."

"Ten Episodes from *Naked Lunch*." *Big Table* 1.1 (1959): 79-137.

These ten pieces predate the publication of *Naked Lunch* in the United States in 1962. They represent another chapter in the fight for free expression because this issue of *Big Table* contains "the complete contents of the suppressed Winter 1959 *Chicago Review*."

"They Just Fade Away." *Evergreen Review* 8.32 (Apr.-May 1964): 62-63, 84-85.

Burroughs: "When Sammy and the boys can't hold the marks and even the Old Doctor packs in – 'Are you all right?' he asks seating himself in the first lifeboat the bag in his lap – 'I'm the Doctor.'"

"Two Episodes from *Nova Express*." *Evergreen Review* 7.29 (Mar.-Apr. 1963): 109-116.

"Gave Proof Through the Night" and "The Fish Poison Con."

Bibliographies

Goodman, Michael B. *William S. Burroughs: An Annotated Bibliography of His Works and Criticism*. New York: Garland, 1975.

Superseded by the reference guide below.

Goodman, Michael B. with Lemuel B. Coley. *William S. Burroughs: A Reference Guide*. New York: Garland, 1990.

A thorough and well-annotated list of books and materials by Burroughs and the corresponding reviews. In-depth treatment of books and articles about Burroughs. A list of miscellaneous references covers TV appearances and sound recordings.

Maynard, Joe, and Barry Miles. *William S. Burroughs: A Bibliography, 1953-1973*. Charlottesville: University of Virginia Press, 1978.

An exhaustive listing of the writings and recordings of Burroughs. The emphasis on publication and printing data is represented by reproductions of more than one hundred covers, wrappers, or dust jackets from Burroughs' books and from periodicals.

Miles, Barry. *William S. Burroughs: El Hombre Invisible*. San Diego: Atticus Books, 1981.
This biography has a current list of primary sources at the back. The index helps the reader find background details on individual titles.

Miles Associates. *A Descriptive Catalog of the William S. Burroughs Archive*. Ollon, Switzerland and London: Covent Garden and Am Here, 1973.
A listing of holdings in an archive in Liechtenstein. Burroughs' "Literary Autobiography" is included.

Skerl, Jennie. "A William S. Burroughs Bibliography." *Serif* 11 (Summer 1974): 12-20.
Burroughs' works are listed chronologically, and criticism is alphabetized.

Interviews

Bockris, Victor, with William Burroughs. *A Report from the Bunker*. New York: Seaver, 1981.
An extensive interview accumulated as Bockris accompanied Burroughs during travels to many cities around the world. A chart clarifies the identities of people referred to in the interviews.

Corso, Gregory, and Allen Ginsberg. "Interviews with William Burroughs." *Journal for the Protection of All Beings* 1 (1961): 79-83.
Agent Lee discusses the early novels, politics, narcotics, and language.

Fox, James. "The Return of the Invisible Man." *Rolling Stone* 23 Oct. 1986: 68-69, 72, 74, 114, 116.

Rather than provide transcribed conversation, Fox narrates a visit to Burroughs in Lawrence, Kansas. Background on Burroughs' life, review of his works, and an impression of his life in Lawrence.

"The Hallucinatory Operators Are Real." *SF Horizons* 2 (1965): 3-12.
Burroughs discusses science fiction and sees no limits on its development.

Knickerbocker, Conrad. "William Burroughs: An Interview." *Paris Review* 35 (Fall 1965): 12-49.
This interview is central to the interpretation of the first four novels as Burroughs comments on his mythmaking and his use of montage and "cut-up." Mention of drug use and cure through apomorphine. See this interview in *Writers at Work: The Paris Review Interviews*, third series, ed. Alfred Kazin (New York: Viking, 1967): 143-174.

Malanga, Gerard. "An Interview with William Burroughs." *The Beat Book*. Eds. Arthur and Glee Knight. California, PA: unspeakable visions of the individual, 1974. 90-112.
Burroughs reviews his life, work, and dreams. He refers to Paul Bowles, Brion Gysin, Richard Seaver, and Terry Southern.

Masterson, Graham, and Andrew Rossabi. "William Burroughs." *Penthouse* Mar. 1972: 44-52, 122.
Burroughs calls attention to "the mental engineering which can make or break mankind."

Mikriamos, Philipe. "The Last European Interview." *The Review of Contemporary Fiction* 4.1 (Spring 1984): 12-18.
This interview actually dates back to 1974. Burroughs comments on the authors who have influenced him and the methods he follows in writing.

Odier, Daniel. *The Job: Interviews with William Burroughs*. New York: Grove Press, 1974.
This book-length interview affords a wide range of topics to Burroughs, who discusses sex, law enforcement, narcotics, and literary techniques. Added texts: "Playback from Eden to Watergate" and "Electronic Revolution." This is a translation and enlargement of *Entretiens avec William Burroughs*, published in Paris by Belfond in

1969. The 1974 translation is an enlargement of a previous translation done in New York by Grove Press in 1970.

Palmer, Robert. "William Burroughs." *Rolling Stone* 11 May 1972: 48-53.
Burroughs and Gysin discuss their collaboration. Burroughs updates his ideas on theory, method, and theme in his novels.

Rivers, J. E. "An Interview with William S. Burroughs." *Resources for American Literary Study* 10.2 (Autumn 1980): 154-166.
The conversation includes references to the obscenity trial of *Naked Lunch*, homosexuality in *Naked Lunch*, Jean Genet, confessional writing, satire, picaresque, and filmic techniques.

Skerl, Jennie. "An Interview with William S. Burroughs." *Modern Language Studies* 12.3 (Summer 1982): 3-17.
This interview monitors Burroughs' thoughts on theory and writing at the beginning of the 1980's.

Tytell, John. "An Interview with William Burroughs." *The Beat Diary*. Eds. Arthur and Kit Knight. California, PA: unspeakable visions of the individual, 1977. 35-49.
Burroughs discusses his life with a critic who pioneered the analysis of the lives and literature of the Beat Generation. Some discussion of the cut-up.

von Ziegesar, Peter. "Mapping the Cosmic Currents: An Interview with William Burroughs." *New Letters: A Magazine of Fine Writing* 53.1 (Fall 1986): 57-71.
Discussion of *Queer* and *Naked Lunch*. Review of Burroughs' theories on the need for evolution and space travel for human survival. Discussion of *Place of Dead Roads*, Burroughs' connection to punk rock, the question of fame, Burroughs' audience, and the Beat literary movement.

Wedge, George, and Steven Lowe. "An Interview with William S. Burroughs." *Cottonwood* 41 (1988): 42-50.
Discussion of Fitzgerald, Proust, Coleridge, and other authors. Burroughs mentions his favorite passages from his own writing that date back "thirty or forty years." Drugs, politics, and law enforcement are also mentioned.

Biographies

Lemaire, Gérard-Georges. *Burroughs*. Paris: Editions Artefact, 1986.
   This book is written in French and may not be fully useful to all readers, but numerous photos and images of book covers have value. A bibliography and discography are included.

Miles, Barry. *William Burroughs: El Hombre Invisible: A Portrait*. London: Virgin Books, 1992; New York: Hyperion, 1993.
   An insightful and thorough biography commenting on Burroughs' works and friends. Miles also clarifies Burroughs' connection to popular culture.

Morgan, Ted. *Literary Outlaw: The Life and Times of William S. Burroughs*. New York: Henry Holt, 1988.
   This biography is much respected for its thoroughness and accuracy. The work is based on extensive interviews and includes a set of photos.

Books About Burroughs' Work

Goodman, Michael B. *Contemporary Literary Censorship: The Case History of Burroughs' "Naked Lunch."* Metuchen, NJ: Scarecrow, 1981.
   A chronicle of the four-year legal struggle to publish and distribute *Naked Lunch* in the United States.

Lydenberg, Robin. *Word Cultures: Radical Theory and Practice in William S. Burroughs' Fiction*. Urbana: University of Illinois Press, 1987.
   A study of Burroughs' innovations in style and method in light of corresponding contemporary literary theory. Lydenberg writes, "I argue that Burroughs' radical notions about language and literary production have constituted a much more substantial attack on the humanistic literary establishment than the unconventional life or the allegedly pornographic fiction for which he is often vilified."

Mottram, Eric. *William Burroughs: The Algebra of Need.* Buffalo, NY: Intrepid Press, 1971; London: Boyars, 1977.

An early study of Burroughs. Opens with discussion of *Junky* and proceeds to *The Book of Breething.* Burroughs displays the influence of Joyce and Eliot, but also applies cubism, surrealism, montage, superimposition, and cutting.

Skerl, Jennie. *William S. Burroughs.* Boston: Twayne, 1985.

This compact yet thorough study of Burroughs is clear and powerfully interpretive, offering insights into his innovations in form and clarifications of his ideas.

Skerl, Jennie, and Robin Lydenberg, eds. *William S. Burroughs: At the Front: Critical Reception, 1959-1989.* Carbondale: Southern Illinois University Press, 1991.

This volume serves as an up-to-date, portable collection of criticism on Burroughs and his work, opening with a survey of the literary reputation; continuing with selected criticism from the 1950's, 1960's, 1970's, and 1980's; and concluding with Burroughs' "My Purpose Is to Write for the Space Age." A selected bibliography is included.

Sections or Chapters

Bowles, Paul. *Without Stopping.* New York: Putnam, 1972.

Biographical background on Burroughs in Tangier and his association with Bowles.

Bryant, Jerry H. *The Open Decision: The Contemporary American Novel and Its Intellectual Background.* New York: Free Press, 1970. 199-228.

Burroughs is a hip satirist who develops figurative implications for drug dependency.

Burkholder, Robert E. "William Seward Burroughs." *Dictionary of Literary Biography, Volume 2, American Novelists Since World War II.* Eds. Jeffrey Hetterman and Richard Layman. Detroit: Gale Research, 1978. 70-75.

Biographical background, survey of novels, review of criticism, and selected bibliography.

Burroughs, William, Jr. *Kentucky Ham*. New York: Dutton, 1973.

As William Burroughs, Jr., discusses his grandparents and his visit to his father in Tangier, he provides insights into his father's life and work. Some material in *Kentucky Ham* appeared earlier in William Burroughs, Jr., "Life with Father," *Esquire* 76 (Sept. 1971): 113-115, 140-141, 144-145. Published in conjunction with *Speed* in *Speed/Kentucky Ham* (Woodstock, NY: the overlook press, 1993). The 1993 text includes a foreword by Ann Charters.

"Burroughs, William S(eward)." *Contemporary Authors*. New Revision Series. Vol. 52. Eds. Jeff Chapman and Paula S. Dear. Detroit: Gale Research, 1996. 62-76.

A review of Burroughs' major works, including various critical interpretations. An assessment of Burroughs' influence on culture and literature. Bibliography of primary and secondary materials.

Charters, Ann. *Kerouac: A Biography*. San Francisco: Straight Arrow, 1973; New York: St. Martin's, 1987.

Charters reveals Burroughs' connection with Kerouac and his friends and demonstrates Burroughs' influence on Kerouac. Charters defines the correspondences between Kerouac's characters and Burroughs. Includes several photos of Burroughs.

Cook, Bruce. *The Beat Generation*. New York: Scribner's, 1971; New York: Quill, 1994.

Offers a chapter on Burroughs, particularly *Naked Lunch*. Part of the chapter is an interview.

Gifford, Barry, and Lawrence Lee. *Jack's Book: An Oral Biography of Jack Kerouac*. New York: St. Martin's, 1978.

Offers insight into the early career of Burroughs.

Ginsberg, Allen, and Neal Cassady. *As Ever: The Collected Correspondence of Allen Ginsberg and Neal Cassady*. Berkeley, CA: Creative Arts, 1977.

Ginsberg and Cassady offer occasional comments on Burroughs and his work.

Glover, David. "Utopia and Fantasy in the Late 1960's: Burroughs, Moorcock, Tolkien." In *Popular Fiction and Social Change*. Ed. Christopher Pawling. New York: St. Martin's, 1984. 185-211.

Glover: "At first sight Burroughs, Moorcock, and Tolkien might seem to make an oddly disparate collection; yet their works rapidly achieved canonical status amongst Underground readers and provided a vocabulary of reference for its journalism, correspondents signing themselves with such names as 'Bradley Martin' and 'Bilbo Baggins.'" Glover adds, "Burroughs rejects politics as a means of achieving change since he identifies it with the conventional mechanisms of the nation state and hence part of the very problem."

Grauerholz, James. "On Burroughs' Art." Santa Fe: Gallery Casa Sin Nombre Catalog, 1988.

Grauerholz: Burroughs "belongs to no current 'school' of art, but is subjectively exploring art-making techniques according to the literary and artistic ideas he began to develop twenty-five years ago." See this article reprinted in *William S. Burroughs: At the Front*, eds. Jennie Skerl and Robin Lydenberg (Carbondale: Southern Illinois University Press, 1991): 239-249.

Harris, Oliver C. G. "Cut-up Closure: The Return to Narrative." *William S. Burroughs: At the Front*. Eds. Jennie Skerl and Robin Lydenberg. Carbondale: Southern Illinois University Press, 1991. 251-262.

Harris: "Resistance through cut-ups to the tyranny of artificially imposed narrative structures, and of individualistic narrative style, gradually gave way to the use of a plurality of inherited styles."

Hendin, Josephine. *Vulnerable People: A View of American Fiction Since 1945*. New York: Oxford University Press, 1978. 54-59.

An interpretation of Burroughs' style as an expression of sadomasochism and rage.

Hoffman, Frederick J. *The Mortal No: Death and the Modern Imagination*. Princeton, NJ: Princeton University Press, 1964. 486-489.

Burroughs' works represent "destructive expression."

Jardine, Alice. *Gynesis: Configurations of Woman and Modernity.* Ithaca: Cornell University Press, 1985. 232-234, 236.

Jardine: "With Burroughs's writing, we are not beyond the sign, we are its masters. The 'nodal points' of the text are separated, reconnected, repeated, left out, added, plugged in and out of one giant nightmare machine. The forces (cancerous and diseased) controlling the individual are ultimately seen as technological and programmatic. And Burroughs declares war on them with ever more advanced technology."

Kazin, Alfred. *Bright Book of Life: American Novelists and Storytellers from Hemingway to Mailer.* Boston: Little, 1973. 262-270.

A discussion of Burroughs as an absurdist. Refers also to Pynchon and Barthelme.

Lawlor, William. "*Nova Express.*" *Magill's Guide to Science Fiction and Fantasy Literature.* Eds. T. A. Shippey and A. J. Sobczak. Pasadena, CA: Salem Press, 1996. 681-682.

Summary and analysis of *Nova Express*.

Lodge, David. *Modes of Modern Writing: Metaphor, Metonymy, and the Typology of Modern Literature.* Ithaca: Cornell University Press, 1977.

Dismissal of *Naked Lunch*.

_____. *The Novelist at the Crossroads and Other Essays in Fiction and Criticism.* Ithaca: Cornell University Press, 1971; London: Routledge, 1971; London: Routledge, 1986.

Dismissal of Burroughs. This piece originally appeared in *Critical Quarterly* 8 (Autumn 1966): 203-212. See this piece reprinted in *William S. Burroughs: At the Front*, eds. Jennie Skerl and Robin Lydenberg (Carbondale: Southern Illinois University Press, 1991): 75-84.

Lydenberg, Robin, and Jennie Skerl. "Points of Intersection: An Overview of William S. Burroughs and His Critics." *William S. Burroughs: At the Front.* Eds. Jennie Skerl and Robin Lydenberg. Carbondale: Southern Illinois University Press, 1991. 3-15.

A decade-by-decade assessment of the critical interpretation given to the work of William Burroughs.

MacAdams, Lewis. "Outlaw, Junkie, Godfather to the Beats: William
S. Burroughs (1914-1997)." *Rolling Stone* 18 Sept. 1997: 52, 54-55.
   A succinct biographical tribute that includes a selection of photos
and additonal comments by Hunter S. Thompson, Lou Reed, and
Gregory Corso.

McCarthy, Mary. "Burroughs' *Naked Lunch.*" *The Writing on the
Wall and Other Essays*. New York: Harcourt, 1970. 42-53.
   Insightful essay bringing light to *Naked Lunch* in the face of other
rejections of Burroughs' work. See this piece reprinted in *William S.
Burroughs: At the Front*, eds. Jennie Skerl and Robin Lydenberg
(Carbondale: Southern Illinois University Press, 1991): 33-40.

McNally, Dennis. *Desolate Angel: Jack Kerouac, the Beat Generation,
and America*. New York: McGraw-Hill, 1979.
   A biography of Kerouac that inevitably comments on Burroughs,
especially *Naked Lunch*.

Mertz, Robert. "The Virus Visions of William Burroughs." *Itinerary
3: Criticism*. Ed. Frank Baldanza. Bowling Green, OH: Bowling
Green University Press, 1977.
   An analysis of Burroughs' attitude, in various novels, toward mass
media.

Nelson, Cary. "The End of the Body: Radical Space in Burroughs."
The Incarnate Word: Literature and Verbal Space. Urbana:
University of Illinois Press, 1973. 208-229.
   Nelson applies reader-response theory in a chapter referring to
various works by Burroughs. This piece is reprinted in *William S.
Burroughs: At the Front*, eds. Jennie Skerl and Robin Lydenberg
(Carbondale: University of Southern Illinois Press, 1991): 119-132.

Oxenhandler, Neal. "Listening to Burroughs' Voice." In *Surfiction:
Fiction Now . . . and Tomorrow*. Ed. Raymond Federman.
Chicago: Swallow, 1975. 181-201.
   Freudian analysis of various novels by Burroughs. This piece is
reprinted in *William S. Burroughs: At the Front*, eds. Jennie Skerl and
Robin Lydenberg (Carbondale: University of Southern Illinois Press,
1991): 133-147.

Palumbo, Donald. "William S. Burroughs." *Dictionary of Literary Biography, Volume 8, Twentieth-Century American Science-Fiction Writers, Part 1.* Eds. David Cowart and Thomas L. Wymer. Detroit: Gale Research, 1981. 92-96.
Survey of novels. Review of criticism. Bibliography.

Pearce, Richard. *Stages of the Clown: Perspectives on Modern Fiction from Dostoevsky to Beckett.* Carbondale: Southern Illinois University Press, 1970.
Naked Lunch illustrates the technique of "the clown," but the novel is flawed.

Porush, David. "Cybernetics and Techno-Paranoia: Kurt Vonnegut, Jr., and William Burroughs." *The Soft Machine: Cybernetic Fiction.* New York: Methuen, 1985. 85-111.
Porush: "[I]n Burroughs's apocalyptic mythology, the soft machine is the pure end-product of control by some malicious and all-powerful conspiracy of government, media, and what Burroughs calls 'the Nova Police,' agents of technology."

Seltzer, Alvin. "Confusion Hath Fuck His Masterpiece." *Chaos in the Novel: The Novel in Chaos.* New York: Schocken, 1974. 330-374.
Analysis of "cut-up."

Skerl, Jennie. "William S. Burroughs." In *The Beats: Literary Bohemians in Postwar America.* Ed. Ann Charters. Detroit: Gale Research, 1983. 45-69.
Skerl: "Burroughs's novels reflect both the Beat sensibility of revolt and the avant-garde tradition of innovation by introducing new subject matter and new techniques into fiction." Includes photos, biographical information, illustrations of original book covers, and bibliographical data.

Solotaroff, Theodore. "The Algebra of Need." *The Red Hot Vacuum.* New York: Atheneum, 1970. 247-253.
Discussion of *Nova Express, The Soft Machine,* and *The Ticket That Exploded.* In the discussion of addiction, the focus is on the "pushers as much as the pushed."

Tanner, Tony. "Rub Out the Word." *City of Words: American Fiction 1950-1970.* New York: Harper and Row, 1971. 109-140.

A positive appraisal of various works by Burroughs, with comparisons of Burroughs with Marshall McLuhan and John Cage. See this piece reprinted in *William S. Burroughs: At the Front*, eds. Jennie Skerl and Robin Lydenberg (Carbondale: Southern Illinois University Press, 1991): 105-113.

Tytell, John. *Naked Angels: The Lives and Literature of the Beat Generation*. New York: McGraw-Hill, 1976; New York: Grove Press, 1986.

Tytell: "Burroughs, like Poe or the French Symbolists, creates an ambiance, an atmosphere of conflicting particles whose points of contact reveal a dark and hidden interior." Tytell examines the life and work of Burroughs as a major player in the Beat movement. Includes various photos of Burroughs. "The Broken Circuit," a chapter from *Naked Angels: The Lives and Literature of the Beat Generation*, is reprinted in *William S. Burroughs: At the Front*, eds. Jennie Skerl and Robin Lydenberg (Carbondale: Southern Illinois University Press, 1991): 149-157. Tytell analyzes the beginnings of the Beats and comments on *Naked Lunch*.

Vernon, John. *The Garden and the Map: Schizophrenia in Twentieth Century Literature and Culture*. Urbana: University of Illinois Press, 1973. 85-109.

Discussion of various works by Burroughs, the cut-up method, and the impression that reality is schizophrenic.

Werner, Craig Hansen. *Paradoxical Resolutions: American Fiction Since James Joyce*. Urbana: University of Illinois Press, 1982. 96-119.

Parallels in the methods of Joyce and Burroughs.

Widmer, Kingsley. *The Literary Rebel*. Carbondale: Southern Illinois University Press, 1965. 155-158.

Widmer discusses *Naked Lunch* and remarks, "Burroughs is more mannered moralist than rebel."

Young, Allen. *Gay Sunshine Interview, Allen Ginsberg with Allen Young*. Bolinas, CA: Grey Fox Press, 1974.

Ginsberg refers to Burroughs' view of sexuality.

Zurbrugg, Nicholas. "Beckett, Proust, and Burroughs and the Perils of 'Image Warfare.'" *Samuel Beckett: Humanistic Perspectives*. Eds. Morris Beja, S. E. Gontarski, and Pierre Astier. Columbus: Ohio State University Press, 1983. 172-187.
Zurbrugg: "Burroughs seems most interesting as an author exploring the social and political potential of the word and image as a 'virus' propagating chaos." This piece is reprinted in *William S. Burroughs: At the Front*, eds. Jennie Skerl and Robin Lydenberg (Carbondale: University of Southern Illinois Press, 1991): 177-188.

Articles About Burroughs' Work

Abel, Lionel. "Beyond the Fringe." *Partisan Review* 30 (Spring 1963): 109-112.
Naked Lunch provides for some readers a satisfaction that elevated literary exploration of "ethical decision" and "speculative wonder" cannot supply.

Adams, Ian. "Society as Novelist." *Journal of Aesthetics and Art Criticism* 25 (Summer 1967): 375-386.
Adams compares *Naked Lunch* with Thackeray's *Vanity Fair*.

Adams, Phoebe. "*Exterminator.*" *Atlantic* Sept. 1973: 118-119.
Adams: "The chapters, taken as individual sketches, are inventive, glitteringly clever attacks" but "as a whole, they become the diatribe of an aging homosexual."

Ansen, Alan. "Anyone Who Can Pick Up a Frying Pan Owns Death." *Big Table* 2 (Summer 1959): 32-41.
Analysis of the early novels and biographical detail about Burroughs in Tangier. Evaluation of Burroughs as an influence on other Beats. See this essay reprinted in Thomas Parkinson, ed., *A Casebook on the Beat* (New York: Crowell, 1961): 107-113 or Jennie Skerl and Robin Lydenberg, eds., *William S. Burroughs: At the Front* (Carbondale: Southern Illinois University Press, 1991): 25-29.

_____. "William Burroughs: A Personal View." *The Review of Contemporary Fiction* 4.1 (Spring 1984): 49-55.
Biography and interpretation by Burroughs' associate.

Baumbach, Jonathan. "Joe the Dead Seeks Immortality." *New York Times Book Review* 3 Jan. 1988: 11.

The Western Lands "is made up of bizarre anecdotes, which fit into one another like Chinese boxes, and comic routines, which tend to be as irreverent and obscene as Lenny Bruce at his most subversive."

Beml, Maxy. "William Burroughs and the Invisible Generation." *Telos* 13 (Fall 1972): 125-131.

"Chaos and derangement" in Burroughs' fiction.

Bergman, Andrew C. J. "The Naked Plate." *New York Times Book Review* 14 Oct. 1973: 14.

Review of *Exterminator!* Bergman: "Despite occasional sparks of collision, Burroughs's satire tends to be both broad and repetitive."

Bliss, Michael. "The Orchestration of Chaos: Verbal Technique in William Burroughs' *Naked Lunch*." *enclitic* 1.1 (1977): 59-69.

A study of *Naked Lunch* with a focus on the use of language to establish control and some discussion of the innovative narrative technique.

Bowles, Paul. "Burroughs in Tangier." *Big Table* 2 (Summer 1959): 42-43.

A brief recollection of Burroughs, Ginsberg, and Bowles in Tangier. See this essay reprinted in Thomas Parkinson, ed., *A Casebook on the Beat* (New York: Crowell, 1961): 114-115.

Bryan, Jeff. "William Burroughs and His Faith in X." *West Virginia University Philological Papers* 32 (1986-1987): 79-89.

Bryan: "Burroughs's two full-length books of nonfiction, *The Job*, and *The Third Mind*, were completed in the middle and late sixties." He adds, "After the *Naked Lunch* tetralogy, Burroughs set himself the task of exploring what writing was, and the results of his research were presented in his nonfiction, before they were applied to the creation of his two larger, later books, *Cities of the Red Night* (1982) and *The Place of Dead Roads* (1985).

Bucher, Francois. "Burroughs' Tree." *The Review of Contemporary Fiction* 4.1 (Spring 1984): 131-134.

Biographical commentary beginning with the bomb on Nagasaki.

Burgess, Anthony. "Yards and Yards of Entrails." *Observer* 13 Feb. 1966: 27.

In this review of *Nova Express*, Burgess remarks, "This forcing of a new look at language on us (and, essentially, at the things language stands for) sounds exciting. Unfortunately, the execution doesn't live up to the prospectus."

Bush, Clive. "Review Article: An Anarchy of New Speech: Notes on the American Tradition of William Burroughs." *Journal of Beckett Studies* 6 (1980): 120-128.

Review of *Cobble Stone Gardens*, by Burroughs, which embodies "familiar Burroughsian themes with a new elegance and energy." The review also covers *The Third Mind* by Gysin and Burroughs, which is "a collection of interviews with [Burroughs], statements about him, and examples of the cut-up technique." Finally, the review turns to *William Burroughs: The Algebra of Need*, by Eric Mottram, which is "the first serious full-length work on Burroughs."

Carr, C. "Hollow Man." *Voice Literary Supplement* Oct. 1986: 20-22.

Review of *The Adding Machine*, *Queer*, and Jennie Skerl's *William S. Burroughs*. Discussion of Burroughs at Naropa in 1981, analysis of the cut-up method, and consideration of Burroughs as a collaborator, misogynist, and pop-art novelist.

Carr, C., and David Ulin. "William S. Burroughs 1914-1917." *Village Voice* 12 Aug. 1997: 51.

For this full-page tribute to Burroughs on the occasion of his death, Carr writes "Addicted to Words," in which he evaluates Burroughs' contribution to contemporary literature, and Ulin writes "Live Fast, Die Old," in which he remarks, "Burroughs' writing was a curious mix of the hard-boiled and the avant-garde."

Ciardi, John. "The Book Burners and Sweet Sixteen." *Saturday Review* 27 June 1959: 22.

A defense of *Big Table* 1 (which included material by Burroughs and other Beats) against censorship by the Post Office. See this article reprinted in *William S. Burroughs: At the Front*, eds. Jennie Skerl and Robin Lydenberg (Carbondale: Southern Illinois University Press, 1991): 19-23.

Cohen, Robert. "Dispatches from the Interzone." *New York Times Book Review* 15 Jan. 1995: 9, 11.
My Education "depicts a life seen almost from beyond itself, through a dense field of shifting, associational patterns, but behind it there is a naked weight of loss and regret."

Cordess, Gérard. "The Science-fiction of William Burroughs." *Caliban* 12 (1975): 33-43.
Analysis of metaphoric implications in various novels.

Didion, Joan. "Wired for Shock Treatments." *Book Week* 27 Mar. 1966: 2-3.
A "book by William Burroughs has about as much intrinsic 'meaning' as the actual inkblot in a Rorschach test." Didion adds, "*The Soft Machine* has only the dulling effect of a migraine attack."

Disch, Thomas M. "Pleasures of Hanging." *New York Times Book Review* 15 Mar. 1981: 14-15.
Disch reviews *Cities of the Red Night*, exclaiming, "Forget morality! Forget art! What Mr. Burroughs offered the rubes back in 1959 and what he offers them today, in somewhat wearier condition, is entrance to a sideshow where they can view his curious id capering and making faces and confessing to bizarre inclinations."

Dorn, Edward. "Notes More or Less Relevant to Burroughs and Trocchi." *Kulchur* 7 (1962): 3-22.
Commentary on theme and form in *Naked Lunch*.

Elliott, George P. "Destroyers, Defilers, and Confusers of Men." *Atlantic Monthly* Dec. 1968: 74-80.
Analysis of satire in Swift and in Burroughs' *Naked Lunch*.

Estrin, Barbara L. "The Revelatory Connection: Inspired Poetry and *Naked Lunch*." *The Review of Contemporary Fiction* 4.1 (Spring 1984): 58-64.
Estrin: "To place a book as seemingly profane as *Naked Lunch* in a genre as ostensibly sacred as inspired literature is neither to elevate the novel nor to deflate the Bible."

Fiedler, Leslie. "The New Mutants." *Partisan Review* 32 (1965): 505-525.
Naked Lunch portrays "post-humanist sexuality."

Fox, Hugh. "Cut-up Poetry and William Burroughs." *West Coast Review* 4 (Fall 1969): 17-19.
With the cut-up, Burroughs succeeds in setting aside the limiting effect of conventions.

Friedberg, Anne. "'Cut-Ups': A *Syn*ema of the Text." *Downtown Review* 1.1 (1979): 3-5.
Friedberg: "The 'cut-up' techniques of William Burroughs echo much of the dadaist fervor against rationality and much irreverence for bourgeois life and art-making." See this article reprinted in *William S. Burroughs: At the Front*, eds. Jennie Skerl and Robin Lydenberg (Carbondale: Southern Illinois University Press, 1991): 169-173.

Géfin, Laszlo K. "Collage, Theory, Reception, and the Cutups of William Burroughs." *Literature and the Other Arts: Perspectives on Contemporary Literature* 13 (1987): 91-100.
Géfin: "Similar to the Dadaists, Burroughs has burdened his method with a considerable ideological load; he claims, for instance, that the cutup initiates 'a movement castrating the continuum of meaning, the breaking up of the Hegelian structure,' with the result that 'the text eventually escapes from the control of its manipulator.'" Géfin adds, "Burroughs applauds the cutup because it, like the collage for the Dadaists, destroys univocality, uniformity, linear structure, and ownership," concluding that "while the 'mind jolt' at the alienating 'seam' may be universal, and even reconstitutive of a 'reading subject,' the kind of semantic reconciliation that would take place should at all times be dependent on the individual horizon of expectations inescapably different in each reader."

Glover, David. "Burroughs' Western." *Over Here: An American Studies Journal* 6.2 (1986): 14-23.
Glover: "[I]n Burroughs' western the gun duel which opens the book is posed as an enigma, and . . . the specter of death . . . shadows the fantasies the author so painstakingly constructs." See this article reprinted in *William S. Burroughs: At the Front*, eds. Jennie Skerl and

Robin Lydenberg (Carbondale: Southern Illinois University Press, 1991): 209-215.

Gold, Herbert. "At Play in the Circles of Hell." *New York Times Book Review* 20 Mar. 1966: 24.
    Review of *The Soft Machine*. Gold: "The lasting idea here is of a morally uninhabitable world, created by an artist robbed of compassion and endowed with such gifts as to make that loss seem irrelevant."

_____. "Instead of Love, the Fix." *New York Times Book Review* 25 Nov. 1962: 4, 69.
    Review of *Naked Lunch*. Gold: Burroughs displays "American racial, commercial, and social prejudices, placed upon a subject matter of perversion and nihilism." Gold adds, "William Burroughs has written the basic work for understanding that desperate symptom which is the beat style of life."

Guzlowski, John Z. "The Family in the Fiction of William Burroughs." *Midwest Quarterly* 30.1 (Autumn 1988): 11-26.
    Guzlowski: In Burroughs' writing, the reader learns of "the maiming effect of the family" because the family is another part of the "control system."

Gysin, Brion. "Cut-ups: A Project for Disastrous Success." *Evergreen Review* 8.32 (April-May 1964): 56-61.
    Gysin explains about Burroughs and Gysin in Tangier and Paris collaborating and using the "cut-up." Gysin provides a clear illustration of the steps in the process.

Hassan, Ihab. "The Literature of Silence: From Henry Miller to Beckett and Burroughs." *Encounter* 28.1 (Jan. 1967): 74-82.
    An interpretation of innovative form in three authors. Burroughs provides "the new map of our hell."

_____. "The Novel of Outrage: A Minority Voice in Postwar American Fiction." *American Scholar* 34.2 (Spring 1965): 239-253.
    An analysis of the response to authority in various novels, including *Naked Lunch*, *The Soft Machine*, and *The Ticket That Exploded*.

_____. "The Subtracting Machine: The Work of William S. Burroughs." *Critique* 6 (Spring 1963): 4-23.
An analysis of theme and form in various novels by Burroughs. See this article reprinted in *William S. Burroughs: At the Front*, eds. Jennie Skerl and Robin Lydenberg (Carbondale: Southern Illinois University Press, 1991): 53-67.

Hendin, Josephine. "*The Wild Boys*." *Saturday Review* 30 Oct. 1971: 46, 49-50.
Hendin: "*Wild Boys* is brutal hagiography, a book of demon saints purged of hope or desire."

Hicks, Granville. "Life in Four Letters." *Saturday Review* 7 Nov. 1964: 23-24.
Hicks: "There are large elements of fantasy in *Naked Lunch*, but *Nova Express* is all fantasy, the purpose of which, so far as I can find out, is to puzzle the reader."

Hilfer, Anthony Channell. "Mariner and Wedding Guest in William Burroughs' *Naked Lunch*." *Criticism* 22 (1980): 252-265.
The narrator in *Naked Lunch*.

Johnston, Allan. "The Burroughs Biopathy: William S. Burroughs' *Junky* and *Naked Lunch* and Reichian Theory." *The Review of Contemporary Fiction* 4.1 (Spring 1984): 107-120.
A review of the main ideas of Reich and their place in *Junky* and *Naked Lunch*.

Kazin, Alfred. "He's Just Wild About Writing." *New York Times Book Review* 12 Dec. 1971: 4, 22.
The Wild Boys "is essentially a reverie in which different items suddenly get animated with a marvelously unexpectable profusion and disorder." See this article reprinted in *William S. Burroughs: At the Front*, eds. Jennie Skerl and Robin Lydenberg (Carbondale: Southern Illinois University Press, 1991): 115-118.

Kerouac, Jack, and Neal Cassady. "First Night of the Tapes." *Transatlantic Review* 33/34 (Winter 1969-1970): 115-125.
Transcript of a conversation between Kerouac and Cassady. Cassady describes life with Burroughs in Texas.

Kimball, Roger. "The Death of Decency." *Wall Street Journal* 8 Aug.
1997: A12.

Irked by tributes to Burroughs and Ginsberg in the *New York
Times*, the *Village Voice*, and other papers, Kimball writes, "Allen
Ginsberg, William Burroughs, and the rest of the Beats really do
mark an important moment in American culture, not as one of its
achievements, but as a grievous example of its degeneration."

"King of the YADS." *Time* 30 Nov. 1962: 96, 98.

Review of *Naked Lunch*. *Time*: "The value of the book is mostly
confessional, not literary." The Beats are a "conspiracy of the spider-
eyed."

Koch, Steven. "Images of Loathing." *Nation* 4 July 1966: 25-26.

Koch: "Burroughs' ideology–the theme explicitly developed by
Nova Express, his least impressive book so far–is based on an image
of consciousness in bondage to the organism; better, of
consciousness as an organism, gripped by tropisms of need." Koch
adds, "*The Soft Machine* . . . is a collection of related, syncretically
developed 'routines'–sections from 2 to 50 pages–that exploit
various images and voices in the surrealistic confidence that
language retains its vibrancy even–perhaps especially–in a state of
radical dissociation."

Kostelanetz, Richard. "From Nightmare to Serendipity: A
    Retrospective Look at William Burroughs." *Twentieth Century
    Literature* 11 (Oct. 1965): 123-130.

Praise for Burroughs' treatment of drugs and the city in *Naked
Lunch*, but doubt about the merit of works produced after *Naked
Lunch*.

Leddy, Michael. "'Departed Have Left No Address':
    Revelation/Concealment Presence/Absence in *Naked Lunch*."
    Review of Contemporary Fiction 4.1 (1984): 33-39.

Leddy: "While Burroughs is conning the reader, he is also conning
himself, becoming entangled in self-contradiction."

Lee, A. Robert. "William Burroughs and the Sexuality of Power."
    20th Century Studies 2 (Nov. 1969): 74-88.

An analysis of imagery, structure, and moral and social themes in
various novels by Burroughs.

LeVot, Andre. "Disjunctive and Conjunctive Modes in Contemporary American Fiction." *Forum* 14 (1976): 44-55.

A new Lost Generation includes Hawkes, Coover, Barthelme, and Burroughs. Nathaniel West anticipated this generation.

Lodge, David. "Objections to William Burroughs." *Critical Quarterly* 8 (Autumn 1966): 203-212.

Lodge finds that Burroughs is "unsatisfying." See this article reprinted in *William S. Burroughs: At the Front*, eds. Jennie Skerl and Robin Lydenberg (Carbondale: Southern Illinois University Press, 1991): 75-84.

Lydenberg, Robin. "Beyond Good and Evil: 'How-To' Read *Naked Lunch*." *Review of Contemporary Fiction* 4.1 (1984): 75-85.

Lydenberg: "In Burroughs' radical vision, all materiality stems ultimately from the materiality of language, a materiality which is masked by abstraction, by a 'blind prose' of euphemisms which obscures and devours fact and reference."

_____. "Cut-Up: Negative Poetics in William Burroughs and Roland Barthes." *Comparative Literature Studies* 15 (1978): 414-430.

Parallels in the methods and themes of Burroughs and Barthes.

_____. "El Hombre Invisible." *Nation* 19 Mar. 1988: 387-389.

In *The Western Lands*, "creativity is no longer depicted as violent aggression, sexual exhilaration, or hallucinatory fantasy–it has instead a peculiarly domestic, almost maternal quality." See this article reprinted in *William S. Burroughs: At the Front*, eds. Jennie Skerl and Robin Lydenberg (Carbondale: Southern Illinois University Press, 1991): 233-237.

McCarthy, Mary. "Burroughs' *Naked Lunch*." *Encounter* 20 (1963): 92-98.

McCarthy provides a lucid interpretaion of *Naked Lunch*, which she sees as a novel based on the form of a circus. See this article reprinted in *William S. Burroughs: At the Front*, eds. Jennie Skerl and Robin Lydenberg (Carbondale: Southern Illinois University Press, 1991): 33-39. See this piece in *The Writing on the Wall and Other Essays* (New York: Harcourt, 1970): 42-53.

McConnell, Frank D. "William Burroughs and the Literature of Addiction." *Massachusetts Review* 8 (1967): 665-680.

Burroughs and Coleridge and the literature of addiction, with references to DeQuincey, Wilde, Lowry, and Algren. *Naked Lunch* dismantles and exposes "a cash-and-carry culture." See this article reprinted in *William S. Burroughs: At the Front*, eds. Jennie Skerl and Robin Lydenberg (Carbondale: Southern Illinois University Press, 1991): 53-67.

McLuhan, Marshall. "Notes on Burroughs." *Nation* 28 Dec. 1964: 517-519.

Naked Lunch and *Nova Express* exemplify McLuhan's theories about the influence of technology. See this article reprinted in *William S. Burroughs: At the Front*, eds. Jennie Skerl and Robin Lydenberg (Carbondale: Southern Illinois University Press, 1991): 69-73.

Malcolm, Donald. "The Heroin of Our Times." 2 Feb. 1963: 114, 117-118, 120-121.

Review of *Naked Lunch*. Malcolm: "It may be fruitful, then, to postpone our consideration of Mr. Burroughs' claims for the work and simply regard it as a raw document of personal history."

Malin, Irving. "Flashes of *Schultz*." *Review of Contemporary Fiction* 4.1 (1984): 143-144.

In *The Last Words of Dutch Schultz*, Burroughs links "art and criminality in an 'associative' way."

Manganotti, Donatella. "The Final Fix." *Kulchur* 4 (Autumn 1964): 76-87.

A study of *The Yage Letters* with references to other works by Burroughs.

Marten, Harry. "Mexican Specters." *New York Times Book Review* 3 Nov. 1985: 22.

Marten says that *Queer* "just trails off, leaving its narrator much as we first found him, alone in a chaotic and sinister world, parading his coping mechanisms and still hoping to connect." Nevertheless, Marten adds that *Queer* "helps us come to grips with the dark humor, violent energy and unsettling vision of this writer who has forced himself into our consciousness and seized a place in our literary history."

Meisel, Perry. "Gunslinger in a Time Warp." *New York Times Book Review* 19 Feb. 1984: 8-9.
Meisel finds that *The Place of Dead Roads* has "a largely naturalistic style and an often conventional mode of storytelling," yet the work "slips and slides in time and place–almost unaccountably until one is again reminded that a transpersonal web links everything together."

Meyer, Adam. "One of the Great Early Counselors: The Influence of Franz Kafka on William S. Burroughs." *Comparative Literature Studies* 27.3 (1990): 211-229.
Meyer: "If we look beneath Kafka's smooth veneer . . . we will see that he is attempting to disrupt conventional language patterns just as much as Burroughs is."

Michelson, Peter. "Beardsly, Burroughs, Decadence, and the Poetics of Obscenity." *Tri-Quarterly* 12 (Spring 1968): 139-155.
Naked Lunch and other works as examples of Decadence following from the works of Beardsly, an early Decadent artist.

Mudrick, Marvin. "Sarroute, Duras, Burroughs, Barthelme, and a Postscript." *Hudson Review* 20 (Autumn 1967): 473-486.
Comparison of Lenny Bruce and William Burroughs. The works after *Naked Lunch* are inferior.

Obejas, Achy. "Beats' Burroughs Survives in Pop, Gay Culture." *Chicago Tribune* 4 Aug. 1997, Sec. 1: 4.
On the occasion of Burroughs' death, Obejas reviews Burroughs' literary achievements and experiments and explains his influence on musicians and visual artists.

O'Brien, Glenn. "Burroughs Live." *Review of Contemporary Fiction* 4.1 (1984): 141-142.
A review of William Burroughs as a speaker.

Palumbo, Donald. "William Burroughs' Quartet of Science-Fiction Novels as Dystopian Social Satire." *Extrapolation* 20 (1979): 321-329.

An interpretation of the Nova mythology in various novels by Burroughs.

Perry, Tony. "Beat Icon William S. Burroughs Dies at 83." *Los Angeles Times* 3 Aug. 1997: A1.

Perry reviews Burroughs' life, his accomplishments, and his role in the Beat Generation.

Peterson, R. G. "A Picture Is a Fact: Wittgenstein and *The Naked Lunch.*" *Twentieth Century Literature* 12 (July 1966): 78-86.

A comparative analysis of Wittgenstein's *Tractatus Logico-Philosophicus* and *Naked Lunch*. Find this essay in *The Beats: Essays in Criticism*, ed. Lee Bartlett (Jefferson, NC: McFarland, 1981): 30-39.

Ploog, Jurgen. "A Burroughs Primer." Trans. Regina Weinreich. *Review of Contemporary Fiction* 4.1 (1984): 131-140.

Biographical perspective on Burroughs with some commentary on the novels.

Pounds, Wayne. "The Postmodern Anus: Parody and Utopia in Two Recent Novels by William Burroughs." *Poetics Today* 8.3-4 (1987): 611-629.

This essay delights with its examination of the "asshole" in Pound, Joyce, and Burroughs, and moves forward to the conclusion that "a progressive reading of Burroughs . . . should read him as one response to Jameson's call for a 'social cartography.'" See this article reprinted in *William S. Burroughs: At the Front*, eds. Jennie Skerl and Robin Lydenberg (Carbondale: Southern Illinois University Press, 1991): 217-232.

Russell, Charles. "Individual Voice in the Collective Discourse: Literary Innovation in Postmodern American Fiction." *Sub-stance: A Review of Theory and Literary Criticism* 27 (1980): 29-39.

A poststructuralist assessment of various contemporary writers. Includes references to Burroughs.

Sante, Luc. "The Invisible Man." *New York Review of Books* 10 May 1984: 12-15.

Review of the twenty-fifth anniversary edition of *Naked Lunch*, *Letters to Allen Ginsberg, 1953-1957*, and *Burroughs*, the film directed by Howard Brookner. The article is a discussion of Burroughs' literary career. Sante: Burroughs "is the dangerous figure in a worn business outfit who haunts schoolyards and mutters vague fragments about planetary conspiracy."

Scheer-Schazler, Brigitte. "Language at the Vanishing Point: Some Notes on the Use of Language in Recent American Literature." *Revue de Langues Vivantes* 42 (1976): 497-508.
Burroughs analyzes control through language. References to Barth, Pynchon, and Nabokov.

Seldon, E. S. "The Cannibal Feast: *Naked Lunch* by William Burroughs." *Evergreen Review* 6.22 (Jan.-Feb. 1962): 110-113.
Naked Lunch marks "one of the most impressive literary debuts of the past century."

Severo, Richard. "William S. Burroughs Dies at 83; Member of Beat Generation Wrote *Naked Lunch.*" *New York Times* 3 Aug. 1997, sec. 1: 31.
A review of Burroughs' life and work on the occasion of his death.

Sharret, Christopher. "The Hero as Pastiche: Myth, Male Fantasy and Simulacra in *Mad Max* and *The Road Warrior.*" *Journal of Popular Film and Television* 13 (1985): 82-91.
In analyzing George Miller's *Mad Max* and *The Road Warrior*, Sharrett says, "Miller seems to be another director dependent on the influence of William Burroughs for the use of his art as social satire and as a projection of an insipient nihilism in postmodern society."

Shaviro, Steven. "Burroughs' Theater of Illusion: *Cities of the Red Night.*" *Review of Contemporary Fiction* 4.1 (1984): 64-74.
About Burroughs' discourse, Shaviro remarks, "[C]ontradictions mutually condition and contaminate one another in such a way that they can neither be separated into simple binary oppositions, nor resolved into unity by dialectical synthesis." See this article reprinted in *William S. Burroughs: At the Front*, eds. Jennie Skerl and Robin Lydenberg (Carbondale: Southern Illinois University Press, 1991): 197-207.

Skau, Michael. "The Central Verbal System: The Prose of William Burroughs." *Style* 15.4 (1981): 401-414.
An investigation of Burroughs' innovative prose methods.

Skerl, Jennie. "A Beat Chronology: 1944-1964." *Moody Street Irregulars: A Jack Kerouac Newsletter* 6/7 (Winter-Spring 1980): 11-14.
The chronology presents Burroughs' life in the context of the lives of other Beat writers. This chronology is revised and expanded as "A Beat Chronology, the First Twenty-Five Years: 1944-1969" in *The Beats: Literary Bohemians in Postwar America*, ed. Ann Charters (Detroit: Gale Research, 1983): 593-606.

_____. "Freedom Through Fantasy in the Recent Novels of William S. Burroughs." *Review of Contemporary Fiction* 4.1 (1984): 124-130.
Skerl: "The four major novels published from 1971 to 1981 create a second metaphorical world which replaces the Nova mythology of Burroughs' earlier work." See this article reprinted in *William S. Burroughs: At the Front*, eds. Jennie Skerl and Robin Lydenberg (Carbondale: Southern Illinois University Press, 1991): 189-207.

_____. "William S. Burroughs: Pop Artist." *Sphinx* 11 (1980): 1-15.
Burroughs as a pop artist exploiting popular culture and a central "carny" metaphor.

Smith, William James. "*Nova Express*." *Commonweal* 8 Jan. 1965: 491.
Smith: "Unfortunately, the independent talent which expressed itself so powerfully in *Naked Lunch* has become, in *Nova Express*, the silliness of extreme hipsterism."

Solotaroff, Theodore. "The Algebra of Need." *New Republic* 5 Aug. 1967: 29-34.
Nova Express, *The Soft Machine*, and *The Ticket That Exploded* "reach a brilliantly lit dead end" yet "they also possess the kind of genuine innovation that keeps the novel alive and the literary enterprise going." See this article reprinted in *William S. Burroughs: At the Front*, eds. Jennie Skerl and Robin Lydenberg (Carbondale: Southern Illinois University Press, 1991): 85-89.

Sorrentino, Gilbert. "Firing a Flare for the Avant-garde." *Book Week* 3 Jan. 1965: 10.

Review of *The Yage Letters* by Burroughs and Ginsberg, *Ace of Pentacles* by John Wieners, *The Holy Grail* by Jack Spicer, and *After 1's* by Louis Zukofsky. One by one, these writers are "important," "accomplished," "dazzling," and "absolutely necessary."

Southern, Terry. "Rolling Over Our Nerve-endings." *Book Week* 8 Nov. 1964: 5, 31.

Review of *Nova Express*. Southern: "The element of humor in *Nova Express* . . . has moral strength of historic proportions."

Stephenson, Gregory. "The Gnostic Vision of William S. Burroughs." *Review of Contemporary Fiction* 4.1 (1984): 40-49.

Stephenson: The Gnostics and Burroughs "view the material world as illusory, the body as the primary impediment to true being and identity, and escape from the body and the world of the senses as man's paramount concern." See this article reprinted in Gregory Stephenson, *The Daybreak Boys: Essays on the Literature of the Beat Generation* (Carbondale: Southern Illinois University Press, 1990): 59-73.

Stimpson, Catherine R. "The Beat Generation and the Trials of Homosexual Liberation." *Salmagundi* 58/59 (Fall-Winter 1982-1983): 373-392.

Stimpson: "The Beats . . . wrote about sex as inevitably as Shelley did eternity. In letters, journals, memoirs, essays, fiction, and poetry, they textualized the body – be it celibate, heterosexual, bisexual, or homosexual."

Streitfeld, David. "William Burroughs: Shooting Star." *Washington Post* 4 Aug 1997: C1.

Streitfeld: "A half-century after the East Coast Jew Ginsberg, the French Canadian Catholic Jack Kerouac and the Midwestern WASP Burroughs shared an apartment in New York, the church of the Beats is stronger than ever, unquestionably the most significant literary congregation in America since the Lost Generation of Hemingway and Fitzgerald, spawn of academic monographs, fat biographies, feature films, celebrations, feuds, imitations and still the occasional denunciation."

Stull, William L. "The Quest and the Question: Cosmology and Myth in the Work of William S. Burroughs." *Twentieth Century Literature* 24.2 (Summer 1978): 225-242.
  The quest theme in *Junky*, "In Search of Yage," and *Naked Lunch*. See this article in *The Beats: Essays in Criticism*, ed. Lee Bartlett (Jefferson, NC: McFarland, 1981): 14-29.

Tanner, James E., Jr. "Experimental Styles Compared: E. E. Cummings and William Burroughs." *Style* 10 (1976): 1-27.
  Parallels in technique. Cummings is ultimately more innovative.

Tanner, Tony. "The New Demonology." *Partisan Review* 32 (Fall 1965): 505-525.
  In a survey of Burroughs' novels, Tanner notes "malign pressures moving in on the individual."

Tytell, John. "Conversation with Allen Ginsberg." *Partisan Review* 41 (1974): 253-262.
  Ginsberg comments extensively on Burroughs.

Wain, John. "The Great Burroughs Affair." *New Republic* 1 Dec. 1962: 21-23.
  Naked Lunch has no value as an artistic composition.

Weinreich, Regina. "The Dynamic Déjà Vu of William Burroughs." *Review of Contemporary Fiction* 4.1 (1984): 55-58.
  Weinreich focuses on *The Third Mind* and praises non-linear technique and in the process refers to many works by Burroughs.

Weinstein, Arnold. "Freedom and Control in the Erotic Novel: The Classic *Liaisons dangereuses* Versus the Surrealist *Naked Lunch*." *Dada/Surrealism* 10/11 (1982): 29-38.
  A comparison of two novels.

Willett, John. "UGH . . ." *Times Literary Supplement* 14 Nov. 1963: 919.
  Willett: "Glug glug. It tastes disgusting, even without the detailed but always callous homosexual scenes and the unspeakable homosexual fantasies–pure verbal masturbation." Check the *Supplement* for weekly correspondence in the issues through January 23, 1964. See the article reprinted in *William S. Burroughs: At the*

Front, eds. Jennie Skerl and Robin Lydenberg (Carbondale: Southern Illinois University Press, 1991): 41-44. See the responses on 45-51.

Wolcott, James. "Night Crawlers." *New Yorker* 16 Jan. 1995: 83-84.
   My Education "is skimmable, like nearly everything Burroughs has written. One channel-surfs through his books, flipping from episode to episode."

Zurbrugg, Nicholas. "Burroughs, Barth, and the Limits of Intertextuality." *Review of Contemporary Fiction* 4.1 (1984): 86-107.
   Zurbrugg: "This article will suggest that by deliberately venturing beyond the over-literary intertextuality confined within 'writing itself,' the intertextual critic may enter a more expansive field of studies in which radical contemporary textual experiments – or *intertextual experiments* – may best be explicated by analogy with the extra-literary conventions peculiar to artistic, musical, and technological discursive spaces, rather than in terms of the literary conventions informing the literary discourse within which conservative theory and practice locates intertextual relations."

_____. "Burroughs, Grauerholz, and Cities of the Red Night: An Interview with James Grauerholz." *The Review of Contemporary Fiction* 4.1 (Spring, 1984): 19-32.
   This interview features Grauerholz, who "has not only organized Burroughs' highly successful reading tours with the poet John Giorno and the New York performance artist, Laurie Anderson, and thereby facilitated his emergence as a masterly reader and verbal performer, but has also played a crucial role in the evolution of . . . *Cities of the Red Night*."

Audio-Visual Materials

Break Through in Grey Room. CD. Brussels, Belgium: Sub Rosa, 1986.
   This disc features experiments in the cut-up technique done in collaboration with Ian Sommerville and Brion Gysin during the

1960's. A short explanation of the cut-up by Burroughs himself was recorded at the Naropa Institute in 1976.

Burroughs: the Movie. Film available in video. Howard Brookner. Black and white and color. Sound. 87 minutes. Video. Citifilmworks, 1983.
Biographical, with interviews and performances. A strong introduction to the writer and his works.

Call Me Burroughs. CD. Santa Monica, CA: Rhino Word Beat, 1995.
A sound recording originally made in 1965 that includes readings from *Naked Lunch* and *Nova Express*.

Commissioner of Sewers. Klaus Maeck. A film available in video. Black and white and color. 60 minutes. Maeck/VAP, 1986. New York: Mystic Fire Video, 1995.
Interview of Burroughs and performances by Burroughs. The focus is on Burroughs' philosophy and writings rather than on his life.

Dead City Radio. CD. Island Records, 1990.
Burroughs reads with the music of Sonic Youth, John Cale, the NBC Symphony, and Chris Stein as background. Includes "Naked Lunch Excerpts," "Ah Pook the Destroyer," "Dr. Benway's House," and "The Lord's Prayer."

Junky. 2 audio cassettes. New York: Penguin AudioBooks, 1997.
A reading by Burroughs of an abridged version of the novel.

Naked Lunch. David Cronenberg. Film available in video. Color. Sound. 115 minutes. Twentieth Century Fox, 1991.
Cronenberg creates a film that captures the bizarre world of *Naked Lunch*. The book is more startling than the film, but the scenes of the hideous talking typewriter capture the spirit of *Naked Lunch*. Based on the life of Burroughs during the composition of the novel rather than the actual text, the film features Peter Weller as Will Lee.

Naked Lunch. 2 audio cassettes. 3 hours. Los Angeles: Warner Audio Video Entertainment, 1995.

Burroughs reads an abridged version of his novel with musical background.

The "Priest" They Called Him. With Kurt Cobain. CD. Portland, OR: Tim Kerr Records, 1993.

This CD features only the the title track. Burroughs recorded his track on September 25, 1992, spinning a "Christmas story" about drug addiction. Cobain's musical background, a wailing guitar interpretation of "Silent Night," was recorded in November 1992, and later combined with Burroughs' material.

Sobieszek, Robert A. *Ports of Entry: William S. Burroughs and the Arts.* Los Angeles: Los Angeles County Museum of Art, 1996.

Catalog of an exhibition held at the Los Angeles County Museum of Art July 18-October 6, 1996. Shotgun paintings, painted doors, and other works of art by Burroughs.

Spare Ass Annie and Other Tales. CD. Island Records, 1993.

Burroughs reads with musical accompaniment by the Disposable Heroes of Hiphoprisy. Selections include "Spare Ass Annie," "The Last Words of Dutch Schultz," "Mildred Pierce Reporting," "Dr. Benway Operates," "Did I Ever Tell You About the Man Who Taught His Asshole to Talk?" and "Words of Advice for Young People."

Towers Open Fire, The Cut-Ups, Bill and Tony, William Buys a Parrot. 35 minutes. Anthony Balch. Films available in video. 1962-1972. New York: Mystic Fire Video, 1995.

Experimental work in film.

Vaudeville Voices. CD. London: Grey Matter, 1994.

Performance of William Burroughs. The first eight tracks are from *Call Me Burroughs* and the ninth track is "Ali's Smile."

William Burroughs. With Kathy Acker. Video. Color. 36 minutes. Ho-Ho-Kus, NJ: Roland Collection, 1995.

Burroughs discusses his relationship to the Beats, his ideas on thinking, the cut-up method, and the background to *Junky, Queer,* and *Naked Lunch.* This tape is available from the Roland Collection, 22-D Hollywood Avenue, Ho-Ho-Kus, NJ 07423.

William S. Burroughs: The Elvis of Letters. CD. Portland: TK
Records, 1990.
   Burroughs and Gus Van Sant perform. Includes "Burroughs
Break," "Word Is Virus," "Millions of Images," and "The Hipster Be-
bop Junkie."

Words of Advice for Young People. LP. Island Records, 1993.
   Burroughs reads his ironic offer of advice based on his
experience.

Addresses on the Internet

LitKicks is a hypertext presentation that features information on
Burroughs and segments on topics such as "The Beat Generation,"
"Beat Connections in Rock Music," "Films About the Beats,"
"Buddhism: The Beat Religion," and "Origin of the Term Beat." Levi
Asher, the developer of this site, which has been on line since July
23, 1994, provides updates on news about the Beats and speeds
access to other sites by providing links. The address is
http://www.charm.net/~brooklyn/, and Levi Asher may be reached
at **brooklyn@netcom.com**.

   At **http://www.primenet.com/~dirtman/wsb.htm**, one finds a
site that serves as a point-and-click jump-off point to many sites
related to Burroughs.

   The Burroughs File is at **http://www.hyperreal.org/wsb/
index.html**. Malcolm Humes, the creator of this site, makes available
an "electronic reference guide" to the literary texts of William
Seward Burroughs, as well as sound recordings and appearances on
video. Also at this site one has point-and-click access to other sites.

   The Unofficial Burroughs Homepage at **http://www.peg.
apc.org/~firehorse/wsb/wsb.html** features snippets from
Burroughs' writings, including *Nova Express*, *Interzone*, and
Electronic Revolution.

   At **http://www.levity.com/corduroy/burroughs.htm** one finds
varied information about Burroughs and links to other sites.

At **http://muse.jhu.edu/journals/postmodern_culture/V005/ 5.2r_wood.html**, one finds Brent Wood's review of *Spare Ass Annie, Dead City Radio*, and other recordings.

At **www.bigtable.com** one finds The *William Burroughs Explorer*.

At **http://www.cs.cmu.edu/afs/cs.cmu.edu/user/ehn/Web/ release/reading_list.html** one finds "links to texts, excerpts, quotations and notes acquired during recreational reading." The list includes *Interzone*, *The Job*, and *Naked Lunch*.

Chapter 4

ALLEN GINSBERG (1926–1997)

yes, yes,
that's what
I wanted,
I always wanted,
I always wanted,
to return
to the body
where I was born
— Allen Ginsberg

Books by Ginsberg

"Howl" and "Kaddish" are quintessentially Beat poems, and any course on Beat writers must include these works. Ginsberg should also be recognized as a literary artist who specializes in oratory and combines music, chanting, and poetry in his public presentations. His veneration for Blake, the blues, rags, and Buddhist chants characterizes his work. Audio and video resources make these aspects of Ginsberg's art evident to students in economical formats. While *Collected Poems 1947-1980* and *Selected Poems 1947-1995* offer a broad selection, some readers prefer the Pocket Poets editions produced by City Lights, particularly *Howl and Other Poems* and *Kaddish and Other Poems*. I also admire "White Shroud" because of its revelation of Ginsberg's lifelong connection to his mother, Naomi.

Airplane Dreams: Compositions from Journals. Toronto: Anansi, 1968; San Francisco: City Lights, 1969.

Michael Schumacher: "48-page miscellany of journal notations, prose, and poetry."

Allen Verbatim: Lectures on Poetry, Politics, Consciousness. Ed. Gordon Ball. New York: McGraw-Hill, 1974.

Ginsberg offers comments on the social issues and the literary milieu of the 1960's. Lectures, which include interaction with various classes and audiences, are titled "Identity Gossip," "Eternity," "Words and Consciousness," "Addition Politics, 1922-1970," "Crime in the Streets Caused by Addiction Politics," "Narcotics Agents Peddling Drugs," "CIA Involvement with Opium Traffic," "Advice to Youth (with Robert Duncan)," "Early Poetic Community (with Robert Duncan)," "Kerouac," "Poetic Breath, and Pound's Usura," "The Death of Ezra Pound," "War and Peace: Vietnam and Kent State," and "Myths Associated with Science."

Ankor Wat. London: Fulcrum Press, 1968.

A long poem by Ginsberg written while he was in Cambodia to visit the ruins of Ankor Wat, which Michael Schumacher describes as a "temple complex built under the guidance of King Suryavarman II in the twelfth century." Photos by Alexandra Lawrence. Schumacher: "a long poem that combined impressionistic sketches of the ruins, travel notes, and political musings."

Chicago Trial Testimony. San Francisco: City Lights, 1975.

The copyright page says, "Verbatim transcript of Allen Ginsberg's testimony as witness for the defendants (David T. Dellinger, et al.) in the 1969 'Chicago Seven' trial." The transcript is published in a comic-book format, with color cartoons of scenes from the court on the cover.

Collected Poems: 1947-1980. New York: Harper and Row, 1984.

Ginsberg: "Herein author has assembled all his poetry books published to date rearranged in straight chronological order to compose an autobiography." The seven texts produced through City Lights are included: *Howl and Other Poems, Kaddish and Other Poems, Reality Sandwiches, Planet News, The Fall of America, Mind Breaths,* and *Plutonian Ode.*

Composed on the Tongue. Ed. Donald Allen. Bolinas, CA: Grey Fox
    Press, 1980.
    This collection of journal notes, interviews, conversations, and
lectures on the making of poetry includes "Encounters with Ezra
Pound," "Improvised Poetics," "A Conversation," "'First Thought,
Best Thought,'" "An Exposition of William Carlos Williams' Poetic
Practice," and "Some Different Considerations in Mindful
Arrangement of Open Verse Forms on the Page."

Empty Mirror: Early Poems. San Francisco: City Lights, 1961.
    Introduction by William Carlos Williams. Louis Simpson: except
for "Hymn" and "Paterson," these early poems are monotonous: "On
the whole the effect is a drab, depressing realism."

The Fall of America: Poems of These States: 1965-1971. San
    Francisco: City Lights, 1972.
    Reviews in *Poetry* and *Hudson Review* are disparaging, but for this
book Ginsberg holds the National Book Award. Helen Vendler:
"Ginsberg has it in mind to write a long 'poem of these states'
(incorporating earlier poems like 'Wichita Vortex Sutra'), which will
finally sum up the physical and spiritual map of America – its natural
rivers, mountains, and coastlines, its manmade cities, superhighways,
and dams, its media (radio, TV, magazines, newspapers, movies), its
social life (bars, universities, dance halls), its political activity
(especially its isolationism, suspicion, and hatred of foreigners), its
poets and musicians (including rock and pop), its mythology (comics
and S. F.), its graffiti, its religion (a poisonous fundamentalism), its
banks, its wars, its violence, its secret police, its history, its
seasons – in short, the whole of our common life."

First Blues: Rags, Ballads, and Harmonium Songs: 1971-1974. New
    York: Full Court, 1975.
    Michael Schumacher: "[A]n honest, if imperfect, look at
[Ginsberg's] spontaneous song composition."

The Gates of Wrath: Rhymed Poems: 1948-1952. Bolinas, CA: Grey
    Fox Press, 1972.
    Ginsberg: "Youthful poetries." Charley Shively: "In *The Gates of
Wrath: Rhymed Poems: 1948-1952* there is a whole section of love
poems from 1947 for Neal Cassady. These are mostly interesting for

historical purposes; they show the immense imprint of Blake's visionary verses on Ginsberg."

Howl and Other Poems. San Francisco: City Lights, 1956.

"Howl," according to Richard Eberhart, "lays bare the nerves of suffering and spiritual struggle. Its positive force and energy comes from a redemptive quality of love, although it destructively catalogues evils of our time from physical deprivation to madness." The first line of this poem is one of the most memorable lines in twentieth-century literature. The censorship trial over the poem energized its audience and supporters. See also *Howl: Original Draft Facsimile*, ed. Barry Miles (New York: Harper and Row, 1986). The edition by Miles presents facsimile manuscript documents and assembles a virtual casebook on the poem.

Indian Journals: March 1962-May 1963: Notebooks, Diary, Blank Pages, Writings. San Francisco: Dave Haselwood/City Lights, 1970.

Ginsberg's reactions to his travels in India. Reed Whittemore: "The significant life of the book is (1) the inner life of the poet reflecting on poetry, America, death, love, personality; (2) the private life of the poet in a room with Orlovsky; and (3) the life of the astonished alien observer seeing for the first time India's squalor and grandeur."

Iron Horse. Toronto: Coach House, 1972.

A long poem based on a train ride July 22-23, 1966. Charley Shively: "Iron Horse is partly a tantric meditation following masturbation in a train. The words are printed over railroad pictures – illuminations in half-tone lying under the tracks of the song, bringing it all back home."

Journals: Early Fifties-Early Sixties. Ed. Gordon Ball. New York: Grove Press, 1977.

Ball: "This book represents edited transcriptions from eighteen separate notebooks ranging incompletely in time from March 1952 (when Ginsberg was twenty-five) to February 1962." Paul Berman: "The *Journals* record his meetings with William Carlos Williams, which influenced him considerably, and a beery run-in with Dylan Thomas in a Greenwich Village bar, which influenced him not at all, and they show how highly he regarded the work of his fellow Beats.

There are reading lists of Pound, Eliot, Rimbaud, Gertrude Stein – the authors one would expect."

Journals Mid-Fifties: 1954-1958. Ed. Gordon Ball. New York: Harper Collins, 1995.

Ball: "The printed text of this volume draws on material entered by Allen Ginsberg in twelve notebooks and related separate pages from June 1954 through mid-July 1958. In terms of his major poems, it represents the period from his entering the Bay Area, where within approximately a year he'd write *Howl*, through his first trips to the Arctic and to North Africa and Europe, when he made brief early notations that would culminate several years later in the completed 'Kaddish.'"

Kaddish and Other Poems: 1958-1960. San Francisco: City Lights, 1961.

Some readers argue that "Kaddish," not "Howl," is Ginsberg's masterpiece. "Kaddish" represents Ginsberg's work in narrative poetry. M. L. Rosenthal: "Naomi's story brings out in every possible way the psychopathology of the violence done by modern existence to the most vulnerable among us. The homosexuality of the poet, his use of drugs, and his rejection of squeamishness to the point where he has cultivated a positive addiction to the revolting are familiar motifs of recent literature."

Mind Breaths: Poems 1972-1977. San Francisco: City Lights, 1978.

Paul Berman: "The resounding successes in *Mind Breaths* are in those poems that, without excessive artifice, confront head-on Ginsberg's new estimations of self and world outlook."

Planet News: 1961-1967. San Francisco: City Lights, 1968.

For Alan Brownjohn, "Television Was a Baby Crawling Toward That Deathchamber" and "Wichita Vortex Sutra" are major poems in this collection. Brownjohn: "The other poems are by this poet's standards, short – many of them pieces of personal meditation in places visited on his travels. Bombay, Warsaw, Prague, London and Wales receive the same hectic treatment as Hollywood and New York, Ginsberg working, as before, to pile up vast accumulations of topical images and references."

Plutonian Ode and Other Poems: 1977-1980. San Francisco: City Lights, 1982.

Paul Berman: "There are rueful Blakean love songs of the sort that are greatly improved in performance. There is an experiment in rigid sapphic metrics. There are three minor additions to 'Don't Grow Old,' the moving kaddish for his father–his tenderest, most distinguished poem of the last decade. And there are a couple of vivid cityscapes, or rather Avenue A-scapes, which he has always been very good at." Berman adds, "The one significant advance from the last book, and the one major success, is an adaptation of Neruda (done with Sidney Goldfarb from an old *Masses & Mainstream* translation)."

Poems All Over the Place: Mostly Seventies. Cherry Valley, NY: Cherry Valley Editions, 1978.

Michael Schumacher: "[T]he most noteworthy work included in the volume was 'The Names,' the addendum to 'Howl' written while Ginsberg was in Paris, and 'Fragment: The Names,' a continuation of the work written a few years later. From these poems one can see how Allen had at one time hoped to extend 'Howl' into his own version, perhaps, of 'Song of Myself.' Other poems in the volume, mostly recent works left out of *Mind Breaths*, included Ginsberg's reflections as he flew to the 1972 Republican National Convention, thoughts recollected from meditation sittings, and a small selection of journal entries."

Reality Sandwiches: 1953-1960. San Francisco: City Lights, 1963.

A. R. Ammons: "The poems in this volume date from 1953-1960, poems both before and after *Howl*. They mostly lack the desperately earnest cry for truth and the sung-tension accuracy of Ginsberg at his best."

Selected Poems 1947-1995. New York: HarperCollins, 1996.

Helen Vendler: "The new generation reading Ginsberg's *Selected* will find in such poems that Ginsberg's 'force field of language' still exerts a powerful imaginative pressure."

To Eberhart from Ginsberg. Lincoln, MA: Penmaen Press, 1976.

Richard Eberhart, a widely respected poet, mentioned Ginsberg favorably in an article in the *New York Times* titled "West Coast Rhythms." *To Eberhart* is directed at this author. A very short selection appears in Lewis Hyde, ed., *On the Poetry of Allen Ginsberg* (Ann Arbor: University of Michigan Press, 1984): 319.

T.V. Baby Poems. London: Cape Goliard, 1967; New York: Grossman, 1968.

A small volume overlapping with *Planet News.* Includes "Television Was a Baby Crawling Toward That Death Chamber," "Portland Coloseum," "First Party at Ken Kesey's with Hell's Angels," "Middle of a Long Poem on 'These States,'" "Uptown," "City Midnight Junk Strains for Frank O'Hara," and "Holy Ghost on the Nod over the Body of Bliss."

The Visions of the Great Rememberer. Amherst, MA: Mulch, 1974.

A running commentary on Jack Kerouac's *Visions of Cody* written in Ginsberg's expressive, poetic style paying homage to Kerouac. See this material appended to Jack Kerouac, *Visions of Cody* (New York: Penguin Books, 1993): 399-430 or in *Saturday Review* Dec. 1972: 60-63.

White Shroud: Poems 1980-1985. New York: Harper and Row, 1986.

In 1983, Ginsberg dreamed vividly of his grandmother, Buba, and his mother, Naomi. "White Shroud" is derived from that dream and reflects Ginsberg's ongoing connection to Naomi more than twenty years after the publication of "Kaddish." Michael Schumacher remarks that "White Shroud" represents "everything Ginsberg hoped to accomplish in dream-derivative poetry" and urges the reading of "Black Shroud," a companion poem that "speaks forcefully about the idea of one's taking irreversible action for the good of another." The volume also includes "Why I Meditate," "Love Comes," "Airplane Blues," "Do the Meditation Rock," and "Written in My Dream by W. C. Williams."

Wichita Vortex Sutra. San Francisco: Coyote Books, 1967.

Paul Carroll: "When the entire poem is seen as being a statement of desire, it seems irrelevant to circumscribe our critical appreciation by such questions as: Does the mantra fail? or Is this an anti-Vietnam poem? What matters is that the poem embodies and sustains throughout the statement of Ginsberg's complex desire to assume the function of poet as priestly legislator and as Baptist announcing the dispensation of peace, compassion, and brotherhood for all Americans."

Works in Periodicals and Editions

For a thorough listing of Ginsberg's contributions to editions and periodicals, see Bill Morgan, *The Works of Allen Ginsberg 1941-1994* (Westport, CT: Greenwood Press, 1995): 97-284.

"America." *Black Mountain Review* 7 (Autumn 1957): 25-29.

This publication comes on the heels of the publication of *Howl and Other Poems*, which included "America."

"The Change." *Fuck You: A Magazine of the Arts* 5.5 (Dec. 1963): 90-106.

Michael Schumacher: "'The Change' expresses [Ginsberg's] vow to live in his own form and accept his death."

"Death and Fame." *New Yorker* 21 Apr. 1997: 80-81.

Dated February 22, 1997, this poem is the work of one who knows that his death is not far off. He anticipates his funeral and thinks of ways he will be remembered: "Everyone knew they were part of the 'History' except the deceased/ who never knew exactly what was happening even when I was alive." On 78-79 of this issue, David Remnick contributes a "postscript" alongside a 1970 photo by Richard Avedon of Allen Ginsberg with his father, Louis Ginsberg.

"An Exposition of William Carlos Williams' Poetics." *Loka 2: A Journal from the Naropa Institute*. Garden City, NY: Doubleday, 1976. 123-140.

Ginsberg: Williams was "trying to compose poems that are indistinguishable from our ordinary speech." See this piece reproduced in *Composed on the Tongue*, ed. Don Allen (Bolinas, CA: Grey Fox Press, 1980): 118-152.

"From 'Kaddish.'" *Yugen* 5 (Aug. 1959): 2-4.

This publication predates the publication of *Kaddish and Other Poems*.

"Howl." *Evergreen Review* 1.2 (May-June 1957): 137-147.

This publication follows the publication of *Howl and Other Poems* and the censorship trial.

"Hymn from 'Kaddish.'" *Beatitude* 1 (May 1959): not paginated.
This selection anticipates the publication of *Kaddish and Other Poems*.

"Kaddish." *Big Table* 1.2 (1959): 19-23.
This selection from Part I of "Kaddish" anticipates the publication of *Kaddish and Other Poems*.

"Kaddish." *Big Table* 1.3 (1959): 7-10.
Parts II-IV are published prior to *Kaddish and Other Poems*.

"Lysergic Acid." *Evergreen Review* 5.18 (May-June 1961): 80-85.
Ginsberg: "I am on the last millionth infinite tentacle of the spiderweb, a worrier/ lost, separated, a worm, a thought, a self."

"May Days 1988." *Broadway 2: A Poets and Painters Anthology*. Ed. James Schuyler and Charles North. Brooklyn: Hanging Loose, 1989. 47-49.
Ginsberg, in this Manhattan poem that is a meditation on death, asks, "How many mornings to be or not to be?"

"Notes for Howl and Other Poems," "Introduction to Gasoline," "'When the Mode of the Music Changes the Walls of the City Shake,'" "Poetry, Violence, and the Trembling Lambs," "Prose Contribution to Cuban Revolution," "How Kaddish Happened," "Some Metamorphoses of Personal Poetry," and "On Improvised Poetics." *The Poetics of the New American Poetry*. Eds. Donald Allen and Warren Tallman. New York: Grove Press, 1973. 318-350.
The editors offer these selections to give an impression of Ginsberg's diverse interpretations of poetics.

"Williams in a World of Objects." *William Carlos Williams: Man and Poet*. Ed. Carroll F. Terrell. Orono, ME: National Poetry Foundation, 1983. 33-39.
Ginsberg: "Williams' work as a poet is very similar to Zen Buddhist mindfulness practice, because it clamps the mind down on objects and brings the practitioner into direct relations with whatever he can find in front of him without making a big deal about it; without satisfying some ego ambition to have something more princely or less painful than what already *is*."

Works in Collaboration with Others

Illuminated Poems. With Eric Drooker. New York: Four Walls Eight Windows, 1996.

Along with familiar titles published since 1948, two new poems by Ginsberg are featured alongside illustrations by Drooker. The drawings are sometimes in color, sometimes in black and white, with a contemporary style that alternates between urban landscapes and the panels of comics.

Straight Hearts' Delight. With Peter Orlovsky. Ed. Winston Leyland. San Francisco: Gay Sunshine Press, 1980.

Michael Schumacher: "[A] documentary of Allen's and Peter's twenty-five year relationship. The ambitious book project included Allen's and Peter's love poems, an excerpt from Allen's interview in *Gay Sunshine*, erotic drawings of Allen and Peter by Robert LaVigne, and a large selection of the Ginsberg-Orlovsky correspondence."

To Eberhart from Ginsberg. With Richard Eberhart. Lincoln, MA: Penmaen Press, 1976.

Includes Eberhart's "West Coast Rhythms." Ginsberg offers a letter about "Howl," and both authors provide additional comments.

The Yage Letters. With William S. Burroughs. San Francisco: City Lights, 1963.

The eleven letters from Burroughs to Ginsberg that make up the section titled "In Search of Yage" were written in 1953 and contribute to a trilogy in conjunction with *Junky* and *Queer*. *The Yage Letters* includes a letter from Ginsberg to Burroughs written in 1960 and Burroughs' reply of the same year. The text concludes with a short piece by Ginsberg titled "To Whom It May Concern" and a piece by Burroughs titled "I am Dying, Meester?"

Correspondence

As Ever: The Collected Correspondence of Allen Ginsberg and Neal Cassady. Ed. Barry Gifford. Berkeley, CA: Creative Arts, 1977.

Mark Schecner remarks, "The correspondence with Neal Cassady extends . . . to 1947 and the tender years at Columbia, and plots the vicissitudes of that difficult relationship into 1963. The Ginsberg who emerges from these pages is the lost and driven young poet seeking respite from his pains through determined reading, mysticism, and sex."

"A Letter to Richard Helms, Director of the Central Intelligence Agency." *On the Poetry of Allen Ginsberg.* Ed. Lewis Hyde (Ann Arbor: University of Michigan Press, 1984): 252-253.
Ginsberg reminds Helms of a wager made regarding the the CIA's involvement in drug traffic in Southeast Asia.

Moore, Mariane. "A Letter to Allen Ginsberg." *On the Poetry of Allen Ginsberg.* Ed. Lewis Hyde (Ann Arbor: University of Michigan Press, 1984): 13-15
Moore offers advice to the young poet.

Bibliographies

Dowden, George. *A Bibliography of Works by Allen Ginsberg: October, 1943-July 1, 1967.* San Francisco: City Lights, 1971.
Superseded by Morgan's new bibliography of Ginsberg's works.

Kraus, Michelle P. *Allen Ginsberg: An Annotated Bibliography, 1969-1977.* Metuchen, NJ: Scarecrow, 1980.
Kraus: "This extensive (1969-1977) bibliography covers not only the traditional literary publications of a Poet, but also cinema shadows, vocal tones tape-recorded, interviews transcribed and printed in whole or part, television apparitions, newspaper images especially underground, niteclub blues, even secret CIA or FBI reports, media documents and fragments of a public self, a sort of work of art, or Happening, named Allen Ginsberg."

Morgan, Bill. *The Response to Allen Ginsberg 1926-1994: A Bibliography of Secondary Sources.* Westport, CT: Greenwood Press, 1996.
A comprehensive listing of translations and secondary sources. All listings are retrievable in the archives at Stanford University.

_____. *The Works of Allen Ginsberg 1941-1994: A Descriptive Bibliography*. Westport, CT: Greenwood Press, 1995.

A thorough inventory of Ginsberg's books and pamphlets, broadsides, contributions to books, contributions to periodicals, photos, recordings, and film, radio, and television appearances. Thoroughly detailed and indexed. Introduction by Ginsberg himself.

Selerie, Gavin. *Allen Ginsberg*. London: Binnacle Press, 1980.

A selected bibliography appears on pages 43-51.

Interviews

Cargas, Harry J. "An Interview with Allen Ginsberg." *Nimrod* 19.1 (Fall/Winter 1974): 24-29.

The discussion includes inspiration, translation, twentieth-century literature, the reason for writing, intoxicants, writing method, daily schedules, and reading habits.

Carroll, Paul. "*Playboy* Interview." *Playboy* Apr. 1969: 81-92, 236-244.

Ginsberg speaks with "authority, profanity, erudition, and often lyricism" about himself, his poetry, his country, and the world.

Clark, Thomas. "Allen Ginsberg: An Interview." *Paris Review* 37 (Spring 1966): 12-55.

Among other things, Ginsberg discusses his visions. Ginsberg: "[P]oetry generally is like a rhythmic articulation of feeling. The feeling is like an impulse that rises within – just like sexual impulses." See this interview in *Writers at Work: The Paris Review Interviews*, 3rd Series (New York: Viking, 1967). See an excerpt in Lewis Hyde, ed., *On the Poetry of Allen Ginsberg* (Ann Arbor: University of Michigan Press, 1984): 120-130. See an excerpt in Park Honan, ed., *The Beats* (London: J. M. Dent, 1987): 178-182.

Colbert, Allison, and Anita Box. "Conversations: A Talk with Allen Ginsberg." *Partisan Review* 38.3 (1971): 289-309.

References to Blake, Williams, and Kerouac. Discussion of Buddhism.

"Craft Interview with Allen Ginsberg." *The Craft of Poetry: Interviews from the New York Quarterly.* Ed. William Packard. New York: Doubleday, 1974. 53-78.
Focus on "the circumstances of the artist's work and not the work itself."

Foley, Jack. "Same Multiple Identity: An Interview with Allen Ginsberg." *Poetry Flash* 272 (June/July 1997): 1, 4, 6, 8-11.
Ginsberg and Foley discuss Ginsberg's work in various forms and analyze the writers who have influenced Ginsberg. Focus on *Selected Poems 1947-1995.*

Freifield, Elazar. "Conversation with Allen Ginsberg." *Tel Aviv Review* 2 (Fall/Winter 1989-1990): 307-314.
A rapid-fire series of short questions and short answers on topics such as the West Bank, Naropa Institute, poetry personalities, China, and ways of writing.

Ganguly, Suranjan. "Allen Ginsberg in India: An Interview." *Ariel* 24.4 (October 1993): 21-32.
Thirty years after his first visit to India, Ginsberg reflects on his experiences and the effects of Indian culture on his life and consciousness. Ginsberg remarks, "India helped me to rediscover that relationship between poetry and song. I heard people singing in the streets, chanting mantras, so I began singing mantra too."

Geneson, Paul. "A Conversation with Allen Ginsberg." *Chicago Review* 27.1 (Summer 1975): 27-35.
Ginsberg establishes that the Naropa Institute should be based on open form and improvisation. See this interview in Donald Allen, ed., *Composed on the Tongue* (Bolinas, CA: Grey Fox Press, 1980): 94-105.

Ginsberg, Allen. "Ginsberg." *Intrepid* 18/19 (1971): 52-61.
On July 1, 1968, Ginsberg sat in "a giant field of flowers and orange buds" and taped himself as he interviewed himself, questioning his own thoughts and ways of thinking.

Koch, Kenneth. "Allen Ginsberg Talks About Poetry." *New York Times Book Review* 23 Oct. 1977: 9, 44-46.
Ginsberg focuses on the circumstances he needs to write well.

Lucie-Smith, Edward. *Mystery in the Universe: Notes on an Interview with Allen Ginsberg*. London: Turret Books, 1965.

These notes appear on five small pages, but they encapsulate much of Ginsberg's thinking and experience, including his vision of Blake in Harlem, his "renunciation of this first vision" in the poem "The Change," his experience in Cuba, Czechoslovakia, and Russia, and his ideas on language as a "vehicle for feeling."

McKenzie, James. "Interview." *The Beat Journey*. Eds. Arthur Knight and Kit Knight. California, PA: unspeakable visions of the individual, 1978. 3-45.

Discussion of the Beat background and the individual lives. "Howl" is discussed as a poem to be performed by the author rather than read silently by others.

Ossman, David. "Allen Ginsberg." *The Sullen Art: Interviews*. New York: Corinth, 1963. 87-95.

A selected interview from a series of radio programs.

Portugués, Paul. "An Interview with Allen Ginsberg." *Boston University Journal* 25.1 (1977): 47-59.

Interview done in July 1976. Focus on meditation.

_____. *The Visionary Poetics of Allen Ginsberg*. Santa Barbara, CA: Ross-Erickson, 1979.

Three exchanges with Ginsberg give broad range to discussions of drugs, religion, and politics.

Portugués, Paul, and Guy Amirthanaygam. "Buddhist Meditation and Poetic Spontaneity." *Writers in East-West Encounters: New Cultural Bearings*. Ed. Guy Amirthanaygam. London: Macmillan, 1982. 10-31.

Two interviews are included here. Paul Portugués conducted the first in July, 1976; Guy Amirthanayagam did the second in October 1977. In the first interview, Ginsberg remarks, "You can't really chase details – you have to remember them, experience them and then remember them, rather than chase after the perfect detail." In the second interview he states, "So books of poetry were never common; manuscripts, occasionally. But mostly it was songs memorized, and composed on occasion according to formulae, by the bard who was a specialist in thinking with his tongue, his words and his thoughts being identical."

Rodman, Selden. "Allen Ginsberg." *Tongues of Fallen Angels*. New York: New Directions, 1974. 183-199.
Rodman narrates a visit to Ginsberg's apartment and Ginsberg's performance with his father, Louis. Ginsberg discusses religion and literature.

Rothschild, Matthew. "An Interview with Allen Ginsberg." *The Progressive* 58.8 (Aug. 1994): 34.
Matthew Rothschild, publisher of *The Progressive*, discusses with Ginsberg his new book *Cosmopolitan Greeting*s and Ginsberg's "current political views." The conversation touches on the need for peace, the "New Left," sexual preference, AIDS, Buddhism, pacifism, and poetry vs. political poetry. Ginsberg objects to the FCC's suppression of literary freedom on broadcasts. The reader also gets an impression of the intensity of daily activity in Ginsberg's life.

Steward, Robert, and Rebekah Presson. "Sacred Speech: A Conversation with Allen Ginsberg." *New Letters* 54.1 (Fall 1987): 72-86.
Ginsberg discusses "fundamental principles of poetry and aesthetics" and "problems with censorship" because of the FCC's restrictions on broadcasts.

Tytell, John. "Conversation with Allen Ginsberg." *Partisan Review* 41.3 (Summer 1974): 253-262.
Ginsberg explains his relationship with Burroughs and the way Burroughs has influenced Ginsberg and Kerouac.

Young, Allen. "Allen Ginsberg." *Gay Sunshine Interviews*. Volume 1. Ed. Winston Leyland. San Francisco: Gay Sunshine, 1978. 95-128.
This interview took place at Ginsberg's farm in Cherry Valley, New York, on September 25, 1972. The discussion focuses on Ginsberg's sexual relations with Cassady, Kerouac, and Peter Orlovsky. Ginsberg mentions Castro and Cuba, offers comment on Carl Solomon at Rockland, and makes reference to the Soviet Union. This interview appeared originally in *Gay Sunshine* 16 (Jan. 1973) and 17 (Mar. 1973).

Biographies

Kramer, Jane. *Allen Ginsberg in America*. New York: Random House, 1969.
Kramer relates her experiences as she accompanies Ginsberg in his daily activities and interactions.

Miles, Barry. *Ginsberg: A Biography*. New York and London: Simon and Schuster, 1989.
A detailed biography of "the most famous living poet on earth, one of America's best-known cultural ambassadors," whose aim has always been to help his fellow human beings.

Schumacher, Michael. *Dharma Lion: A Critical Biography of Allen Ginsberg*. New York: St. Martin's, 1992.
A thorough biography that provides interpretation and background for the understanding not only of Ginsberg but also of the Beats as a whole.

Books About Ginsberg's Work

Bowering, George. "How I Hear 'Howl.'" *Beaver Kosmos Folio* 1. Toronto: Coach House Press, 1969.
Explication and interpretation of "Howl." According to Bowering, the interpretation is based on the recording of "Howl" rather than the text. See a selection in Lewis Hyde, ed., *On the Poetry of Allen Ginsberg* (Ann Arbor: University of Michigan Press, 1984): 370-378.

Burns, Glen. *Great Poets Howl: A Study of Allen Ginsberg's Poetry, 1943-1955*. Frankfurt am Main: Peter Lang, 1983.
Burns: "What I offer the reader . . . is a detailed study of Ginsberg's development up until 'Howl,' following a deconstructive analysis of the criticism he has received and followed by a brief survey of his poetry after 'Howl.'"

Clark, Tom. *The Great Naropa Poetry Wars*. Santa Barbara, CA: Cadmus, 1980.

This report on "a hot gossip item on the coast-to-coast literary scene" tells about a confrontation in which Chogyam Trungpa's associates forced W. S. Merwin and Dana Naone to become naked in front of others at a Buddhist retreat. Clark appends various letters, editorials, and comments, as well as an interview with Ginsberg.

Ehrlich, J. W., ed. *Howl of the Censor: Lawrence Ferlinghetti, Defendant*. San Carlos, CA: Nourse, 1961.

A lawyer from the *Howl and Other Poems* obscenity trial, in which Ferlinghetti, the book's publisher, faced prosecution, evaluates obscenity and censorship in America. Includes a full transcript of the trial, the decision, and "Howl," the title poem of the work in question.

Hyde, Lewis, ed. *On the Poetry of Allen Ginsberg*. Ann Arbor: University of Michigan Press, 1984.

This volume collects a diverse selection of materials by and about Allen Ginsberg, including many important reviews and commentaries by critics. A bibliography is included.

Merrill, Thomas F. *Allen Ginsberg*. Rev. ed. Boston: Twayne, 1988.

This volume updates Merrill's *Allen Ginsberg* (New York: Twayne, 1969), providing additional analysis in light of the publication of *Collected Poems 1947-1980*, but the bibliography of the secondary sources in the earlier volume is more thorough. Both editions feature a chapter on *Reality Sandwiches*, and one may compare Merrill's "Allen Ginsberg's *Reality Sandwiches*" in Lee Bartlett, ed., *The Beats: Essays in Criticism* (Jefferson, NC: McFarland, 1981): 90-106. Merrill discusses *Empty Mirror*, *Howl and Other Poems*, *Kaddish and Other Poems*, *Reality Sandwiches*, and *Wichita Vortex Sutra*.

Morgan, Bill, and Bob Rosenthal, eds. *Best Minds: A Tribute to Allen Ginsberg*. New York: Lospecchio, 1986.

Dozens of writers, poets, and scholars offer short works in honor of Allen Ginsberg's sixtieth birthday.

Mottram, Eric. *Allen Ginsberg in the Sixties*. Brighton, England: Unicorn Bookshop, 1972.

A twenty-six page pamphlet. Mottram: "[P]ower and paranoia" draw Ginsberg's attention, as do "self-exploration and cosmic consciousness." See an excerpt in Lewis Hyde, ed., *On the Poetry of Allen Ginsberg* (Ann Arbor: University of Michigan Press, 1984): 260-267.

Portugués, Paul. *The Visionary Poetics of Allen Ginsberg.* Santa Barbara, CA: Ross-Erikson, 1978.
Blake's influence on the visionary elements in Ginsberg's writings. An interview is included. See an excerpt in Lewis Hyde, ed., *On the Poetry of Allen Ginsberg* (Ann Arbor: University of Michigan Press, 1984): 131-140.

Sections or Chapters

America Through American Eyes: An Exhibit of Recent Books that Reflect Life in the United States. Sept. 1979. ERIC # ED178427.
Directed at an audience in the Soviet Union, this annotated bibliography strives to list works that are comprehensible to people whose native language is not English but whose wish is to know about popular culture and art in the United States. Allen Ginsberg is among the many authors referred to.

Bliss, Shepherd. "Men, Poetry, and the Military: a Memoir." *On the Poetry of Allen Ginsberg.* Ed. Lewis Hyde. Ann Arbor: University of Michigan Press, 1984. 314-316.
Bliss, born into a family rooted in military tradition, explains how learning about Allen Ginsberg changed Bliss's life.

Bloom, Harold. *Figures of Capable Imagination.* New York: Seabury Press, 1976. 260.
Bloom: "The genuine painfulness of reading through 'Kaddish' is not an *imaginative* suffering for the reader, but is precisely akin to the agony we sustain when we are compelled to watch the hysteria of strangers."

_____. "On Ginsberg's *Kaddish.*" *Ringers in the Tower: Studies in Romantic Tradition.* Chicago: University of Chicago Press, 1971. 213-215.
Bloom: "The poem opens, movingly, with the son and poet walking the streets of the city, remembering the death of his mother

three years before. It passes, through sustained and harrowing memories of childhood and youth, to an agonized summary of the hopelessness of love confronted by the separating power of mental disease."

Breslin, James E. B., ed. *From Modern to Contemporary: American Poetry 1945-1965*. Chicago: University of Chicago Press, 1984. 77-109.
An extended discussion of "Howl," recognizing the poem as a touchstone for the Beat Generation.

Breslin, Paul. "Allen Ginsberg as Representative Man: The Road to Naropa." *The Psycho-Political Muse: American Poetry Since the Fifties*. Chicago: University of Chicago Press, 1987. 22-41.
Breslin: "Reading 'Howl' and 'Kaddish' together, one confronts a recurrent problem for psycho-political poetry: Does psychology explain politics, as in 'Kaddish,'or does politics explain psychology, as in 'Howl'?"

Cargas, Henry J. *Daniel Berrigan and Contemporary Protest Poetry*. New Haven, CT: College and University Press, 1972.
Cargas: "[A]s we study Jones and Berrigan and Ginsberg, we begin to understand that . . . they cannot accept the notion that their work is separate from their lives." Cargas surveys Ginsberg's works, emphasizing "Wichita Vortex Sutra."

Carroll, Paul. *The Poem in Its Skin*. Chicago: Big Table, 1968. 81-109.
In this collection of interpretive essays about ten poets, Carroll includes analysis of Ginsberg's "Wichita Vortex Sutra." See this discussion of Ginsberg in Lewis Hyde, ed., *On the Poetry of Allen Ginsberg* (Ann Arbor: University of Michigan Press, 1984): 292-213.

Charters, Sam. "Allen Ginsberg: 'American Change.'" *Some Poems/Poets: Studies in American Underground Poetry Since 1945*. Berkeley, CA: Oyez, 1971.
Charters: "Only someone who was sure of his attitudes toward his society could find an imagery as coherent, as consistent, as Ginsberg finds in his responses to something as casual as loose money."

Christensen, Paul. "Allen Ginsberg." In *The Beats: Literary Bohemians in Postwar America* Ed. Ann Charters. Detroit: Gale Research, 1983. 214-241.

Christensen: "Although Ginsberg's image now may be that of a poet who has freed himself from all inhibitions and who thrives upon expressing his complete self from base instinct to religious exaltation, the young Ginsberg was, if anything, the opposite in nature: cautious, careful, with a reverence for poetic convention and the European verse tradition." Biographical background, survey of major works, photos, illustrations of original book covers, and bibliographical data.

Cusic, Don. "Allen Ginsberg." *The Poet as Performer*. Lanham, MD: University Press of America, 1991. 75-85.

Ginsberg "has emerged . . . as a poet whose poetry depends on live performance for its lifeblood."

Dickey, James. *Babel to Byzantium*. New York: Grosset, 1968.

Includes harsh reviews of *Howl and Other Poems* and *Kaddish and Other Poems* originally published in 1957 and 1961.

Donoghue, Denis. *Connoisseurs of Chaos: Ideas of Order in Modern American Poetry*. New York: Macmillan, 1965. 49.

Donoghue: "In 'A Supermarket in California,' Ginsberg [does] everything that is required of a poet except the one essential thing – to write his poem."

Engel, Dave. "The Allen Ginsberg Chair of Disembodied Poetics." *Portage 1978*. Ed. Dave Engel. Stevens Point, WI, 1978.

Ginsberg's visit to Stevens Point in 1978 is recounted in witty fashion as Engel describes how the selection of Ginsberg's seat came to pass.

Faas, Ekbert. "Allen Ginsberg." *Towards a New American Poetics: Essays and Interviews*. Santa Barbara, CA: Black Sparrow, 1979. 269-288.

An essay on Ginsberg precedes an interview. Faas surveys the work of Ginsberg through *The Fall of America*, accounting for the "horrific" in Ginsberg's poems. See this discussion of Ginsberg in Lewis Hyde, ed., *On the Poetry of Allen Ginsberg* (Ann Arbor: University of Michigan Press, 1984): 434-450.

Géfin, Laszlo. "Ellipsis and Riprap: The Ideograms of Ginsberg and Snyder." *Ideogram: History of a Poetic Method*. Austin: University of Texas Press, 1982. 117-134.

Ginsberg did not become a committed or dogmatic surrealist. In his search for a non-logical, "elliptical" mode of expression, he utilized all possible manifestations of the form, whether found in haiku, Williams, Cézanne, or surrealism. See this material in Lewis Hyde, ed., *On the Poetry of Allen Ginsberg* (Ann Arbor: University of Michigan Press, 1984): 272-287.

"Ginsberg, Allen." *Contemporary Authors*. New Revision Series. Vol. 41. Ed. Susan M. Trosky. Detroit: Gale Research, 1994. 169-177.

A narrative of Ginsberg's literary career, including his principal works, his political activism, his association with the Naropa Institute, and various critical views. Bibliography of primary and secondary sources.

Heffernan, James. "Politics and Freedom: Refractions of Blake in Joyce Cary and Allen Ginsberg." *Romantic and Modern*. Ed. George Bornstein. Pittsburgh: University of Pittsburgh Press, 1977.

Heffernan: "Blake is only one of the many influences on Ginsberg, who owes at least as much (if not more) to Whitman, to his Paterson mentor Williams, and to his contemporaries Kerouac, William Burroughs, and Neal Cassady." Heffernan adds that while Ginsberg "uses Blake in the cause of political freedom, he also knows that Blake is a prophet of ultimate freedom: the kind of freedom that comes from individual imagination." See an excerpt of this material in Lewis Hyde, ed., *On the Poetry of Allen Ginsberg* (Ann Arbor: University of Michigan Press, 1984): 256-259.

Holmes, John Clellon. "The Consciousness Widener." *Nothing More to Declare*. New York: Dutton, 1967.

Holmes comments on his friendship with Ginsberg and expresses his admiration for "Howl." See this essay also in Holmes, *Representative Men* (Fayetteville: University of Arkansas Press, 1988): 85-102. In this book, Holmes updates "The Consciousness Widener" to 1986 with the essay "Tally at Three Score": 103-110.

Howard, Richard. "Allen Ginsberg." *Alone with America: Essays on the Art of Poetry in the United States Since 1950*. Enlarged edition. New York: Atheneum, 1980. 145-152.

Howard: "Ginsberg is not concerned with the poem as art. He is after 'the poem *discovered* in the mind and in the process of writing it out on the page as notes, transcriptions.'"

Investigative Poetry Group. *The Party: A Chronological Perspective on a Confrontation at a Buddhist Seminary*. Woodstock, NY: Poetry, Crime & Culture Press, 1977.

Ed Sanders and his students at Naropa Institute investigate an incident at a Buddhist retreat involving the forced disrobing of W. S. Merwin, a visiting poet.

Kostelanetz, Richard. "Allen Ginsberg: Artist as Apostle, Poet as Preacher." *Representative Men: Cult Heroes of Our Time*. Ed. Theodore L. Gross. New York: Free Press, 1970. 257-275.

Kostelanetz describes Ginsberg's personality, home life, family relations, and biographical background; the notoriety of "Howl," the change in critical opinions; the variety of forms revealed in Ginsberg's poetry; the periods in the development of Ginsberg as an artist; confessionalism; political activism; and Ginsberg's role as "the most widely acclaimed unofficial American cultural ambassador."

McClure, Michael. "Allen for Real: Allen Ginsberg." *Lighting the Corners*. Albuquerque: University of New Mexico College of Arts and Sciences, 1993. 161-172.

Jerry Aronson interviews Michael McClure, who comments on how he met Ginsberg and what the reading at the Six Gallery in 1955 was like.

Martin, Robert K. *The Homosexual Tradition in American Poetry*. Austin: University of Texas Press, 1979. 165-170.

Commentary on "Howl," Ginsberg's connection to Whitman, *Planet News*, and *The Fall of America*. Martin: "Ginsberg's successful selling of himself as a representative of the avante-garde has mangaged to conceal the fact that he has little new to say and no new way to say it, and that his joylessness is far from the world of the more traditional gay poets of the same time."

Mersmann, James F. *Out of the Vietnam Vortex: A Study of Poets and Poetry Against the War*. Lawrence: University of Kansas Press, 1974. 31-75, 205-246.

Includes chapter "Allen Ginsberg: Breaking Out." Mersmann: "Ginsberg's war protest is clearly an honest outgrowth of his biography and his experience of America." References to *Ankor Wat*, *The Empty Mirror*, *Howl and Other Poems*, *Planet News*, and *Reality Sandwiches*. Includes chapter "Other Poems and Poets Against the War," with references to Ginsberg, DiPrima, Ferlinghetti, McClure, and Kupferberg.

Miller, James E. "Dreaming of the Lost America of Love: Allen Ginsberg's 'Fall of America.'" *The American Quest for a Supreme Fiction*. Chicago: University of Chicago Press, 1979. 276-316.

Miller: "If the first two sections of *The Fall of America* are engagement and outrage, 'Elegies' and 'Ecologues' are despair and withdrawal." The short final section, according to Miller, "suggests something in the nature of a conclusion – or capitulation."

Miloscz, Czeslaw. "The Image of the Beast." *Visions from San Francisco Bay*. New York: Farrar, Straus & Giroux, 1982.

Milosz: "Chanting his song, Whitman's turned inside out, Allen Ginsberg was Everyman." See a selection in Lewis Hyde, ed., *On the Poetry of Allen Ginsberg* (Ann Arbor: University of Michigan Press, 1984): 268-271.

Molesworth, Charles. "Republican Objects and Utopian Moments: The Poetry of Robert Lowell and Allen Ginsberg." *The Fierce Embrace*. Columbia: University of Missouri Press, 1979. 37-60.

Molesworth: "Ginsberg's lyric shaping often begins with a chanting, meditative flattening out of the daily order, an unwinding of the logical mind's coils of expended pressure. His poems then often end with an anagogic leap, a sudden breakthrough of new awareness." See a selection in Lewis Hyde, ed., *On the Poetry of Allen Ginsberg* (Ann Arbor: University of Michigan Press, 1984): 288-291.

Ower, John. "Allen Ginsberg." *Dictionary of Literary Biography*, 5, *American Poets Since World War II*. Ed. Donald J. Greiner. Detroit: Gale Research, 1980. 269-286.

Biographical background, survey of major works, bibliographical references, photos.

Parkinson, Thomas. "Phenomenon or Generation." *A Casebook on the Beat*. New York: Crowell, 1961. 276-290.

A valuable assessment of the period with appreciation for Ginsberg's input. Parkinson: "Allen Ginsberg's public posture on literary matters is that of an innocent who writes from impulse, but he knows better."

Perloff, Marjorie. "A Lion in Our Living Room: Reading Allen Ginsberg in the Eighties." *Poetic License: Essays on Modernist and Postmodernist Lyric*. Evanston, IL: Northwestern University Press, 1990. 199-230.

Perloff focuses on *Collected Poems* (New York: Harper and Row, 1985) and surveys the critical response to Ginsberg. She asserts, "What the *Collected Poems* show us is that Ginsberg is, finally, a very *funny* poet. To read 'Howl' as a serious indictment of American culture, a culture that denies the possibility of spiritual illumination, is to ignore the poet's self-deprecatory humor, his ability to laugh at himself and his friends."

Phillips, Robert. *The Confessional Poets*. Carbondale: Southern Illinois University Press, 1973.

A study of confessional writers that consciously excludes Ginsberg. Phillips explains his reasoning in his introduction.

Rexroth, Kenneth. "Disengagement: The Art of the Beat Generation." In *The Alternative Society: Essays from the Other World*. New York: Herder and Herder, 1970. 1-16.

Published in *New World Writing* in 1957, this essay evaluates the avant-garde movement among painters, musicians, and literary artists. San Francisco is praised for "intense literary activity." Rexroth: "The avant-garde has not only not ceased to exist. It's jumping all over the place. Something's happening, man."

Rosenthal, M. L. "Allen Ginsberg." *The New Poets: American and British Poetry Since World War II*. New York: Oxford University Press, 1967. 89-112.

Rosenthal recognizes Ginsberg's excellence as a confessional poet. See a selection in Lewis Hyde, ed., *On the Poetry of Allen Ginsberg* (Ann Arbor: University of Michigan Press, 1984): 111-113.

Rosenthal, M. L., and Sally M. Gall. *The Modern Poetic Sequence: The Genius of Modern Poetry*. New York: Oxford University Press, 1983. 422-428.

An exposition of "Kaddish," which is filled with strengths, but nevertheless "falls short of its possibilities."

Simpson, Louis. "The Eye Altering Alters All." *A Revolution in Taste: Studies of Dylan Thomas, Allen Ginsberg, Sylvia Plath, and Robert Lowell*. New York: Macmillan, 1978. 45-82.

An essay on Ginsberg provides background on the genesis of the Beats in general. See a selection in Lewis Hyde, ed., *On the Poetry of Allen Ginsberg* (Ann Arbor: University of Michigan Press, 1984): 114-116.

Stepanchev, Stephen. *American Poetry Since 1945: A Critical Survey*. New York: Harper and Row, 1965.

A chapter on Ginsberg, who in "Howl" represents the Beats as a whole. Some discussion of "Kaddish" and *Reality Sandwiches*.

Thurley, Geoffrey. *The American Moment: American Poetry in the Mid-Century*. London: Edward Arnold, 1977.

Thurley: "Ginsberg is basically a Jewish reformer-moralist, trying desperately hard to be an Anglo-Saxon seer–a Blake, a Whitman, a Shelley. His shouting rant deafens truth, and the numinous end of the language spectrum is burnt out by overuse." See a selection in Lewis Hyde, ed., *On the Poetry of Allen Ginsberg* (Ann Arbor: University of Michigan Press, 1984): 394-400.

Tytell, John. *Naked Angels*. New York: McGraw-Hill, 1976.

A biographical and critical interpretation of Ginsberg by a pioneering critic of the Beats. Tytell: "Ginsberg, like Blake, is seeking to purge language of stultifying formalisms." See a selection in Lewis Hyde, ed., *On the Poetry of Allen Ginsberg* (Ann Arbor: University of Michigan Press, 1984): 171-179.

Vance, Thomas H. "American Poetry of Protest, from World War II to the Present." *Amerikanische Literatur im 20. Jahrhundert*. Ed.

Alfred Weber and Dietmar Haack. Gottingen: Vanderhock & Ruprecht, 1971. 249-270.

This analysis includes discussion of "Howl," and Vance finds that Ginsberg "has the gift of making the details of the urban, technological environment a part of his nervous system, of absorbing them directly into the stream of his emotional and imaginative experience."

Articles About Ginsberg's Work

Aiken, William. "Denise Levertov, Robert Duncan, and Allen Ginsberg: Modes of the Self in Projective Poetry." *Modern Poetry Studies* 10.2/3 (1981): 200-240.

Aiken: "[T]he spontaneous synthetic power of a poet like Allen Ginsberg becomes important if projective poetics is to have more than just a fanciful appeal." Discussion of "Wichita Vortex Sutra," which is a "rare integration of visual and aural, phenomenal and personal attentions."

Alexander, Floyce. "Allen Ginsberg's Metapolitics: From Moloch to the Millenium." *Research Studies of Washington State University* 38 (June 1970): 157-173.

Alexander: "Ginsberg's poetry embodies his effort to break through the crust of civilization which exalts the static, rational virtues of the mind and denies the body its dynamic power to generate an imaginative alternative to the contemporary political and spiritual decay." See a selection in Lewis Hyde, ed., *On the Poetry of Allen Ginsberg* (Ann Arbor: University of Michigan Press, 1984): 254-255.

Alvarez, A. "Ginsberg and the Herd Instinct." *Observer* [London] 14 May 1961.

Alvarez: "Kaddish" is "at once moving and curiously detached; the sufferings of his mother were so overwhelming they leave him no time for his own." Alvarez adds that the language "is the violent emotional shorthand of the analyst's couch, held together by a strong narrative thread." See a selection in Lewis Hyde, ed., *On the Poetry of Allen Ginsberg* (Ann Arbor: University of Michigan Press, 1984): 92-93.

Ammons, A. R. "Ginsberg's New Poems." *Poetry* 104 (June 1964): 186-187.

Discussion of Ginsberg's line, questioning the success of poems in *Reality Sandwiches*. See a selection in Lewis Hyde, ed., *On the Poetry of Allen Ginsberg* (Ann Arbor: University of Michigan Press, 1984): 184-185.

Atlas, James. "A Modern Whitman." *Atlantic* Dec. 1984: 132-136.

Atlas, speaking of *Collected Poems* (1985), says, "There aren't many memorable lines in even the best of Ginsberg's work, but it has a virtue rare in contemporary poetry: it's never dull."

Bartlett, Jeffrey. "Howl in High School" and "Allen Ginsberg Today." *North Dakota Quarterly* (Spring 1982): 68-75, 76-80.

Born in 1950, Bartlett recounts his personal experience in learning about the writings of the Beats and drawing reactions from teachers and others in McKinney, Texas, in 1968. "Howl in High School" is now reprinted in *One Vast Page* (Berkeley, CA: Provine Press, 1991). Dated 11-12 Jan. 1982, "Allen Ginsberg Today" depicts Ginsberg as someone "hungry for experience and a place in the great world," a person "determinedly on the leading edge of hipness and protest." He adds, "Ginsberg presents a mirror of present-day consciousness, which he had a hand in forming."

Bawer, Bruce. "The Phenomenon of Allen Ginsberg." *New Criterion* 3.6 (Feb. 1985): 1-14.

Ginsberg is "the only poet in America who is not just a member of the august American Academy of Arts and Letters but a bona fide celebrity." Bawer surveys Ginsberg's career and evaluates his connection to the Beats. Bawer laments Ginsberg's endorsement of drugs and the poor example of open form he has set for aspiring poets.

Berman, Paul. "Intimations of Mortality." *Parnassus: Poetry in Review* 8.1 (Fall-Winter 1979): 283-293.

This review of *Journals: Early Fifties, Early Sixties* and *Mind Breaths* evaluates Ginsberg's "visionary, prophetic poetry" in contrast to ordinary perceptions. See a selection in Lewis Hyde, ed., *On the Poetry of Allen Ginsberg* (Ann Arbor: University of Michigan Press, 1984): 342-353.

"Big Day for Bards at Bay." *Life* 9 Sept. 1957: 105-108.
Discussion of the San Francisco poets and the obscenity trial for *Howl and Other Poems*.

Bingham, June. "The Intelligent Square's Guide to Hippieland." *The New York Times Magazine* 24 Sept. 1967: 25, 68-73.
What is Hip and what is Beat? What religious views appear? What is Ginsberg's role?

Borawski, Walta. "Curls Curses & Cum." *Boston Gay Review* (Fall 1978): 12-13.
Borawski: "There are poems about things besides fucking, sucking, rimming and death; but though each poem reflects warm gentility of soul, grabs out with brotherly/loverly touches, *Mind Breaths* is hardly a happy book."

Breslin, James. "Allen Ginsberg: The Origins of 'Howl' and 'Kaddish.'" *Iowa Review* 8.2 (Spring 1977): 82-108.
Breslin's interpretation of "Howl" and "Kaddish" is based on biographical and autobiographical sources. See a selection in Lewis Hyde, ed., *On the Poetry of Allen Ginsberg* (Ann Arbor: University of Michigan Press, 1984): 401-433. The piece also appears in Lee Bartlett, ed., *The Beats: Essays in Criticism* (Jefferson, NC: McFarland, 1981): 66-89.

Brinnin, John Malcolm. "The Theory and Practices of Poetry." *New York Times Book Review* 2 Mar. 1975: 4-5.
Review of Allen Ginsberg, *Allen Verbatim*; Donald Allen and Warren Tallman, eds., *The Poetics of the New American Poetry*; William Packard, *The Craft of Poetry*; M. L. Rosenthal, *Poetry and the Common Life*; and Muriel Rukeyser, *The Life of Poetry*. Brinnin uses these texts to evaluate the state of contemporary poetry.

Brownjohn, Alan. "Fblup." *New Statesman* 10 Jan. 1969: 52.
A review of *Planet News* and *Ankor Wat*, pointing out several successes amidst a background of weakness. See a selection in Lewis Hyde, ed., *On the Poetry of Allen Ginsberg* (Ann Arbor: University of Michigan Press, 1984): 189-191.

Buckley, Christopher, and Paul Slansky. "Yowl: For Jay McInerny." *New Republic* 8 Dec. 1986: 48-49.

A satire of the yuppie lifestyle set in a form imitating Ginsberg's "Howl." Done on the thirtieth anniversary of the publication of "Howl."

"California's Young Writers, Angry and Otherwise." *Library Journal* 83 (15 June 1958): 1850-1854.
Brief treatment of principal Beat writers, including Ginsberg.

Carroll, Paul. "Death Is a Letter That Was Never Sent." *Evergreen Review* 5.19 (July-Aug. 1961): 114.
A positive review of *Kaddish and Other Poems*. Carroll: "For the first time in our poetry we have a poet who celebrates the ancient ritual – Invoking of the God. These poems are both invocation and confrontation. In them, Ginsberg asks and gives no quarter." See a selection in Lewis Hyde, ed., *On the Poetry of Allen Ginsberg* (Ann Arbor: University of Michigan Press, 1984): 94-95.

Carruth, Hayden. "Chants, Oracles, Body-Rhythms." *New York Times Book Review* 19 Mar. 1978: 15.
According to Carruth, in *Mind Breaths* Ginsberg "has returned to poems of the imagination, poems arising from within, complexes of feeling that come to consciousness with their own structure already in them." See a selection in Lewis Hyde, ed., *On the Poetry of Allen Ginsberg* (Ann Arbor: University of Michigan Press, 1984): 321-323.

Ciardi, John. "Epitaph for the Dead Beats." *Saturday Review* 6 Feb. 1960: 11-13.
While Ciardi attacks the weaknesses of the Beats, he offers valuable insights. Ciardi remarks, "I find that first part of 'Howl' a compelling piece of writing. I also find it impossible to believe (though I may be confessing my own square blindness in saying so) that any man could put together without revision as tight a catalogue as I find there." See this article in Thomas Parkinson, ed., *A Casebook on the Beat* (New York: Crowell, 1961): 257-265.

Cohen, Mortimer J. "Is This Poetry?" *Jewish Exponent* 10 Nov. 1961: 21.
Cohen finds "that Allen Ginsberg possesses a more creative and more powerful poetic fire" than Harvey Shapiro, but Cohen is troubled by "a kind of illegitimate use of Jewish tradition."

Cox, Harvey. "An Open Letter to Allen Ginsberg." *Commonweal* 21 Apr. 1967: 147-149.

Ginsberg questioned Cox, "What is Christianity going to do about the Hippies?" Cox in this letter says, "I confess I still perversely hope that you and most of the hippies will drop back in some day."

Dennison, George. "Symposium: The Writer's Situation." *New American Review* 9 (Apr. 1970): 93-99.

Dennison: "The formal structure of Ginsberg's poetry–the 'nonlinear' accumulation of detail; the long breath of the rhapsodic voice–is identical with the attitude of compassion and his subject of the natural sanctification of being." See a selection in Lewis Hyde, ed., *On the Poetry of Allen Ginsberg* (Ann Arbor: University of Michigan Press, 1984): 451-453.

Dickey, James. "Confession Is Not Enough." *New York Times Book Review* 9 July 1961: 14.

In a review that touches on *The Maximus Poems* and *The Distances* by Olson, *Mountain Fire, Thornbush* by Harvey Shapiro, and *Kaddish and Other Poems* by Ginsberg, Dickey expresses distaste for *Kaddish and Other Poems*.

———. "From Babel to Byzantium." *Sewanee Review* 65 (Summer 1957): 508-530.

Dickey finds that Ginsberg lacks craft. Dickey remarks, "Ginsberg's writings are of the familiar our-love-against-their-machines-and-money variety, strongly akin to those of Henry Miller, Kenneth Patchen, and Kenneth Rexroth."

Diggory, Terrence. "Ginsberg's Voice." *American Book Review* 7 (Sept.-Oct. 1985): 13-14.

Diggory: "If the tone is that of elegy, the texture of Ginsberg's voice is that of paranoia, the obsessional, disjointed, unmodulated stream of exclamation that Ginsberg claimed as his own in 'Howl' but revealed in 'Kaddish' to be originally the voice of his mad mother."

"The Disorganization Man." *Time* 9 June 1958: 98, 100, 102.

This review of Gene Feldman and Max Gartenberg, eds., *The Beat Generation and the Angry Young Men* turns into an attack on underground movements. *Time*: "A good mind is hard to find among the Beats, but the leading theoreticians of hipdom are probably Jack Kerouac and Clellon (*Go*) Holmes. Each insists that the Beat Generation is on a mystic search for God." Referring to the underground movement in England, the article declares, "The Angry Young Man is a rebel with a cause, a disorganization man in transition who will eventually make his peace with a society in which he means to make good." See a selection in Lewis Hyde, ed., *On the Poetry of Allen Ginsberg* (Ann Arbor: University of Michigan Press, 1984): 54-55.

Dougherty, Jay. "From Society to Self: Ginsberg's Inward Turn in Mind Breaths." *Sagetriebe* 6.1 (Spring 1987): 81-92.
   Dougherty: "In some of the poetry of *Mind Breaths* – and, again, one cannot make sweeping generalizations about all of the poems here – there is the implication that, for the individual, the only way out of the madness created by societies askew, run by governments which, in conflicting with other governments, create more chaos and, hence, anxiety for the individual, is to take refuge in the Self, to retreat, in a sense, into one's 'Separate Identity' and to live out the remainder of one's life there."

Eberhart, Richard. "West Coast Rhythms." *New York Times Book Review* 2 Sept. 1956: 7.
   Eberhart: "Poetry has become a tangible force, moving and unifying its auditors, releasing the energies of the audience through spoken, even shouted verse, in a way at present unique to this region." See a selection in Lewis Hyde, ed., *On the Poetry of Allen Ginsberg* (Ann Arbor: University of Michigan Press, 1984): 24-25.

Eckman, Frederick. "Neither Tame Nor Fleecy." *Poetry* 90 (Sept. 1957): 386-397.
   A review touching on nine books, including Ginsberg's *Howl and Other Poems*. Eckman: "The poem is an explosion" but the collection is "a very shaggy book, the shaggiest I've ever seen."

Elman, Richard. "Beyond Self-Absorption." *Nation* 12 Nov. 1977: 500-501.
   A review of *Journals: Early Fifties, Early Sixties*. Elman: "I got the sense [that the journals] were carefully edited, though not necessarily cleaned up, so that I was able to see the young man struggling to be an artist, and the developing artist as a man on almost every page."

See a selection in Lewis Hyde, ed., *On the Poetry of Allen Ginsberg* (Ann Arbor: University of Michigan Press, 1984): 324-329.

Farrell, B. "Guru Comes to Kansas." *Life* 27 May 1966: 78-80.
A description of readings by Ginsberg in the midwest.

Ferlinghetti, Lawrence. "Horn on *Howl*." *Evergreen Review* 1.4 (1957): 145-158.
Ferlinghetti chronicles the events in the effort to censor *Howl and Other Poems* and catalogs statements made in defense of the book during the trial. See a selection in Lewis Hyde, ed., *On the Poetry of Allen Ginsberg* (Ann Arbor: University of Michigan Press, 1984): 42-53, or in Ann Charters, ed., *The Portable Beat Reader* (New York: Viking, 1992): 254-263.

"Fried Shoes; Beatniks." *Time* 9 Feb. 1959: 16.
Scorn for Ginsberg, Corso, and Orlovsky in Chicago.

Fuller, J. G. "Trade Winds: Ginsberg Trial." *Saturday Review* 5 Oct. 1957: 5-7.
A post-trial review of the case against *Howl and Other Poems*. An assessment of the poetry scene in San Francisco following the trial.

Gertmenian, Donald. "Remembering and Rereading 'Howl.'" *Ploughshares* (Fall 1975): 151-163.
In "Howl," Gertmenian notices "sorrows of human limitation" and "a vein of Romantic experience."

Ginsberg, Louis. "To Allen Ginsberg." *Prairie Schooner* 33.2 (Summer 1959): 172.
Ginsberg's father counsels his son in this poem. See this poem in Lewis Hyde, ed., *On the Poetry of Allen Ginsberg* (Ann Arbor: University of Michigan Press, 1984): 84.

Glaser, Alice. "Back on the Open Road for Boys." *Esquire* July 1963: 48-49, 115.
Glaser recounts her visit with Ginsberg and Peter Orlovsky in Benares. Photos.

Gold, Herbert. "Hip, Cool, Beat – and Frantic." *Nation* 16 Nov. 1957: 349-355.

Writers like Ginsberg and Kerouac "are unauthentic exactly to the degree that they are literary."

Golffing, Francis, and Barbara Gibbs. "The Public Voice: Remarks on Poetry Today." *Commentary* 28 (July 1959): 63-69.
Ginsberg and others as a part of the ongoing development of poetry.

Grossman, Allen. "Allen Ginsberg: The Jew as an American Poet." *Judaism* 11.4 (Fall 1962): 303-308.
Grossman: "Ginsberg has had the sense to perceive that the only significant Jewish poetry will also be a significant American poetry in the sense that its style will be dictated by the universe of recognition formed by the discourse of American poetry as a whole, and not by the universe of recognition constituted by the parochial concern to which the typical Yiddish-American writer addrsses himself." See a selection in Lewis Hyde, ed., *On the Poetry of Allen Ginsberg* (Ann Arbor: University of Michigan Press, 1984): 102-110.

Hahn, Stephen. "The Prophetic Voice of Allen Ginsberg." *Prospectus: Annual of American Cultural Studies* 2 (1976): 527-567.
Discussion of prophecy in Ginsberg.

Hampton, Wilborn. "Allen Ginsberg, 70, Master of Beat Poets, Dies." *New York Times* 6 Apr. 1997: 1, 21.
Hampton: "As much through the strength of his own irrepressible personality as through his poetry, Mr. Ginsberg provided a bridge between the Underground and the Transcendental." Photos included.

Haselmayer, Louis A. "Beat Prophet and Beat Wit." *Iowa English Yearbook* 6 (1961): 9-13.
Haselmayer: "Ginsberg regards his role as a poet in terms of the prophet or bard who is called upon to denounce the evils of the age. His task is to picture with intense realistic detail the contemporary scene and to arouse in the reader or listener the same reaction of disgust and despair. Hebrew prohecy of the Old Testament has molded Ginsberg's self-image, his poetic line and his descriptive imagery."

Hazel, Robert. "Prefigures." *Nation* 11 Nov. 1961: 381.
Review of *Empty Mirror*. Hazel: "In these early poems there is a chemistry of personal analysis: each poem the test tube of a particular agony, ennui, sexual injury or religious outcry."

Henry, William A., III. "In New York: 'Howl' Becomes a Hoot." *Time* 7 Dec. 1981: 8.
This review of Ginsberg's reading of "Howl" at Columbia University on the twenty-fifth anniversary of its publication treats the poem as a dated document performed with irony before an audience ill-equipped to comprehend. See a selection in Lewis Hyde, ed., *On the Poetry of Allen Ginsberg* (Ann Arbor: University of Michigan Press, 1984): 367-369.

Hollander, John. "Poetry Chronicle." *Partisan Review* 24 (Spring 1957): 296-304.
Hollander finds that *Howl and Other Poems* is a "dreadful little volume" and "a very short and very tiresome book." In an addendum to the review included in Lewis Hyde, ed., *On the Poetry of Allen Ginsberg* (Ann Arbor: University of Michigan Press, 1984): 26-28, Hollander regrets not acknowledging the quality of "America" and "In a Supermarket in California."

Howard, Richard. "Allen Ginsberg: O Brother of the Laurel a Joke or a Crown of Thorns." *Minnesota Review* 9 (1969): 50-56.
Ginsberg's "presence" empowers his prophecy.

_____. "*Collected Poems*." *Boston Review* 9 (Sept. 1984): 33.
Collected Poems (1985) "may not be poetry at all," yet "it is always testimony."

Hunsberger, Bruce. "Kit Smart's Howl." *Wisconsin Studies in Contemporary Literature* 6 (Winter/Spring 1965): 34-44.
Hunsberger: "Scholars find the chief value of the *Jubilate Agno* to be its abundant biographical data for Smart's life. A midcentury American reader, however, is struck by the similarities of Christopher Smart's two-hundred-year-old *Jubilate Agno* and Allen Ginsberg's ultramodern 'Howl.'" See a selection in Lewis Hyde, ed., *On the Poetry of Allen Ginsberg* (Ann Arbor: University of Michigan Press, 1984): 158-170.

Hyde, Lewis. "States of Altering Consciousness." *New York Times Book Review* 30 Dec. 1984: 5-6.

Hyde: "The difference between the mind reflected in 'Howl' and the one that guides the recent 'Plutonian Ode' is striking. 'Howl' assumes armies of darkness and light, devouring gods and tender lambs, and it urges us to choose sides. 'Plutonian Ode' . . . does not moralize."

Ignatow, David. "Accents of Death and Endurance." *New Leader* 31 July-7 Aug. 1961: 24-25.

Review of *Kaddish and Other Poems*. "Kaddish" to Ignatow "is a poem coarse and crying, wicked and pitiful, at the point before a man cracks. Slowly, in inflections blasphemous and obscene, always frightened and enraged, the poem turns to God, and help comes." He adds, "This poem, I believe, will be read many years from now as one of the great modern acts of faith, rising classically out of the extremes of human life."

Jacobson, Dan. "America's Angry Young Men: How Rebellious Are the San Francisco Rebels?" *Commentary* Dec. 1957: 475-479.

The Beats in San Francisco.

Jarman, Mark. "Generations and Contemporaries." *Hudson Review* 38 (1985-1986): 327-340.

In an evaluation of thirteen poets born between 1900 and 1960, Jarman advises readers of *Collected Poems* (1985) to focus on pages 126-365 to see how Ginsberg "anticipated American life, especially the youth subculture built around music and drugs."

Johnson, Mark. "Discovery of Technique: Allen Ginsberg's 'These States.'" *Contemporary Poetry* 4.2 (1981): 23-46.

Johnson: Mark Schorer's "technique as Discovery" includes a denunciation of those who employ a technique that "forgives both innocence and slovenliness." Yet Johnson argues that "Ginsberg writes poetry exactly in the technique Schorer maligns, though its result is neither innocent nor slovenly."

Jones, Landon Y., Jr. "Response 1966." *Princeton Alumni Weekly* 17 May 1966: 6-9.

A student's reaction to a reading by Ginsberg.

Klingenberg, E. "Ginsberg's Czech Expulsion." *Censorship* 3 (Summer 1965): 31-33.

Ginsberg rises in popularity, becoming the King of May, but his confiscated notebook provides Czech authorities with evidence to expel Ginsberg from the country. This London publication is reproduced in part in Lewis Hyde, ed., *On the Poetry of Allen Ginsberg* (Ann Arbor: University of Michigan Press, 1984): 240-243.

Kostelanetz, Richard. "Ginsberg Makes the World Scene." *New York Times Magazine* 11 July 1965: 22-23.

Kostelanetz recognizes Ginsberg for his international fame and gives the story of his visit to Czechoslovakia. Photos.

Kotlowitz, R. "Performing Arts: 'Kaddish' on Record." *Harper's Magazine* Oct. 1966: 134-135.

Ginsberg's recording of *Kaddish* draws praise for its poetic effect but reservations about Ginsberg's reading voice.

Kramer, Jane. "Profiles: Allen Ginsberg." *New Yorker* 17 Aug. 1968: 32-73 and 24 Aug. 1968: 38-91.

Articles that anticipate Jane Kramer's *Allen Ginsberg in America*.

Leary, Timothy. "In the Beginning, Leary Turned on Ginsberg . . ." *Esquire* July 1968: 83-85, 116-117.

Timothy Leary chronicles "November 26, 1960, the sunny Sunday afternoon [he] gave Allen Ginsberg the mushrooms." Leary explains the beginnings of their leadership in the psychedelic revolution. See a selection in Lewis Hyde, ed., *On the Poetry of Allen Ginsberg* (Ann Arbor: University of Michigan Press, 1984): 231-239.

Lehman, David. "When the Sun Tries to Go On." *Poetry* 114.6 (Sept. 1969): 401-409.

This review of *Ankor Wat* says that the "nonstop movement from scene to scene, voice to voice, so vitally builds and sustains an undercurrent of urgency and dread." See a selection in Lewis Hyde, ed., *On the Poetry of Allen Ginsberg* (Ann Arbor: University of Michigan Press, 1984): 192-194.

Lyon, George W., Jr. "Allen Ginsberg: Angel Headed Hipster." *Journal of Popular Culture* 3.3 (Winter 1969): 391-403.

Lyon: "In this paper I will attempt to devise a meaningful understanding of the art and charisma of Allen Ginsberg." Lyon focuses on Ginsberg's efforts to bring order through art to the chaos of family, society, and culture. Lyon: "Ginsberg has found in mythology and mysticism a feeling of oneness with the universe, with God, which has enabled him to live freely and sanely and personally in a world that is cruel, brutal, and impersonal."

MacCaig, Norman. "Poemburgers." *New Statesman* 5 July 1963: 20.
      Positive review of *Reality Sandwiches*.

McFadden, J. P. "Howling in the Wilderness." *National Review* 12 Sept. 1959: 338-339.
      McFadden's narration of his visit to a reading by an unidentified Beat poet criticizes the Beats in general and Ginsberg in particular.

McG. Thomas, Robert, Jr. "Ginsberg Is Remembered in Word and Spirit." *New York Times* 13 Apr. 1997, Metro sec.: 37.
      Summary of the memorial at St. Mark's Church.

McGrath, Charles. "Street Singer." *New York Times Book Review* 27 Apr. 1997: 43.
      McGrath finds that Ginsberg "liberated poetry from the library and took it boldly into the cafes and onto the street corner." Ginsberg's poem, "Gone Gone Gone," written 10 Nov. 1996, is printed alongside McGrath's tribute.

MacKinnon, Lachlan. "A Loss of Beat." *Times Literary Supplement* 24 May 1985: 574.
      In this review of Lewis Hyde, ed., *On the Poetry of Allen Ginsberg*, and Allen Ginsberg, *Collected Poems*, MacKinnon remarks, "Ginsberg's *Collected Poems* shows us the prodigious squandering of an enormous potential. He has learnt his manners from his masters, but has not understood the coherence of their forms with their subjects, and has been too lazy to shape his material as it, like any material, demands."

Marin, Peter. "Spiritual Obedience." *Harper's Magazine* Feb. 1979: 43-58.
      Of the Naropa Institute, Marin says, "Sometimes the entire institute seems like an immense joke played by Trungpa on the

world, the attempt of a grown child to reconstruct for himself a simple world." Marin recounts Trungpa's control of "P" and "W," who are taken from their room and forced to be naked in front of all the others at a Buddhist retreat.

Middlebrook, Diane. "Bound to Each Other." *Parnassus: Poetry in Review* 2.2 (Spring-Summer 1974): 128-135.

Middlebrook: "Some of the poems in *The Gates of Wrath* are lovely," yet the volume "represents in Ginsberg's work the stage of poetic slavery."

Molesworth, Charles. "Language, and Sweet Music Too." *Nation* 23 Feb. 1985: 213-215.

Molesworth proposes that Ginsberg's *Collected Poems* (1985) may be read as a dialogue, fugue, example of ethnic literature, or "exfoliation of a single vision that occurred to a young poet in East Harlem in 1948."

Moramarco, Fred. "Moloch's Poet: A Retrospective Look at Ginsberg's Poetry." *American Poetry Review* Sept.-Oct 1982: 10-17.

Moramarco interprets Ginsberg's "Siesta in Xalba and Return to the States," a poem included in *Reality Sandwiches*, as a statement that Ginsberg cannot continue to bask in the idle pleasures of rest in Mexico but must dedicate his imagination to "transcribing the world that worships Moloch." Ginsberg's work is not "an aberrant diversion from mainstream American literary traditions" but instead "a central expression of that tradition." See a selection in Lewis Hyde, ed., *On the Poetry of Allen Ginsberg* (Ann Arbor: University of Michigan Press, 1984): 222-230.

Mottram, Eric. "The Wild Good and the Heart Ultimately: Ginsberg's Art of Persuasion." *Spanner* 2.5 (July 1978): 70-118.

Mottram: "In a form which is not confessional but declaratory, Ginsberg bears witness to his criticism and his emotion in a time of local and international destruction of creative life and perpetuation of the competitive war machine."

Oppen, George. "Review." *Poetry* 100 (Aug. 1961): 329-331.

"Kaddish" is strong, but the accompanying poems are uneven.

Parkinson, Thomas. "Reflections on Allen Ginsberg as a Poet."
    Concerning Poetry 2 (1968): 21-24.
    A discussion of *Planet News* includes comparisons with C. S.
Lewis's *Out of the Silent Planet*.

Peck, John. "Pollution, Purification, and Song." *Tri-Quarterly* 75
    (Spring/Summer 1989): 121-148.
    Peck: "When writers as dissimilar as Ginsberg and Bonnefoy
project the fantasied cultural conditions of archaic song . . . they are
responding to the impulse of mnemosyne to father a humane order
beyond rather than behind us."

Perlman, Dan. "How Captain Hanrahan Made 'Howl' a Bestseller."
    Reporter 12 Dec. 1957: 20.
    A compact and engaging summary of the trial of Ferlinghetti over
the publication and sale of Ginsberg's *Howl and Other Poems*.

Perry, Tony. "Poet Allen Ginsberg Dies at 70." *Los Angeles Times* 6
    Apr. 1997: A1.
    Perry reviews Ginsberg's life and relates comments on his death
from Lawrence Ferlinghetti, Bob Dylan, Gordon Ball, and others.

Pinckney, Darryl. "The May King." *Parnassus: Poetry in Review* 10.1
    (Spring/Summer 1982): 99-116.
    Of *Straight Hearts' Delight* by Ginsberg and Orlovsky, Pinckney
says, "The letters . . . between Ginsberg and Peter Orlovsky are
rough going but worthwhile for those interested in their relationship
as literary history." In *Scratching the Beat Surface* by Michael
McClure, Pinckney finds "something of the cultural climate that
launched Ginsberg on his search for the systemless system."

Podhoretz, Norman. "A Howl of Protest in San Francisco." *New
    Republic* 16 Sept. 1957: 20.
    Podhoretz: "I would say that the avant-garde 'renaissance' in San
Francisco is a product of Rexroth's publicistic impulses. No new
territory is being staked out by these writers." See a selection in
Lewis Hyde, ed., *On the Poetry of Allen Ginsberg* (Ann Arbor:
University of Michigan Press, 1984): 34-35.

_____. "The Know-Nothing Bohemians." *Partisan Review* 25 (Spring
    1958): 305-311, 313-316, 318.

Dismissal of the Beats, especially Kerouac. Ginsberg's lines about anal sex with motorcyclists are singled out for a special attack. See this article in Thomas Parkinson, *A Casebook on the Beat* (New York: Crowell, 1961): 201-212 or Scott Donaldson, ed., *"On the Road": Text and Criticism* (New York: Viking Critical Library, 1979): 357-367.

Portugués, Paul. "Allen Ginsberg's Paul Cézanne and the Pater Omnipotens Aeterna Deus." *Contemporary Literature* 21 (Summer 1980): 435-449.

Portugués compares the influence of Cézanne on Ginsberg with that of Blake. Ginsberg's "feelings, intuitions, and musings on Cézanne's methods inspired him to investigate such possibilities for his own poetry." Ginsberg "felt, as did Cézanne, that it was possible to transcend and realize the essence of nature." See a selection in Lewis Hyde, ed., *On the Poetry of Allen Ginsberg* (Ann Arbor: University of Michigan Press, 1984): 141-157.

Pritchett, V. S. "The Beat Generation." *New Statesman* 6 Sept. 1958: 292, 294.

Mixed review of the principal Beats.

Reilly, Evelyn. "Naked Allen Ginsberg." *Parnassus* 16.2 (1991): 161-171.

Review of Barry Miles, *Ginsberg: A Biography*. Ginsberg is an "energetic citizen and abundant poet" but Reilly longs for "a more thoughtful biographer."

"Remembering Allen Ginsberg." *Village Voice* 15 Apr. 1997: 1, 36-39.

This memorial includes Ann Douglas, "Remembering Allen Ginsberg," Robert Pinsky, "Defiant America," Robert Creeley, "Voice of the People," C. Carr, "Rebel Scholar," Elsa Dorfman, "Looking for Allen," Richard Goldstein, "Queer Shoulder to the Wheel," Lee Renaldo, "The Kiss," David Amram, "Circle of Friends," Gary Indiana, "Speaking the Unspeakable," and Bobbie Louise Hawkins, "True Faith." Also included are a series of photos and a short collection of materials connected to Ginsberg in previous issues of the *Village Voice*.

Rexroth, Kenneth. "A Hope for Poetry." *Holiday Magazine* Mar. 1966: 147-151.

Rexroth assesses and categorizes American poetry after World War II and discusses the Black Mountain school and the San Francisco Poetry Renaissance, with final focus on Kerouac, Ginsberg, Corso, Snyder, Ferlinghetti, and Dylan.

_____. "The New American Poets." *Harper's Magazine* June 1965: 65-71.
Rexroth: "With the exception of the neo- and post-Beats of the unprintable school . . . the last five years of American poetry give the impression of being a little more at ease."

_____. "San Francisco Letter." *Evergreen Review* 1.2 (Summer 1957): 5-14.
Rexroth responds to a range of publications assaulting Ginsberg's "Howl" and proclaims that Ginsberg "will be the first genuinely popular, genuine poet in over a generation." Rexroth comments on what it means to be "disaffiliated" and calls attention to Everson, Lamantia, Duncan, Ginsberg, and Ferlinghetti. Rexroth comments on jazz programs at The Cellar. See a selection in Lewis Hyde, ed., *On the Poetry of Allen Ginsberg* (Ann Arbor: University of Michigan Press, 1984): 32-33.

_____. "San Francisco's Mature Bohemians." *Nation* 23 Feb. 1957: 159-162.
Ginsberg carries on the tradition of Sandburg but tends to fall into popular entertainment.

Richman, Robert. "Allen Ginsberg Then and Now." *Commentary* 80 (July 1985): 50-55.
Richman surveys the career of Allen Ginsberg, who is "radical scourge, hero of the counterculture, mystic, now the proud holder of a six-figure book deal and seemingly irrevocable status as a major American poet."

Rodman, Selden. "Three Neurotics." *National Review* 1 Sept. 1978: 1094-1095.
In this review of *Journals: Early Fifties, Early Sixties*, Rodman finds that "obsessions become absurd and pitiful." Rodman: "Ginsberg's inability to make poetry out of anything except what he hates may account for his changeover from poet to guru." See a

selection in Lewis Hyde, ed., *On the Poetry of Allen Ginsberg* (Ann Arbor: University of Michigan Press, 1984): 330.

Rosenberg, Harold. "Six American Poets." *Commentary* Oct. 1961: 349.
Short positive review of *Kaddish and Other Poems*.

Rosenblatt, Roger. "A Major Minor Poet." *New Republic* 4 Mar. 1985: 33-35.
Referring to *Collected Poems* (1985), Rosenblatt says, "What these eight hundred pages prove is that Ginsberg has always been a minor poet; that is, a poet who has produced a few remarkable pieces, but the bulk of whose work shows no philosophical growth."

Rosenthal, M. L. "Poet and Public Figure." *New York Times Book Review* 14 Aug. 1966: 4-5.
Poets as social as well as literary forces. Ginsberg is recognized as key figure in such a movement.

_____. "Poet of the New Violence." *Nation* 23 Feb. 1957: 162.
Rosenthal: Ginsberg "has brought a terrible psychological reality to the surface with enough originality to blast American verse a hairsbreadth forward in the process." He adds that "this is poetry of genuine suffering." See a selection in Lewis Hyde, ed., *On the Poetry of Allen Ginsberg* (Ann Arbor: University of Michigan Press, 1984): 29-31.

Rumaker, Michael. "Allen Ginsberg's 'Howl.'" *Black Mountain Review* 7 (Autumn 1957): 228-237.
Rumaker: "The onrush of the lines is vigorous, has energy. The focus, where the poem gets off, is anger. Which supplies the force and is maintained on a pretty even pitch throughout. But the anger, as such, is not enough to make the poem." See a selection in Lewis Hyde, ed., *On the Poetry of Allen Ginsberg* (Ann Arbor: University of Michigan Press, 1984): 36-40. See an update of Rumaker's view of "Howl" on 36.

Schecner, Mark. "The Survival of Allen Ginsberg." *Partisan Review* 46.1 (Spring 1979): 105-112.
Review of *Journals: Early Fifties, Early Sixties, As Ever: The Collected Correspondence of Allen Ginsberg and Neal Cassady* and

Mind Breaths. Schecner: "These journals and letters, by and large, have little to tell us about Ginsberg's survival, but much to show us about his early desperation." He adds, "The correspondence with Neal Cassady extends . . . to 1947 and the tender years at Columbia, and plots the vicissitudes of that difficult relationship into 1963." About the poems in *Mind Breaths*, Schecner says, "They put forth the standard brew of homosexuality, metaphysics, pacifism, stirring declamation and muddled prophecy, and home-cooked Buddhism, which is as familiar now as the morning coffee and about as shocking." See a selection in Lewis Hyde, ed., *On the Poetry of Allen Ginsberg* (Ann Arbor: University of Michigan Press, 1984): 331-341.

Scully, James. "Search for Passion." *Nation* 16 Nov. 1963: 329.

Discussion of *Reality Sandwiches*. Scully: Though some poems are weak because of "a lapse of mental integrity or a breakdown of language," Ginsberg's writings "do touch home." See a selection in Lewis Hyde, ed., *On the Poetry of Allen Ginsberg* (Ann Arbor: University of Michigan Press, 1984): 186-188.

Seelye, John. "The Sum of '48." *New Republic* 12 Oct. 1974: 23-24.

In this review of *Allen Verbatim*, Seelye says, "This collection of lectures and conversations is a pocket epitome of the Beat genesis, for it too begins in hope in 1971, and ends two years later in sadness and a sense of defeat. It begins by sortieing out into Young America, Ginsberg launching a private campaign against institutional corruption, and ends by a threatened withdrawal into a sanctuary of silence. Toward the end of the book Gordon Ball includes an interview not given until 1972, an impromptu and touching tribute to Ezra Pound, inspired by the announcement of the poet's death." See a selection in Lewis Hyde, ed., *On the Poetry of Allen Ginsberg* (Ann Arbor: University of Michigan Press, 1984): 216-220.

Shapiro, Harvey. "Exalted Lament." *Midstream* 7 (Autumn 1961): 95.

Shapiro: "My view of Ginsberg's achievement [in 'Kaddish'] is that he has said what he wanted to say with all the force of his original impulse, and with nothing left out." See a selection in Lewis Hyde, ed., *On the Poetry of Allen Ginsberg* (Ann Arbor: University of Michigan Press, 1984): 86-91.

Sheppard, R. Z. "Mainstreaming Allen Ginsberg." *Time* 4 Feb. 1985: 72.

R. Z. Sheppard: "*Collected Poems* (1985) is only the first step in drawing Ginsberg to mainstream publication and ratifying his presence between two covers."

Shively, Charles. "Allen Ginsberg: A Prophet on the Electric Networks." *Gay Sunshine* June-July 1973: 14-15.
Review of *The Fall of America, Iron Horse, Bixby Canyon*, and *The Gates of Wrath*. Shively admires Ginsberg as a poet and example for the gay community, but questions Ginsberg's reasoning and observations. See a selection in Lewis Hyde, ed., *On the Poetry of Allen Ginsberg* (Ann Arbor: University of Michigan Press, 1984): 210-215.

_____. "25 Rainbows on My Windowsill." *Gay Sunshine* Autumn-Winter 1980: 22-23.
Shively: *Straight Hearts' Delight* by Ginsberg and Orlovsky "leaves a lot out (don't we all withhold evidence?); yet it provides wonderful clues and questions about how love, poetry, sex, relationships, the world and revolution are (and can be) linked together." He adds, "The letters and poetry are so completely honest because the authors and editors have undertaken a minimum of deletion and disguises." See a selection in Lewis Hyde, ed., *On the Poetry of Allen Ginsberg* (Ann Arbor: University of Michigan Press, 1984): 354-360.

Sisk, John P. "Beatniks and Tradition." *Commonweal* 17 Apr. 1959: 74-77.
Ginsberg and other Beat principals in historical context. Sisk: "Ginsberg's 'Howl' is a very American poem and Kerouac's *On the Road* is a very American novel. By this I do not mean that they are for that reason either good or bad as literature, but simply that they give us back as in a distorting mirror the anarchism and antinomianism, the dream of utopian freedom and innocence to be found in a commitment to instinct and feeling." See this article in Thomas Parkinson, ed., *A Casebook on the Beat* (New York: Crowell, 1961): 194-200.

Smith, Dinitia. "How Allen Ginsberg Thinks His Thoughts." *New York Times* 8 Oct. 1996: C13.
Ginsberg says that Norman Podhoretz, long-time opponent of the Beats, has "been a great help." News of the release of *Selected Poems* and the CD *Ballad of the Skeletons*.

"Social Study." *Vanity Fair* Mar. 1994: 186.
 Allen Ginsberg responds to *Vanity Fair*'s "Proust Questionnaire," giving short answers to questions about happiness, lies, sex, beauty, literature, and life. A one-page interview with photo.

Sorrentino, Gilbert. "Firing a Flare for the Avant-Garde." *Book Week* 3 Jan. 1965: 10.
 Review of *The Yage Letters* by Burroughs and Ginsberg, *Ace of Pentacles* by John Wieners, *The Holy Grail* by Jack Spicer, and *After 1's* by Louis Zukofsky. One by one, these writers are "important," "accomplished," "dazzling," and "absolutely necessary."

Spector, Robert D. "The Poet's Other Voices, Other Rooms." *Saturday Review* 1 Feb. 1964: 37.
 Discussion of *Reality Sandwiches* and the connection between Ginsberg and Whitman.

Stephenson, Gregory. "'Howl': A Reading." *Palantir* 23 (1983): 11-18.
 Stephenson: "I want to consider 'Howl' as essentially a record of psychic process and to initiate its relationship to spiritual and literary traditions and to archetypal patterns." See a version of this essay in *The Daybreak Boys* (Carbondale: Southern Illinois University Press, 1990): 50-59. See a selection in Lewis Hyde, ed., *On the Poetry of Allen Ginsberg* (Ann Arbor: University of Michigan Press, 1984): 386-393.

Stimpson, Catherine R. "The Beat Generation and the Trials of Homosexual Liberation." *Salmagundi* 58/59 (Fall-Winter 1982-1983): 373-392.
 Stimpson: "The Beats . . . wrote about sex as inevitably as Shelley did eternity. In letters, journals, memoirs, essays, fiction, and poetry, they textualized the body–be it celibate, heterosexual, bisexual, or homosexual."

Tallman, Warren. "Mad Song: Allen Ginsberg's San Francisco Poems." *Open Letter* 3rd Series 6 (Winter 1976-1977): 37-47.
 Tallman: "The resourcefulness of the phrasing in all of the San Francisco poems argues a resourceful, a supermarket sensibility and the impact of that phrasing, particularly of the images of burning, argues a hard-pressed one, almost run down by ten thousand

unnatural shocks fresh in from the city street fields." See a selection in Lewis Hyde, ed., *On the Poetry of Allen Ginsberg* (Ann Arbor: University of Michigan Press, 1984): 379-385.

Tilling, Diana. "The Other Night in Heaven." *The Fifties* 3 (1959): 54-56.
Satire of an article by Diana Trilling apparently written by Robert Bly. See a selection in Lewis Hyde, ed., *On the Poetry of Allen Ginsberg* (Ann Arbor: University of Michigan Press, 1984): 75-77.

Trilling, Diana. "The Other Night at Columbia: A Report from the Academy." *Partisan Review* 26 (Spring 1959): 214-230.
Trilling: "Ginsberg at Columbia on Thursday night was not Ginsberg at Chicago – according to *Time*, at any rate – or Ginsberg at Hunter either, where Kerouac ran the show, and a dismal show it must have been, with Kerouac drinking on the platform and clapping James Wechsler's hat on his head in a grand parade of contempt – they were two of four panelists gathered to discusss 'Is there such a thing as a Beat Generation?' – and leading Ginsberg out from the wings like a circus donkey." See a selection in Lewis Hyde, ed., *On the Poetry of Allen Ginsberg* (Ann Arbor: University of Michigan Press, 1984): 56-74.

Tytell, John. "Allen Ginsberg Howls Again." *Soho News* 18-24 Nov. 1981: 6.
Tytell praises Allen Ginsberg's reading at Columbia University on the occasion of the twenty-fifth anniversary of the publication of *Howl and Other Poems*.

Vendler, Helen. "American X-Rays: Forty Years of Allen Ginsberg's Poetry." *New Yorker* 4 Nov. 1996: 98-102.
Vendler's review of *Selected Poems 1947-1995* is an appraisal of Ginsberg in general that is both generous and controversial.

———. "A Lifelong Poem Including History." *New Yorker* 13 Jan. 1986: 77-84.
Vendler evaluates *Collected Poems* (1985) and finds that Ginsberg is "a descriptive rather than a topical poet, that his strengths are geographical and domestic rather than erotic, and that at his best he is a rueful intellectual, and not a populist."

_____. "My Fiercest Liberator: A Tribute to Allen Ginsberg."
Harvard (Sept.–Oct. 1997): 62-64.

Vendler: "The anthologies will sharply reduce him, and in fifty
years he may be remembered (as almost all poets are) as the author
of fifteen or twenty poems."

_____. "Poets." *New Yorker* 18 Sept. 1978: 165-173.

A review of several books turns to Ginsberg's *Mind Breaths* and
Journals: Early Fifties, Early Sixties. Vendler likes "Mugging" and
journal entries about Ginsberg's "despairs and his travels."

_____. "Review of *The Fall of America*." *New York Times Book
Review* 15 Apr. 1973: 14, 16, 18.

Vendler: "It may be boring to read [*The Fall of America*]
aloud–West Coast to East, East to West, 'L. A. to Wichita,' 'Kansas
City to St. Louis,' 'Bayonne Turnpike to Tuscarora,' and so on, but it
is true that Ginsberg lights up the territory when it is familiar to me,
and so maybe the ideal reader of this poem is someone who knows
Kansas City and Wichita and Salt Lake and Bixby Canyon and
Sonora Desert as I do not." See a selection in Lewis Hyde, ed., *On
the Poetry of Allen Ginsberg* (Ann Arbor: University of Michigan
Press, 1984): 203-209.

Weinberger, Eliot. "Dharma Demogogy." *Nation* 19 Apr. 1980: 470-
476.

Summary of Investigative Poetry Group, *The Party*, and Tom
Clark, *The Great Naropa Poetry Wars*. Weinberger: At Naropa, "the
presence of well-known writers and artists has legitimized Trungpa's
activities . . . and is a further justification in his experiment in
monarchy."

Wesling, D. "Berkeley: Free Speech and Free Verse." *Nation* 8 Nov.
1965: 338-340.

Report on a reading at Berkeley that included Ginsberg and other
Beats.

White, C. "A Tortured Romanticism." *Manchester Guardian* 1 Aug.
1963: 11.

Review of *Reality Sandwiches*. White: "In the best poems, mostly
the latter ones, there is a pattern of exotic, world-evading ecstasy
followed by abrupt deflation, an innocence of thought and emotion,

which seem perfectly spontaneous until one examines the changes in vocabulary which bring this about."

Whittemore, Reed. "From 'Howl' to OM." *New Republic* 25 July 1970: 17-18.

In this review of *Indian Journals*, Whittemore says, "For the devotee the fascination of the *Indian Journals* will presumably be in seeing where and how the saint who brought OM to Chicago had his basic–i.e. oriental–training. For me, the nonbeliever, the fascination is mostly less pleasant: it is the fascination of seeing close up the kind of cheaply acquired religious experience–hop the plane, get the drugs–that has come to take hold of so many so fast in the last few years." See a selection in Lewis Hyde, ed., *On the Poetry of Allen Ginsberg* (Ann Arbor: University of Michigan Press, 1984): 200-202.

Will, George. "Ginsberg Turned Paranoia into Marketable Commodity." *Rocky Mountain News* 10 Apr. 1997: 56A.

In the week following Ginsberg's death, Will argues that Ginsberg had "a talent that rarely rose to mediocrity, but with a flair for vulgar exhibitionism." This syndicated column also ran in slightly shorter form in *The Washington Post* 9 Apr. 1997: B7, the *Baltimore Sun* 10 Apr 1997: 17A, and the *Detroit News* 11 Apr. 1997: A11.

Wilson, Robert Anton. "The Poet as Radar System." *Liberation* Nov. 1962: 25-26.

In this review of *Kaddish and Other Poems*, Wilson focuses on the connection between Pound and Ginsberg. Wilson explores Ginsberg's special metrical techniques. Ginsberg is an "extremely delicate instrument" and "the soul of the poet today." See a selection in Lewis Hyde, ed., *On the Poetry of Allen Ginsberg* (Ann Arbor: University of Michigan Press, 1984): 96-100.

Zweig, Paul. "A Music of Angels." *Nation* 10 Mar. 1969: 311-313.

In this review of *Planet News*, Zweig writes, "Ginsberg has confidence that form, once rhetorical shapes have been discarded, can arise from life itself, referring backward and forward, in the fashion of a psychic genre, to a larger shape of human experience. Here Ginsberg writes the 'night-ode' or whatever name we give it: a form more ample for our total needs than sonnet, epic, or other hanger for old clothes." See a selection in Lewis Hyde, ed., *On the*

Poetry of Allen Ginsberg (Ann Arbor: University of Michigan Press, 1984): 195-199.

Audio-Visual Materials

Allan and Allen's Complaint. Directed by Nam June Paik. Produced by Nam June Paik and Shigeko Kubota. Video. Color. Sound. 30 minutes. San Francisco: Send Video Arts, 1982.

Tape package: "[P]oet Allen Ginsberg greets his father via videotape . . . "; "expressionistic 'painting' of the screen with fractured images and high-speed loops." Contact Send Video Arts, 1250 17th St., San Francisco, CA 94110.

Allen Ginsberg: Holy Soul Jelly Roll: Poems and Songs 1949-1993. Four CD's. Produced by Hal Willner. Santa Monica, CA: Rhino Records, 1994.

This widely available set of CD's is a comprehensive collection of Ginsberg's poems and songs, including "Pull My Daisy," "Howl," and a complete reading of "Kaddish."

Allen Ginsberg: Literary Video. Directed and produced by Lewis MacAdams and John Dorr. 87 minutes. Video. Los Angeles, CA: Lannan Foundation in Association with Metropolitan Pictures and EZTV, 1989.

Tape package: "Allen Ginsberg . . . gives an energetic mostly-poetry-some-music performance of work from *Collected Poems: 1947-1980* and unpublished manuscripts. He read on February 25, 1989, accompanied by Donald Was." An interview with Lewis MacAdams is blended with the reading. The Lannan Foundation makes this video available through Small Press Distribution, Inc. (800-869-7553) at moderate cost.

Allen Ginsberg. With R. D. Laing. Video. Color. 61 minutes. Ho-Ho-Kus, NJ: Roland Collection, no date.

Ginsberg discusses the intimacy of poetry, poems and dreams, and the role of meditation. This tape is available from the Roland Collection, 22-D Hollywood Avenue, Ho-Ho-Kus, NJ 07423.

Allen Ginsberg Meets Nanao Sakaki. New York: Thin Air Video, 1988.

Catalog description: "Beat poet of the West meets Beat poet of Japan in this international event. Poets energetically recite own work; Ginsberg serves as occasional translator."

The American Poetry Review Presents Allen Ginsberg. Video. 103 minutes. Color. VHS. Philadelphia: American Poetry Review, 1993.

Ginsberg reads "Dream Record June 8, 1955," "A Supermarket in California," "Sunflower Sutra," "Don't Grow Old (Wasted Arms)," "Do the Meditation Rock," "To Aunt Rose," "Wales Visitation," "Birdbrain," and excerpts from "Howl" and "Kaddish." He also does a selection of material from other authors, including Blake, William Carlos Williams, and Shelley.

Beat Legends: Allen Ginsberg. New York: Thin Air Video, 1994.

This 92-minute cassette does not include "Howl" or "Kaddish," but includes a broad selection of others, including "CIA Dope Calypso," "Wales Visitation," "Cosmopolitan Greetings," "Whom Bomb," and "Going to the World of the Dead."

Charters, Ann. *Beats and Company*. Garden City, NY: Doubleday, 1986.

Photos by Ann Charters in large format. Accompanying passages by Ann Charters make the photo collection an appealing introduction to the Beats.

_____. *Scenes Along the Road: Photographs of the Desolation Angels 1944-1960*. New York: Portents/Gotham Book Mart, 1970; San Francisco: City Lights, 1984.

Snapshots of the Beats in four chapters: "New York 1944-1954," "On the Road 1947-1956," "San Francisco and Berkeley 1954-1959," and "Mexico and Abroad 1951-1960." Comments on the snapshots by Ginsberg are included. Three poems by Ginsberg refer to persons in the snapshots: "Neal's Ashes," "Memory Gardens," and "In a Car."

First Blues. Audio Cassette. Folkways/Smithsonian Records, 1981.

This cassette is a reissue of an LP *First Blues: Rags, Ballads, and Harmonium Songs*, produced by Ann Charters, through Folkway Records in New York in 1981. Allen reads "4 AM Blues," "New York

Blues," "NY Youth Call Annunciation," "Come Back Christmas," "MacDougal Street Blues," "CIA Dope Calypso," "Put Down Yr Cigarette Rag," "Slack Key Guitar," "Siratoka Beach Croon," "Bus Ride Ballad Road to Suva," "Prayer Blues," and "Dope Fiend Blues." This cassette should not be confused with *First Blues*, John Hammond Records, 1983, a double LP on which Ginsberg reads "Going to San Diego," "Vomit Express," "Jimmy Berman Rag," "Sickness Blues," "Broken Bone Blues," "Stay Away from the White House," "Hardon Blues," "Guru Blues," "Everbody Sing," "Gospel Noble Truths," "Bus Ride Ballad Road to Suva," "Prayer Blues," "Love Forgiven," "Father Death Blues," "Capitol Air," and several poems by others.

Ginsberg, Allen. *Allen Ginsberg: Photographs*. Altadena, CA: Twelvetrees Press, 1990.
    Introduction by Corso. Afterword by Ginsberg. Oversize volume featuring black and white photos of Ginsberg and his milieu from the 1940's through the 1980's. Captions beneath the photos are printed in Ginsberg's own hand, but are reproduced at the back of the book in standard type. Biographies of photo subjects are appended at the back.

_____. *The Ballad of the Skeletons*. Mercury Records, 1996.
    In November 1995, Ginsberg's poem "The Ballad of the Skeletons" appeared in *Nation*, and this poem is now recorded on CD with musical support from Lenny Kaye, Philip Glass, Marc Ribot, and Paul McCartney. The poem, with musical score, is included in *Selected Poems 1947-1995* (New York: HarperPerennial, 1997): 401-405.

_____. *Snapshot Poetics: Allen Ginsberg's Photographic Memoir of the Beat Era*. San Francisco: Chronicle Books, 1993.
    A collection of black and white photos taken by Ginsberg during the period 1953-1991. There is some repetition of photos from *Allen Ginsberg: Photographs*, and this volume is slender and paperbound. Ginsberg's captions appear in his hand and are set in type at the back of the text. Biographies of the subjects of the photos also appear at the end. Ginsberg provides a discussion of his photos, his subjects, and the people who influenced the way he thought about photos.

Ginsberg Memorial Tribute. New York: Thin Air Video, 1997.
Corso, Patti Smith, Lou Reed, Ann Charters, Peter Orlovsky, and many others pay homage to Ginsberg.

Ginsberg Sings Blake: Songs of Innocence and Experience. New York: Thin Air Video, 1996.
Catalog description: "Ginsberg in concert with Steven Taylor (vocals, guitar) in a hearty neo-renaissance revival of Blake's classics."

Heart Beat. A film by John Byrum. Orion/Warner Brothers. 1979.
The film promises a lot with stars Sissy Spacek, John Hurt, and Nick Nolte, but is a disappointment.

Howls, Raps, and Roars: Recordings from the San Francisco Poetry Renaissance. 4 CD box. Berkeley, CA: Fantasy Records, 1993.
Vintage recordings of "Howl," "Footnote to Howl," "A Supermarket in California," "Transcription of Organ Music," "America," "In Back of the Real," "Strange New Cottage in Berkeley," "Europe! Europe!," "Kaddish, Part 1," "Sunflower Sutra," "Patna-Benares Express," and "May 22 (1962) Calcutta."

Hydrogen Jukebox. CD. [Opera by Philip Glass]. Libretto by Allen Ginsberg. Elektra/Nonesuch, 1993.
Excerpts of "Iron Horse," "Jaweh and Allah Battle," "To P. O.," "Wichita Vortex Sutra," "Howl," "Nagasaki Days," and "Throw Out the Yellow Journalists."

The Life and Times of Allen Ginsberg. Produced by Jerry Aronson. Black and white and color. 83 minutes. New York: First Run Icarus Films, 1993.
This tape includes an interview and readings of "Song (The Weight of the World)," "Tears," "Don't Grow Old (Old Poet)," "Father Death Blues," and "Broken Bones Blues" and readings of excerpts from "Howl," "Kaddish," "Kral Majales," "Wales Visitation," and "Plutonian Ode."

A Moveable Feast: Profiles of Contemporary American Authors—Allen Ginsberg. Video. Color. Sound. 30 minutes. In Our Time Arts Media, Inc., Atlas Video. 1991.

This tape of Ginsberg is part of a series of eight half-hour tapes. Ginsberg's tape features Ginsberg commenting on Naomi and Kerouac. Ginsberg reads from "Kaddish."

Addresses on the Internet

At **charm.net/~brooklyn/** Levi Asher presents *LitKicks*, and Allen Ginsberg is a principal topic. In a wide range of topics covered at the site, including features on individual authors, the Beats in general, films about the Beats, Beat news, and the Beats and rock music, Ginsberg is often referred to. A bibliography on Ginsberg as well as a tribute to Ginsberg on the occasion of his death also appear.

At **http://www.ginzy.com/** Mongo BearWolf presents *Allen Ginsberg: Shadow Changes into Bone*, which describes itself as "the clearinghouse for all things Ginsberg." Poems, photos and drawings of Ginsberg and by Ginsberg, interviews, articles, announcements, humor, reviews, links, and other information appear at this site.

By visiting **http://levity.com/corduroy/ginsberg.htm**, one may examine a biography of Ginsberg by John Tytell, interviews with Ginsberg, tributes, and links to other sites. This site is done by Dharmageddon.

One finds an extended interview with Allen Ginsberg at **http://www.iuma.com/Seconds/html/issue28/Allen_Ginsberg.html**.

One finds selections of poetry by Ginsberg at **http://ezinfo.ucs.indiana.edu/~avigdor/poetry/ginsberg.html**.

Chapter 5

JACK KEROUAC (1922–1969)

What a man wishes to hide, revise, and unsay is
precisely what Literature is waiting and bleeding for –
–Jack Kerouac

Books by Kerouac

Jack Kerouac was prolific, both as a poet and as a prose writer, and making representative selections for a class is difficult. Certainly *On the Road* is a standard reading for any course on the Beats, but opinions vary about which texts might serve as further examples of Kerouac's writing. Some choose the lengthy and difficult *Visions of Cody*, citing the novel as Kerouac's masterpiece and noting its connection to *On the Road*. Others favor *The Dharma Bums* for its accessibility, its development of religious ideas, and its introduction of personalities and events from the Beat scene. *Visions of Gerard* and *Dr. Sax* earn consideration for their treatment of the youthful period in the Duluoz legend, which, according to Kerouac, lends structure to the body of Kerouac's prose.

In recent years more attention has been paid to Kerouac's work as a poet, including *Mexico City Blues* and *Scattered Poems*, and one should not overlook Kerouac's writings on spontaneous prose and the origin, definition, and history of the Beat literary movement.

As a central figure among the Beats acknowledged for his leadership in innovation and his influence on other writers, perhaps Kerouac deserves more emphasis than any other author in a course on the Beats.

Big Sur. New York: Farrar, Straus, and Cudahy, 1962; London: Deutsch, 1963.

Ginsberg: "a humane, precise account of the extraordinary ravages of alcohol delerium tremens on Kerouac." He adds, "Here we meet San Francisco's poets & recognize hero Dean Moriarty ten years after *On the Road*." Kerouac chooses "to end with 'Sea,' a brilliant poem appended, on the hallucinatory Sounds of the Pacific Ocean at Big Sur."

Book of Blues. New York: Penguin Books, 1995.

A collection of poetry: "San Francisco Blues," "Richmond Hill Blues," "Bowery Blues," "MacDougal Street Blues," "Desolation Blues," "Orizaba 210 Blues," "Orlanda Blues," and "Cerrada Medellin Blues." Creeley in his introduction: "Much is painful, even at times contemptible – the often violent disposition toward women, the sodden celebrations of drink – but it is nonetheless fact of a world still very much our own."

Book of Dreams. San Francisco: City Lights, 1961.

Kerouac, in the foreword: "The reader should know that this is just a collection of dreams that I scribbled after I woke up from my sleep." He adds, "The heroes of *On the Road*, *The Subterraneans*, etc., reappear here doing further strange things for no other reason than that the mind goes on, the brain ripples, the moon sinks, and everybody hides their heads under pillows with sleepingcaps."

Desolation Angels. New York: Coward-McCann, 1965; London: Deutsch, 1966.

Duluoz is a fire lookout on Desolation Peak but later does some "passing through" in Mexico, New York, Tangiers, France, London, and America.

The Dharma Bums. New York: Viking, 1958; London: Deutsch, 1959.

Ray Smith witnesses the literary scene in San Francisco, goes mountain climbing with Japhy Ryder, travels across the continent, visits family, returns to California to live in a cabin, and finally ventures to Washington, where he serves as a fire lookout.

Doctor Sax: Faust Part Three. New York: Grove, 1959; London: Deutsch, 1977.

Warren French: "*Doctor Sax* is the voice of 'Francis Martin' producing one of Kerouac's most difficult and puzzling works." French adds, "Kerouac is trying to create here, possibly from early writings of his own, the kind of lurid allegory that aspiring fourteen-year-olds think ponderous, a successful recapturing of the excessess of juvenilia that Joyce accomplished also in *A Portrait of the Artist as a Young Man*."

Good Blonde & Others. Ed. Donald Allen. San Francisco: Grey Fox Press, 1993.

Donald Allen gathers many of Kerouac's writings for magazines such as *Playboy*, *Esquire*, and *Evergreen Review*, creating a convenient collection for the reader. This volume features an introduction by Robert Creeley and includes "Good Blonde," "The Great American Bus Ride," "Essentials of Spontaneous Prose," "Belief & Technique for Modern Prose," and other writings.

Heaven and Other Poems. Ed. Donald Allen. Bolinas, CA: Grey Fox Press, 1977.

Nine poems, including "Heaven." Features an illustration of Dr. Sax done by Kerouac for the children of the Cassadys. Also includes autobiographical summaries of Kerouac from 1957, as well as letters to friends and "List of Essentials for the Belief and Technique of Modern Prose."

Kerouac's Last Word: Jack Kerouac in "Escapade." Ed. Tom Clark. Sudbury, MA: Water Row, 1986.

Has a supplement of three articles by Jack Kerouac, in addition to his contributions to the magazine *Escapade*.

Lonesome Traveler. New York: McGraw-Hill, 1960; London: Deutsch, 1963.

Includes "Piers of the Homeless Night," "Mexico Fellaheen," "The Railroad Earth," "Slobs of the Kitchen Sea," "New York Scenes," "Alone on a Mountaintop," "Big Trip to Europe," and "The Vanishing American Hobo."

Maggie Cassidy. New York: Avon, 1959; London: Panther, 1960.

A first-person narrative by Jackie Duluoz that recounts adolescent affection. Ann Charters senses "a mood of excited joy."

Mexico City Blues. New York: Grove, 1959.

Ann Charters: "Most of *Mexico City Blues* was loose sketching, and the choruses were based on what Kerouac saw and heard around him at the moment of writing his poems. Some choruses were more formally structured like a line of recognizable melody in the middle of a free form jazz improvisation."

Old Angel Midnight. San Francisco: Grey Fox Press, 1993.

Dennis McNally: This poem is "extremely long and devoid of meaning in the common sense, a high argument between Jack and God in a universe of hurricane winds that swept his words around like confetti."

On the Road. New York: Viking, 1957; London: Deutsch, 1958.

Gilbert Millstein: the publication of *On the Road* is "a historic occasion insofar as the exposure of an authentic work of art is of any great moment in any age in which the attention is fragmented and the sensibilities are blunted by the superlatives of fashion." Millstein adds that the novel is "beautifully executed, the clearest and most important utterance yet made by the generation Kerouac himself named years ago as 'beat.'" Millstein declares that *On the Road* represents the Beats in the same way that *The Sun Also Rises* represented the Lost Generation.

Pic. New York: Grove, 1971; London: Deutsch, 1973.

In 1969, Kerouac, according to Dennis McNally, "decided to complete a tale he'd begun eighteen years earlier, just after finishing *On the Road*. It was called *Pic*, short for the name of his childhood card baseball game star 'Pictorial Review Jackson.' It was a simple, gentle tale of a black nine-year-old North Carolina boy, as much a dialect study of country Carolina speech as a novel."

Pomes All Sizes. San Francisco: City Lights, 1992.

Ginsberg: "Here's a treasure–in the mainstream of American Literature, random as this collection is, of notebook jottings, little magazine items–containing lovely, familiar classic Kerouacisms, nostalgic gathas from 1955 Berkeley cottage days, pure sober tender Kerouac of your yore, pithy exquisite later drunken laments and bitter nuts and verses."

The Portable Jack Kerouac. Ed. Ann Charters. New York: Viking, 1995.

This volume "features excerpts from most of the 'true story novels' that [Kerouac] considered chapters in his *Legend of Duluoz*, the story of his lifetime." Also includes poems, literary essays, and letters.

Pull My Daisy. New York: Grove Press, 1961; London: Evergreen, 1961.

Kerouac's film script for a famous underground film narrated by Kerouac and featuring Ginsberg and Corso on film.

Satori in Paris. New York: Grove Press, 1966; London: Deutsch, 1967.

A description of Kerouac's trip to Paris in June 1965, written in one week with the help of a bottle of cognac.

Scattered Poems. Ed. Ann Charters. San Francisco: City Lights, 1971.

Ann Charters selects these poems from various literary magazines and unpublished manuscripts.

The Scripture of the Golden Eternity. New York: Totem/Corinth Books, 1960; London: Centaur, 1960.

Ann Charters: "Kerouac's particular brand of Buddhism, mixed as it was with his Catholicism, can be found in *The Scripture of the Golden Eternity*," which is "a hymn of praise to 'One that is what is, the golden eternity, or God, or, Tathagata – the name.'"

Some of the Dharma. New York: Viking Penguin, 1997.

Ann Charters: "[An] account of Buddhism" meant to serve "as a study guide" for Allen Ginsberg. Published in an oversize format, *Some of the Dharma* is a writer's notebook begun in 1953 and finished in 1956. The book is a collection of observations on Buddhism, poems, haiku, prayers, fragments, and personal thoughts.

The Subterraneans. New York: Grove Press, 1958; London: Deutsch, 1960.

Kerouac's account of his love relationship with a black woman, including some expressions of Reich's sexual theories. Tom Clark: "*The Subterraneans* was the triumph and epitome of the spontaneous writing technique Kerouac had been refining for the past two years.

The first person prose of this novel achieves a unified sound like a great bop solo. It has a tensile strength that bears strains and torques of complex feeling; its extended sentences hold together despite sudden shifts of mood."

The Town and the City. New York: Harcourt Brace, 1950; London: Eyre and Spottiswoode, 1951.
    Kerouac's first published novel recounts the story of the Martin family, whose life changes when the Martins leave a small town and begin life in the big city. The prose style reflects Kerouac's admiration of Thomas Wolfe.

Trip Trap: Haiku Along the Road from San Francisco to New York. Bolinas, CA: Grey Fox, 1973.
    Albert Saijo and Lew Welch contribute to this collection that includes various haiku by Kerouac.

Tristessa. New York: Avon, 1960; London: World, 1963.
    A love affair with a Mexican woman who is a prostitute and drug addict. Gerald Nicosia: "*Tristessa* is a love story between the narrator and all creation. Kerouac eulogizes the flow of love (and Light) into the universal void, a flow to which man contributes, thereby redeeming all his agonizing mysteries."

Two Early Stories. New York: Aloe Editions, 1973.
    "The Brothers" and "Une Veille de Noel" are two stories originally published in *The Horace Mann Quarterly*.

Vanity of Duluoz: An Adventurous Education, 1935-1946. New York: Coward-McCann, 1968; London: Deutsch, 1969.
    Tom Clark: "Kerouac's generally jocular tone allowed him to introduce 'tragic' material into his story without putting himself through the emotional rigors of his trademark 'confessional' style."

Visions of Cody. New York: McGraw-Hill, 1972; London: Deutsch, 1969.
    Ginsberg: "Jack Kerouac didn't write this book for money, he wrote it for love, he *gave* it away to the world; not even for fame, but as an explanation and prayer to his fellow mortals, and gods, with naked motive, and humble piety search – That's what makes it a work of primitive genius that stands next to Douanier Rousseau, and

sits well beside Tom Wolfe's Time & River (which Thos. Mann from his European Eminence said was the great prose of America) & sits beside Tolstoi for its prayers."

Visions of Gerard. New York: Farrar Straus, 1963; London: Deutsch, 1964.

Warren French: "Considered as a saint's life, *Visions of Gerard* is a remarkable achievement for a twentieth-century writer generally regarded as an instigator of a counterculture. One can see through this portrait of Ti Jean Duluoz and his lost brother how strong a hold traditional culture had on the author. This is one of Kerouac's most readable books, and indeed it appears to be the only one that has commanded some success and respect in his home town."

Publications in Periodicals

For a thorough listing of Kerouac's contributions to periodicals, see Ann Charters, *Jack Kerouac: A Bibliography* (New York: Phoenix Book Shop, 1975): 79-94.

"After Me, the Deluge." *Chicago Tribune* 28 Sept. 1969, Sunday magazine sec.: 3.

Kerouac bemoans the state of the world, literary and otherwise, and says, "I'll drop out–Great American tradition." See this item in Jack Kerouac, *Good Blonde & Others*, ed. Donald Allen (San Francisco: Grey Fox Press, 1993): 192-198, under the title "What Am I Thinking About?" See this item in Ann Charters, ed., *The Portable Jack Kerouac* (New York: Viking, 1995): 573-578.

"Aftermath: The Philosophy of the Beat Generation." *Esquire* Mar. 1958: 24, 26.

Kerouac: Being beat "never meant juvenile delinquents; it meant characters of special spirituality who didn't gang up but were solitary Bartlebies staring out the dead wall window of our civilization." See this item in Jack Kerouac, *Good Blonde & Others*, ed. Donald Allen (San Francisco: Grey Fox Press, 1993): 47-50. See this item in Ann Charters, ed., *The Portable Jack Kerouac* (New York: Viking, 1995): 559-562.

"Are Writers Made or Born?" *Writers' Digest* 42.1 (January 1962): 13-14.

Kerouac: "When the question is therefore asked, 'Are writers made or born?' one should first ask, 'Do you mean writers with talent or writers with originality?'" See this item in Jack Kerouac, *Good Blonde & Others*, ed. Donald Allen (San Francisco: Grey Fox Press, 1993): 77-79. See this item in Ann Charters, ed., *The Portable Jack Kerouac* (New York: Viking, 1995): 488-490.

"Beatific: On the Origins of the Beat Generation." *Playboy* June 1959: 31-32, 42, 79.

Kerouac: "The word 'beat' originally meant poor, down and out, deadbeat, on the bum, sad, sleeping in subways. Now that the word is belonging officially, it is being made to stretch to include people who do not sleep in subways but have a certain new gesture, or attitude, which I can only describe as a new *more*." See this item in Jack Kerouac, *Good Blonde & Others*, ed. Donald Allen (San Francisco: Grey Fox Press, 1993): 55-65. See this item in Ann Charters, ed., *The Portable Jack Kerouac* (New York: Viking, 1995): 565-573. See this item in Thomas Parkinson, ed., *A Casebook on the Beat* (New York: Crowell, 1961): 68-76.

"The Beginning of Bop." *Escapade* 3.9 (April 1959): 4-5, 52.

Kerouac says, "Bop began with jazz" and narrates an imaginary performance by famous musicians. See this item in Jack Kerouac, *Good Blonde & Others*, ed. Donald Allen (San Francisco: Grey Fox Press, 1993): 126-131. See this item in Ann Charters, ed., *The Portable Jack Kerouac* (New York: Viking, 1995): 555-559.

"Belief & Technique for Modern Prose." *Evergreen Review* 2.8 (Spring 1959): 57.

Kerouac provides a "List of Essentials" that suggestively stimulates a frame of mind for writing. See this item in Jack Kerouac, *Good Blonde & Others*, ed. Donald Allen (San Francisco: Grey Fox Press, 1993): 72-73; Ann Charters, ed., *The Portable Jack Kerouac* (New York: Viking, 1995): 483-484; and Thomas Parkinson, ed., *A Casebook on the Beat* (New York: Crowell, 1961): 67-68.

"Essentials of Spontaneous Prose." *The Black Mountain Review* 7 (Autumn 1957): 226-228, 230-237.

Kerouac creates a glossary for his method, focusing on "Set-up," "Procedure," "Method," "Scoping," etc. See this item in Jack Kerouac, *Good Blonde & Others*, ed. Donald Allen (San Francisco: Grey Fox Press, 1993): 69-71, in Ann Charters, ed., *The Portable Jack Kerouac* (New York: Viking, 1995): 484-485, or in Thomas Parkinson, ed., *A Casebook on the Beat* (New York: Crowell, 1961): 65-67.

"The First Word: Jack Kerouac Takes a Look at Jack Kerouac." *Escapade* 12.1 (Jan. 1967): 4.

Kerouac favors "spontaneous composition" and objects to "laborious and dreary lying called craft and revision by writers." See this item in Jack Kerouac, *Good Blonde & Others*, ed. Donald Allen (San Francisco: Grey Fox Press, 1993): 189-191 and Ann Charters, ed., *The Portable Jack Kerouac* (New York: Viking, 1995): 486-490.

"Good Blonde." *Playboy* Jan. 1965: 139-140, 192-194.

Kerouac: "[W]ho will ever believe I got a ride like this from a beautiful chick like that practically naked in a bathingsuit, wow, what does she expect me to do next?" See this item in Jack Kerouac, *Good Blonde & Others*, ed. Donald Allen (San Francisco: Grey Fox Press, 1993): 3-18. See a selection from this item in Ann Charters, ed., *The Portable Jack Kerouac* (New York: Viking, 1995): 281-290.

"The Great Western Bus Ride." *Esquire* Mar. 1970: 136-137, 158.

Kerouac: "When I bought my ticket from San Francisco clear to New York City via the Pacific Northwest the clerk thought I was crazy." See this item in Jack Kerouac, *Good Blonde & Others*, ed. Donald Allen (San Francisco: Grey Fox Press, 1993): 31-39.

"He Went on the Road." *Life* 29 June 1962: 22.

Kerouac recalls Eddie Gilbert, a fellow student at Horace Mann School for Boys. See this item as "Among the Fantastic Wits" in Jack Kerouac, *Good Blonde & Others*, ed. Donald Allen (San Francisco: Grey Fox Press, 1993): 92-95.

"Home at Christmas." *Glamour* Dec. 1961: 72-73, 145.

Kerouac's Christmas memories focus on food and family. See this item in Jack Kerouac, *Good Blonde & Others*, ed. Donald Allen (San Francisco: Grey Fox Press, 1993): 117-125 or Ann Charters, ed., *The Portable Jack Kerouac* (New York: Viking, 1995): 43-49.

"How to Meditate" and "Hitch Hiker." *Floating Bear* 34 (1967): 129.
    See these short poems in Ann Charters, ed., *The Portable Jack Kerouac* (New York: Viking, 1995): 466, 467.

"In the Ring." *Atlantic* Mar. 1968: 110-111.
    Kerouac remembers the fixing of a match and a wrestler's decision not to take a fall. See this item in Jack Kerouac, *Good Blonde & Others*, ed. Donald Allen (San Francisco: Grey Fox Press, 1993): 151-155 or Ann Charters, ed., *The Portable Jack Kerouac* (New York: Viking, 1995): 497-500.

"Jazz of the Beat Generation." *New World Writing* 7 (1955): 7-16.
    Sal, Dean, and Carlo experience the intensity of jazz performances. See this item in Ann Charters, ed., *The Portable Jack Kerouac* (New York: Viking, 1995): 222-232.

"Lamb, No Lion." *Pageant* Feb. 1958: 160-161.
    Kerouac: "Beat doesn't mean tired, or bushed, so much as it means *beato*, the Italian for beatific: to be in a state of beatitude, like St. Francis, trying to love all life, trying to be utterly sincere with everyone, practicing endurance, kindness, cultivating joy of heart." See this item in Jack Kerouac, *Good Blonde & Others*, ed. Donald Allen (San Francisco: Grey Fox Press, 1993): 51-54 or Ann Charters, ed., *The Portable Jack Kerouac* (New York: Viking, 1995): 562-565.

"The Last Word." *Escapade* 4.2 (June/October 1959): 72.
    Kerouac playfully comments on literature, baseball, music, politics, and religion. See this item in Jack Kerouac, *Good Blonde & Others*, ed. Donald Allen (San Francisco: Grey Fox Press, 1993): 159-188 or Ann Charters, ed., *The Portable Jack Kerouac* (New York: Viking, 1995): 585-587.

"The Mexican Girl." *Paris Review* 11 (Winter 1955): 9-32.
    This story is incorporated in *On the Road*. Sal lives a simple and blissful life with Terry while doing agricultural work at subsistence wages. Illustrated by Albert Eisenlau. Lead story in the issue. See this item in Ann Charters, ed., *The Portable Jack Kerouac* (New York: Viking, 1995): 173-192.

"October in the Railroad Earth." *Black Mountain Review* 7 (Autumn 1957): 30-37 and *Evergreen Review* 1.2 (1957): 119-136.

Kerouac: "I hear far off in the sense of coming night that engine calling our mountains." This material is part of *Lonesome Traveler*. See a selection from this item in Ann Charters, ed., *The Portable Jack Kerouac* (New York: Viking, 1995): 232-245. See this item in Thomas Parkinson, ed., *A Casebook on the Beat* (New York: Crowell, 1961): 31-65.

"Old Angel Midnight." *Big Table* 1.1 (Spring 1959): 7-42.

Kerouac: "Friday afternoon in the universe and in all directions in & out you got your men women dogs children horses ponies . . . " See a selection from this item in Ann Charters, ed., *The Portable Jack Kerouac* (New York: Viking, 1995): 544-548.

"On the Road to Florida." *Evergreen Review* 14.74 (Jan. 1970): 43-47, 64.

Kerouac recounts his journey with photographer Robert Frank. Photos by Frank accompany the narrative. See this item in Jack Kerouac, *Good Blonde & Others*, ed. Donald Allen (San Francisco: Grey Fox Press, 1993): 24-39 or Ann Charters, ed., *The Portable Jack Kerouac* (New York: Viking, 1995): 500-505.

"Poem." *Pax Broadside* 17 (1962).

See this poem in Ann Charters, ed., *The Portable Jack Kerouac* (New York: Viking, 1995): 464-465.

"Poem on Doctor Sax." *Bastard Angel* 1 (Spring 1972): 7.

See this poem in Ann Charters, ed., *The Portable Jack Kerouac* (New York: Viking, 1995): 468.

"A Pun for Al Gelpi." Lowell House Printers Broadside. Harvard University, 1966.

See this poem in Ann Charters, ed., *The Portable Jack Kerouac* (New York: Viking, 1995): 465.

"Rimbaud." *Yugen* 6 (1960): 41-45.

See this poem in Ann Charters, ed., *The Portable Jack Kerouac* (New York: Viking, 1995): 458-463.

"Two Poems Dedicated to Thomas Merton." *Monks Pond* 2 (Summer 1968): 70-72.

See these poems in Ann Charters, ed., *The Portable Jack Kerouac* (New York: Viking, 1995): 466.

"Written Address to the Italian Judge." *Evergreen Review* 7.31 (Oct./Nov. 1963): 108-110.
Kerouac: "*The Subterraneans* is an attempt on my part to use spontaneous modern prose to execute the biography of someone else in a given circumstance and time, as completely as possible without offending." See this item in Jack Kerouac, *Good Blonde & Others*, ed. Donald Allen (San Francisco: Grey Fox Press, 1993): 47-50.

Correspondence

Charters, Ann, ed. *Jack Kerouac: Selected Letters 1940-1956*. New York: Viking, 1995.
These letters come before the success of *On the Road* in 1957 and reveal a pre-fame impression of Kerouac.

_____. *The Portable Jack Kerouac*. New York: Viking, 1995.
Charters includes letters to Norma Blickfelt, Neal Cassady, John Clellon Holmes, Allen Ginsberg, Sterling Lord, and Ann Charters.

Dear Carolyn. California, PA: unspeakable visions of the individual, 1983.
Letters to Carolyn Cassady.

Bibliographies

Anstee, Rod. *Jack Kerouac: The Bootleg Era: An Annotated List*. Sudbury, MA: Water Row Press, 1994.
An annotated list of fifty-nine items that were published in underground limited editions. Anstee notes that the estate is now releasing most material, making bootleg material unnecessary.

Charters, Ann. *A Bibliography of Works by Jack Kerouac, 1939-1975*. New York: Phoenix Book Shop, 1975.

Despite the date of publication, this work remains a valuable guide to Kerouac's works. Primary materials such as books, pamphlets, broadsides, contributions to periodicals and anthologies, translations, recordings, and interviews are cited.

Jack Kerouac. Catalog Five: The Walter Reuben Collection of Jack Kerouac. Santa Barbara, CA: Bradford Morrow, 1979.

This work describes much of the material in Ann Charters' bibliography but also provides information on manuscripts, archives, and foreign editions. Introduction by William S. Burroughs. Many illustrations.

Milewski, Robert J. *Jack Kerouac: An Annotated Bibliography of Secondary Sources, 1944-1979.* Metuchen, NJ: Scarecrow, 1981.

A thoroughly annotated and indexed listing of materials about Kerouac. The date of publication limits access to current material, but this bibliography is a key source.

Interviews

Berrigan, Ted. "The Art of Fiction LXI: Jack Kerouac." *Paris Review* 11.43 (1968): 60-105.

Kerouac credits the correspondence of Neal Cassady with suggesting the spontaneous method for composing *On the Road.* He also discusses Buddhism, haiku, drugs, and the Beat Generation. Aram Saroyan and Duncan McNaughton participate in the interview. This classic interview with Kerouac is reprinted in *Writers at Work, The Paris Review Interviews,* Fourth Series, ed. George Plimpton (New York: Penguin, 1977): 360-395. The interview is also in Scott Donaldson, ed., *"On the Road": Text and Criticism* (New York: Penguin Books, Viking Critical Library, 1979).

Buckley, William F. *Firing Line with William Buckley: Transcripts 1966-1967.* St. Paul, MN: International Microfilm Press, 1972.

A transcript of Kerouac's appearance on the Buckley show is available on film fiche 50. Clips of this material are included in the videos *On the Road with Jack Kerouac* and *What Happened to Kerouac?*

"Excerpts from an Interview with Jack Kerouac." *Street Magazine* 1.4
  (Spring 1975): not paginated.
  Kerouac refers to his travels in France, members of his milieu,
and authors such as Hemingway and Whitman. The interview was
conducted at the art studio of Stanley Twardowiscz in Northport.
Various haiku written by Kerouac are in this issue, too. These
excerpts are drawn from a series of interviews in *Athanor* 1.1 (1971):
1-17, *Athanor* 1.2 (1971): 1-15, and *Athanor* 1.3 (1972): 1-24.

McClintock, Jack. "This Is How the Ride Ends." *Esquire* Mar 1970:
  138-139.
  An article on Kerouac includes statements from an interview.
Kerouac expresses admiration for William F. Buckley, Jr., and
Thomas Wolfe.

White, Michael, ed. *Safe in Heaven Dead: Interviews with Jack
  Kerouac*. New York: Hanuman Books, 1990.
  White offers snippets from the various published interviews of
Kerouac from 1957 through 1969. White cites the source for each
snippet and sees Berrigan's interview in *Paris Review*, Al Aronowitz's
interview in the *New York Post*, and the *Athanor* interview as
"substantive." This book is small enough to slip into a shirt pocket.

Biographies

Cassady, Carolyn. *Heart Beat: My Life with Jack and Neal*. Berkeley,
  CA: Creative Arts, 1976.
  Copyright page: "*Heart Beat* is an excerpt from a work in progress
tentatively titled *The Third Word*." The book includes "Part One:
Spring 1952" and "Part Two: Fall-Winter 1952-1953." Includes letters
from Kerouac, Cassady, and Ginsberg. This memoir is superseded
by *Off the Road: My Years with Cassady, Kerouac and Ginsberg*. The
movie based on *Heart Beat*, despite its cast of stars, is a
disappointment.

_____. *Off the Road: My Years with Cassady, Kerouac and Ginsberg*.
  New York: William Morrow, 1990.
  This work reveals the development of the love relationship
between Neal Cassady and Carolyn Cassady, tracing the entry of

various members of Cassady's milieu, and divulging Carolyn Cassady's reflections on her life among the principal Beats.

Charters, Ann. *Jack Kerouac*. New York: St. Martin's, 1983.
Charters: "[W]ritten in the first years of the 1970's, published by Straight Arrow in January 1973, and last revised for a paperback edition in 1974." Includes identity key to connect real-life people and fictional characters. Part I: 1922-1951. Part Two: 1951-1957. Part Three: 1957-1969.

Clark, Tom. *Jack Kerouac*. New York: Paragon House, 1990.
Begins before Lowell, tracing some details of Kerouac's ancestry and family name. Details personal romance and sexuality. Identifies literary readings. Follows desperation in efforts to find success as a writer. Discusses entry to Buddhism as well as the arrival of fame and the problems of fame. Includes numerous photos of Kerouac, his friends, and the covers of early editions of his books.

Gifford, Barry, and Lawrence Lee. *Jack's Book: An Oral Biography of Jack Kerouac*. New York: St. Martin's, 1978.
The authors interview friends who survive Kerouac "to talk with them about Jack's life and their own lives." The aim is to create "a big, transcontinental conversation, complete with interruptions, contradictions, old grudges, and bright memories, all of them providing a reading of the man himself through the people he chose to populate his work."

Holmes, John Clellon. *Gone in October*. Hailey, ID: Limberlost Press, 1985.
Includes the poem "Going West Alone," a brief introduction, and a selection of essays about Kerouac, including "Rocks in Our Beds," "The Great Rememberer," "Gone in October," and "Tender Hearts in Boulder."

_____. *Passionate Opinions*. Fayetteville: University of Arkansas Press, 1987.
Includes three essays on Kerouac: "The Great Rememberer," "Perpetual Visitor," and "Gone in October."

Johnson, Joyce. *Minor Characters*. New York: Houghton Mifflin, 1983.

This work accounts for Johnson's maturation and the struggles of women among the male writers of the Beat Generation. Johnson describes her relationship with Kerouac, especially the effect of the success of *On the Road* in 1957.

McNally, Dennis. *Desolate Angel: Jack Kerouac, the Beats, and America*. New York: Random House, 1979.

McNally traces the life of Kerouac from his beginnings in Lowell, intermixing references to corresponding historical events and sections of the autobiographical novels, clarifying the differences between fact and Kerouac's myth making. McNally: "In mid-December 1956, almost six years after composition, *On the Road* was officially accepted by Viking for publication the following September. Jack's long vigil was over, but it was perhaps too late for festivities. The six-year wait to publish again had demanded too much of Jack, had stripped him of every personal resource but his work itself."

Montgomery, John. *Kerouac West Coast: A Bohemian Pilot's Detailed Navigational Instructions*. Palo Alto, CA: Fels and Firn, 1976.

A memoir referring to Kerouac and his literary companions by the man depicted as Henry Morley in Kerouac's *The Dharma Bums*. This book is an updating and expansion of Montgomery's *Jack Kerouac: A Memoir* (Fresno, CA: Giligia Press, 1970).

Nicosia, Gerald. *Memory Babe: A Critical Biography of Jack Kerouac*. Berkeley, CA: University of California Press, 1994.

The 767 pages of this volume make it the longest and most thoroughly developed biography of Kerouac. Includes an excellent set of well-printed photos. Nicosia: "Jack Kerouac, like the rest of us, was a creature of flesh and blood, and his life was torn with passions, loves and hates and angers that shoved his life in contradictory directions even as they affected his unshakeable calling to be a writer."

Turner, Steve. *Jack Kerouac: Angelheaded Hipster*. New York: Viking, 1996.

An illustrated biography that takes advantage not only of interviews and the available scholarship but also some special material made available to the author by the Kerouac estate.

Books About Kerouac's Work

Allsop, Kenneth. *Hard Travellin': The Hobo and His History*. London: Hodder and Stoughton, 1967.
Kerouac's characters and the spirit of the American hobo.

Anctil, Pierre, Louis Dupont, Rémi Ferland, and Eric Waddell, eds. *Un Homme Grand: Jack Kerouac at the Crossroads of Many Cultures*. Ottawa: Carleton University Press, 1990.
This volume collects nineteen papers presented at the International Jack Kerouac Gathering held in Quebec City in October, 1987. Some of the work is in French, but there are essays by Charters, Ferlinghetti, Ginsberg, Nicosia, and others.

Beaulieu, Victor-Lévy. *Jack Kerouac: A Chicken Essay*. Trans. Sheila Fischman. Toronto: Coach House, 1975.
French-Canadian heritage in Kerouac.

Challis, Chris. *Quest for Kerouac*. London: Faber and Faber, 1984.
This work is about Challis as much as it is about Kerouac. Challis retraces the haunts of Kerouac during a visit to the United States.

Clark, Tom. *Kerouac's Last Word: Jack Kerouac in "Escapade."* Sudbury, MA: Water Row Press, 1986.
Kerouac made thirteen contributions to *Escapade*, including "The Beginning of Bop," "The Last Word," and "The First Word." Clark provides a thorough introduction.

Donaldson, Scott, ed. *"On the Road": Text and Criticism*. New York: Penguin Books, the Viking Critical Library, 1979.
On the Road, articles about Kerouac and the Beats, and an appreciative introduction with attention paid to the critical reception experienced by Kerouac.

French, Warren G. *Jack Kerouac*. Boston: Twayne, 1986.
A thoughtful consideration of Kerouac that steers effectively between praise and scorn.

Gaffié, Luc. *Jack Kerouac: The New Picaroon*. New York: Postillion, 1977.

The picaresque novel as written by Kerouac. Focus on *On the Road*, *The Dharma Bums*, and *Desolation Angels*.

Gifford, Barry. *Kerouac's Town*. Berkeley, CA: Creative Arts Book Company, 1977.
This book offers an impression of Lowell, Massachusetts (Kerouac's home town), including photos by Marshall Clements. Part Two is an interview with Stella Kerouac.

Ginsberg, Allen. *Allen Verbatim: Lectures on Poetry, Politics, Consciousness*. Ed. Gordon Ball. New York: McGraw-Hill, 1974.
Ginsberg frequently comments on Kerouac's themes and methods.

_____. *The Visions of the Great Rememberer: With Letters by Neal Cassady and Drawings by Basil King*. Amherst, MA: Mulch, 1974.
Ginsberg recalls Kerouac and Cassady. The piece is an expansion of "The Great Rememberer," which appeared as an introduction to *Visions of Cody* (New York: McGraw-Hill, 1972) and was reprinted in *Saturday Review* Dec. 1972: 60-63.

Hipkiss, Robert A. *Jack Kerouac: Prophet of a New Romanticism*. Lawrence: Regents Press of Kansas, 1976.
How are themes developed in the novels of Kerouac? Consideration of the "Beat quest for meaning" and the "despairing of man's future." Evaluation of Kerouac's connections to Salinger, Purdy, Knowles, and Kesey.

Holmes, John Clellon. *Nothing More to Declare*. New York: Dutton, 1967.
The article "The Philosophy of the Beat Generation" from *Esquire* Feb. 1958: 35-38, is included: 116-126. The chapter "The Great Rememberer" is also in Scott Donaldson, ed., *"On the Road": Text and Criticism* (New York: Penguin Books, Viking Critical Library, 1979).

_____. *Representative Men*. Fayetteville: University of Arkansas Press, 1988.
Holmes' compassionate insight about Kerouac informs several essays. Three essays relate directly to Kerouac: "The Great Rememberer," "Perpetual Visitor," and "Gone in October."

Huebel, Harry R. *Jack Kerouac*. Boise, ID: Western Writers Series, 1979.

This monograph offers an account of Kerouac's life and works and provides a useful bibliography.

Hunt, Timothy A. *Kerouac's Crooked Road: Development of a Fiction*. Hamden, CT: Archon, 1981.

Hunt: "I think it is quite clear that *Visions of Cody* was originally titled *On the Road*, that it was written after what is now published as *On the Road*, and that *Visions of Cody* was meant to replace *On the Road*." Hunt's study "begins from the premise that Kerouac's writing is neglected, even though he himself is not, and it attempts to look carefully at two key texts: *On the Road*, the basis of any reputation Kerouac currently has, and *Visions of Cody*, . . . the ultimate basis of Kerouac's claims as a writer."

Jarvis, Charles E. *Visions of Kerouac*. Lowell, MA: Ithaca Press, 1974.

Focus on Kerouac's home town. A second edition of this title (1974) includes an article by Paul Jarvis, "Who Conceived Jack Kerouac–Family or America?": 217-228.

Jones, Granville H. *Jack Kerouac and the American Conscience. Lectures on American Novelists*. Pittsburgh: Carnegie Institute of Technology Department of English, 1963.

A study of autobiographical method in Kerouac. Jones: "Kerouac is certainly not alone as a writer who uses his own experiences in his works; most writers do in one way or another." See this item in Scott Donaldson, ed., *"On the Road": Text and Criticism* (New York: Penguin Books, Viking Critical Library, 1979): 485-503.

Jones, James T. *A Map of Mexico City Blues*. Carbondale: Southern Illinois University Press, 1992.

According to Jones, Burroughs' approach is "neither/nor." No allegorizing is permitted and Burroughs "never forces his text beyond signification." In contrast, Kerouac's approach is "both/and." Kerouac's work includes "multiple allegories deployed dialectically," pitting "fiction against poetry, memory against egolessness, society against solitude, sign against sound, Catholicism against Buddhism, control against spontaneity, narrative against lyric."

Low, Pamela, ed. *Soundings/East* 2.2 (Fall/Winter 1979).
   This issue is a transcript of audio tapes recorded at a symposium on Jack Kerouac held at Salem State College during the spring semester of 1973. Includes Ginsberg, Orlovsky, Corso, Jay McHale (conference organizer), Jarvis, Latham, Twardowicz, Beaulieu, and Holmes.

Montgomery, George. *The Shadow Knew*. Clarence Center, NY: Textile Bridge Press, 1989.
   The Shadow by Maxwell Grant (Walter Gibson) introduced the young Jack Kerouac to "the great Lamont Cranston who with great knowledge cleverly became The Shadow." Montgomery argues that Kerouac's *Dr. Sax* was influenced by stories written by Gibson.

Montgomery, John, comp. *The Kerouac We Knew: Unposed Portraits, Action Shots*. Kentfield, CA: Fels and Firn, 1982.
   This slender volume is compiled in honor of the Kerouac Conference at Naropa Institute in 1982. The book collects nine essays and a few photos.

Morton, James. *The Distance Instead Is the Feeling*. Glasgow, Scotland: Dream of Jazz Press, 1986.
   Morton: "In Jack Kerouac's romantic novel, *The Subterraneans*, the condition of human separateness is explored within the context of sexual love, developed by the themes of internal conflict (and the individual's projected view of it) and the healing power of the imagination."

Parker, Brad. *Kerouac: An Introduction*. Lowell, MA: The Lowell Corporation for the Humanities, 1989.
   Parker traces Kerouac's life and works, offers a few photos and illustrations, and provides an appendix on Lowell.

Peace, Warren. *Jack and the Beatstalkers*. San Francisco: U. S. Record Club, 1991.
   Peace reviews the recordings of Jack Kerouac, including *Poetry for the Beat Generation*, *Blues and Haikus*, and *Readings on the Beat Generation*. The review originally appeared in *Moody Street Irregulars* (Spring 1985): 11-16.

Walsh, Joy. *Jack Kerouac: Statement in Brown*. Clarence Center, NY: Textile Bridge Press, 1984.
Walsh offers nine essays on Kerouac, commenting on his connection to Reich, the Duluoz Legend, the "long, symphonic sentence," and other ideas.

Watts, Alan W. *Beat Zen, Square Zen, and Zen*. San Francisco: City Lights, 1959.
What are some manifestations of Zen, and which form of Zen does *The Dharma Bums* represent? See this item in Ann Charters, ed., *The Portable Beat Reader* (New York: Viking Penguin, 1992).

Weinreich, Regina. *The Spontaneous Poetics of Jack Kerouac: A Study of the Fiction*. Carbondale: Southern Illinois University Press, 1987.
Weinreich: "Kerouac's writing is an attempt to discover form, not to imitate it, and to discover experience in the act of writing about it, as if the language of the 'mental spontaneous process' could expose some human experience as yet unknown simply because no writer had dared to set it down unimpinged by 'craft' in the traditional sense. Yet the obvious irony of this stubborn refusal to revise is that any writer as concerned with the revision process as to oppose it so dogmatically must have this method of refinement keenly fixed in his mind."

Sections or Chapters

Allen, Eliot D. "That Was No Lady–That Was Jack Kerouac's Girl." *Essays in Modern American Literature*. Ed. Richard E. Langford. Deland, FL: Stetson University Press, 1963. 97-102.
Allen: "Mr. Kerouac's girls are almost all physically attractive. And taken all together, they are about as unrepresentative of the women of ordinary American life as they could be." See this item reprinted in Scott Donaldson, ed., *"On the Road": Text and Criticism* (New York: Penguin Books, Viking Critical Library, 1979): 504-509.

Bartlett, Lee. "The Dionysian Vision of Jack Kerouac." *The Beats: Essays in Criticism*. Ed. Lee Bartlett. Jefferson, NC: McFarland, 1981. 115-126.

In the novels after *The Town and the City*, Kerouac tries "to move progressively into the realm of the visionary artist, to surrender himself to the womb of the collective unconscious, bodying forth the Dionysian ideal."

Charters, Ann. "Jack Kerouac." *The Dictionary of Literary Biography. Volume 2. American Novelists Since World War II*. Eds. Jeffrey Hetterman and Richard Layman. Detroit: Gale Research, 1978. 255-261.
Charters surveys Kerouac's novels and reviews his place in the literary community. Analysis of Kerouac's technical innovation.

Cook, Bruce. *The Beat Generation*. New York: Charles Scribner's Sons, 1971; New York: Quill, 1994.
Written after the death of Kerouac, the study accounts for the Beat literary movement, especially Kerouac.

Dardess, George. "Jack Kerouac." *The Beats: Literary Bohemians in Postwar America*. Ed. Ann Charters. Detroit: Gale Research, 1983. 278-303.
Background on the life and the development of Kerouac's writing style. Survey of major works. Various photos, an illustration of the original manuscript of *On the Road*, and bibliographical data.

Duffy, B. I. "The Three Worlds of Jack Kerouac." *Recent American Fiction: Some Critical Views*. Ed. Joseph J. Waldmeier. Boston: Houghton Mifflin, 1963. 175-184.
A discussion of Kerouac's milieu and method with attention to the Beat Generation and spontaneous composition.

Eaton, V. J., and T. Q. Myers, eds. *Catching Up with Kerouac*. Phoenix, AZ: Literary Denim, 1984.
Articles by Gerald Nicosia, Harold R. Goldman, Ronna Johnson, Jake Leed, Jennie Skerl, Arthur Winfield Knight, Joy Walsh,, and Gregory Stephenson. Poems by Michael McClure and John Clellon Holmes. Photos by Chris Felver. Interview of Herbert Huncke by William Gargan.

Everson, William. "Archetype West." *Regional Perspectives: An Examination of America's Literary Heritage*. Ed. John Gordon Burke. Chicago: American Library Association, 1973. 207-306.

Though not a West Coast writer, Kerouac is analyzed for his connection to writers of the region. See a variation of this item in *Archetype West: The Pacific Coast as a Literary Region* (Berkeley, CA: Oyez, 1976).

Feied, Frederick. *No Pie in the Sky: The Hobo as American Cultural Hero in the Works of Jack London, John Dos Passos, and Jack Kerouac*. New York: Citadel, 1964.
Some discussion of the hobo's quest in *On the Road* and *The Dharma Bums*.

Fitch, Robert Elliot. *Odyssey of the Self-Centered Self, or Rake's Progress in Religion*. New York: Harcourt, Brace and World, 1961.
Commentary on Kerouac's characters and their philosophical implications.

Frohock, W. M. "Jack Kerouac and the Beats." *Strangers to This Ground: Cultural Diversity in Contemporary American Writing*. Dallas: Southern Methodist University Press, 1961. 132-147.
Kerouac's *The Subterraneans* as key to understanding the Beats.

Fuller, Edmund. "The Hipster or the Organization Man?" *Man in Modern Fiction: Some Minority Opinions on Contemporary American Writing*. New York: Random House, 1958. 133-165.
Includes some comparison of *On the Road* with Herman Wouk's *The Caine Mutiny*.

Glicksberg, Charles I. "The Sexualized World of the Beat Generation." *The Sexual Revolution in Modern American Literature*. The Hague: Nijhoff, 1971. 143-170.
Discusses Kerouac's presentations of sexuality.

Hassan, Ihab. *Radical Innocence: Studies in the Contemporary Novel*. Princeton, NJ: Princeton University Press, 1961.
Some discussion of the Beats and Kerouac' s novels.

"Jack Kerouac." *Dictionary of Literary Biography Documentary Series: An Illustrated Chronicle*. Vol. 3. Ed. Mary Bruccoli. Detroit: Gale Research, 1982. 71-122.

This encyclopedia article features a collection of some of the most important and famous photos depicting Kerouac's youth, family, and literary milieu. The covers of the first editions of Kerouac's books are displayed, as well as various inscriptions written on copies for friends. Some correspondence, including a letter of recommendation for Kerouac by Neal Cassady. Interview of Kerouac by Farrar, Straus and Cudahy for a publicity release. A selection of articles by and about Jack, including reviews of *The Town and the City*, *On the Road*, *The Dharma Bums*, *Mexico City Blues*, *Vanity of Duluoz*, and *Visions of Cody*.

Jahoda, Gloria. "Strangers in a Strange Land." *River of the Golden Ibis*. New York: Holt, Rinehart and Winston, 1973. 370-382.
   Kerouac in Florida and the events prior to his death in 1969.

Jones, LeRoi, ed. *The Moderns: An Anthology of New Writing in America*. New York: Corinth Press, 1963.
   The introduction includes analysis of Kerouac's style. The anthology includes Kerouac's "Manhattan Sketches," which is also available in Jack Kerouac, *Good Blonde & Others*, ed. Donald Allen (San Francisco: Grey Fox Press, 1993): 99-113. See also Jones' letter to *Evergreen Review* in response to Kerouac's "The Essentials of Spontaneous Prose." Jones' letter appears in *Evergreen Review* 2.8 (Spring 1959): 253-256.

Kazin, Alfred. *Contemporaries*. Boston: Little Brown, 1962.
   Includes a comparison of Kerouac and Mailer.

"Kerouac, Jean-Louis Lebrid de." *Contemporary Authors*. Volumes 5-8. Eds. Barbara Harte and Carolyn Riley. Detroit: Gale Research, 1963. 636-638.
   An introduction to Kerouac's life, his literary output, his theory of spontaneity, and the response of the critics.

"Kerouac, Jean-Louis Lebris de." *Contemporary Authors*. New Revision Series. Vol. 54. Eds. Jeff Chapman and John D. Jorgenson. Detroit: Gale Research, 1997. 235-245.
   This study reviews the life of Kerouac and assesses the changes in the critical reception of his works. Useful listing of primary and secondary materials.

Krim, Seymour. "Introduction." *Desolation Angels*. New York: Bantam, 1966.

Krim: "If critics were to give grades for Humanity, Kerouac would score pure A's each time out; his outcries and sobbing chants into the human night are unphony, to me at least unarguable."

_____. "The Kerouac Legacy." *Shake It For the World, Smartass* (New York: Dial Press, 1970.

Kerouac's writing style sustains the world's interest in the Beats.

McNally, Dennis. "Prophets on the Burning Shore: Jack Kerouac, Gary Snyder, and San Francisco." *A Literary History of the American West*. Fort Worth: Texas Christian University Press, 1987. 482-495.

McNally provides general background on Kerouac and Snyder and their connection to San Francisco, remarking that "Kerouac saw himself as a recording angel for his times, a solitary witness self-obsessed but stormily moving; Snyder's work as a poet is shamanistic, an invocation to an ancient and fully felt tradition, less turbulent but perhaps more grounded and enduring."

Miller, Henry. "Preface." *The Subterraneans*. New York: Avon, 1958.

Appreciative remarks. Miller refers to "weird, hauntingly ubiquitous characters" and "nightmarish, ventilated joy-rides." See this reprinted in Thomas Parkinson, ed., *A Casebook on the Beat* (New York: Crowell, 1961): 230-231.

Mottram, Eric. "Introduction." *The Scripture of the Golden Eternity*. 2nd edition. New York: Corinth Books, 1970.

Interpretation of *The Scripture*.

O'Brien, John, ed. *The Review of Contemporary Fiction* 3.2 (Summer 1983): 4-95.

This issue is dedicated to Jack Kerouac and Robert Pinget, and the section devoted to Kerouac contains twenty-one selections, including pieces by William Burroughs, William Crawford Woods, Arthur Winfield Knight, Ronna Johnson, Larry Kart, Joy Walsh, Tim Hunt, Jim Burns, Albert Huerta, George Rideout, Eric Mottram, John Clellon Holmes, Regina Weinreich, Tom Clark, Thomas McGonigle, Chris Challis, and George Dardess.

Ohashi, Kenzaburo, and Hisao Kanaseki, Kichinosuke Ohashi, and
  Masuru Suwa. "Symposium: Beat Literature." *American Literature – the 1950's*. Ed. Kenzaburo Ohashi. Tokyo: Tokyo Chapter of
  the American Literature Society of Japan, 1976. 269-279.
  Three speakers offer Japanese perspectives on the Beat
movement. The discussion includes the San Francisco Renaissance,
the Beat struggle against literary tradition, Beat religion, Kerouac's
place among the Beats, and the atmosphere on the West Coast and
at Black Mountain College.

Overland, Orm. "West and Back Again." *"On the Road": Text and
  Criticism*. Ed. Scott Donaldson. New York: Penguin Books, the
  Viking Critical Library, 1979. 451-464.
  Overland: "While the protagonist of *The Town and the City* often
tries to break away from the strong ties of home, the protagonist of
On the Road has home as haven and refuge when the complications
of freedom pile up."

Pivano, Fernanda, and Luigi Castigliano, eds. *On the Road*. Milano,
  Italy: Edizione Scholastiche Mondadori, 1974.
  This edition in English marketed in Italy features a general intro-
duction on Kerouac by Pivano.

Portugués, Paul. *The Visionary Poetics of Allen Ginsberg*. Santa Bar-
  bara, CA: Ross-Erickson, 1978.
  Some discussion of Kerouac's influence on Ginsberg, especially
Ginsberg's debt to "The Essentials of Spontaneous Prose."

Smith, Howard. "Jack Kerouac: Off the Road, into the Vanguard,
  and Out." *The Village Voice Reader*. Ed. Daniel Wolf and Edwin
  Fancher. New York: Grove Press, 1963. 236-238.
  Report on a reading by Kerouac.

Spevack, Marvin. "Young Voices on the American Literary Scene:
  The Beat Generation." *The Spirit of a Free Society: Essays in
  Honor of Senator James William Fulbright on the Occasion of the
  German Fulbright Program*. Heidelberg: Quelle and Meyer, 1962.
  313-330.
  Who are the Beats and how do Kerouac and Ginsberg represent
the Beats? How does Kerouac use the picaresque in his novels?

Spiller, Robert E., et al., eds. *Literary History of the United States*. 4th rev. ed. New York: Macmillan, 1974. 1430-1432, 1466-1477.
Commentary on Ginsberg, Snyder, Kerouac, and other Beats.

Stevenson, David L. "James Jones and Jack Kerouac: Novelists of Disjunction." *The Creative Present: Notes on Contemporary American Fiction*. Eds. Nona Balakian and Charles Simmons. Garden City, NY: Doubleday, 1963. 195-212.
Neither Kerouac nor Jones is "truly a writer."

Straumann, Heinrich. *American Literature in the Twentieth Century*. 3rd rev. ed. New York: Harper and Row, 1965. 80-82.
Some discussion of the Beats, with Kerouac as a principal example of Beat writing, particularly in *The Subterraneans*.

Tallmer, Jerry. "Introduction." *Pull My Daisy*. New York: Grove Press, 1959.
Discussion of Robert Frank's film.

Waterman, Walter E. "The Novels of Jack Kerouac: An Attempted Rescue." *Flight and Search: Three Essays on the Modern American Novel*. Georgia State College School of Arts and Sciences Research Paper Number 7. Atlanta: School of Arts and Sciences Research Papers, Georgia State College, 1965. 23-41.
Discussion of *On the Road*, *The Subterraneans*, *The Dharma Bums*, *Maggie Cassidy*, and *Tristessa*.

Webb, Howard W. "The Singular Worlds of Jack Kerouac." *Contemporary American Novelists*. Ed. Harry T. Moore. Carbondale: Southern Illinois University Press, 1964. 120-133.
Kerouac's life on the road and his origins in Lowell. Commentary on *The Town and the City*, *The Subterraneans*, *On the Road*, *The Dharma Bums*, and *Maggie Cassidy*. Webb: Kerouac "is not hostile to civilization as his presentation of the Lowell world makes clear; but he is opposed to the destruction of joy, tenderness, and spirituality in American life."

Wechsler, James A. "The Age of Unthink." *Reflections of an Angry Middle-Aged Editor*. New York: Random House, 1960. 3-16.
Wechsler reports on his participation on a panel discussion on the Beat Generation at Hunter College on November 6, 1958. Jack

Kerouac, Kingsley Amis, Ashley Montagu, and Wechsler were the speakers before an overflow audience. Wechsler on Kerouac: "There were times when he sounded like a jaded traveling salesman telling obscene bedtime stories to the young; there were others when the melancholy of his cadences achieved a mildly hypnotic effect, so that one listened to it as if hearing an obscure but appealing fragment of music. There were also many intervals that can only be described as gibberish."

West, Paul. *The Modern Novel. Volume 2. The United States and Other Countries*. London: Hutchinson University Library, 1963.
Some discussion of Kerouac's novels.

Widmer, Kingsley. "The Beat in the Rise of the Populist Culture." *The Fifties: Fiction, Poetry, Drama*. Ed. Warren French. Deland, FL: Everett Edwards, 1970. 155-173.
What is the Beat literary movement, and why is Jack Kerouac a disappointing example of Beat writing? Widmer: "[T]he Beats helped regenerate the cultural rebellion and allied social dissidence which the hot-and-cold-war cultural nationalism of the preceding decade and a half had muted in literary and social awareness."

_____. "The Hobo Style." Kingsley Widmer, *The Literary Rebel*. Carbondale: Southern Illinois University Press, 1965. 91-107.
Widmer's commentary on "the modern American tramp as an image of rebellion" includes references to Kerouac's *On the Road*, *The Dharma Bums*, *Big Sur*, and *Lonesome Traveler*. Widmer declares, "Despite some of the badness of the writing and the intelligence, [Kerouac's] yearning flights reveal much essential awareness of the cold sense of defeat in the American scene, with its elaborately meaningless places and dubious authorities and dissociated young."

Articles About Kerouac's Work

Albright, Alex. "Before He Went West, He Had to Go South: Kerouac's Southern Aesthetics." *North Carolina Humanities* (Spring 1993): 53-71.

Albright: "[T]he *Road* manuscript . . . includes, in published form, *On the Road*, *Visions of Cody*, and *Pic*, the last book he completed before he died. *On the Road* was the commercial success; *Visions of Cody*, he felt, his masterpiece; and *Pic* is the most interesting of the three when discussed in terms of its potential. These three, and *Vanity of Duluoz*, provide the basis for seeing Kerouac's use of the South as directional symbol: in order for his literary Everyman, first articulated in his vast *Road* manuscript, to be free to explore the vast possibility represented by the American West (and to fully understand America), he must first explore the South."

_____. "Satori in Rocky Mount: Kerouac in North Carolina." *The Southern Quarterly* 24.3 (Spring 1986): 35-48.
An analysis of Rocky Mount, North Carolina, a town that is referred to in five of Kerouac's novels.

Amis, Kingsley. "The Delights of Literary Lecturing." *Harper's Magazine* Oct. 1959: 181-182.
Some commentary on Kerouac as an effective speaker.

Amram, David. "In Memory of Jack Kerouac." *Evergreen Review* 14.74 (Jan. 1970): 41.
A memoir in honor of Kerouac.

Aronowitz, Alfred G. "The Beat Generation–Beaten?" *New York Post* 27 Dec. 1957: 5, 10.
Commentary on Kerouac as a public speaker.

_____. "The Yen for Zen." *Escapade* Oct. 1960: 50-52, 70.
Aronowitz: "Although Kerouac is not exactly a Zen Buddhist, he has his share of satori, enough, in fact, to share with others. His spontaneous prose, for example, is a form of enlightenment, or at least he intends it as such." See also the series of articles Aronowitz wrote for the *New York Post* in March of 1959. Milewski cites articles on March 9, 10, 11, 16, and 19 as especially relevant to Kerouac.

Ashida, Margaret E. "Frogs and Frozen Zen." *Prairie Schooner* 34.3 (Fall 1960): 199-206.
Ashida: "[T]he Beats have turned with ease to Zen, with its appealing non-rational, non-verbal mysticism, its reliance on the individual's spontaneous, intuitive insights and actions, and its

sanctification of each moment of existence." However, "the Beats have taken what pleases them and ignored what does not, meanwhile parading their unique interpretation of Zen as the real thing."

Askew, Melvin W. "Quests, Cars, and Kerouac." *University of Kansas City Review* 28 (1962): 231-240.

Mixed view of Kerouac, acknowledging *On the Road* for its insight into American traditions, but questioning values demonstrated by characters. See this item in Scott Donaldson, ed., *"On the Road": Text and Criticism* (New York: Penguin Books, Viking Critical Library, 1979): 383-396.

Balakian, Nona. "The Prophetic Vogue of the Anti-heroine." *Southwest Review* 47 (1962): 134-141.

Balakian analyzes female characters in Kerouac. See this item reprinted in *Critical Encounters: Literary Views and Reviews, 1953-1977* (Indianapolis: Bobbs-Merrill, 1978).

Basinski, Michael. "Ti Jean in Lowell." *Moody Street Irregulars: A Jack Kerouac Newsletter* 1.1 (1978): 13-15.

Influences during Kerouac's childhood.

"The 'Beat' Generation." *Current Affairs Bulletin* [Australia] 7 Dec. 1959: 35-48.

What does it mean to be Beat, and how well does Kerouac fulfill the definition?

Birkerts, Sven. "Off the Road." *The New Republic* 24 Apr. 1995: 43.

This article is ostensibly a review of *The Portable Jack Kerouac* and *Jack Kerouac: Selected Letters 1940-1956* (both edited by Ann Charters), but Birkerts expands his article to consider Kerouac's life and literary career.

Blackburn, William. "Han Shan Gets Drunk with the Butchers: Kerouac's Buddhism in *On the Road, The Dharma Bums*, and *Desolation Angels*." *Literature East and West* 21.1-4 (Jan.-Dec. 1977): 9-22.

Blackburn: "Kerouac, obsessed as he was with the lost innocence of his childhood, with his piercing awareness of human suffering, and with his sense of himself as a holy wanderer seeking an end to this suffering, seems to have found in the career of Prince Siddhartha (later the Buddha) both an emblem of his own life and a pattern for his major fiction."

"Blazing and the Beat." *Time* 24 Feb. 1958: 104.
Negative review of *The Subterraneans*.

Breslin, James E. "The Beat Generation: A View from the Left." *Village Voice* 16 Apr. 1958: 3.
Breslin reports on "a literary Sunday Meeting" held by the Young Socialist League, at which Michael Harrington attacked Kerouac for "retreating back from the realm of palpable reality." Breslin notes that various members of the audience rose to Kerouac's defense.

Bubin, Louis D., Jr. "Two Gentlemen of San Francisco: Notes on Kerouac and Responsibility." *Western Review* 23 (Spring 1959): 278-283.
Bubin on Kerouac: "Wild though his novels are, full of the most absurd kind of empurpled romanticism and windblown rhetoric, they are written with a strained but quite genuine sense of style, a talent for characterization, an eccentric but unmistakable originality."

Campbell, James. "Kerouac & Co." *New Edinburgh Review* 47 (1979): 11-14.
This article is ostensibly a review of *Jack's Book* by Barry Gifford and Lawrence Lee, but Campbell goes on to assess Kerouac as a talented and committed writer who nevertheless is, as James Baldwin says, "as fast asleep as [the] above-ground 'enemy.'"

Charters, Ann. "Kerouac's Literary Method and Experiments: The Evidence of the Manuscript Notebooks in the Berg Collection." *Bulletin of Research in the Humanities* 84.4 (Winter 1981): 431-450.
Materials acquired in 1974 for the Berg Collection at the New York Public Library enabled Charters to conclude that "Kerouac varied his literary method at different times." Charters presents published versions alongside manuscript versions to show that Kerouac sometimes revised and sometimes did not.

Ciardi, John. "The Book Burners and Sweet Sixteen." *Saturday Review* 27 June 1959: 22, 30.

Ciardi may not have a wholly positive view of the Beats, but he defends intellectual freedom.

Clark, Tom. "Kerouac's Inner Journey to Find Light and Meaning." *Washington Times* 7 Sept. 1997: B8.

Clark: By the end of *Some of the Dharma*, "Kerouac has entirely reverted from teacher to writer, from the glossing of synopsized precepts out of the Buddhist canon to the embedding of a far-flung range of expressive autobiographical and poetic texts in complex, collage-like page structures."

Cook, Bruce. "King of the Road." *Washington Post* 31 Aug. 1997: X15.

Cook: "Kerouac's charged, lightning-swift prose gives the reader the sense that all that is told is happening in the great Now. This is why, when read by teenagers and college kids today, it seems new, written just for them."

Coolidge, Clark. "Kerouac." *American Poetry Review* 24.1 (Jan./Feb. 1995): 43-49.

Coolidge: "I was thinking about Kerouac's work as being in motion in a cycle between these aspects of the work: Sketching, he's right in front of the things, leading to the Memory Blowing, writing the words coming off the memory or the notebooks from the experience, perhaps leading then on to the BabbleFlow."

Dardess, George. "The Delicate Dynamics of Friendship: A Reconsideration of Jack Kerouac's *On the Road*." *American Literature* 46 (May 1974): 200-206.

Dardess: "*On the Road* is a love story, not a travelog (and certainly not a call to Revolution)." See this article in Lee Bartlett, ed., *The Beats: Essays in Criticism* (Jefferson, NC: McFarland, 1981): 127-132.

_____ . "Jack Kerouac as Religious Teacher." *Moody Street Irregulars: A Jack Kerouac Newsletter* 1.1 (1978): 4-6.

Kerouac and the quest for religious fulfillment.

_____ . "The Logic of Spontaneity: A Reconsideration of Kerouac's 'Spontaneous Prose Method.'" *Boundary* 2.3 (Spring 1975): 729-745.

The role and function of spontaneous writing in Emerson, Thoreau, and Kerouac.

D'Orso, Michael. "Man Out of Time: Kerouac, Spengler, and the 'Faustian Soul.'" *Studies in American Fiction* 11.1 (Spring 1983): 19-30.

D'Orso: "Embodying Spengler's contemporary 'Faustian' man, Kerouac's protagonists yearn for something they cannot comprehend or define." D'Orso adds, "Kerouac filled his novels with characters who exemplify the 'passionate thrust' of Spengler's 'infinity craving' Faustian."

Dunn, William. "A 'Beat' Era Love Story: She Recalls Marriage to Author Kerouac." *Detroit News* 19 Aug. 1979: 1A, 18A-19A.
Kerouac's first wife remembers Kerouac.

Farzan, Massud. "The Bippie in the Middle: Jack Kerouac (1922-1969)." *London Magazine*, New Series 9.11 (1970): 62-69.
An appreciation of Kerouac's various works at the time of his death.

Fiedler, Leslie. "Death of the Novel." *Ramparts* Winter 1964: 2-14.
A low appraisal of contemporary writing, with the Beats, including Kerouac, as examples of decline. See this item expanded in *Waiting for the End* (New York: Stein and Day, 1964): 138-178.

Fleischmann, Wolfgang B. "A Look at the 'Beat Generation' Writers." *Carolina Quarterly* 11.2 (1959): 13-20.
An effort to sort out a group that is not easily sorted out. See this item in Joseph J. Waldmeier, ed., *Recent American Fiction: Some Critical Views* (Boston: Houghton Mifflin, 1963).

_____. "Those 'Beat' Writers." *America* 26 Sept. 1959: 766-768.
The Beats, their history, and their place in literary history, with attention to Kerouac and Ginsberg.

Gelfant, Blanche. "Residence Underground: Recent Fiction of the Subterranean Things." *Sewanee Review* 83 (Summer 1975): 406-438.
Kerouac, Burroughs, and Pynchon as authors of the "subterranean city novel."

Goldman, Ivan. "Visit in Summer of 1947–Jack Kerouac's Denver Friends Formed Theme for Novel." *Denver Post* 29 Dec. 1974: 34.

Some background for Kerouac's treatment of Denver and the special characters in *On the Road*. Milewski cites a series of articles on this topic in the *Denver Post*: see December 30, 1974: 12; December 31, 1974: 21; and January 1, 1975: 49.

Gribetz, Sid. "Kerouac's Angels." *Moody Street Irregulars: A Jack Kerouac Newsletter* 4 (1979): 7-8.

Gribetz: "Different from his macho milieu, [Kerouac] achieved tender altruism in love." Gribetz adds, "American women should appreciate Kerouac more."

Gussow, Adam. "Bohemia Revisited: Malcolm Cowley, Jack Kerouac, and *On the Road*." *Georgia Review* 38.2 (Summer 1984): 291-311.

Gussow: "The true source of Cowley's dispute with Kerouac lay not so much in Cowley's insistence on *story*, but in a second, more fundamental principle: his insistence on *craft*."

Hart, John E. "Future Hero in Paradise: Kerouac's *The Dharma Bums*." *Critique: Studies in Modern Fiction* 14.3 (1973): 52-62.

Analysis of *The Dharma Bums*. Consideration of previous literary figures, such as Odysseus, Don Quixote, Rasselas, and Nick Adams, who also embark on journeys.

Hazo, Samuel. "The Poets of Retreat." *Catholic World* Oct. 1963: 33-39.

What does it mean to be Beat, and how can the Beats earn their place in literary history?

Hinchcliffe, Arnold P. "The End of a Dream?" *Studi Americani* 5 (1959): 315-323.

This material is in English and offers some analysis of *On the Road*.

Holder, Wayne. "The Road Goes on Forever." *Moody Street Irregulars: A Jack Kerouac Newsletter* 3 (1979): 6

Analysis of Dean in *On the Road*.

Holmes, John Clellon. "Existentialism and the Novel: Notes and Questions." *Chicago Review* 13.2 (1959): 144-151.
The philosophical base for Kerouac's characters. See this item in John Clellon Holmes, *Passionate Opinions* (Fayetteville: University of Arkansas Press, 1987): 161-175 under the title "The Broken Places: Existential Aspects of the Novel."

_____. "First Reader of *On the Road* in Manuscript: An Excerpt from the Journals of John Clellon Holmes." *Moody Street Irregulars: A Jack Kerouac Newsletter* 5 (1979): 11.
The earliest reactions to *On the Road*.

_____. "An Insider's View of Some Old Friends." *Books* Dec. 1966: 5.
Kerouac, despite his greatness, is often misunderstood.

_____. "The Philosophy of the Beat Generation." *Esquire* Feb. 1958: 35-38.
Who are the Beats and how do they fit into a historical and social context? See this item in John Clellon Holmes, *Passionate Opinions* (Fayetteville: University of Arkansas Press, 1987): 65-77 and in Scott Donaldson, ed., *"On the Road": Text and Criticism* (New York: Penguin Books, Viking Critical Library, 1979): 368-379.

Hull, Keith N. "A Dharma Bum Goes West to Meet the East." *Western American Literature* 11 (Winter 1977): 321-329.
Structure in *The Dharma Bums* based on the exchange between Ray and Japhy.

Jackson, Carl T. "The Counterculture Looks East: Beat Writers and Asian Religion." *American Studies* 29 (Spring 1988): 51-70.
Jackson: "[T]he Beats may be considered the vanguard in a significant shift in post-World War II American religious consciousness, marked by rejection of institutional religion, a questioning of Christian values, and an affirmation of the possibility of a new religious meaning to be found through mystical experience, hallucinogenic drugs and Asian religions." Includes photos of Kerouac, Snyder, and Ginsberg.

Jacobson, Dan. "America's 'Angry Young Men': How Rebellious Are the San Francisco Rebels?" *Commentary* Dec. 1957: 475-479.
A discussion of the Beats that both praises and questions.

Johnson, Joyce. "Lighting Out for the Territory." *Book World* 12 Mar. 1995: 1, 14.

Review of *Jack Kerouac; Selected Letters, 1940-1956*, ed. Ann Charters. Johnson, who received various letters from Kerouac in the spring of 1957, writes, "[T]hese 600 pages of his letters bring Kerouac to life almost palpably – his sweetness, unworldliness, and generosity; his rolling moods; the courage and integrity with which he dedicated himself to his calling; his vulnerability to profound loneliness and nearly suicidal despair."

Kazin, Alfred. "Psychoanalysis and Contemporary Literary Culture." *Psychoanalysis and the Psychoanalytic Review* 45 (1958): 41-51.

The focus is on contemporary writers in general, but some attention is paid to Kerouac's quest. See this reprinted in *Partisan Review* 26 (1959): 45-55.

Kerouac, Joan. "My Ex-Husband, Jack Kerouac, Is an Ingrate." *Confidential* Aug. 1961: 18-19, 53-54.

Joan Haverty, who was briefly married to Kerouac, discusses Kerouac.

Kramer, Peter. "Kerouac Remembered Mama." *Books* July 1965: 2.

Gabrielle Kerouac, Jack's mother, describes her son.

Krim, Seymour. "King of the Beats." *Commonweal* 2 Jan. 1959: 359-360.

A review of *The Dharma Bums* that develops into a consideration of Kerouac's contribution to literature: "Kerouac, by throwing over the literary restraints, has succeeded in letting some of the real experience of our decade escape into his pages in crude, free-swinging, even shapeless form."

Lauerman, Connie. "'On the Road' Again: Jack Kerouac Is Back, as Popular and Misunderstood an Icon as He Ever Was." *Chicago Tribune* 27 Nov. 1994, Arts Section: 7.

Lauerman reviews the revival of interest in Kerouac, but notices that Kerouac's legend seems more important than the artistry of his works.

Leer, Norman. "Three American Novels and Contemporary Society: A Search for Commitment." *Wisconsin Studies in Contemporary Literature* 3.3 (1962): 67-86.
Some commentary on *The Dharma Bums* as a "novel of inquiry" in which Zen Buddhism directs the search for identity.

Lomas, Herbert. "Benzedrine to Booze." *London Magazine*, New Series 14.5 (1974-1975): 73-86.
Kerouac as a weak writer.

Lombreglia, Ralph. "The Only People for Him." *Atlantic* Aug. 1996: 88-93.
This article purports to be a review of *The Portable Jack Kerouac* and *Selected Letters: 1940-1956*, and Lombreglia does praise Charters, but most of the article is an assessment of Kerouac's life and literary career, with the conclusion that the story of that life is "a cautionary tale."

McKelley, James C. "The Artist and the West: Two Portraits Drawn by Jack Kerouac and Sam Shepard." *Western American Literature* 26.4 (February 1992): 293-301.
McKelley: "In his depiction of Sal and Dean, Kerouac has construed a paradigm for a certain type of artistic production, one consistent with the western American myth of exploration and discovery."

Mahoney, Stephen. "The Prevalence of Zen." *Nation* 1 Nov. 1958: 311-315.
Zen and *The Dharma Bums*.

Morissette, Father Armand "Spike." "A Catholic View of Kerouac." *Moody Street Irregulars: A Jack Kerouac Newsletter* 5 (1979): 7-8.
Kerouac's youth in Lowell and his connection to the Catholic faith.

Mosley, Edwin M. "Lost and Hollow, Beat and Angry–The Significant Gestures of Two Generations." *Ball State Teachers College Forum* 1.2 (1960-1961): 44-54.
On the Road and the picaresque novel.

Nicosia, Gerald. "Kerouac's Daughter: The Beat Goes On." *The Chicago Sun-Times* 21 Oct. 1979, Living Section: 5, 9.
Jan Kerouac remembers her father.

Nolan, Dick. "The City." *San Francisco Examiner* 26 Aug. 1959, sec. 2: 1.
Defense of *Maggie Cassidy*.

Norris, Hoke. "The Big Table Has Scant Menu." *Chicago Sun-Times* 5 Apr. 1959, sec. 3: 4.
Early negative reaction to Kerouac and his milieu.

Oates, Joyce Carol. "Down the Road: Jack Kerouac's Highs and Lows, Reconsidered in Two Collections." *New Yorker* 27 Mar. 1995: 96-100.
This article is ostensibly a review of Charters' *The Portable Jack Kerouac* and *Jack Kerouac: Selected Letters 1940-1956*, but Oates evaluates much of Kerouac's literary production and the critical response to it.

Oliphant, Robert. "Public Voices and Wise Guys." *Virginia Quarterly Review* 37.4 (1961): 522-537.
Narrators in the modern novel and Kerouac's "public voice."

Pinck, D. "Digging the San Franciscans." *New Republic* 3 Mar. 1958: 20.
Review of *The Subterraneans*. Pinck: "Perhaps reluctantly one must acknowledge an occasional astonishingly fine poetic run of words," but in general, "Kerouac is simply ignorant."

Plummer, William. "Jack Kerouac: The Beat Goes On." *The New York Times Magazine* 30 Dec. 1979: 18-23, 39-41, 44.
Plummer notes that while the sale of Jack Kerouac's books is holding steady, the interest in Kerouac's personality and legend is growing. Plummer then provides biographical background on Kerouac and the Beats.

Podhoretz, Norman. "The Know-Nothing Bohemians." *Partisan Review* 25 (1958): 305-318.
Podhoretz: "Kerouac apparently thinks that spontaneity is a matter of saying whatever comes into your head, in any order you

happen to feel like saying it." Podhoretz's attack on the Beats serves as a springboard for the defense of the Beats, as is revealed by reprints of the article in Seymour Krim, ed., *The Beats* (Greenwich, CT: Fawcett, 1960), Thomas Parkinson, ed., *A Casebook on the Beat* (New York: Crowell, 1961), and Scott Donaldson, ed., *"On the Road": Text and Criticism* (New York: Penguin Books, Viking Critical Library, 1979). See Podhoretz's piece also in *Doings and Undoings: The Fifties and After in American Writing* (New York: Farrar Straus, 1964): 143-158.

Poteet, Maurice. "The Delussons and the Martins: Some Family Resemblances." *Moody Street Irregulars: A Jack Kerouac Newsletter* 5 (1979): 4-6.
A comparison of characters, setting, and events in *The Town and the City* and Jacques Ducharme's *The Delusson Family*.

_____. "The 'Little (Known) Literature' of Kerouac's 'Little Canada.'" *Moody Street Irregulars: A Jack Kerouac Newsletter* 5 (1979): 4-6.
Is there a link between Kerouac's literature and the literature of "Little Canada"?

Primeau, Ronald. "'The Endless Poem': Jack Kerouac's Midwest." *Great Lakes Review* 2.2 (1976): 19-26.
What is the image of the midwest in *On the Road*?

Pritchett, V. S. "The Beat Generation." *New Statesman* 6 Sept. 1958: 292, 294, 296.
Appreciation of the Beats and Kerouac.

Prothero, Steven. "On the Holy Road: The Beat Movement as Spiritual Protest." *Harvard Theological Review* 84 (Apr. 1991): 205-222.
Prothero: "The beats shared, in short, not an identifiable geographical goal but an undefined commitment to a spiritual search."

Rexroth, Kenneth. "San Francisco's Mature Bohemians." *Nation* 23 Feb. 1957: 159-162.
The rise of new writing in San Francisco, with praise for the work of Kerouac.

Roberts, John G. "The Frisco Beat." *Mainstream* 11.7 (1958): 11-26.
    Discussion of San Francisco writers, including the Beats and Ker-
ouac.

Robertson, David. "Real Matter, Spiritual Mountain: Gary Snyder
    and Jack Kerouac on Mount Tamalpais." *Western American
    Literature* 27.3 (Nov. 1992): 209-226.
    Robertson: "This article . . . consists of historical and
photographic documentation plus my own imaginative response to
[Kerouac's and Snyder's] journey and to the place where it
occurred." Robertson blends Kerouac's *The Dharma Bums*, a work
of fiction, with his documentary of Snyder and Kerouac and offers an
explanation: "That Kerouac in *Dharma Bums* is accurately reporting
Snyder's thought is demonstrated by entries in the latter's journals of
1955 and 1956."

Ross, Andrew M. "Crisis: The Personal Versus the Social." *Moody
    Street Irregulars: A Jack Kerouac Newsletter* 4 (1979): 4-6.
    Discussion of hardships Kerouac faced. Analysis of *Big Sur*.

Scott, James F. "Beat Literature and the American Teen Cult."
    American Quarterly 14 (1962): 150-160.
    The immaturity of the Beats and Kerouac.

Seelye, John D. "The American Tramp: A Version of the Pi-
    caresque." *American Quarterly* 15 (1963): 535-553.
    The wanderer and the frontiersman in Kerouac.

Sheed, Wilfrid. "Beat Down and Beatific." *New York Times Book Re-
    view* 2 Jan. 1972: 2, 21.
    Appreciation of the Beats. This item appears in *The Good Word
and Other Words* (New York: Dutton, 1978): 121-126.

Sorrell, Richard S. "Novelists and Ethnicity: Jack Kerouac and Grace
    Metalious as Franco-Americans." *MELUS* 9.1 (Spring 1982): 37-
    52.
    Sorrell: The "common Franco-American background" of Kerouac
and Metalious is not "the sole key to understanding the lives and
literature of Jack Kerouac and Grace Metalious," but the effect of
their ethnicity is recognizable.

Stevens, Jay. "Classic Jack." *Yankee* 58.9 (Sept. 1994): 72-77, 144, 146.
Stevens reviews the tour of Lowell given by Roger Brunelle and Reggie Ouellette as part of the Lowell Celebrates Kerouac! activities in 1994.

Sutherland, Donald. "Petronius and the Art of the Novel." *Denver Quarterly* 13.3 (1978): 7-16.
A comparison of Kerouac and Petronius.

Tallman, Warren. "Kerouac's Sound." *Tamarack Review* 11 (Spring 1959): 58-74.
Kerouac's prose as writing based on the sounds of jazz and aimed at capturing spontaneity. See this item in Thomas Parkinson, ed., *A Casebook on the Beat* (New York: Crowell, 1961): 215-229. It is also reprinted in *Evergreen Review* 4.11 (1960): 153-169 and Scott Donaldson, ed., *"On the Road": Text and Criticism* (New York: Penguin Books, Viking Critical Library, 1979): 513-530. One also finds this item in *Open Letter*, 3rd Series 6 (1976-1977): 7-19.

"Time Erases Silence on Marriage to Writer." *Milwaukee Sentinel* 21 Aug. 1979, Part 1: 3.
Kerouac's first wife discusses the marriage.

Tytell, John. "The Beat Generation and the Continuing American Revolution." *American Scholar* 42 (1973): 308-317.
What process led to the rise of the Beats? How does *On the Road* depend on experience and energy while *The Dharma Bums* depends on Zen and meditation?

Ulin, David L. "Bent on Self-Destruction." *Newsday* 7 Sept 1997: G12.
Ulin: "As *Some of the Dharma* progresses . . . it becomes less a book about Buddhism than a series of internal snapshots, incorporating concerns about career, notes on relationships, and discussions of family to portray the contradictions Kerouac could not resolve. Again and again here, he makes a statement – about drinking, say, or the futility of literary aspirations – only to turn around a page or two later and take the opposing point of view."

Vaidyanathan, T. G. "Jack Kerouac and Existentialist Anxiety." *Osmania Journal of English Studies* 2 (1962): 61-66.

Vaidyanathan discusses the quest for spiritiual satisfaction in Kerouac.

Van Den Haag, Ernest. "Kerouac Was Here." *Social Problems* 6 (1958): 21-28.
Dismissal of the Beats in general and Kerouac in particular. A similar piece by Van Den Haag is "Kerouac and the Beat: 'They've Nothing to Say and They Say It Badly'" in *Village Voice* 5 Nov. 1958: 5. Another similar piece by Van Den Haag is "Conspicuous Consumption of Self" in *National Review* 11 Apr. 1959: 658-660.

Vopat, Carole Gottlieb. "Jack Kerouac's *On the Road*: A Re-evaluation." *Midwest Quarterly* 14 (1973): 385-407.
How are the Beats depicted in *On the Road*? Are they in search of identity or are they avoiding the establishment of identity? See this material in Scott Donaldson, ed., *"On the Road": Text and Criticism* (New York: Penguin Books, Viking Critical Library, 1979): 431-450.

Wakefield, Dan. "Jack Kerouac Comes Home." *Atlantic Monthly* July 1965: 69-72.
Commentary on *On the Road* and *Desolation Angels*.

_____. "Night Clubs." *Nation* 4 Jan. 1958: 19-20.
A report on a reading by Kerouac.

Walsh, Joy. "Jack Kerouac: An American Alien in America." *Moody Street Irregulars: A Jack Kerouac Newsletter* 1.1 (1978): 8-10.
Kerouac's relationship to his ethnic heritage and to America. See this item in *Jack Kerouac: Statement in Brown: Collected Essays By Joy Walsh* (Clarence Center, NY: Textile Bridge Press, 1984).

_____. "Kerouac: A Reichian Interpretation." *Moody Street Irregulars: A Jack Kerouac Newsletter* 1.2 (1978): 3-5.
Psychoanalytic perspective on Kerouac. See this item in *Jack Kerouac: Statement in Brown: Collected Essays By Joy Walsh* (Clarence Center, NY: Textile Bridge Press, 1984).

Widmer, Kingsley. "The American Road: The Contemporary Novel." *University of Kansas City Review* 26 (1960): 309-317.

Some discussion of *The Dharma Bums* and *On the Road*, with focus on the road in literature, which is representative of "American yearning."

Wolfe, Bernard. "Angry at What?" *Nation* 1 Nov. 1958: 316, 318-322.
Discussion of English writers and Kerouac, particularly about Kerouac's problem with women.

Woods, Crawford. "Reconsideration: Jack Kerouac." *New Republic* 2 Dec. 1972: 26-30.
Renewed challenges to Kerouac's artistry.

Woolfson, Peter. "The French-Canadian Heritage of Jack Kerouac as Seen in His Autobiographical Works." *Revue De Louisiane/Louisiana Review* 5.1 (1976): 35-43.
Focus on Kerouac's works "centered around his early years at home," including *Visions of Gerard, Dr. Sax, The Town and the City*, and *Vanity of Duluoz*. Woolfson: "Kerouac's Franco-American heritage is deep and it remains a base to which he frequently retreats." Kerouac's works reveal "value orientations that appear to be French-Canadian in origin."

Audio-Visual Materials

The Jack Kerouac Collection. Audio cassettes. Produced by James Austin. Santa Monica, CA: Rhino Records, 1990.
A widely available and diverse selection of readings and performances. Material comes from previously released but now unavailable albums, including *Poetry for the Beat Generation*, a set of fourteen tracks done with Steve Allen's accompaniment on piano, among them "October in the Railroad Earth" and selections from *Mexico City Blues, Old Angel Midnight*, and *Heaven and Other Poems*. The recording *Blues and Haikus*, which features the musical backup of Al Cohn and Zoot Sims, has selections from *Scattered Poems, Some of the Dharma, Book of Blues*, and "Conclusion of the Railroad Earth." The collection also includes *Readings by Jack Kerouac on the Beat Generation*, among them a piece from *Desolation Angels*, fragments of poems, a selection from *Old Angel Midnight*, "The Beginning of Bop," a selection from *The*

Subterraneans, and the famous readings from *Visions of Cody* and *On the Road* on the Steve Allen Show in 1959. Liner notes to the collection are rich and varied. David Perry contributes a biographical essay, a brief survey of major works, and information about the original recordings. Jan Kerouac, Allen Ginsberg, Jerry Garcia, Stephen Ronan, Ann Charters, Steve Allen, Bob Thiele, William Burroughs, Michael C. Ford, Robert Frank, Ray Manzarek, Edith Kerouac Parker, Michael McClure, and Harvey Robert Kubernik contribute comments. Gerald Nicosia provides two pieces: "Kerouac as Musician" and "Kerouac at the Brandeis Forum: The Origin of 'The Origin of the Beat Generation.'" The liner notes feature many large photos and a bibliography.

A Jack Kerouac Romnibus. CD-ROM. New York: Penguin Electronics, 1995.
This CD-ROM features *The Dharma Bums* in hypertext. Also available are various paintings by Kerouac, images of artifacts and letters related to his life, music, commentaries from scholars, and a time line of his life.

Jack Kerouac's Road: A Franco-American Odyssey. Film available in video. Color. Sound. Herménégilde Chiasson. The National Film Board of Canada, 1987.
Focus on French-Catholic background. Interview of Kerouac conducted in French with subtitles in English. Comments from Ginsberg and Ferlinghetti.

Kerouac, Jack. *The Dharma Bums.* Two cassettes. Three hours. San Bruno, CA: Audio Literature, 1991.
Allen Ginsberg reads, in an abridged form, the novel by Jack Kerouac.

_____. *Mexico City Blues.* Two cassettes. Three hours. Boston: Shambhala Lion Editions, 1996.
Allen Ginsberg reads poetry by Kerouac. Unabridged.

_____. *On the Road.* Two cassettes. Three hours. St. Paul, MN: Penguin-Highbridge, 1993.
An abridged version of Kerouac's novel read by John Carradine.

_____. *Visions of Cody.* Two cassettes. Three hours. New York: Penguin Audiobooks, 1996.

An abridged version of Kerouac's giant novel read by Graham Parker.

Kerouac – Kicks Joy Darkness. Salem, MA: Rykodisc, 1997.

Promotional flier: "Four beat poets, two punk priestesses, a few folkies, two movie stars, and many rocksters render" selected works of Jack Kerouac, including many unpublished pieces "with the same sense of discovery, excitement, spontaneity and lust for life that Jack brought to all of his writing." The material is "a spoken word tribute with music."

McDarrah, Fred. *Kerouac and Friends.* New York: William Morrow, 1985.

Includes not only many black and white photos by Fred McDarrah of Kerouac, but various articles, including satirical material from *Mad*.

McDarrah, Fred, and Gloria McDarrah. *Beat Generation: Glory Days in Greenwich Village.* New York: Schirmer Books, 1996.

A chapter documents a collaborative poem done by Kerouac, Lew Welch, and Al Saijo at the apartment of Gloria Schoffel. A photo of Kerouac at the Artist's Studio captures Jack as he reads *On the Road*.

On the Road with Jack Kerouac. Color. Sound. 73 minutes. Active Home Video, 1990. New York: Mystic Fire Video, 1995.

This video makes available a slightly shortened version of John Antonelli's 90-minute film *Kerouac* (1984). Biographical study emphasizing youth in Lowell. Interviews with artists in Kerouac's milieu. Soundtrack features Ellington, Sims, and Mingus. Clips of appearances on *The Steve Allen Show* and *Firing Line with William Buckley*.

The Poetable Jack Kerouac and Selected Letters 1940-1956. New York: Thin Air Video, 1995.

Ann Charters reads from Kerouac's notes and postcards. Ginsberg reads from *Mexico City Blues*. Music in tribute to Kerouac is provided by Dave Van Ronk, Ed Sanders, David Amram, Graham Parker, and Lee Renaldo.

What Happened to Kerouac? Directed by Richard Lerner and Lewis MacAdams. 1985. Film available in video. Color. Sound. Video. 96 minutes. Vidmark, 1987.

Focuses on the adult Kerouac and his fall into alcoholism. Good sampling of scenes from Kerouac's appearances on *The Steve Allen Show* and William Buckley's *Firing Line*.

Addresses on the Internet

LitKicks by Levi Asher features biographical and bibliographical information on Kerouac, as well as news and announcements, at **http://www.charm.net/~brooklyn**.

Alex von Halem provides point-and-click access to other sites on Kerouac at **http://www.dtx.net/~vonhalem/kerouac.html**.

At   **http://www.nytimes.com/books/97/09/07/home/kerouac. html** one finds a listing of reviews and other articles related to Kerouac published in the *New York Times*, the *New York Times Book Review*, and the *New York Times Magazine*. Some of the dates posted for the articles and reviews are inaccurate, but one can gain access to each listed piece by clicking on the title. Reviews include John Brooks, "Of Growth and Decay," *New York Times Book Review* 5 Mar 1950: 6; Gilbert Millstein, "Books of the Times," *New York Times* 5 Sept. 1957: 27; David Dempsey, "In Pursuit of 'Kicks,'" *New York Times Book Review* 8 Sept. 1957: 4; David Dempsey, "Diary of a Bohemian," *New York Times Book Review* 23 Feb. 1958: 5; Nancy Wilson Ross, "Beat Buddhist," *New York Times Book Review* 5 Oct. 1958: 5, 14; David Dempsey, "Beatnik Bogeyman on the Prowl," *New York Times Book Review* 3 May 1959: 28-29; David Dempsey, "The Choice Jack Made," *New York Times Book Review* 19 July 1959: 4; Kenneth Rexroth, "Discordant and Cool," *New York Times Book Review* 29 Nov. 1959: 14; Daniel Talbot, Beat and Screaming," *New York Times Book Review* 19 June 1960: 4; Daniel Talbot, "On the Road Again," *New York Times Book Review* 27 Nov. 1960: 38; William Wiegand, "A Turn in the Road for the King of the Beats," *New York Times Book Review* 16 Sept 1962: 4, 43; Saul Maloff, "A Yawping at the Grave," *New York Times Book Review* 8 Sept. 1963: 4-5; Saul Maloff, "A Line Must Be Drawn," *New York Times Book*

Review 2 May 1965: 4; Andrew Sarris, "More Babbitt Than Beatnik," *New York Times Book Review* 26 Feb 1967: 5; Peter Sourian, "One-Dimensional Account," *New York Times Book Review* 18 Feb. 1968: 4, 51; and Aaron Latham, "Visions of Cody," *New York Times Book Review* 28 Jan. 1973: 42-43. (A comprehensive listing of reviews of Kerouac's work may be found in Robert Milewski, *Jack Kerouac: An Annotated Bibliography of Secondary Sources, 1944-1979*: 19-56.) Other articles posted on this internet site include Joseph Lelyveld, "Jack Kerouac, Novelist, Dead; Father of Beat Generation," *New York Times* 22 Oct. 1969: 47; William Plummer, "Jack Kerouac: The Beat Goes On," *New York Times Magazine* 30 Dec. 1979: 18-21, 23, 39; William E. Schmidt, "Beat Generation Elders Meet to Praise Kerouac," *New York Times* 30 July 1982: A8; Richard Hill, "Kerouac at the End of the Road," *New York Times Book Review* 29 May 1988: 1, 11; Kristan Schiller, "Kerouac's 'On the Road' and Its New Jersey Ties," *New York Times* 4 Dec. 1994, sec. 13NJ: 9C; and Ann Douglas, "On the Road Again," *New York Times Book Review* 9 Apr. 1995: 2, 21.

At http://www.freeyellow.com/members/upstartcrow/page3.html one finds reviews of Kerouac's *Some of the Dharma*, including "*Some of the Dharma*," *Kirkus Reviews* 1 July 1997, nonfiction section; "*Some of the Dharma*; Book Reviews," *Publishers Weekly* 14 July 1997: 72; and Tom Clark, "Kerouac's Inner Journey to Find Light and Meaning," *Washington Times* 7 Sept. 1997: B8. This site also provides links to the *Kerouac Quarterly* and The New York Public Library Kerouac Collection.

Audio selections from Rhino Records' *The Jack Kerouac Collection* can be heard at http://www-hsc.usc.edu/ ~gallaher/k_speaks/soundsource.html and also at http://www-hsc.usc.edu/~gallaher/kspeaks/kerouacspeaks.html.

A description of the annual festival Lowell Celebrates Kerouac! in Lowell, Massachusetts, is at http://members.aol.com/ LCKerouac/festival.htm.

A sampling of *A Jack Kerouac Romnibus*, the CD-ROM on Kerouac from Penguin Electronics, is available at http://www.mindinmotion.com/kerouac/index.html.

A selection from *The Subterraneans* is available at http://ie.uwindsor.ca/Jazz/welcome.html.

Highlights of Kerouac's career and three photos of him may be found at **http://www.cmgww.com/historic/kerouac/kerouac.html**.

Chapter 6

OTHER BEATS

The dog trots freely in the street
and has his own dog's life to live
and to think about
and to reflect upon
touching and tasting and testing everything
investigating everything
                    – Lawrence Ferlinghetti

The bibliographical paragraphs for this chapter are intended to address questions that teachers often have in mind when they prepare for doing a particular author in class. How is the author connected to the Beats? What are the major works of the author? Is there a volume of selected or collected writings that provides a sampling of an author, perhaps with an introductory chapter and notes? Are there introductory studies and collections of articles that can facilitate the work of students, especially in places where libraries have limited collections of periodicals? What recordings, videos, visual aids, or computer materials can be acquired to supplement and vary work in class? These bibliographical paragraphs stand by themselves and do not require the reader to figure out codes and then flip through the book; however, the generational links among authors make the scanning of the bibliography as a whole worthwhile in the consideration of any given author, and the author index facilitates access to the full bibliography. Finally, the selection of authors here is bound to

241

stimulate objections because a particular author or editor, for a particular reader, may or may not seem worthy of inclusion.

Donald Allen (1912-   )

Donald Allen may not be a Beat artist himself, but as an editor, anthologist, and publisher he is consummately Beat. Allen's anthology *The New American Poetry: 1945-1960* (New York: Grove Press, 1960), with its refreshing selections of poems, its inclusion of poetic statements by Beat artists, and its biographical information about the authors was a central text for the Beat literary movement. Allen combined with George F. Butterick to edit *The Postmoderns: The New American Poetry Revised* (New York: Grove Press, 1982), which updated the previous anthology. Donald Allen and Warren Tallman, eds., *The Poetics of the New American Poetry* (New York: Grove Press, 1973) gave space to many Beat writers to express their theories. See also Donald Allen and Robert Creeley, eds., *The New Writing in the USA* (Harmondsworth: Penguin, 1967). Without the support of Donald Allen, dozens of books of Beat writing would never have appeared in print, and Allen is the editor of numerous collections of poems, stories, letters, and other materials. In particular, Allen and Barney Rosset, as editors of *Evergreen Review*, gave many opportunities to Beat writers. Allen's correspondence is included at various collections of archives, but the principal site is the University of California, San Diego, where sixty-seven boxes of material are held. Michael Davidson, *Guide to the Donald Allen/Four Seasons Archive* (San Diego: University of California, 1978) is a pamphlet that explains the contents of the archive. A large photo of Allen appears in Ann Charters, *Beats and Company* (Garden City, NY: Doubleday, 1986): 59.

Amiri Baraka (1934-   )

The LeRoi Jones/Amiri Baraka Reader, ed. William J. Harris (NY: Thunder's Mouth Press, 1991) identifies periods in Baraka's development (including his Beat period) and presents a general selection including material from *Preface to a Twenty Volume Suicide*

Note, Blues People, The Dead Lecturer, Dutchman, Tales, and *The Autobiography of LeRoi Jones/Amiri Baraka.* A bibliography is included. In *Transbluency: Selected Poems 1961-1995,* ed. Paul Vangelisti (New York: Marsilio Publishers, 1995) substantial selections from ten volumes of poetry are in chronological order. *Funk Lore* (Los Angeles: Littoral Books, 1996) is the first book to follow *Transbluency.* Baraka's connection to the Beats is revealed by his inclusion in important anthologies related to the movement, including Ann Charters, ed., *The Portable Beat Reader* (New York: Viking Penguin, 1992), Anne Waldman, ed., *The Beat Book* (Boston: Shambhala, 1996), and Donald Allen, ed., *The New American Poetry: 1945-1960* (New York: Grove Press, 1960). Baraka himself is noted for his work as an editor of Beat writers in publications like *Yugen* and *Floating Bear.* See also LeRoi Jones, ed., *The Moderns: An Anthology of New Writing in America* (New York: Corinth Books, 1963). Baraka contributes "Expressive Language," "Hunting Is Not Those Heads on the Wall," and "State/meant" to Donald Allen and Warren Tallman, eds., *The Poetics of the New American Poetry* (New York: Grove Press, 1973): 373-383. Useful works for students are Kimberly Benston, ed., *Imamu Amiri Baraka (LeRoi Jones): A Collection of Critical Essays* (Englewood Cliffs, NJ: Prentice Hall, 1978) and Lloyd W. Brown, *Amiri Baraka* (Boston: Twayne, 1980). See also Stephen Gardner, "Amiri Baraka (LeRoi Jones)" in *The Dictionary of Literary Biography, Volume 5, American Poets Since World War II,* ed. Donald J. Greiner (Detroit: Gale Research, 1980): 21-27. An interview appears in David Ossman, *The Sullen Art* (New York: Corinth, 1963). Houston A. Baker, "'These Are Songs If You Have the/Music': An Essay on Imamu Baraka," *Minority Voices* 1.1 (Spring 1977): 1-18, provides interpretation, and A. Robert Lee, "Black Beats: The Signifying Poetry of LeRoi Jones/Amiri Baraka, Ted Joans, and Bob Kaufman" appears in *The Beat Generation Writers,* ed. A. Robert Lee (London: Pluto Press, 1996). Additional bibliographical information may be found in Theodore Hudson, *From LeRoi Jones to Amiri Baraka: The Literary Works* (Durham, NC: Duke University Press, 1973): 198-209, Thomas M. Inge, *Black American Writers: Bibliographical Essays, Volume 2: Richard Wright, Ralph Ellison, James Baldwin, and Amiri Baraka* (New York: St. Martin's, 1978): 121-178, and Werner Sollors, *Amiri Baraka/LeRoi Jones: The Quest for a "Populist Modernism"* (New York: Columbia University Press, 1978): 301-328. Videos include *Amiri Baraka: Literary Video* (Los Angeles: Lannan Foundation, 1991), *Recent*

Readings/NY, Volume 5: Baraka-Natumbo (New York: Thin Air Video, 1996), and *Dutchman* (San Francisco: California Newsreel, 1994). *Dutchman* on video is a convenient option for viewing Beat drama, and *The Lectures*, Volume 3 (New York: Thin Air Video, 1996) includes Baraka commenting on the state of the art of poetry in 1990.

Paul Blackburn (1926-1971)

Blackburn is associated with the Beats because for a time he edited and distributed *Black Mountain Review*, a journal that featured some writers connected to the Beat movement. Furthermore, he organized numerous readings that featured Beat writers, and the collection of tapes that documents these readings is now at the University of California, San Diego. Blackburn is included in Donald Allen's famous anthology *The New American Poetry: 1945-1960* (New York: Grove Press, 1960). *Early Selected y Mas* (Los Angeles: Black Sparrow Press, 1972) includes *The Dissolving Fabric* (1955), *The Nets* (1961), and *Brooklyn-Manhattan Transit* (1960), as well as *The Reardon Poems* (1967) and other uncollected poems. This volume of selected poems is superseded by *The Collected Poems of Paul Blackburn*, ed. Edith Jarolim (New York: Persea Books, 1985) and *The Selected Poems of Paul Blackburn*, ed. Edith Jarolim (New York: Persea Books, 1989). Blackburn's translations of French Troubadour poets appear in *Proensa: An Anthology of Troubadour Poetry*, ed. George Economou (Berkeley, CA/Los Angeles: University of California Press, 1978), and personal and autobiographical poems are in *Journals*, ed. Robert Kelley (Los Angeles: Black Sparrow Press, 1975). Edith Jarolim, "Paul Blackburn," in *The Beats: Literary Bohemians in Postwar America*, ed. Ann Charters (Detroit: Gale Research, 1983): 24-32, offers a worthy introduction. Articles include James Dickey, "Toward a Solitary Joy," *Hudson Review* 14 (Winter 1961-1962): 607-613, Stephen Fredman, "Paul Blackburn the Translator," *Chicago Review* 30 (Winter 1979): 152-156, Edith Jarolim, "Paul Blackburn: Twenty-two Poems/Introduction," *Sulfur* 4 (1982): 60-64, M. L. Rosenthal, "Paul Blackburn, Poet," *New York Times Book Review* 11 Aug. 1974: 27, and Gilbert Sorrentino, "Singing Virtuoso," *Parnassus* 4.2 (Spring-Summer 1976): 57-67. See also M. L. Rosenthal, *The New*

York Poets (New York: Oxford University Press, 1967) and Jerome Rothenberg, "A Preface, for Paul Blackburn," in *The Doctor Generosity Poets*, ed. Charles Shahoud Hanna (Wescosville, PA: Damascus Road Press, 1975). Marjorie Perloff, "On the Other Side of the Field: The Collected Poems of Paul Blackburn," in *Poetic License* (Evanston, IL: Northwestern University Press, 1990): 251-265 finds that Blackburn's output is better reflected in a selection of a hundred pages of poetry than in an exhaustive volume. Interviews appear in David Ossman, "Paul Blackburn," *The Sullen Art* (New York: Corinth Books, 1963): 22-26, L. S. Dembo, "An Interview with Paul Blackburn," *Contemporary Literature* 13 (Spring 1972): 133-143, and Patricia Norton and John O'Connell, "Craft Interview with Paul Blackburn," *The Craft of Poetry*, ed. William Packard (Garden City, NY: Doubleday, 1974): 11-17. For a complete listing of Blackburn's writings, see Kathleen Woodward, *Paul Blackburn: A Checklist* (San Diego: Archive for New Poetry, University of California, San Diego, 1980). See a photo in Ann Charters, *Beats and Company* (Garden City, NY: Doubleday, 1986): 89.

Paul Bowles (1910-   ) and Jane Bowles (1917-1973)

Millicent Dillon, ed., *The Portable Paul and Jane Bowles* (New York: Viking, 1994) provides handy access to a wide variety of materials, and Dillon's introduction and annotations help the reader new to Paul and Jane Bowles. Paul Bowles has written for various little magazines, but his connection to the Beats is perhaps clearest in *The Sheltering Sky* (New York: Ecco Press, 1978), a novel previously published by New Directions in New York in 1949. Paul Bowles' work, with its treatment of the underground in North Africa and the expression of personal emptiness in the twentieth century, is clearly related to the work of William S. Burroughs. Other works include Paul Bowles, *Without Stopping: An Autobiography* (New York: Putnam, 1972), *The Delicate Prey* (New York: Ecco Press, 1972), *The Selected Writings of Paul Bowles* (New York: Ecco Press, 1993), *Let It Come Down* (Los Angeles: Black Sparrow Press, 1980), and *The Spider's House* (Los Angeles: Black Sparrow Press, 1955). See also Caroline G. Bokinsky, "Paul Bowles," in *The Dictionary of Literary Biography, Volume 5, American Poets Since World War II*, ed. Donald J. Greiner (Detroit: Gale Research, 1980): 92-96. Jane Bowles' writings include *Feminine Wiles* (Los Angeles: Black Sparrow Press, 1976) and *Out in the World: Selected Letters of Jane Bowles 1935-1970* (Los Angeles: Black Sparrow Press, 1985). See "Jane Bowles: A Life at the End of the World" in Brenda Knight, ed., *The Women of the Beat Generation* (Berkeley, CA: Conari Press, 1996): 18-27, and Jennie Skerl, *A Tawdry Place of Salvation: The Art of Jane Bowles* (Carbondale: Southern Illinois University Press, 1997). On the companion cassette tapes to *The Women of the Beat Generation* (San Bruno, CA: Audio Literature, 1996), Mary Norbert Korte reads several selections by Jane Bowles. See John W. Aldridge, "Paul Bowles: The Cancelled Sky" in *After the Lost Generation: A Critical Study of the Writers of Two Wars* (New York: McGraw-Hill, 1951): 184-193, Oliver Evans, "Paul Bowles and the 'Natural Man'" in *Recent American Fiction*, ed. Joseph J. Waldmeir (Boston: Houghton Mifflin, 1963): 141-143, Ihab H. Hassan, "The Pilgrim as Prey: A Note on Paul Bowles," in *Radical Innocence: Studies in the Contemporary American Novel* (Provincetown, NJ: Princeton University Press, 1961): 86-87, Theodore Solotaroff, "Paul Bowles: The Desert Within" in *The Red Hot Vacuum, and Other Pieces on the Writing of the Sixties* (New York: Atheneum, 1970): 254-260, and Heinrich Straumann, *American Literature in the Twentieth Century* (New York: Harper and Row, 1965): 79-80. A video *Paul Bowles in Morocco* (New York: Mystic Fire Video, 1995) presents Paul Bowles speaking about his life, reading from his work, and leading a tour of Morocco.

Richard Brautigan (1935-1984)

Sometimes called the "last Beat," Richard Brautigan gained widespread popularity during the era of flowers in San Francisco. At first inspection, Brautigan seems to favor humor, but a dark perspective lurks always beneath the surface. *A Confederate General from Big Sur, Dreaming of Babylon, and The Hawkline Monster* (Boston: Houghton Mifflin, 1991) is a gathering of multiple works, as is *Trout Fishing in America, The Pill Versus the Springhill Mine Disaster, and In Watermelon Sugar* (Boston: Houghton Mifflin/Seymour Lawrence, 1989). Works of poetry include *Rommel Drives on Deep into Egypt* (New York: Delacorte Press/Seymour

Lawrence, 1970), *The Pill Versus the Springhill Mine Disaster* (San Francisco: Four Seasons Foundation, 1968), *Loading Mercury with a Pitchfork* (New York: Simon and Schuster, 1976), *June 30th, June 30th* (New York: Delacorte Press/Seymour Lawrence, 1977), and *The Galilee Hitch-Hiker* (San Francisco: White Rabbit Press, 1958). Novels include *The Abortion: An Historical Romance 1966* (New York: Simon and Schuster, 1971), *A Confederate General from Big Sur* (New York: Grove Press, 1964), *Dreaming of Babylon: A Private Eye Novel 1942* (New York: Delacorte Press/Seymour Lawrence, 1977), *The Hawkline Monster: A Gothic Western* (New York: Simon and Schuster, 1974), *In Watermelon Sugar* (San Francisco: Four Seasons Foundation, 1968), *Sombrero Fallout: A Japanese Novel* (New York: Simon and Schuster, 1976), *The Tokyo-Montana Express* (New York: Delacorte Press/Seymour Lawrence, 1980), *Trout Fishing in America* (San Francisco: Four Seasons Foundation, 1967), and *Willard and His Bowling Trophies: A Perverse Mystery* (New York: Simon and Schuster, 1975). A collection of stories is *Revenge of the Lawn: Stories 1962-1970* (New York: Simon and Schuster, 1971). A good starting point is Caroline G. Bokinsky, "Richard Brautigan," in *The Dictionary of Literary Biography, Volume 5, American Poets Since World War II*, ed. Donald J. Greiner (Detroit: Gale Research, 1980): 96-99. See Edward Halsey Foster, *Richard Brautigan* (Boston: Twayne, 1983), Marc Chenetier, *Richard Brautigan* (New York: Methuen, 1983), Keith Abbot, *Downstream from Trout Fishing in America: A Memoir of Richard Brautigan* (Santa Barbara, CA: Capra Press, 1989), Jay Boyer, *Richard Brautigan* (Boise, ID: Boise State University, 1987), and Terence Malley, *Richard Brautigan* (New York: Warner Paperback Library, 1972). See also Michael McClure, "Ninety-One Things About Richard Brautigan," in Michael McClure, *Lighting the Corners* (Albuquerque: University of New Mexico College of Arts and Sciences, 1993): 36-68. Erik Weber, *Richard Brautigan, 1967-1978: Photographs* (San Francisco: E. Weber, 1990) offers a visual perspective on this colorful author. *Listening to Richard Brautigan* (Hollywood, CA: Harvest, 1970) features Brautigan reading in an LP album format. At the Woodberry Poetry Room at Harvard College Library, one can find reel tapes of Ron Loewinsohn lecturing at Harvard on Whalen, Snyder, and Brautigan on April 22 and 27, 1970. John F. Barber, *Richard Brautigan: An Annotated Bibliography* (Jefferson, NC: McFarland, 1990) provides in-depth bibliographical information.

Bonnie Bremser (Brenda Frazer, 1939-   )

Troia: Mexican Memoirs (New York: Croton Press, 1969) is a travel narrative that invites comparisons with Kerouac's *On the Road* (1957). Bremser's work was republished as *For Love of Ray* (London: London Magazine Editions, 1971), and the new title reveals the narrative's emphasis on Brenda Frazer's relationship with poet and fugitive Ray Bremser. In Michael Perkins, "Bonnie Bremser," *The Beats: Literary Bohemians in Postwar America*, ed. Ann Charters (Detroit: Gale Research, 1983): 33-35, one finds background on Bremser's life and book. An excerpt of *Troia* appears in Ann Charters, ed., *The Portable Beat Reader* (New York: Viking, 1992). See also Amy Friedman, "'I Say My New Name': Women Writers of the Beat Generation," *The Beat Generation Writers*, ed. A. Robert Lee (London: Pluto Press, 1996): 200-216, Ann Charters, *Beats and Company* (Garden City, NY: Doubleday, 1986): 101, and "Brenda Frazer: Transformed Genius," in Brenda Knight, ed., *The Women of the Beat Generation* (Berkeley, CA: Conari Press, 1996): 269-278. On the companion cassette tapes to *The Women of the Beat Generation* (San Bruno, CA: Audio Literature, 1996), Brenda Frazer reads an excerpt from *Troia: Mexican Memoirs*.

Ray Bremser (1934-   )

Bremser's work includes *Poems of Madness* (New York: Paperbook Gallery, 1965), *Angel* (New York: Tompkins Square Press, 1967), *Drive Suite* (San Francisco: Nova Broadcast Press, 1968), *Black Is Black Blues* (Buffalo: Intrepid Press, 1971), and *Blowing Mouth/The Jazz Poems 1958-1970* (Cherry Valley, NY: Cherry Valley Editions, 1978). Bremser's work appears in Donald Allen, ed., *The New American Poetry* (New York: Grove Press, 1960), Seymour Krim, ed., *The Beats* (Greenwich, CT: Fawcett, 1960), and Ann Charters, ed., *The Portable Beat Reader* (New York: Viking Penguin, 1992). Arnold Moodnik and Mikail Horowitz, "Ray Bremser," *The Beats: Literary Bohemians in Postwar America*, ed. Ann Charters (Detroit: Gale Research, 1983): 35-42, provides background. See Ann Charters, *Beats and Company* (Garden City, NY: Doubleday, 1986): 100-101. *Bremser: The Jazz Poems* (New

York: Thin Air Video, 1996) features Bremser reading "The Christmas Poem or Letter," "Frankenstein," and "Monk in Moonshot."

Chandler Brossard (1922-   )

Brossard's novel *Who Walk in Darkness* (New York: New Directions, 1952) invites comparisons with Kerouac's *The Town and the City* (1950). Brossard was the editor of *The Scene Before You: A New Approach to American Culture* (New York: Rinehart, 1958). For production at the Crystal Palace, a cabaret playhouse owned by Jay Landesman, Brossard wrote several plays: *Harry the Magician* (1961), *Some Dreams Aren't Real* (1962), and *The Man with Ideas* (1962). A selection from Brossard appears in Seymour Krim, ed., *The Beats* (Greenwich, CT: Fawcett, 1960). Sam Charters, "Chandler Brossard," *The Beats: Literary Bohemians in Postwar America*, ed. Ann Charters (Detroit: Gale Research, 1983): 43-45, offers background information. See also Chandler Brossard, "Hidalgo Redeemed," *The Review of Contemporary Fiction* 13.1 (1993); take note of *The Review of Contemporary Fiction* 7.1 (1987), which is an issue devoted to Brossard and includes bibliographical information.

Lenny Bruce (Leonard Alfred Schneider, 1926-1966)

Lenny Bruce was a stand-up comedian whose material precipitated an obscenity trial and a 1964 conviction for giving an obscene performance. Bruce dedicated the rest of his life to demonstrating that the conviction was wrongheaded. His autobiography *How to Talk Dirty and Influence People* (New York: Fireside, 1992) was originally published in 1965. The play *Lenny* by Julian Barry (1971) was later produced as a film *Lenny* (1974), in which Dustin Hoffman played the role of Bruce. A sound recording of the play is also available (Beverly Hills, CA: Blue Thumb, no date). A conversation between Hugh Hefner and Bruce is on *Playboy's Penthouse (The Beat Episode)*, a black and white video (1959). *Lenny Bruce Performance Film* (1968), a black and white video produced by John Magnuson, features Lenny Bruce on stage.

As of 1992, Rhino Home Video offered this title. "Shorty Peterstein Interview," "Djinni in the Candy Store," "Enchanting Transylavania," "How to Relax Your Colored Friends at Parties," "Lima, Ohio," "Comic at the Palladium," and "In Which the Artist Discusses 'The Lie'" are included on *Howls, Raps, and Roars: Recordings from the San Francisco Poetry Renaissance* (Berkeley, CA: Fantasy Records, 1993). See William Karl Thomas, *Lenny Bruce: The Making of a Prophet* (Hamden, CT: Archon Books, 1989) and Frank Kofsky, *Lenny Bruce: The Comedian as Social Critic and Secular Moralist* (New York: Monad Press/Pathfinder Press, 1974).

Charles Bukowski (1920-1994)

Born in Germany, Bukowski came to the United States when he was still a toddler. He grew up in Los Angeles and became an employee of the United States Postal Service. For *Open City*, a Los Angeles newspaper, Bukowski contributed a regular column titled "Notes of a Dirty Old Man." These columns were later collected in *Notes of a Dirty Old Man* (San Francisco: City Lights, 1973). Bukowski's connection to the Beats is clear in one of the columns, which recounts a meeting with Neal Cassady in Los Angeles a few days before Cassady's death in Mexico on February 4, 1968, and this column is reprinted in Ann Charters, ed., *The Portable Beat Reader* (New York: Viking Penguin, 1992) and David Kherdian, ed., *Beat Voices* (New York: Henry Holt, 1995). Bukowski is the author of more than forty-five books, among them the poetry collections *The Days Run Away Like Wild Horses Over the Hills* (Los Angeles: Black Sparrow Press, 1969), *Mockingbird Wish Me Luck* (Los Angeles: Black Sparrow Press, 1972), *Burning in Water Drowning in Flame: Selected Poems 1955-1973* (Los Angeles: Black Sparrow Press, 1974), *Love Is a Dog from Hell* (Santa Barbara, CA: Black Sparrow Press, 1977), *War All the Time: Poems 1981-1984* (Santa Barbara, CA: Black Sparrow Press, 1984), *The Roominghouse Madrigals: Early Selected Poems 1946-1966* (Santa Rosa, CA: Black Sparrow Press, 1988), and *The Last Night of the Earth Poems* (Santa Rosa, CA: Black Sparrow Press, 1992). *Ham on Rye: A Novel* (Santa Barbara, CA: Black Sparrow Press, 1982) gives an impression of Bukowski as a writer of fiction. Among his most recently published materials are *Betting on the Muse: Poems and Stories* (Santa Rosa, CA: Black Sparrow Press, 1996) and *Bone Palace Ballet: New Poems* (Santa Rosa, CA: Black Sparrow Press, 1997). Douglas Blazek, ed., *A Bukowski Sampler* (Madison, WI: Quixote Press, 1969) is updated by John Martin, ed., *Run with the Hunted: A Charles Bukowski Reader* (New York: Harper Perennial, 1994), and for this collection an audio cassette of the same title is available (New York: Caedmon/Harper Audio, 1993). Available correspondence includes Seamus Cooney, ed., *The Bukowski/Purdy Letters: A Decade of Dialogue, 1964-1974* (Santa Barbara, CA: Paget Press, 1983) and Seamus Cooney, ed., *Living on Luck: Selected Letters 1960's-1970's, Volume 2* (Santa Rosa, CA: Black Sparrow Press, 1995). Studies of Bukowski include William Joyce, *Miller, Bukowski and Their Enemies: Essays on Contemporary Culture* (Greensboro, NC: Avisson Press, 1996), Hugh Fox, *Charles Bukowski: A Critical and Bibliographical Study* (Los Angeles: Abyss Publications, 1969), Gerald Locklin, *Charles Bukowski: A Sure Bet* (Sudbury, MA: Water Row Press, 1996), Bob Graalman, "Charles Bukowski," in *The Dictionary of Literary Biography, Volume 5, American Poets Since World War II*, ed. Donald J. Greiner (Detroit: Gale Research, 1980): 112-116, and Russell Harrison, *Against the American Dream: Essays on Charles Bukowski* (Santa Rosa, CA: Black Sparrow Press, 1994). Gay Brewer, *Charles Bukowski* (New York: Twayne, 1997) is a valuable full-length study of Bukowski, and Neeli Cherkovski, *Bukowski: A Life* (South Royalton, VT: Steerforth Press, 1997) replaces a previous biography by Cherkovski published in 1991. In Rudi Horemans, ed., *Beat Indeed!* (Antwerp, Belgium: EXA, 1985) one finds Chris Challis, "Bukowski, Drain a Last, Tired Beer" and Rudi Horemans, "Charles Bukowski's Playful Perversions," and these selections provide background and interpretation. On CD, one may acquire *Bukowski Reads His Poetry* (Santa Rosa, CA: Black Sparrow Graphic Art, 1995); a video *Bukowski at Bellevue* (Santa Rosa, CA: Black Sparrow Press, 1988) is also available. *The Movie, "Barfly": An Original Screenplay by Charles Bukowski for a Film by Barbet Schroeder* (Santa Rosa, CA: Black Sparrow Press, 1987) is available for comparison with the film itself. On the internet, if one sends the message **subscribe bukowski name** to **listproc@bigendian.com**, one can join an on-line exchange of ideas on Bukowski.

William S. Burroughs, Jr. (1947-1981)

The original separate editions of *Speed* (New York: Olympia Press, 1970) and *Kentucky Ham* (New York: Dutton, 1973) are now published as *Speed/Kentucky Ham* (Woodstock, NY: The Overlook Press, 1993). Ann Charters provides an introduction for this combined volume. Jennie Skerl and James Grauerholz, "William S. Burroughs, Jr.," *The Beats: Literary Bohemians in Postwar America*, ed. Ann Charters (Detroit: Gale Research, 1983): 69-75, provides an overview of Burroughs, who is the son of William S. Burroughs, Sr., and Joan Vollmer. See also Aram Saroyan, "A Death in the Family," *Village Voice* 22-28 Apr. 1981: 41. See Arthur Winfield Knight, "Journal Notes: William Burroughs, Jr., in Boulder," in Rudi Horemans, ed., *Beat Indeed!* (Antwerp, Belgium: EXA, 1985): 105. A pair of cassettes of a reading and an interview at the New School of Social Research (31 Mar. 1981) includes Stephen King, Herbert Lieberman, and William S. Burroughs, Jr. Colgate University has the tapes as part of its library holdings.

Paul Carroll (1927-   )

Carroll's connection to the Beats stems from Carroll's role as editor of *Chicago Review* (1958-1959) and his publication of various materials by Kerouac, Ginsberg, Burroughs, and other Beats. The material provoked controversy, sparked largely by Jack Mabley, "Filthy Writing on the Midway," *Chicago Daily News* 25 Oct. 1958. To circumvent oppression of *Chicago Review*, Irving Rosenthal and Paul Carroll worked together to produce *Big Table*, an independent journal that featured in the spring of 1959 excerpts from William S. Burroughs' *Naked Lunch* and Jack Kerouac's *Old Angel Midnight*. Later issues featured selections from *Kaddish and Other Poems* by Ginsberg, *Her* by Ferlinghetti, and other pieces. *Big Table* ran for five issues and published material by Beat and non-Beat authors. *The Poem in Its Skin* (Chicago: Big Table, 1968) offers interpretations of ten poems, including work by Ginsberg, Creeley, and O'Hara. Carroll's discussion of Ginsberg's "Wichita Vortex Sutra" appears in Lewis Hyde, ed., *On the Poetry of Allen Ginsberg* (Ann Arbor: University of Michigan Press, 1984): 292-313. Carroll's books of poems include *Odes* (Chicago: Big Table, 1969), *The Luke Poems* (Chicago: Big Table, 1971), and *New & Selected Poems* (Chicago: Yellow Press, 1978). See Douglas K. Macdonald, "Paul Carroll," *The Beats: Literary Bohemians in Postwar America*, ed. Ann Charters (Detroit: Gale Research, 1983): 75-80. For selections of previously published material, see Paul Carroll, *Chicago Tales* (Chicago: Big Table Press, 1991). Paul Carroll interviews Lawrence Ferlinghetti (Mar. 1975) on WFMT in Chicago. The University of California, Berkeley, holds the tape at the Bancroft Poetry Archive. Carroll's poem "Father" is in Donald Allen, *The New American Poetry* (New York: Grove Press, 1960).

Carolyn Cassady (1923-   )

Carolyn Cassady is associated with the Beat Generation because of her marriage to Neal Cassady and the three-way relationship among Jack Kerouac, Neal Cassady, and Carolyn Cassady. Her memoir *Heart Beat: My Life with Jack and Neal* (Berkeley, CA: Creative Arts, 1976) recounts this relationship. This work was later converted into a feature film *Heart Beat*, with Sissy Spacek, Nick Nolte, and John Hurt, but the production was disappointing. *Off the Road: My Years with Cassady, Kerouac, and Ginsberg* (New York: Penguin, 1990) is a more thorough memoir than *Heart Beat*. For additional reflection on the Beats, see "As I See It," *The Beats: Literary Bohemians in Postwar America*, ed. Ann Charters (Detroit: Gale Research, 1983): 607-620. Joy Walsh, "Carolyn Cassady," *The Beats: Literary Bohemians in Postwar America*, ed. Ann Charters (Detroit: Gale Research, 1983), gives biographical and background information. In Barry Gifford, ed., *As Ever: The Collected Correspondence of Allen Ginsberg and Neal Cassady* (Berkeley, CA: Creative Arts, 1977), Carolyn Cassady provides a foreword. See Carolyn Cassady, "Life with Jack and Neal," in *The Beat Vision*, eds. Arthur Knight and Kit Knight (New York: Paragon, 1987): 29-51, Ann Charters, *Beats and Company* (Garden City, NY: Doubleday, 1986): 54, and "Carolyn Cassady: Karmic Grace" in Brenda Knight, ed., *The Women of the Beat Generation* (Berkeley, CA: Conari Press, 1996): 57-76. On the companion cassette tapes to *The Women of the Beat Generation* (San Bruno, CA: Audio Literature, 1996), Carolyn Cassady reads an excerpt from *Off the Road*. For Neal Cassady,

Grace Beats Karma: Letters from Prison 1958-1960 (New York: Blast Books, 1993), Carolyn Cassady provides a foreword, notes, and a letter to Jack Kerouac (22 Apr. 1959). *The New York Beat Generation Show: Volume Two: Women and the Beats* (New York: Thin Air Video, 1995) includes a brief interview with Carolyn Cassady. Carolyn Cassady also appears in John Antonelli's *Kerouac*, a film which has been reproduced as a video under the title *On the Road with Jack Kerouac*. The same film is now available in video as *Kerouac* (New York: Mystic Fire Video, 1995).

Neal Cassady (1926-1968)

Cassady is the real-life person corresponding to Dean Moriarty and Cody Pomeray in the novels of Jack Kerouac. Cassady's autobiography, *The First Third and Other Writings* (San Francisco: City Lights, 1971), which was revised and expanded in 1981, reveals the struggles of Neal's early life, and *As Ever: The Collected Correspondence of Allen Ginsberg and Neal Cassady* (Berkeley, CA: Creative Arts, 1977) provides information about the literary and romantic ties between Cassady and Ginsberg. A lengthy letter (23,000 words) known as the "Joan Anderson letter" exists now only as a 5,000 word fragment, but from this letter, which is now included in *The First Third* under the title "To Have Seen a Specter Isn't Everything . . . " (146-160), Kerouac took inspiration for spontaneous composition based on real life. William Plummer, *The Holy Goof* (Englewood Cliffs, NJ: Prentice Hall, 1981) is a biography now republished (New York: Paragon, 1990). Cassady is described in "The Gandy Dancer 1981" in John Clellon Holmes, *Representative Men* (Fayetteville: University of Arkansas Press, 1988): 201-210. See "Prison Letters from Neal Cassady to Carolyn Cassady" in *Pearl* 13-14 (Summer 1992 and Winter 1993) or *Grace Beats Karma: Letters from Prison 1958-1960* (New York: Blast Books, 1993). Gerald Nicosia, "Neal Cassady," *The Beats: Literary Bohemians in Postwar America*, ed. Ann Charters (Detroit: Gale Research, 1983): 92-114, provides detailed treatment of Cassady's life and literary influence. See Steven Watson, "Neal Cassady," *The Birth of the Beat Generation* (New York: Pantheon, 1995): 78-94, Gregory Stephenson, "Friendly and Flowing Savage: The Literary Legend of Neal Cassady," in *The Daybreak Boys* (Carbondale: University of Southern Illinois Press,

1990): 154-171, and Clive Bush, "'Why Do We Always Say Angel?':
Herbert Huncke and Neal Cassady," in *The Beat Generation Writers*,
ed. A. Robert Lee (London: Pluto Press, 1996): 128-157. Gian
Berriault, "Neal's Ashes," *Rolling Stone* 12 Oct. 1972: 32, 34, 36,
reviews the legend of Cassady and clarifies it through an interview
with Carolyn Cassady. "Pierre Delattre Remembers Neal Cassady,"
The Beat Vision, eds. Arthur Knight and Kit Knight, is an interview
that reflects on Cassady. A video *Neal Cassady in the Backhouse, On
the Road* (Key-Z Productions, 1990) runs 52 minutes and is available
at the library at Northern Illinois University. *Neal Cassady Drive
Alive* is an audio tape available from Key-Z productions.

Andy Clausen (1943-)

Clausen calls himself a "rebeat" poet. He draws inspiration from
his meeting with Neal Cassady in 1968. He taught briefly at Naropa
in 1980. His poetry has won him friendship with Corso and
Ginsberg, who have combined with him for readings on various oc-
casions. His books include *Extreme Unction* (Salt Lake City: Litmus,
1974), *Shoe Be Do Be Ee-Op* (Oakland: Renegade Press, 1975), and
Austin, Texas, Austin, Texas (Austin: Place of Herons Press, 1981).
See Tom Swartz and Michel Wojczuk, "Andy Clausen," *The Beats:
Literary Bohemians in Postwar America*, ed. Ann Charters (Detroit:
Gale Research, 1983): 115-117. See Clausen in *Renegade: The Bay
Area Review of North American Migrant and Off-the-Wall Literature*
(Berkeley, CA: Cross Cut Saw, 1977). *Recent Readings/NY, Volume
14: Micheline-Clausen* (New York: Thin Air Video, 1996) divides a
cassette between performances of Clausen and Jack Micheline.

Gregory Corso (1930-)

Gregory Corso is often regarded as a principal member of the
Beat Generation, along with Jack Kerouac, Allen Ginsberg, and
William Burroughs. When Corso emerged from prison in 1950, he
met Allen Ginsberg, who took an interest in the young poet's work
and introduced Corso to Kerouac, Burroughs, and John Clellon
Holmes. Corso's first book, *The Vestal Lady on Brattle* (Cambridge,

MA: Richard Brukenfeld, 1955) was published with funds raised among students at Harvard and Radcliffe. Ferlinghetti recognized Corso by publishing *Gasoline* (San Francisco: City Lights, 1958). Selections from these two books, along with selections from *The Happy Birthday of Death* (New York: New Directions, 1960), *Long Live Man* (New York: New Directions, 1962), *Elegiac Feelings American* (New York: New Directions, 1970), and *Herald of the Autochthonic Spirit* (New York: New Directions, 1981) are in *Mindfield: New and Selected Poems* (New York: Thunder's Mouth Press, 1989), which includes a substantial selection from Corso's major works and some previously unpublished poems. Forewords are written by Ginsberg and Burroughs, and drawings by Corso adorn the text. Other writings include *The American Express* (Paris: Olympia Press, 1961), a work in prose. Corso's efforts at playwrighting include *In This Hung-Up Age: A One-Act Farce Written 1954*, in *New Directions in Prose and Poetry* 18, ed. James Laughlin (New York: New Directions, 1964): 149-161, *Standing on a Streetcorner: A Little Play*, in *Evergreen Review* 6 (Mar./Apr. 1962): 63-78, and *That Little Black Door on the Left*, in *Pardon Me, Sir, But Is My Eye Hurting Your Elbow?*, compiled by Bob Booker and George Foster (New York: Geis, 1967): 159-163. "Variations on a Generation," a prose commentary on beatness, is included in Thomas A. Parkinson, ed., *A Casebook on the Beat* (New York: Crowell, 1961): 88-97, and a selection from "Variations" is in *The Portable Beat Reader*, ed. Ann Charters (New York: Viking Penguin, 1992), along with other selected material by Corso. "Some of My Beginning . . . and What I Feel Right Now" is another prose commentary, and it is included in *Poets on Poetry*, ed. Howard Nemerov (New York: Basic Books, 1966): 172-181. See also Gregory Corso, *Poems, Interview, Photographs* (Louisville, KY: White Fields Press, 1994), in which Corso offers "On My Way Here," "Gregorian Rant," and an interview set in combination with a series of recent photos. See also Robert King, "Gregory Corso: An Interview," in *The Beat Diary*, eds. Arthur Winfield Knight and Kit Knight (California, PA: unspeakable visions of the individual, 1977): 4-24. Corso is also included in Donald Allen, ed., *The New American Poetry* (New York: Grove Press, 1960), Donald Allen and George F. Butterick, eds., *The New American Poetry Revised* (New York: Grove Press, 1982), Seymour Krim, ed., *The Beats* (Greenwich, CT: Fawcett, 1960), Anne Waldman, *The Beat Book* (Boston: Shambhala, 1996), Park Honan, *The Beats* (London: J. M. Dent, 1987), Elias Wilentz, ed.,

The Beat Scene (New York: Corinth Books, 1960), and David Kherdian, ed., *Beat Voices* (New York: Henry Holt, 1995). Robert A. Wilson, *A Bibliography of Works by Gregory Corso, 1954-1965* (New York: Phoenix Book Shop, 1966) provides a listing of primary sources; secondary sources include Gregory Stephenson, *Exiled Angel: A Study of the Work of Gregory Corso* (London: Hearing Eye, 1989), which is the only full-length study of Corso's poetry, offering individual chapters on principal collections of poetry. Thomas McClanahan, "Gregory Corso," in *The Dictionary of Literary Biography, Volume 5, American Poets Since World War II*, ed. Donald J. Greiner (Detroit: Gale Research, 1980): 142-148 offers analysis and bibliographical references. "Corso, (Nunzio) Gregory" in Susan M. Trosky, ed., *Contemporary Authors*, New Revision Series, Volume 41 (Detroit: Gale Research, 1994): 82-86 is a similar study. Neeli Cherkovski, "Revolutionary of the Spirit: Gregory Corso" is a chapter in *Whitman's Wild Children* (San Francisco: Lapis, 1988). Bruce Cook, "An Urchin Shelley" appears in *The Beat Generation* (New York: Quill, 1994). Carolyn Gaiser, "Gregory Corso: A Poet the Beat Way" is in Thomas Parkinson, ed., *A Casebook on the Beat* (New York: Crowell, 1961). Edward Halsey Foster, "Corso," is a major portion of *Understanding the Beats* (Columbia: University of South Carolina Press, 1992). Richard Howard, "Gregory Corso: 'Surely There'll Be Another Table,'" is one of many chapters in *Alone with America* (New York: Atheneum, 1969). Gregory Stephenson, "The Arcadian Map: Notes on the Poetry of Gregory Corso" is a chapter in *The Daybreak Boys: Essays on the Literature of the Beat Generation* (Carbondale: Southern Illinois University Press, 1990). John Fuller, "The Poetry of Gregory Corso," *London Magazine*, new series 1 (Apr. 1961): 74-77 offers a brief perspective. Nancy Grayson, "How Does a Poem Teach: 'Poets Hitchhiking on the Highway' and the Process of Critical Reading" appears in *CEA Forum* 13, 3-4 (1983): 24-26. Dennis Grunes, "The Mythifying Memory: Corso's 'Elegiac Feelings American'" is included in *Contemporary Poetry: A Journal of Criticism* 2.3 (1977): 51-61. Geoffrey Thurley, "The Development of the New Language: Michael McClure, Philip Whalen, and Gregory Corso" is reproduced in *The Beats: Essays in Criticism* (Jefferson, NC: McFarland, 1981): 165-180. "Gregory Corso" is a chapter in *The Beat Vision*, eds. Arthur Winfield Knight and Kit Knight (New York: Paragon, 1987): 151-184. See Ann Charters, *Beats and Company* (Garden City, NY: Doubleday, 1986): 48-50, 53, 121, 122, 124, 148. Jim Philip, "Journeys in the Mindfield: Gregory Corso Reconsidered," appears in *The Beat Generation Writers*, ed. A. Robert Lee (London: Pluto Press, 1996): 61-73, Marilyn Schwartz, "Gregory Corso," in *The Beats: Literary Bohemians in Postwar America* (Detroit: Gale Research, 1983): 117-140 offers valuable background, and William Lawlor, "Gregory Corso," in *Cyclopedia of World Authors*, eds. Frank N. Magill, McCrea Adams, and Juliane Brand (Pasadena, CA: Salem Press, 1997): 459-460 offers a compact summary of Corso's life and literary production. See also Gerald J. Dullea, "Ginsberg and Corso: Image and Imagination," *Thoth* 11 (1971): 17-27. A video *Beat Legends: Gregory Corso* (New York: Thin Air Video, 1994) reveals the spirit and personality of the poet. *Howls, Raps, and Roars: Recordings from the San Francisco Poetry Renaissance* (Berkeley, CA: Fantasy Records, 1993) is a set of CD's that features Corso reading "In the Fleeting Hand of Time," "Vision of Rotterdam," "The Last Warmth of Arnold," "Mexican Impressions," "Botticelli Spring," "Sun–A Spontaneous Poem," "Ode to Coit Tower," and "I Am 25." A film *Gregory Corso Reads from the U.S. Constitution and Bill of Rights* (James Rasin and Jerry Poynton, 1992) may be hard to acquire. Those interested in Corso's artwork may want to examine *The Saturn Family: Drawings by Gregory Corso* (Charleston: Parchment Gallery, 1981). One can see and hear Corso on *The New York Beat Generation Show: Volume One: History and Overview: The Censorship Years* (New York: Thin Air Video, 1995) and Maria Beatty, *Gang of Souls* (New York: Mystic Fire Video, 1988).

Robert Creeley (1926–   )

Robert Creeley has a long, distinguished career apart from any interconnections with the Beats, but a principal link to the Beat movement developed when Creeley served as editor of *Black Mountain Review* and brought together in a single volume Kerouac, Burroughs, Ginsberg, McClure, Whalen, and Snyder with Black Mountain writers Jonathan Williams, Joel Oppenheimer, Denise Levertov, Charles Olson, and Robert Creeley. Ginsberg served as contributing editor. Creeley's first book was *Le Fou* (Columbus, OH: Golden Goose Press, 1952), but he had more success with *For Love: Poems 1950-1960* (New York: Scribner's, 1962). *Selected Poems* (New York: Scribner's, 1976) is superseded by *The Collected*

Poems: 1945-1975 (Berkeley: University of California Press, 1982).
Other works published in Berkeley by the University of California
Press are *The Collected Prose* (1988), *The Collected Essays* (1989),
and *Selected Poems* (1991). Correspondence includes *Charles Olson
and Robert Creeley: The Complete Correspondence*, ed. George F.
Butterick (Santa Barbara, CA: Black Sparrow Press, 1980) and *Irving
Layton and Robert Creeley: The Complete Correspondence, 1953-
1958*, eds. Ekbert Faas and Sabrina Reed (Montreal: McGill-Queens
University Press, 1990). Interviews are presented in Donald Allen,
ed., *Contexts of Poetry: Interviews 1961-1971* (Bolinas, CA: Four
Seasons Foundation, 1973) and Ekbert Faas, *Towards a New
American Poetry: Essays and Interviews* (Santa Barbara, CA: Black
Sparrow Press, 1979), in which each interview is complemented with
an essay. A valuable collection of materials is John Wilson, ed.,
Robert Creeley's Life and Work: A Sense of Increment (Ann Arbor:
University of Michigan Press, 1987), and several articles on Creeley,
including some discussions of his prose, make up about one third of
Review of Contemporary Fiction 15.3 (1995). Tom Clark, ed., *Robert
Creeley and the Genius of the American Commonplace* (New York:
New Directions, 1993) is a biography that also includes Creeley's
short autobiography. Bibliographical information is to be found in
Willard Fox, *Robert Creeley, Edward Dorn, and Robert Duncan: A
Reference Guide* (Boston: G. K. Hall, 1989). Creeley's poems are
featured in Donald Allen, ed., *The New American Poetry* (New York:
Grove Press, 1960) and Donald Allen and George F. Butterick, eds.,
The Post Moderns: The New American Poetry Revised (New York:
Grove Press, 1982). To Donald Allen and Warren Tallman, eds., *The
Poetics of the New American Poetry* (New York: Grove Press, 1973),
Creeley contributes "A Note on Ezra Pound," "Louis Zukofsky: *All:
The Collected Short Poems, 1923-1958*," "Introduction to *The New
Writing in the USA*," "I'm Given to Write Poems," and "Linda
Wagner: An Interview with Robert Creeley." Useful studies include
Edward Halsey Foster, "Robert Creeley: Poetics of Solitude," in
Understanding the Black Mountain Poets (Columbia: University of
South Carolina Press, 1995): 81-121, Frank Day, "Robert Creeley," in
*The Dictionary of Literary Biography, Volume 5, American Poets
Since World War II*, ed. Donald J. Greiner (Detroit: Gale Research,
1980): 152-159, Sherman Paul, *The Last America of Love: Rereading
Robert Creeley, Edward Dorn, and Robert Duncan* (Baton Rouge:
Louisiana State University Press, 1981), Steven Watson, "Robert
Creeley," *The Birth of the Beat Generation* (New York: Pantheon,

1995): 220-225, Richard Howard, "Robert Creeley," in *Alone with America* (New York: Atheneum, 1969): 65-74, Ekbert Faas, "Robert Creeley," in *The Beats: Literary Bohemians in Postwar America*, ed. Ann Charters (Detroit: Gale Research, 1983): 141-148, Paul Carroll, "The Scene in the Wicker Basket," in *The Poem in Its Skin* (Chicago: Big Table Press, 1968): 31-38, Michael McClure, "These Decades Are Echoes," in Michael McClure, *Lighting the Corners* (Albuquerque: University of New Mexico College of Arts and Sciences, 1993): 173-177, and William Lawlor, "Robert Creeley's 'I Know a Man': A Metaphysical Conceit," *Iowa Review* 15.2 (Spring-Summer, 1985): 173-175. See Ann Charters, *Beats and Company* (Garden City, NY: Doubleday, 1986): 129-131; a video *Robert Creeley* (Los Angeles: Lannan Foundation, 1990) features a reading done on 16 Apr. 1990 and an interview with Lewis MacAdams. On the internet, **http://wings.buffalo.edu/epc/authors/creeley** includes a site in commemoration of Creeley's seventieth birthday, available at **http://wings.buffalo.edu/epc/authors/creeley/70th**. *Seventieth Birthday Reading* (New York: Thin Air Video, 1996), features readings from all stages of Creeley's career.

Diane DiPrima (1934-   )

This Kind of Bird Flies Backward (New York: Totem Press, 1958) was DiPrima's first poetry book, and it included an introduction by Lawrence Ferlinghetti. This book was followed by the collection of stories *Dinners and Nightmares* (New York: Corinth Books, 1961). *Selected Poems 1956-1975* was first published in 1975 but the same publisher soon released an enlarged edition titled *Selected Poems 1956-1976* (Plainfield, VT: North Atlantic Books, 1977). In *Memoirs of a Beatnik* (New York: Olympia, 1969), DiPrima plays with popular perceptions of the Beat movement. In addition to her prolific work as a writer, she is central among the Beats as an editor. She was involved in the production of *Yugen* and *Kulchur*, two magazines that frequently featured the Beats, and served as editor for *Floating Bear*, a journal that may now be examined in a compiled format: *The Floating Bear: A Newsletter*, eds. Diane DiPrima and LeRoi Jones (La Jolla, CA: McGilvery, 1974). DiPrima was also a founder of Poets Press, which produced twenty-nine titles. Also a playwright, DiPrima helped to found New York's American Theater for Poets and saw her plays produced by the Living Theatre. See Diane DiPrima, *Zip Code: The Collected Plays of Diane DiPrima* (St. Paul, MN: Coffee House Press, 1992). Her work is included in Ann Charters, ed., *The Portable Beat Reader* (New York: Viking Penguin, 1992), Carole Tonkinson, ed., *Big Sky Mind* (New York: Riverhead Books, 1995), David Kherdian, ed., *Beat Voices* (New York: Henry Holt, 1995), Anne Waldman, ed., *The Beat Book* (Boston: Shambhala, 1996), Florence Howe, ed., *See No Masks!: An Anthology of Twentieth-Century Women Poets*, newly revised and expanded (New York: Harper Perennial, 1993), Seymour Krim, ed., *The Beats* (Greenwich, CT: Fawcett, 1960), and Donald Allen and George F. Butterick, eds., *The Postmoderns: The New American Poetry Revised* (New York: Grove Press, 1982). For an interview, see "Anne Waldman Talks with Diane DiPrima," *The Beat Vision*, eds. Arthur Winfield Knight and Kit Knight (New York: Paragon, 1987), 139-145. Jack Foley's interview of Diane DiPrima broadcast on 15 and 22 Apr. 1990 is held at the Bancroft Poetry Archive at the University of California, Berkeley. A cassette of a reading done in July 1987 is available from the Naropa Institute. Secondary materials include George F. Butterick, "Diane DiPrima," in *The Beats: Literary Bohemians in Postwar America*, ed. Ann Charters (Detroit: Gale Research, 1986): 149-160, which is not entirely supportive of DiPrima. Ann Charters, "Diane DiPrima and the Loba Poems: Poetic Archetype as Spirit Double" in *Beat Indeed!*, ed. Rudi Horemans (Antwerp, Belgium: EXA, 1985): 107-116 presents interpretation of myth. See also Amy L. Friedman, "'I Say My New Name': Women Writers of the Beat Generation," in *The Beat Generation Writers* (London: Pluto Press, 1996): 200-216, Gretchen H. Munroe, "Diane DiPrima" in *The Dictionary of Literary Biography, Volume 5, American Poets Since World War II*, ed. Donald J. Greiner (Detroit: Gale Research, 1980): 202-205, "Diane DiPrima, Poet Priestess," in Brenda Knight, ed., *Women of the Beat Generation* (Berkeley, CA: Conari Press, 1996): 123-140, Joel Oppenheimer, "Floating Bear," *Village Voice* 13 June 1974: 36, David Rosenthal, "Art and Revolution," *Nation* 3 Jan. 1972: 24, 26, and Ann Charters, *Beats and Company* (Garden City, NY: Doubleday, 1986): 73-77, 154. Bill Zavatsky reviews *Selected Poems* in *The New York Times Book Review* 17 Oct. 1976: 32-36. One can see and hear Diane DiPrima on Maria Beatty, *Gang of Souls* (New York: Mystic Fire Video, 1988) and *Fried Shoes Cooked Diamonds* (New York: Mystic Fire Video, 1978). *Recollections of My Life as a Woman* (New York:

Thin Air Video, 1996) features DiPrima commenting on "family, womanhood, aging, anarchy, and The Bomb." On the companion cassette tapes to *The Women of the Beat Generation* (San Bruno, CA: Audio Literature, 1996), Diane DiPrima reads several selections.

Kirby Doyle (1932-   )

Doyle's first book of poems was *Sapphobones* (Kerhonkson, NY: Poet's Press, 1966), a collection of thirty-six poems written 1957-1959. The first novel, which bears some comparison to the style and themes of Burroughs, was *Happiness Bastard* (North Hollywood, CA: Essex House, 1968). In 1981, Doyle became the editor of the legendary magazine *Beatitude*. Doyle's poetry is gathered in *The Collected Poems of Kirby Doyle* (San Francisco: Greenlight Press, 1983). Raymond Foye, "Kirby Doyle," in *The Beats: Literary Bohemians in Postwar America*, ed. Ann Charters (Detroit: Gale Research, 1983): 161-168 provides background. One may hear Doyle read from "Angel Faint" on *Howls, Raps and Roars: Recordings from the San Francisco Poetry Renaissance* (Berkeley, CA: Fantasy Records, 1993), a collection of CD's.

Robert Duncan (1919-1988)

Robert Duncan distinguishes himself from the Beats, but he shares with them the emphasis on personal confession, the opposition to society's power structure, and the questioning of literary conformity. Duncan's first book was *Heavenly City Earthly City* (Berkeley, CA: Bern Porter, 1947). He established himself as a prominent experimentalist with *The Opening of the Field* (New York: Grove Press, 1960). The Beat Generation's affinity for Duncan is revealed in Ferlinghetti's publication of *Selected Poems* (San Francisco: City Lights, 1959) and in the inclusion of Duncan in Donald Allen, ed., *The New American Poetry: 1945-1960* (New York: Grove Press, 1960). *Selected Poems*, ed. Robert Bertholf (New York: New Directions, 1993) now supersedes the 1959 volume. Robert Bertholf, *Robert Duncan: A Descriptive Bibliography* (Santa Rosa,

CA: Black Sparrow Press, 1986) and Willard Fox, *Robert Creeley, Edward Dorn, and Robert Duncan: A Reference Guide* (Boston: G. K. Hall, 1989) offer bibliographical data. Always respected as a theorist on poetic form, Duncan is the author of "Toward an Open Universe," *Poets on Poetry*, ed. Howard Nemerov (New York: Basic Books, 1966): 133-146. In Donald Allen and George F. Butterick, eds., *The Poetics of the New American Poetry* (New York: Grove, 1973): 185-225, Duncan contributes "Notes on Poetics Regarding Olson's Maximus," "Ideas of the Meaning of Form," and "Towards an Open Universe." An interview with Duncan, as well as an essay about the poet, appears in Ekbert Faas, *Towards a New American Poetics: Essays and Interviews* (Santa Barbara, CA: Black Sparrow Press, 1978): 55-85. Michael McClure, "Talking with Robert Duncan" and "Robert Duncan: A Modern Romantic" appear in Michael McClure, *Lighting the Corners* (Albuquerque: University of New Mexico College of Arts and Sciences, 1993): 69-93. Mark Andrew Johnson, *Robert Duncan* (Boston: Twayne, 1988) is a useful introduction for students, and a worthwhile collection of articles is Robert Bertholf and Ian W. Reid, *Robert Duncan: Scales of the Marvelous* (New York: New Directions, 1979). Other secondary materials are Edward Halsey Foster, "Robert Duncan: Aspirations of the Word," in *Understanding the Black Mountain Poets* (Columbia: University of South Carolina Press, 1995): 122-162, James Dickey, "Robert Duncan," in *Babel to Byzantium* (New York: Farrar, Straus, and Giroux, 1968): 173-177, Michael Davidson, *The San Francisco Renaissance: Poetics and Community at Mid-Century* (New York: Cambridge University Press, 1989): 125-149, Davidson, "Robert Duncan," in *The Beats: Literary Bohemians in Postwar America*, ed. Ann Charters (Detroit: Gale Research, 1983): 169-180, Norman Finkelstein, *The Utopian Movement in Contemporary American Poetry* (Lewisburg, PA: Bucknell University Press, 1988), Sherman Paul, *The Lost America of Love: Rereading Robert Creeley, Edward Dorn, and Robert Duncan* (Baton Rouge: Louisiana State University Press, 1981), Nathaniel Mackey, "The World-Poem in Microcosm: Robert Duncan's 'The Continent,'" *ELH* 47 (Fall 1980): 590-618, Steven Watson, "Robert Duncan," *The Birth of the Beat Generation* (New York: Pantheon, 1995): 200-205, George F. Butterick, "Robert Duncan," in *The Dictionary of Literary Biography, Volume 5, American Poets Since World War II*, ed. Donald J. Greiner (Detroit: Gale Research, 1980): 217-229, and Ann Charters, *Beats and Company* (Garden City, NY: Doubleday, 1986): 55.

Bob Dylan (Robert Zimmerman, 1941-   )

Dylan is a cultural hero in his own right, but some of his work reveals his connection to the artists of the Beat Generation. His work is interdisciplinary, combining poetry and various forms of music, including folk and rock; in addition, Dylan is individualistic, challenging conformity and misguided authority. Produced and marketed through Columbia Records, albums like *The Freewheelin' Bob Dylan* (1963), *The Times They Are A-Changin'* (1964), *Another Side of Bob Dylan* (1964), *Bringing It All Back Home* (1965), *Highway 61 Revisited* (1965), and *Blonde on Blonde* (1966) represent Dylan's transition from folk protest to social protest in the rock format. Following a motorcycle accident, Dylan spent some time without releasing an album, but *John Wesley Harding* (1968) marked the arrival of a softened tone and the influence of country music. *Nashville Skyline* (1969), *Self-Portrait* (1970) and *New Morning* (1970) carried the style of *John Wesley Harding* forward. The book *Tarantula* (New York: Macmillan, 1974) is in the cut-up format associated with William S. Burroughs. The albums *Planet Waves* (1974) and *Blood on the Tracks* (1974) led up to *Desire* (1975), which proved to be Dylan's best-selling album and which included liner notes by Allen Ginsberg. Rolling Thunder Revue, discussed in Sam Shephard, *Rolling Thunder Logbook* (New York: Viking, 1977), was a tour by Dylan in New England that featured Joan Baez, Allen Ginsberg, Peter Orlovsky, Ramblin' Jack Elliot, and Roger McGuinn. Other albums include *Street Legal* (1978), *Slow Train Coming* (1979), *Saved* (1980), and *Shot of Love* (1981). Biographies include Robert Shelton, *No Direction Home: The Life and Music of Bob Dylan* (New York: William Morrow, 1986) and Bob Spitz, *Dylan: A Biography* (New York: McGraw-Hill, 1989). Dave Engel, *Just Like Bob Zimmerman's Blues: Dylan in Minnesota* (Rudolph, WI: River City Memoirs-Mesabi, 1997) offers photos, documents, and text to unfold the early life of Dylan. See also William McKeen, *Bob Dylan: A Bio-Bibliography* (Westport, CT: Greenwood Press, 1993), Michael Gray, *The Art of Bob Dylan* (New York: St. Martin's, 1981), Craig McGregor, *Bob Dylan: a Retrospective* (New York: William Morrow, 1972), and Anthony Scaduto, *Bob Dylan* (New York: New American Library, 1973). A chapter "Bob Dylan" appears in Don Cusic, *The Poet as Performer* (Lanham, MD: University Press of America, 1991): 87-101. *The Songs of Bob Dylan from 1966-1975* (New York:

Knopf/Cherry Lane, 1980) presents lyrics and music for numerous selections. See Joseph Wenke, "Bob Dylan," *The Beats: Literary Bohemians in Postwar America*, ed. Ann Charters (Detroit: Gale Research, 1983): 180-188 and Michael McClure, "Bob Dylan: The Poet's Poet," in Michael McClure, *Lighting the Corners* (Albuquerque: University of New Mexico College of Arts and Sciences, 1993): 26-35. D. A. Pennebaker, *Bob Dylan: Don't Look Back* (New York: Ballantine Books, 1968) is a publication that corresponds to the film *Don't Look Back* by D. A. Pennebaker, who writes, "The film was made without a script. This [book] is simply a transcript of what happened and what was said." The book also includes lyrics of early Dylan songs, interviews, and many photos from the 1965 tour of England. On the internet, one finds information at **http://www.bobdylan.com**.

Larry Eigner (1927-1996)

Larry Eigner was "palsied from a 1927 birth injury" and spent his life confined to a wheelchair. Nevertheless, he became an important poet of his time, winning a place in Donald Allen, ed., *The New American Poetry* (New York: Grove Press, 1960), Donald Allen and George F. Butterick, eds., *The Postmoderns: The New American Poetry Revised* (New York: Grove Press, 1982), and Douglas Misserli, ed., *From the Other Side of the Century: A New American Poetry, 1960-1990* (Los Angeles: Sun and Moon Press, 1994). A photo of Eigner appears in Ann Charters, *Beats and Company* (Garden City, NY: Doubleday, 1986): 112. See Larry Eigner, *Areas Lights Heights: Writings, 1954-1989* (New York: Roof Books, 1989). Irving P. Leif, *Larry Eigner: A Bibliography of His Works* (Metuchen, NJ: Scarecrow Press, 1989) identifies primary materials. Robert Kocik and Joseph Simas, eds., *Larry Eigner Letters* (Paris: Moving Letters Press, 1987) gives access to correspondence. "Larry Eigner: Interview, Autobiography, Poems" is in *Kaleidoscope* 5 (Spring 1982). See also Michael McClure, "Larry Eigner 1927-1996" in *Sulfur* 38 (Spring 1996): 4 and *A Tribute to Larry Eigner and His Work* (Detroit: Gale Research, 1996), a sixty-two page book with an accompanying cassette tape. See the introductory article "Larry Eigner" by Idris McElveen in *The Dictionary of Literary Biography*,

Volume 5, American Poets Since World War II, ed. Donald J. Greiner
(Detroit: Gale Research, 1980): 242-248.

William Everson
(Brother Antoninus, 1912-1994)

The career of William Everson divides into three periods. The
first occurs prior to his acceptance of Roman Catholicism in 1949,
and poems related to this period may be found in the various versions of *The Residual Years*, which culminated in a final enlarged
version *The Residual Years: Poems 1934-1948* (New York: New
Directions, 1968). The second period, roughly from 1949 to 1969, is
Everson's time as a Catholic, culminating in his service as a
Dominican friar. *The Veritable Years, 1949-1966* (Santa Barbara, CA:
Black Sparrow Press, 1978) corresponds to the second period. The
third period, which involves Everson's life after 1969, is marked by
Everson's exit from the Dominican brotherhood and his marriage to
Susanna Rickson. *The Integral Years* is the title intended for the
collection which corresponds to Everson's third period, but that
collection was not ready at the time of Everson's death. Albert
Gelpi, ed., *The Blood of the Poet: Selected Poems/William Everson*
(Seattle: Broken Moon Press, 1994) offers a variety of Everson's
poems, and *Prodigious Thrust* (Santa Rosa, CA: Black Sparrow
Press, 1996) includes an afterword by Allan Campo. Everson's work
is anthologized in Donald Allen, ed., *The New American Poetry* (New
York: Grove Press, 1960), Donald Allen and George F. Butterick,
eds., *The Postmoderns: The New American Poetry Revised* (New
York: Grove Press, 1982), and Ann Charters, ed., *The Portable Beat
Reader* (New York: Viking Penguin, 1992). For bibliographical
information, see Lee Bartlett and Allan Campo, *William Everson: A
Descriptive Bibliography* (Metuchen, NJ: Scarecrow Press, 1977). See
also David Kherdian, ed., *Six San Francisco Poets* (Fresno, CA:
Giligia Press, 1965). An interview with Everson appears in David
Meltzer, ed., *Golden Gate: Interviews with Five San Francisco Poets*
(San Francisco: Wingbow Press, 1976): 67-115. Additional interviews
are in Clifton Ross, ed., *The Light and the Shadow: Five Interviews
with William Everson, Plus Corresponding Poems* (Berkeley, CA:
New Earth Publications, 1996). See also William Everson, *Naked
Heart: Talking on Poetry, Mysticism, and the Erotic* (Albuquerque:

University of New Mexico College of Arts and Sciences, 1992). Secondary materials include Albert Gelpi, "Everson/Antoninus: Contending with the Shadow" in *The Beats: Essays in Criticism*, ed. Lee Bartlett (Jefferson, NC: McFarland, 1981): 40-52, Ann Charters, *Beats and Company* (Garden City, NY: Doubleday, 1986): 58, James A. Powell, "William Everson (Brother Antoninus)" in *The Beats: Literary Bohemians in Postwar America*, ed. Ann Charters (Detroit: Gale Research, 1986): 189-199, Donna Nance, "William Everson," in *The Dictionary of Literary Biography, Volume 5, American Poets Since World War II*, ed. Donald J. Greiner (Detroit: Gale Research, 1980): 242-248, William E. Stafford, *The Achievement of Brother Antoninus: A Comprehensive Selection of His Poems with a Critical Introduction* (Chicago: Scott Foresman, 1967), Lee Bartlett, ed., *Benchmark and Blaze: The Emergence of William Everson* (Metuchen, NJ: Scarecrow Press, 1979), which collects twenty-two essays on the life and writings of Everson and offers a selected bibliography, James Dickey, "Brother Antoninus," in *Babel to Byzantium* (New York: Farrar, Straus, and Giroux, 1968): 124-126, and Neeli Cherkovski, *Whitman's Wild Children* (Venice, CA: Lapis Press, 1988). See also Lee Bartlett, *William Everson* (Boise, ID: Boise State University Press, 1985). An issue of *Quarry West* is published as *The Poet as Printer, William Everson: The Fine Press Artists' Book* (Santa Cruz, CA: Porter College-University of California, Santa Cruz, 1995) and discusses Everson's special skills as a printer.

Richard Fariña (1937-1966)

Fariña's *Been Down So Long It Looks Like Up to Me* (New York: Random House, 1966) is now available in a paperback with an introduction by Thomas Pynchon (New York: Penguin Books, 1983). The novel presents the journey of Gnossos Pappadopoulis through the psychedelic world of the 1960's and bears comparison to the legendary journeys of Sal and Dean in Jack Kerouac's *On the Road*. Works by Fariña appeared in *Poetry*, *Atlantic*, and *Mademoiselle*; his plays were produced at Cornell University and at the Image Theater in Cambridge, Massachusetts. With his wife Mimi, Fariña gained prominence as a folk singer, with the album *Reflections in a Crystal Wind* enjoying critical recognition. Selections performed by Mimi and Richard Fariña are on *Troubadors of the Folk Era, Volume One* (Santa Monica, CA: Rhino, 1992), *Vanguard Folk Sampler* (Santa Monica, CA: Vanguard, 1996), *Folk Music at Newport, Part One* (Santa Monica, CA: Vanguard, 1995), *Legendary Folk Singers* (Santa Monica, CA: Vanguard, 1994), *The Best of Mimi and Richard Fariña* (Santa Monica, CA: Vanguard, 1988), *Celebrations for a Gray Day* (Santa Monica, CA: Vanguard, 1995), and *Reflections in a Crystal Wind* (Santa Monica, CA: Vanguard, 1995). Michael Friedman, *Richard Fariña, Long Time Coming, Long Time Gone* (New York: EMR Publishing, 1969) presents a biographical narrative by Friedman. A collection of Fariña's works is *A Long Time Coming and a Long Time Gone* (New York: Random House, 1969). See a chapter on Fariña in Gregory Stephenson, *The Daybreak Boys* (Carbondale: Southern Illinois University Press, 1990): 131-138.

Lawrence Ferlinghetti (1919-   )

Though not usually associated with the beginnings of the Beat Generation in New York City following World War II, Lawrence Ferlinghetti is a central figure in the Beat literary movement of the 1950's. Ferlinghetti's industry as a writer, his inventiveness in combining poetry and jazz, his success in establishing the first bookstore to sell only paperbacks, and his uncompromising efforts in publishing works that tested the limits of law and social acceptance make him not only an important figure in the bohemian struggle but also a major figure in his own right. To launch the Pocket Poets Series, Ferlinghetti published his own *Pictures of the Gone World* (San Francisco: City Lights, 1955), which is now available in an enlarged edition with eighteen new poems (San Francisco: City Lights, 1995). The Pocket Poets Series continued with works by Kenneth Rexroth and Kenneth Patchen, but the publication of Allen Ginsberg's *Howl and Other Poems* (San Francisco: City Lights, 1956) brought Ferlinghetti's publishing house to national attention as charges of obscenity were made and the American Civil Liberties Union succeeded in vindicating Ferlinghetti. As a result, the Beat movement became associated with freedom of expression, with Ferlinghetti acknowledged as a key player in the making of that freedom, as he went on to publish in the Pocket Poets Series works by Gregory Corso, Bob Kaufman, Jack Kerouac, Frank O'Hara, Philip

Lamantia, Janine Pommy Vega, Diane DiPrima, and many others. Ferlinghetti furthered his work in publishing through his association with *City Lights* and *Beatitude*, two journals which featured Beat and non-Beat writers and which led to the now famous *City Lights Anthology* and *Beatitude Anthology*. *A Coney Island of the Mind* (Norfolk, CT: New Directions, 1958) is Ferlinghetti's most perennially popular book and is now enlarged (New York: New Directions, 1968). In addition to the twenty-nine poems from the Coney Island sequence, the volume includes poems selected from *Pictures of the Gone World* and a special series of poems intended for oral presentation with jazz accompaniment. Other collections of poetry include *Endless Life: Selected Poems* (New York: New Directions, 1981), *Landscapes of Living and Dying* (New York: New Directions, 1979), *Open Eye, Open Heart* (New York: New Directions, 1973), *The Secret Meaning of Things* (New York: New Directions, 1969), *Starting from San Francisco* (Norfolk, CT: New Directions, 1961), *and Who Are We Now?* (New York: New Directions, 1976). A collection that gathers material from the entire career is *These Are My Rivers: New and Selected Poems* (New York: New Directions, 1994). A new collection of poetry whose title plays on the enduring *A Coney Island of the Mind* is *A Far Rockaway of the Heart* (New York: New Directions, 1997). Though best known as a poet, Ferlinghetti is also the author of creative prose, such as *Back Roads to Far Places* (New York: New Directions, 1971), the novel *Her* (Norfolk, CT: New Directions, 1966), *Tyranus Nix?* (New York: New Directions, 1969), and the novel *Love in the Days of Rage* (New York: Dutton, 1988). Travel writings include *The Mexican Night* (New York: New Directions, 1970), *A Trip to Italy and France* (New York: New Directions, 1980), and *Seven Days & Nicaragua Libre* (San Francisco: City Lights, 1984). Among his periodical publications are "Lawrence Ferlinghetti: Horn on 'Howl'" *Evergreen Review* 1.4 (1957): 145-158 and "Notes on Poetry in San Francisco" *Chicago Review* 12 (Spring 1958): 3-5. The plays are *Routines* (New York: New Directions, 1964) and *Unfair Arguments with Existence* (New York: New Directions, 1963). As a collaborator, Ferlinghetti has written *Open Eye*, bound as one book with *Open Head* by Allen Ginsberg (Melbourne, Australia: Sun Books, 1972); with Nancy Joyce Peters, Ferlinghetti is the author of *Literary San Francisco: A Pictorial History from Its Beginnings to the Present Day* (San Francisco: City Lights/Harper and Row, 1980). Neeli Cherkovski, *Ferlinghetti: A Biography* (New York: Doubleday, 1979), is a straightforward biography, with photos, thorough index, and short bibliography. Barry Silesky, *Ferlinghetti: The Artist in His Time* (New York: Warner Books, 1990) updates Cherkovski and is longer. Critical studies include Michael Skau, *Constantly Risking Absurdity: The Writings of Lawrence Ferlinghetti* (Troy, NY: Whitson, 1989), and Larry Smith, *Lawrence Ferlinghetti: Poet-at-Large* (Carbondale: Southern Illinois University Press, 1983). See also David Kherdian, "Lawrence Ferlinghetti," in *Six Poets of the San Francisco Renaissance* (Fresno, CA: Giligia Press, 1978), in which a chapter describes a day in the life of the poet and publisher. Thomas Parkinson, "Phenomenon or Generation," in *A Casebook on the Beat* (New York: Crowell, 1961), offers some interpretation. Gregory Stephenson presents a general view of Ferlinghetti's writings in "The 'Spiritual Optics' of Lawrence Ferlinghetti" in *The Daybreak Boys: Essays on the Literature of the Beat Generation* (Carbondale: University of Southern Illinois Press, 1990). See also Neeli Cherkovski, *Whitman's Wild Children* (Venice, CA: Lapis Press, 1988). Anne Janette Johnson, "Ferlinghetti, Lawrence (Monsanto)," in *Contemporary Authors*, New Revision Series, Volume 41, ed. Susan M. Trosky (Detroit: Gale Research, 1994): 132-138 offers a survey of Ferlinghetti's career and bibliographical information. Johnson's essay draws mainly from Larry Smith, "Lawrence Ferlinghetti," in *The Beats: Literary Bohemians in Postwar America* (Detroit: Gale Research, 1983): 199-214 and Thomas McClanahan, "Lawrence Ferlinghetti," in *Dictionary of Literary Biography, Volume 5, American Poets Since World War II* (Detroit: Gale Research, 1980): 248-254. David Meltzer, ed., *Golden Gate: Interviews with Five San Francisco Poets* (San Francisco: Wingbow Press, 1976) is a revised edition of *The San Francisco Poets* (New York: Ballantine, 1971) and presents an extended interview with Ferlinghetti. Another interview is Thaddeus Vane, "Lawrence Ferlinghetti: A Candid Conversation with the Man Who Founded the Beat Generation," *Penthouse* Aug. 1965: 24, 26, 71-73. Other studies include Crale D. Hopkins, "The Poetry of Lawrence Ferlinghetti: A Reconsideration," *Italian Americana* (1974): 59-76, Louis A. Haselmayer, "Beat Prophet and Beat Wit," *Iowa English Yearbook* 6 (1961): 9-13, Peter Stack, "Ferlinghetti: Offbeat Beatnik," *San Francisco Chronicle* 26 Nov. 1995: 29, Brother Edward Kent, "Daredevil Poetics: Ferlinghetti's Definition of a Poet," *English Journal* 59.9 (Dec. 1970): 1243-1244, 1251 [ERIC NO. EJ030019]; Michael Mahon,

"Pala at Dominguez Hills," *Change* 3.6 (October 1971): 45-50 [ERIC NO. EJ046229], which describes how an English teacher learns about Ferlinghetti and Yeats and a method for approaching a class, Russell O'Neill, "A Fling with Ferlinghetti," *English Journal* 58.7 (October 1969): 1025-1027, 1031 [ERIC NO. 009445], Anne Tobias, "A Poet for Teachers and Students: Lawrence Ferlinghetti," *English in Texas* 19.3 (Spring 1988): 15-19 [ERIC NO. ED302850], Christina Waters, "The Poet and Political Gadfly as Painter," *Chronicle of Higher Education* 25 Apr. 1990: 56, and William Lawlor, "Lawrence Ferlinghetti," in *Cyclopedia of World Authors*, eds. Frank N. Magill, McCrea Adams, and Juliane Brand (Pasadena, CA: Salem Press, 1997): 667-668. L. A. Ianni, "Lawrence Ferlinghetti's Fourth Person Singular and the Theory of Relativity," *Wisconsin Studies in Contemporary Literature* 8 (1967): 392-406 is reprinted in Lee Bartlett, ed., *The Beats: Essays in Criticism* (Jefferson, NC: McFarland, 1981): 53-65. Bill Morgan, *Lawrence Ferlinghetti: A Comprehensive Bibliography to 1980* (New York: Garland, 1982) features an introduction by Ferlinghetti and foreword by Larry Smith, illustrations of title pages and covers, and detailed descriptions of works by Ferlinghetti. Morgan adds a list of recordings and film appearances and a chronological listing of articles and books about Ferlinghetti and cites many newspaper notices. Lawrence Ferlinghetti, *When I Look at Pictures* (Salt Lake City: Peregrine Smith Books, 1990) is a beautiful book that combines poetry by Ferlinghetti that refers to major works of art with fine prints of the original paintings. *Howls, Raps and Roars: Recordings from the San Francisco Poetry Renaissance* (Berkeley, CA: Fantasy, 1993) is a collection of four CD's that includes readings of "Autobiography," "Statue of St. Francis," and "Moscow in the Wilderness, Segovia in the Snow" by Ferlinghetti. One can see and hear Ferlinghetti on *The New York Beat Generation Show: Volume One: History and Overview: The Censorship Years* (New York: Thin Air Video, 1995) and on *The Coney Island of Lawrence Ferlinghetti* (New York: Mystic Fire Video, 1996), a video that features Ferlinghetti's comments on counter-cultural literature and includes Ginsberg, Corso, Baraka, McClure, Whalen, Waldman, and Cherkovski. This tape is available at the Bancroft Library at the University of California, Berkeley. Still another tape is *Ferlinghetti, City Lights, and the Beats in San Francisco: From the Margins to the Mainstream* (San Francisco: Cloud House Poetry Archives, 1996).

Brion Gysin (1916-   )

Gysin's association with the Beat Generation stems mainly from his collaborations with William S. Burroughs and, on one occasion, Gregory Corso. With Burroughs, Sinclair Beiles, and Corso, Gysin wrote *Minutes to Go* (Paris: Two Cities, 1960; San Francisco: Beach Books, 1968); with Burroughs, Gysin wrote *The Exterminator* (San Francisco: Auerhahn Press/Dave Haselwood Books, 1960) and *Oeuvre Croisse* (Paris: Flammarion, 1976), which was later published as *The Third Mind* (New York: Viking, 1978; London: Calder, 1979). Gysin and Burroughs combined to make the cut-up a prominent part of twentieth-century literature. See Terry Wilson, "Brion Gysin," in *The Beats: Literary Bohemians in Postwar America*, ed. Ann Charters (Detroit: Gale Research, 1983): 241-247. See an excerpt from "The Beat Hotel, Paris" in Ann Charters, ed., *The Portable Beat Reader* (New York: Viking, 1992): 473-475. He is also included in *Literary Visions* (New York: Jack Tilton Gallery, 1988). Brion Gysin, *Smack My Crack* (New York: Giorno, 1987) is a single audio cassette.

Bobbie Louise Hawkins (1930-   )

A regular member of the writing faculty at Naropa Institute, Hawkins has established herself as a prolific writer and an innovative educator, especially in connection with Beat literature. The collections of her work that offer the broadest samplings are *Almost Everything* (Toronto: Coach House Press, 1982) and *My Own Alphabet: Stories, Essays, and Memoirs* (Minneapolis: Coffee House Press, 1989). Other books include *One Small Saga: A Novella* (Minneapolis: Coffee House Press, 1984), *The Sanguine Breast of Margaret* (Twickenham, Middlesex, England: North and South, 1992), and *Rainbow* (Buffalo, NY: Just Buffalo, 1975). In 1995 in Boulder, Colorado, various titles appeared: *Some Small Poems* (Rodent Press), *Fragrant Trappings* (Bijou Books), *Bitter Sweet* (Bijou Books), and *Sensible Plainness* (Bijou Books). Hawkins' work is included in *New Directions in Prose and Poetry* (New York: New Directions, 1978). Washington University holds a collection of Robert Creeley's papers, and among them is correspondence with Bobbie Louise Hawkins; the University of California, San Diego, has a collection of Charlie Vermont's papers, and some letters by Bobbie Louise Hawkins are included. At the University of California, San Diego, the library holds a tape of Hawkins reading on May 15, 1985. An LP album *Live at the Great American Music Hall* (Chicago: Flying Fish, 1980) features humorous monologues by Hawkins. A video *Knowing Words* (Twickenham, Middlesex, England: Solaris, 1993) features Hawkins "talking about her life and writing, reading from her work, with archive footage and photos." See also Gloria Frym, *Second Stories: Conversations with Women Whose Artistic Careers Began After Thirty-Five* (San Francisco: Chronicle Books, 1979).

John Clellon Holmes (1926-1988)

The centerpiece of John Clellon Holmes' association with the Beat Generation is the novel *Go* (New York: Scribner's, 1952), which includes characters who correspond directly to Allen Ginsberg, Jack Kerouac, and Neal Cassady. In addition, Holmes is well known for his contribution to *The New York Times Magazine* titled "This Is the Beat Generation" on 16 Nov. 1952. "The Philosophy of the Beat Generation," *Esquire* Feb. 1958: 35-38 added to Holmes' identity as a commentator on the Beats. These two essays, as well as "The Name of the Game" and "The Game of the Name," may be found in *The Beats: Literary Bohemians in Postwar America*, ed. Ann Charters (Detroit: Gale Research, 1983): 627-642. In New York, Thunder's Mouth Press has published editions of *Go* (1988), *The Horn* (1988), and *Get Home Free* (1988), which include various prefaces, introductions, forewords, and afterwords. In Fayetteville, the University of Arkansas Press has published *Passionate Opinions: The Cultural Essays* (1988), which includes "This Is the Beat Generation," "The Philosophy of the Beat Generation," "The Beat Poets: A Primer," and introductions to Holmes' various novels. The same press has published *Representative Men: The Biographical Essays* (1988), *Displaced Person: The Travel Essays* (1987), and *Night Music: Selected Poems* (1989), which contains poems from previous collections *Dire Coasts, Death Drag,* and *The Bowling Green Poems*. Holmes' "Unscrewing the Locks: The Beat Poets" is in Lee Bartlett, ed., *The Beats: Essays in Literary Criticism* (Jefferson, NC: McFarland, 1981). See Richard Kirk

Ardinger, "John Clellon Holmes," in *The Beats: Literary Bohemians in Postwar America*, ed. Ann Charters (Detroit: Gale Research, 1983): 247-262, Cynthia Hamilton, "The Prisoner of Self: The Work of John Clellon Holmes," in *The Beat Generation Writers*, ed. A. Robert Lee (London: Pluto, 1996): 114-127, Gregory Stephenson, "Homeward from Nowhere: Notes on the Novels of John Clellon Holmes" in *The Daybreak Boys* (Carbondale: Southern Illinois University Press, 1990): 90-104, John Clellon Holmes, "Crazy Days, Numinous Nights: 1948-1950," in *The Beat Vision*, eds. Arthur Winfield Knight and Kit Knight (New York: Paragon, 1987): 73-88, Theo D'haen, "John Clellon Holmes's Intertextual Beat," in Rudi Horemans, ed., *Beat Indeed!* (Antwerp, Belgium: EXA, 1985): 163-171, and Ann Charters, *Beats and Company* (Garden City, NY: Doubleday, 1986): 7-10, 79-81, 121, 122, 124, 149. A discussion limited to Holmes' poetry is Jaap Van Der Bent, "The Maples Will Enleaf Again, and Consciousness Relent: The Poetry of John Clellon Holmes," *American Poetry Review* 23.6 (Nov./Dec. 1994): 55-61. A review of Holmes' volume of poems titled *Night Music* is Frank Miele, "John Clellon Holmes and the Burden of Maturity," *The Literary Review* 33 (Spring 1990): 381-387. For interviews, see John Tytell, "An Interview with John Clellon Holmes," in *The Beat Book*, eds. Arthur Winfield Knight and Glee Knight, which is the fourth volume in the series called *unspeakable visions of the individual* (1974): 37-52, Timothy Hunt, "Interview with John Clellon Holmes," *Quarterly West* 5 (Winter 1978): 50-58, Timothy Hunt, "An Interview with John Clellon Holmes," in *The Beat Journey*, eds. Arthur Winfield Knight and Kit Knight, which is volume eight in *unspeakable visions of the individual* (1978): 147-166, or Arthur Winfield Knight and Kit Knight, eds., *Interior Geographies: An Interview with John Clellon Holmes* (Warren, OH: Literary Denim Press, 1981). Bibliographical data may be found in Richard K. Ardinger, *An Annotated Bibliography of Works by John Clellon Holmes* (Pocatello: Idaho State University Press, 1979).

Herbert Huncke (1915-1996)

Sometimes heralded as the quintessential Beat figure, Herbert Huncke corresponds to Kerouac's Elmo Hassel, Junky, and Huck. In

Burroughs, Huncke corresponds to Herman in *Junky*, and in Holmes' *Go* he is Ancke. Allen Ginsberg with Eric P. Nash, "The Hipster's Hipster," *The New York Times Magazine* 29 Dec. 1996: 39, includes a selection from the *The Herbert Huncke Reader* (New York: William Morrow, 1997). A selection from the autobiography *Guilty of Everything* (New York: Paragon House, 1990) appears in *Low Rent: A Decade of Prose and Photographs from the Portable Lower East Side* (New York: Grove Press, 1994). Other works by Huncke include *Huncke's Journal* (New York: Poets Press, 1965), *Elsie John and Joey Martinez* (New York: Pequod Press, 1979), and *The Evening Sun Turned Crimson* (Cherry Valley, NY: Cherry Valley Editions, 1980). See "Elsie John" and "Joey Martinez" in Ann Charters, ed., *The Portable Beat Reader* (New York: Viking, 1992): 145-152. See Arthur Winfield Knight, "Herbert Huncke," in *The Beats: Literary Bohemians in Postwar America*, ed. Ann Charters (Detroit: Gale Research, 1983): 262-267, Clive Bush, "'Why Do We Always Say Angel?': Herbert Huncke and Neal Cassady," in *The Beat Generation Writers* (London: Pluto, 1996): 128-157, and Steven Watson, "Herbert Huncke," in *The Birth of the Beat Generation: Visionaries, Rebels, and Hipsters 1944-1960* (New York: Pantheon, 1995): 72-76. John Tytell, "An Interview with Herbert Huncke" appears in *unspeakable visions of the individual*, 3.1-2 (1973): 3-15. See also Ann Charters, *Beats and Company* (Garden City, NY: Doubleday, 1986): 41, 152. A tape of Huncke's reading with Lawrence Ferlinghetti on 21 Mar. 1987 in Lowell, Massachusetts, is available at the Bancroft Poetry Archive at the University California, Berkeley. *Huncke and Louis*, a ten-minute video by Laki Vazakas (1995), offers insight about Huncke and his companion. *In New Orleans 1938*, a twelve-minute video by Jerry Poynton (1995), features Edgar Oliver, an actor, reading "New Orleans 1938," a story by Huncke. Huncke comments on Kerouac in the video *Kerouac* (New York: Mystic Fire Video, 1995), which is a release of John Antonelli's film *Kerouac*. *Huncke's Last Reading/Memorial Tribute* (New York: Thin Air Video, 1996) combines a presentation by Huncke done in New York in January 1996 with a memorial to Huncke done in September 1996.

Ted Joans (1928-   )

All of Ted Joans and No More (New York: Excelsior Press, 1961) is a generous sampling of Joans' work. His writing also appears in Elias Wilentz, ed., *The Beat Scene* (New York: Corinth Books, 1960), Seymour Krim, ed., *The Beats* (Greenwich, CT: Fawcett, 1960), and David Kherdian, ed., *Beat Voices* (New York: Henry Holt, 1995). See Joans' "The Surrealist Griot" in Michael Fabre, ed., *Black American Writers in France, 1840-1980* (Urbana: University of Illinois Press, 1991). Joans contributes "Worthy Beat Women: Recollection by Ted Joans" to Brenda Knight, ed., *The Women of the Beat Generation* (Berkeley, CA: Conari Press, 1996). Joans' "Discursive Strategies in James Baldwin's Essays" appears in Jakob J. Kollhofer, ed., *James Baldwin: His Place in American Literary History* (New York: Peter Lang, 1991). "Gerald Nicosia Talks with Ted Joans" is an interview published in Arthur Winfield Knight and Kit Knight, eds., *The Beat Vision* (New York: Paragon, 1987): 271-283. "Ted Joans Interviewed by Jack Foley" is a 1989 cassette available at the Bancroft Poetry Archive at the University of California, Berkeley. Three cassettes document the appearance of Ted Joans (with Jayne Cortez) at the New School for Social Research on 3 Apr. 1984, and the tapes are held at the library at Colgate University. See James A. Miller, "Ted Joans," in *The Beats: Literary Bohemians in Postwar America*, ed. Ann Charters (Detroit: Gale Research, 1983): 268-270; see also A. Robert Lee, "Black Beats: The Signifying Poetry of LeRoi Jones/Amiri Baraka, Ted Joans, and Bob Kaufman" in A. Robert Lee, ed., *The Beat Generation Writers* (London: Pluto Press, 1996): 158-177.

Joyce Johnson (1935-   )

Joyce Johnson is a successful writer in her own right, but her connection to the Beat Generation, for many readers, stems mainly from her love relationship with Jack Kerouac. In fact, she was with Kerouac on the evening he picked up the *New York Times* (5 Sept. 1957) with Gilbert Millstein's stunning review of *On the Road*. *Minor Characters* (New York: Washington Square Press, 1984), the winner of the National Book Critics Circle Award in 1984, is a memoir by

Johnson that traces her maturation, recognizes the struggle of various women on the Beat scene to gain artistic recognition, and unfolds Johnson's connection to Kerouac. Johnson also discusses the Kerouac relationship in "Outlaw Days," *The Beats: Literary Bohemians in Postwar America*, ed. Ann Charters (Detroit: Gale Research, 1983): 621-625. Other works include *Bad Connections* (New York: Putnam, 1978), *In the Night Cafe* (New York: Dutton, 1989), and *What Lisa Knew: The Truths and Lies of the Steinberg Case* (New York: Putnam, 1990). An excerpt of *Minor Characters* appears in Ann Charters, ed., *The Portable Beat Reader* (New York: Viking, 1992), in Park Honan, ed., *The Beats* (London: J. M. Dent, 1987), and in Phyllis Rose, ed., *The Norton Book of Women's Lives* (New York: Norton, 1993). Johnson contributes "My Amoeba" to Gloria Norris, ed., *The Seasons of Women: An Anthology* (New York: Norton, 1996); Johnson is included in Susan Nuenzig Cahill, ed., *Writing Women's Lives: An Anthology of Autobiographical Narratives by Twentieth-Century American Women Writers* (New York: Harper Perennial, 1994); and "The Children's Wing" appears in *Prize Stories 1987: The O. Henry Awards* (Garden City, NY: Doubleday, 1987). Some of Johnson's correspondence is kept in the archive of Edward Dorn at the library of the University of Connecticut. A photo of Joyce Johnson is in Ann Charters, *Beats and Company* (Garden City, NY: Doubleday, 1986): 117. Joyce Johnson is featured in *Kerouac* (1984), a film by John Antonelli later released as *On the Road with Jack Kerouac* (Active Home Video, 1990) but now distributed as *Kerouac* (New York: Mystic Fire Video, 1995). See "Joyce Johnson: A True Good Heart" in Brenda Knight, ed., *The Women of the Beat Generation* (Berkeley, CA: Conari Press, 1996): 167-181. On the companion cassette tapes to *The Women of the Beat Generation* (San Bruno, CA: Audio Literature, 1996), Johnson reads an excerpt from *Minor Characters*. *The New York Beat Generation Show: Volume Two: Women and the Beats* (New York: Thin Air Video, 1995) features commentary by Joyce Johnson.

Hettie Jones (1934-   )

The work that most clearly connects Jones to the Beat Generation is *How I Became Hettie Jones* (New York: Dutton, 1990), which has recently been republished (New York: Grove Press, 1997).

In this memoir she recounts her love relationship with LeRoi Jones, who shared with Hettie an association with many Beat writers and publishers, particularly through their editing of *Yugen* and their operation of Totem Press. LeRoi Jones has written "For Hettie," part of a recording held at the Archive of Recorded Poetry at the Library of Congress. Hettie Jones' other works include *The Trees Stand Shining: Poetry of the North American Indians* (New York: Dial, 1971) and *Big Star Fallin' Mama: Five Women in Black Music* (New York: Viking, 1995). Jones adapted stories for *Coyote Tales* (New York: Holt, Rinehart, and Winston, 1974). In Brenda Knight, ed., *The Women of the Beat Generation* (Berkeley, CA: Conari Press, 1996): 183-195, see "Hettie Jones: Mother Jones." On the companion cassette tapes to *The Women of the Beat Generation* (San Bruno, CA: Audio Literature, 1996), Jones reads several selections. See Hettie Jones on *The New York Beat Generation Show: Volume Two: Women and the Beats* (New York: Thin Air Video, 1995).

Lenore Kandel (1932-   )

Lenore Kandel's association with the Beat Generation may stem from her correspondence to Ramona Schwarz, a character in the novel *Big Sur* by Jack Kerouac. She is also connected to the Beats because of her notorious collection of poems *The Love Book* (San Francisco: Stolen Paper Editions, 1966), which was frank in its celebration of physical love and precipitated a five-week obscenity trial. Eventually the book was vindicated. *Word Alchemy* (New York: Grove Press, 1967) reveals development in Kandel's technique. The focus is still mostly on sex, but drugs and insanity are also treated. "In Transit" and "Small Prayer for Falling Angels" are in David Kherdian, ed., *Beat Voices* (New York: Henry Holt, 1995): 102-106. Kandel's "Poetry Is Never Compromise" appears in Donald Allen and Warren Tallman, eds., *The Poetics of the New American Poetry* (New York: Grove Press, 1973): 450-452. See Donna Nance, "Lenore Kandel," in *The Beats: Literary Bohemians in Postwar America*, ed. Ann Charters (Detroit: Gale Research, 1983): 270-274, Leonard Wolf, "Lenore Kandel," in *Voices from the Love Generation* (Boston: Little Brown, 1968): 19-37, Bruce Cook, *The Beat Generation* (New York: Quill, 1994): 208-212, Barry Gifford and Lawrence Lee, *Jack's Book* (New York: St. Martin's, 1978): 283-290, and "Lenore Kandel:

Word Alchemist," in Brénda Knight, ed., *The Women of the Beat Generation* (Berkeley, CA: Conari Press, 1996): 279-285. On the companion cassette tapes to *The Women of the Beat Generation* (San Bruno, CA: Audio Literature, 1996), Kandel reads three selections.

Bob Kaufman (1925-1986)

Cranial Guitar: Selected Poems, ed. Gerald Nicosia (Minneapolis: Coffee House Press, 1996) features an introduction by David Henderson and takes poems from *Golden Sardine* (San Francisco: City Lights, 1965), *Solitudes Crowded with Loneliness* (New York: New Directions, 1965), and *The Ancient Rain* (New York: New Directions, 1981) and offers some "uncollected works." "Blues Note" and "Abomunist Manifesto" are included in Anne Waldman, ed., *The Beat Book* (Boston: Shambhala, 1996): 302-313. Kaufman is prominent among the West Coast Beats for his leadership in making poetry events happen in North Beach, despite resistance from local authorities. As one of the founders of *Beatitude*, he provided a forum for creative activity. Broadsides such as "Abomunist Manifesto" (1959), "Second April" (1959), and "Does the Secret Mind Whisper?" (1960) are characteristic of his creativity and innovation. "Jazz Chick," "O-Jazz-O," "On," and "Round About Midnight" appear in Ann Charters, ed., *The Portable Beat Reader* (New York: Viking Penguin, 1992). Valuable introductory remarks are provided in Barbara Christian, "Whatever Happened to Bob Kaufman," in *The Beats: Essays in Criticism* (Jefferson, NC: McFarland, 1981): 107-114. See Maria Damon, "Victors of Catastrophe" and Mona Lisa Saloy, "Black Beats and Black Issues" in *Beat Culture and the New America: 1950-1965* (New York: Whitney Museum of American Art/Flammarion, 1995): 141-149, 153-165. Damon's "'Unmeaning Jargon'/Uncanonized Beatitude: Bob Kaufman Poet" is a chapter in her book *The Dark End of the Street: Margins in American Vanguard Poetry* (Minneapolis: University of Minnesota Press, 1993): 32-76. See also Steven Watson, "Bob Kaufman," in *The Birth of the Beat Generation* (New York: Pantheon, 1995): 225-227, Eileen Kaufman, "Laughter Sounds Orange at Night," in *The Beat Vision*, eds. Arthur Winfield Knight and Kit Knight (New York: Paragon, 1987): 259-267, "Eileen Kaufman: Keeper of the Flame," in Brenda Knight, ed., *The Women of the Beat Generation* (Berkeley, CA: Conari Press,

1996), and Neeli Cherkovski, *Whitman's Wild Children* (Venice, CA: Lapis Press, 1988). A. D. Winans, "Bob Kaufman," in *The Beats: Literary Bohemians in Postwar America*, ed., Ann Charters (Detroit: Gale Research, 1983): 275-279 and Winans, *Bob Kaufman* (San Francisco: A. D. Winans, 1986) provide useful commentary. See also A. Robert Lee, "Black Beats: The Signifying Poetry of LeRoi Jones/Amiri Baraka, Ted Joans, and Bob Kaufman," in *The Beat Generation Writers* (London: Pluto Press, 1996): 158-177. A pair of cassettes titled *Bob Kaufman Poet* (1991) includes commentary on Kaufman by Baraka, Ginsberg, and Ferlinghetti and is available at the Bancroft Poetry Archive at the University of California, Berkeley.

Jan Kerouac (1952-1996)

The estranged daughter of the legendary Jack Kerouac, Jan Kerouac is a writer relevant to students of the Beat. An excerpt from *Baby Driver: A Story About Myself* (New York: St. Martin's, 1981) appears in Ann Charters, ed., *The Portable Beat Reader* (New York: Viking Penguin, 1992). Her second book is *Trainsong* (New York: Henry Holt, 1988). *Parrot Fever: Excerpts from a Novel* (Santa Cruz, CA: Pica Pole Press, 1994) presents two chapters from the work *Parrot Fever*. See Gerald Nicosia, "Jan Kerouac," in *The Beats: Literary Bohemians in Postwar America*, ed. Ann Charters (Detroit: Gale Research, 1983): 303-306 and "Jan Kerouac: The Next Generation," in Brenda Knight, ed., *Women of the Beat Generation* (Berkeley, CA: Conari Press, 1996): 309-318. On the companion cassette tapes to *The Women of the Beat Generation* (San Bruno, CA: Audio Literature, 1996), an excerpt from Jan Kerouac's *Trainsong* is read by Mary Norbert Korte. Jan Kerouac may be seen on video on *What Happened to Kerouac?*, a video directed by Richard Lerner and Lewis MacAdams in 1985 (Vidmark, 1987) and on *The New York Beat Generation Show: Volume Two: Women and the Beats* (New York: Thin Air Video, 1995), a video prepared at the 1994 conference on the Beats held at New York University. See also Daniel Pinchbeck, "Children of the Beats," *New York Times Magazine* 5 Nov. 1995: 38-43. In Gerald Nicosia, "Kerouac's

Daughter: The Beat Goes On," *Chicago Sun-Times* 21 Oct. 1979, *Living* section: 5, 9, Jan Kerouac remembers her father.

Ken Kesey (1935-   )

Kesey's first and most celebrated work is the novel *One Flew Over the Cuckoo's Nest* (New York: Viking, 1962), which pits a nonconformist against society. *Sometimes a Great Notion* (New York: Viking, 1964) also enjoyed success and was followed by *Ken Kesey's Garage Sale* (New York: Viking, Intrepid Trips, 1973). Kesey's activities with the Merry Pranksters, including Neal Cassady, and the journeys on the bus, Further, earned Kesey a reputation as a figure leading the transition from the Beat world to the Hippie world. Kesey's Merry Pranksters are popularized and made legendary in Tom Wolfe, *The Electric Kool-Aid Acid Test*. Other links to the Beats include Ginsberg's poem "First Party at Ken Kesey's with Hell's Angels" (1965) and Kesey's tributes to Neal Cassady: *The Day After Superman Died* (Northridge, CA: Lord John Press, 1980) and the manuscript *Over the Border*, which Ann Charters describes as "a morality play conceived in the modern form of a psychedelic comic-book film scenario." Kesey is also connected with *Spit in the Ocean*, a magazine begun in 1974. The sixth issue is a memorial to Neal Cassady, and other issues feature guest editors Timothy Leary, Ken Babbs, and Lee Marrs. Introductory volumes about Kesey include Barry H. Leeds, *Ken Kesey* (New York: Frederick Ungar, 1988) and Stephen L. Tanner, *Ken Kesey* (Boston: Twayne, 1983). For students, George Searles, *A Casebook on Ken Kesey's "One Flew Over the Cuckoo's Nest"* (Albuquerque: University of New Mexico Press, 1992) gathers valuable reference material. Paul Perry, *On the Bus: The Complete Guide to the Legendary Trip of Ken Kesey and the Merry Pranksters and the Birth of the Counterculture* (New York: Thunder's Mouth Press, 1990) and Peter O. Whitmer, *Aquarius Revisited: Seven Who Created the Sixties Counterculture That Changed America* (New York: Citadel Press, 1991) demonstrate Kesey's links to many ideas and actions associated with the Beat movement. Ann Charters, "Ken Kesey," in *The Beats: Literary Bohemians in Postwar America*, ed. Ann Charters (Detroit: Gale Research, 1983): 306-316 provides concise background material and offers an impressive list of journal articles about Kesey. See also

Ann Charters, *Beats and Company* (Garden City, NY: Doubleday, 1986): 125, 128, 136-141, 151. *Still Kesey* is a video by Key-Z Productions (1986), which can be found on the internet at **http://www.continet.com/key-z**. On the internet, one can try "The Far Gone Interview" at **http://www.imv.com/lit/fargone/kesey.htm** or check out the unofficial home page of Ken Kesey at **http://www.peak.org/~clapp/kesey/**.

Seymour Krim (1922-   )

Seymour Krim earns prominence among the Beats primarily for his role as editor and critic. He is the editor of the anthology *The Beats* (Greenwich, CT: Fawcett, 1960), which features Kerouac, Mailer, Ginsberg, Ferlinghetti, and others. Although Krim has written for establishment publications such as *Commentary, Partisan Review, Hudson Review, Harper's,* and the *New York Times,* he has also served as editor for *Swank, Provincetown Review, Nugget, Show, Evergreen Review,* and *Element,* providing publication opportunities for numerous Beat writers. In a truncated version of *Views of a Cannoneer* (New York: Excelsior Press, 1961), which later appeared in full length (New York: Dutton, 1968), as well as *Shake It for the World, Smartass* (New York: Dial, 1970) and *You and Me* (New York: Holt, Rinehart and Winston, 1974), Krim appreciates the Beats and articulates the principles of a literature based on honest self-revelation. Krim is also noteworthy for his introductions published with important Beat texts, including Kerouac's *Desolation Angels* and Holmes' *Go. What's This Cat's Story? The Best Of Seymour Krim* (New York: Paragon House, 1991) offers a sampling of Krim's work. See Krim, "The Insanity Bit," in Park Honan, ed., *The Beats* (London: J. M. Dent, 1987): 125-142. Joseph Wenke, "Seymour Krim," in *The Beats: Literary Bohemians in Postwar America,* ed. Ann Charters (Detroit: Gale Research, 1983): 316-320 gives Krim's general background. Theodore Solotaroff, *The Red Hot Vacuum and Other Pieces on the Writing of the Sixties* (New York: Atheneum, 1970) includes a review of Krim. A cassette *Seymour Krim Reads Excerpts from the Siege* (Columbia, MO: American Audio Prose Library, 1985) offers an impression of Krim, and a cassette *Seymour Krim Interview* (1984) is available from the same source.

Tuli Kupferberg (1923-   )

Tuli Kupferberg's "Greenwich Village of My Dreams" appears in David Kherdian, *Beat Voices* (New York: Henry Holt, 1995): 33-35 and Park Honan, ed., *The Beats* (London: J. M. Dent, 1987): 59-61. "Greenwich Village," along with "1001 Ways to Beat the Draft," also appears in Ann Charters, ed., *The Portable Beat Reader* (New York: Viking Penguin, 1992): 385-394. Kupferberg's association with the spirit of the Beats is most notable in his participation in a musical group called The Fugs, which included Ed Sanders and Ken Weaver. *The Fugs First Album* (1964) challenged the limits of censorship and questioned American politics and values. In 1958, Kupferberg founded the magazine *Birth*, which included various Beat writers and led to Birth Press, which enabled Kupferberg to publish many of his own books, including *Beating* (1959), *Selected Fruits and Nuts, From One Crazy Month in Spring Not So Long Ago* (1959), and *Snow Job Poems 1946-1959* (1959). Kupferberg and Sylvia Tapp share an admiration for children and have published books of photos of children and writings by children, including works by Beat writers when they were children. See *First Glance: Childhood Creations of the Famous* (1978) and *As They Were Too* (1979). Joseph Wenke, "Tuli Kupferberg," in *The Beats: Literary Bohemians in Postwar America*, ed. Ann Charters (Detroit: Gale Research, 1983): 320-324 chronicles Kupferberg's life and work. See also Ann Charters, *Beats and Company* (Garden City, NY: Doubleday, 1986): 14. "The First National Anthem" by Tuli Kupferberg is included in *Shimmy Disc* (New York: JAF, 1989), a collection of music videos. "Arse Longer Vita Herring" by Tuli Kupferberg is available on *Breathe on the Living* (Dayton, OH: Nexus, 1989), a collection of three sound discs. Kupferberg's letters to Ed Sanders are at the University of Connecticut with Ed Sanders' papers. A tape recording of an interview of Kupferberg with David Ossman on the radio show *The Sullen Art* is available from the library at the University of Toledo.

Joanne Kyger (1934-   )

Joanne Kyger was associated with the literary scene in North Beach in 1957, participating in poetry sessions with Robert Duncan and Jack Spicer. *The Tapestry and the Web* (San Francisco: Four Seasons Foundation, 1965) appeared with the support of Donald Allen, and this publication was soon followed by the presentation of Kyger, along with Ginsberg, Welch, Sanders, Berrigan, and others, at the Berkeley Poetry Conference in the summer of 1965. Other titles include *Places to Go* (Los Angeles: Black Sparrow, 1970), *Just Space: Poems 1979-1989* (Santa Rosa, CA: Black Sparrow, 1991), *Phenomenological* (Canton, NY: Institute of Further Studies, 1989), and *Book for Sensi: Poems* (Pacifica, CA: Big Bridge Press, 1990). Kyger's travels to Japan, India, and Latin America have extended her connection to Beat writers. She has strong interests in Buddhism and Native American culture. Kyger's work is included in Anne Waldman, ed., *The Beat Book* (Boston: Shambhala, 1996): 238-259; see also David Kherdian, ed., *Beat Voices* (New York: Henry Holt, 1995), which includes Kyger's "My Father Died This Spring." Donald Allen and George F. Butterick, eds., *The Postmoderns: The New American Poetry Revised* (New York: Grove Press, 1982) includes a half dozen poems by Kyger. See Bill Berkson, "Joanne Kyger," in *The Beats: Literary Bohemians in Postwar America*, ed. Ann Charters (Detroit: Gale Research, 1983): 324-328, Amy L. Friedman, "'I Say My New Name': Women Writers of the Beat Generation," in A. Robert Lee, ed., *The Beat Generation Writers* (London: Pluto, 1996): 200-216, Ann Charters, *Beats and Company* (Garden City, NY: Doubleday, 1986): 71, 72, 142, and "Dharma Sister," in Brenda Knight, ed., *The Women of the Beat Generation* (Berkeley, CA: Conari Press, 1996): 196-204. On the companion cassette tapes to *The Women of the Beat Generation* (San Bruno, CA: Audio Literature, 1996), Joanne Kyger reads several selections. In the papers of Gary Snyder housed at the University of California, Davis, correspondence with Joanne Kyger is included. See Joanne Kyger on *The New York Beat Generation Show: Volume Two: Women and the Beats* (New York: Thin Air Video, 1995).

Philip Lamantia (1927-   )

Lamantia is sometimes regarded as the link between surrealists and the Beats. One finds "Fud at Foster's" in David Kherdian, ed., *Beat Voices* (New York: Henry Holt, 1995): 109 and Park Honan, ed., *The Beats* (London: J. M. Dent, 1987): 58-59. "Fud," as well as

"High," "I Have Given Fair Warning," "The Night Is a Space of White Marble," and "There Is This Distance Between Me and What I See," appear in Ann Charters, ed., *The Portable Beat Reader* (New York: Viking Penguin, 1992): 317-320. In *Popular Culture in America* (Minneapolis: University of Minnesota Press, 1987), Lamantia's "Radio Voices: A Child's Bed of Sirens" is included. Lamantia's "Voice, USA, 1959" is in *Shaped Poetry* (San Francisco: Arion Press, 1981). "Put Down the Whore of Babylon" is in Seymour Krim, ed., *The Beats* (Greenwich, CT: Fawcett, 1960). *Bed of Sphinxes: New and Selected Poems 1943-1993* (San Francisco: City Lights, 1997) provides access to diverse materials. Books include *Erotic Poems* (Berkeley, CA: Bern Porter Books, 1946), *Ekstasis* (San Francisco: Auerhahn Press, 1959), *Narcotica* (San Francisco: Auerhahn Press, 1959), *Destroyed Works* (San Francisco: Auerhahn Press, 1962), and *Selected Poems 1943-1966* (San Francisco: City Lights, 1967). See Nancy J. Peters, "Philip Lamantia," in *The Beats: Literary Bohemians in Postwar America*, ed. Ann Charters (Detroit: Gale Research, 1983): 329-336, which includes a list of references for the study of Lamantia. See also Steven Watson, "Philip Lamantia," in *The Birth of the Beat Generation* (New York: Pantheon, 1995): 215-217, and Neeli Cherkovski, *Whitman's Wild Children* (Venice, CA: Lapis Press, 1988). Lamantia reads "Rest in Peace, Al Capone" and "All Hail Pope John XXIII" on *Howls, Raps, and Roars: Recordings from the San Francisco Poetry Renaissance* (Berkeley, CA: Fantasy Records, 1993).

Fran Landesman (1927-) and Jay Landesman (1919-)

Jay Landesman edited *Neurotica*, a journal that, apart from student magazines, was the first place a poem by Allen Ginsberg appeared in print. Other writers for *Neurotica* included Kenneth Patchen, Marshall McLuhan, Anatole Broyard, Judith Malina, and Gershon Legman. *Neurotica* has been published twice in collected editions (New York: Hacker Art Books, 1963; London: Jay Landesman, 1981). The Landesmans were also active in theater and music, with Jay combining with his brother, Fred, to open a cabaret theater, the Crystal Palace, in St. Louis. Lenny Bruce, Barbra Streisand, Phyllis Diller, the Smothers Brothers, and Chicago's

Second City Players made appearances. The Landesmans combined to produce *The Nervous Set*, which John Clellon Holmes calls the first and only Beat musical. Jay Landesman and Theodore J. Flicker prepared the material as a musical play, with lyrics by Fran Landesman and musical score by Tommy Wolfe. The play opened at the Henry Miller Theatre in the spring of 1959 and an original cast album was recorded. Fran later wrote lyrics for *Molly Darling*, which opened at the St. Louis Municipal Opera in 1963. See Jay Landesman, *Jay Walking* (London: Weidenfeld and Nicolson, 1992) and Jay Landesman, *Rebel Without Applause* (Sag Harbor, NY: Permanent Press, 1987), which was later republished by Paragon House in New York in 1990. For references, see John Clellon Holmes, "Jay and Fran Landesman," in *The Beats: Literary Bohemians in Postwar America*, ed. Ann Charters (Detroit: Gale Research, 1983): 337-344. Holmes writes about Jay Landesman and *Neurotica* in *Representative Men: The Biographical Essays* (Fayetteville: University of Arkansas Press, 1988): 11-18, 51-72.

Timothy Leary (1920-1996)

Though known as the insatiable experimenter of the psychedelic period, Timothy Leary held a Ph.D. in Clinical Psychology from the University of California, Berkeley (1950). He directed clinical research and psychology at the Kaiser Foundation Hospital, Oakland, California (1954-1959) and became a lecturer at Harvard University. In December of 1960, Leary met with Allen Ginsberg and Peter Orlovsky and gave them psilocybin. See chapter 9 in Leary, *High Priest* (New York: World, 1968), which was recently republished (Berkeley, CA: Ronin Publications, 1995). See also "In the Beginning, Leary Turned on Ginsberg," *Esquire* July 1968: 83-85, 116-117, which is reproduced in Lewis Hyde, ed., *On the Poetry of Allen Ginsberg* (Ann Arbor: University of Michigan Press, 1984): 231-239. For *Jail Notes* (New York: Douglas, 1970), Ginsberg provides an introduction. Ginsberg gave references to many artists, writers, and musicians who might want to experiment with psilocybin. At Ginsberg's suggestion, Charles Olson also tried psilocybin, and Olson describes the experience in "Under the Mushroom," an interview in *Muthologos* (1977). William Seward Burroughs was also enlisted for experimentation, but Burroughs did not appreciate Leary and rejected drugs as a means of social improvement. Leary's plan for establishing the future appears in *The Politics of Ecstasy* (New York: Putnam's, 1968) and in "Interview: Timothy Leary," *Playboy* Sept. 1966. Leary entered prison in 1970 but escaped and lived internationally as a fugitive until he was apprehended in Afghanistan. See Timothy Leary, Ralph Metzner, and Richard Albert, *The Psychedelic Experience: A Manual Based on the Tibetan Book of the Dead* (New Hyde Park, NY: University Books, 1964) and *Psychedelic Prayers After the Tao Te Ching* (Kerhonkson, NY: Poets Press, 1966). For a concise review of Leary's life and work, see Martin A. Lee and Bruce Shlain, "Timothy Leary," in *The Beats: Literary Bohemians in Postwar America*, ed. Ann Charters (Detroit: Gale Research, 1983): 344-351. Bibliographical data are presented in Ken Thomas, *Timothy Leary: Print, Audio, and Video Sources, 1947-Present* (St. Louis, MO: K. Thomas, 1991) and Michael Horowitz, *An Annotated Bibliography of Timothy Leary* (Hamden, CT: Archon Books, 1988). Video resources include *Timothy Leary: A Portrait in the First Person* (Princeton, NJ: Films for the Humanities and Sciences, 1994) and *Fried Shoes Cooked Diamonds* (New York: Mystic Fire Video, 1978), in which Allen Ginsberg talks with Leary. A recent interview appears in *Mavericks of the Mind: Conversations for the New Millenium* (Freedom, CA: Crossing Press, 1993). A chapter on Leary appears in Peter O. Whitmer, *Aquarius Revisited* (New York: Citadel Press, 1991). Leary's autobiography is *Flashbacks: A Personal and Cultural History of an Era: An Autobiography* (Los Angeles: J. P. Tarcher, 1990).

Lawrence Lipton (1898-1975)

Lipton's *The Holy Barbarians* (New York: Messner, 1959) is a sociological interpretation of the Beat Generation. Among many other things, Lipton describes Ginsberg's undressing during a poetry reading when challenged by a heckler. Lipton refers to Ginsberg, Rexroth, Patchen, Perkoff, Corso, and Ferlinghetti. "Poetry and the Vocal Tradition," *Nation* 14 Apr. 1956: 319-324 and "Youth Will Serve Itself," *Nation* 10 Nov. 1956: 389-392 demonstrate Lipton's connection to ideas associated with the Beats. *Jazz Canto* (1958) is an anthology on record prepared by Lipton featuring musicians such as the Chico Hamilton Quintet and Gerry Mulligan, with poetry from Dylan Thomas, William Carlos Williams, Walt Whitman, Langston Hughes, Philip Whalen, and Lawrence Ferlinghetti. The material is read by John Carradine, Hoagy Carmichael, Ben Wright, Roy Glenn, and Bob Dorough. In addition to *The Holy Barbarians*, Lipton is the author of *The Erotic Revolution: An Affirmative View of the New Morality* (Los Angeles: Sherbourne Press, 1965). See also *Bruno in Venice West and Other Poems* (Van Nuys, CA: Venice West Publishers, 1976). Nettie Lipton, "Lawrence Lipton," in *The Beats: Literary Bohemians in Postwar America*, ed. Ann Charters (Detroit: Gale Research, 1983): 352-356 offers background on Lipton, and John Arthur Maynard, *Venice West: The Beat Generation in Southern California* (New Brunswick, NJ: Rutgers University Press, 1991) includes numerous references to the activities and writings of Lipton. A photo of Lipton reading poetry in Venice, California, appears as part of "Squaresville U.S.A. Vs. Beatsville," *Life* 21 Sept. 1959: 31-37.

Joanna McClure (1930-   )

Joanna McClure has associated with almost all of the Beat writers, including Ginsberg, Kerouac, Rexroth, Lamantia, O'Hara, Jones, DiPrima, and Snyder. Her relationship with Robert Duncan and his lover, Jess Collins, helped Joanna McClure develop as an artist, especially as she read in Duncan' s personal library. She attended the reading at the Six Gallery on October 7, 1955. Her books include *Wolf Eyes* (San Francisco: Bearthm Press, 1974) and *Extended Love Poem* (Berkeley, CA: Arif Press, 1978), which are collections of earlier works. Joanna and Michael McClure correspond to the McLears in Kerouac's *Big Sur*. See Michael McClure, "Joanna McClure," in *The Beats: Literary Bohemians in Postwar America*, ed. Ann Charters (Detroit: Gale Research, 1983): 376-381. See also "Joanna McClure: West Coast Villager," in Brenda Knight, ed., *The Women of the Beat Generation* (Berkeley, CA: Conari Press, 1996): 214-222. On the companion cassette tapes to *The Women of the Beat Generation* (San Bruno, CA: Audio Literature, 1996), Joanna McClure reads several selections.

Michael McClure (1932-   )

Michael McClure was a major force among West Coast writers of the Beat Generation and the San Francisco Renaissance. He was one of the readers at the Six Gallery on October 7, 1955. His work as an editor, environmental advocate, poet, playwright, essayist, novelist, and linguistic innovator is revealed in his extensive production. He was editor of *Ark II/Moby I*, a journal that published poets representative of the San Francisco Beats and the Black Mountain group. One finds his pictographic poetry in *Passage* (Big Sur, CA: Jonathan Williams, 1956), *Hymns to Saint Geryon and Other Poems* (San Francisco: Auerhahn Press, 1959), and *A Fist-Full (1956-1957)* (Los Angeles: Black Sparrow, 1974). Books include *Dark Brown* (London: Auerhahn Press, 1961) and *Ghost Tantras* (San Francisco: privately printed, 1964). McClure's work in other forms is found in *Meat Science Essays* (San Francisco: City Lights, 1963) and the novel *The Mad Club* (New York: Bantam, 1970). Along with Ferlinghetti and Meltzer, he was editor of *Journal for the Protection of All Beings*. In 1966, *NET Presents* broadcast *USA Poetry: Michael McClure and Brother Antoninus*. McClure read sound poetry and beast-language poems to lions, who apparently responded to the poet. McClure has written many plays, among them *The Beard* (New York: Grove Press, 1967). The play was challenged by police for obscenity in San Francisco and Berkeley, but intervention by the ACLU led to the dropping of charges. When the play was produced by students at California State University, Fullerton, newspapers voiced objections and a committee from the state senate investigated. *Dream Table* (San Francisco: Dave Haselwood, 1965) brought forward the concept of "poetry decks." Each package contained thirty cards, each with two words, suitable for the spontaneous generation of poems through the selection and distribution of the cards. A tape from the San Francisco Poetry Archive shows McClure lecturing to teachers on the use of poetry decks in teaching creative writing. See an essay about poetry decks in Anne Waldman's *Talking Poetics from Naropa Institute* (1979). *Love Lion* (New York: Mystic Fire Video, 1991) features McClure and Ray Manzarek (formerly the keyboard player of the Doors) combining in performance. One can also see McClure and Manzarek on *The Beat Generation: Volume One: History and*

Overview: The Censorship Years (New York: Thin Air Video, 1995). *Star* (New York: Grove Press, 1970) offers selected material from the 1960's. *Scratching the Beat Surface* (San Francisco: North Point Press, 1982) offers powerful interpretation of the Beat movement. An excerpt of this book and other material are included in Ann Charters, ed., *The Portable Beat Reader* (New York: Viking, 1992): 264-287 and 556-560. *Lighting the Corners: On Art, Nature, and the Visionary* (Albuquerque: University of New Mexico College of Arts and Sciences, 1993) collects various writings and furthers McClure's analysis. "The Ring" and "Point Lobos: Animism" are in David Kherdian, ed., *Beat Voices* (New York: Henry Holt, 1995): 97-99. In Anne Waldman, ed., *The Beat Book* (Boston: Shambhala, 1996): 315-332, one finds a selection of poems. Nine poems and a statement on poetics are included in Donald Allen, ed., *The New American Poetry: 1945-1960* (New York: Grove Press, 1960): 334-351, 421-424. Four poems are included in Donald Allen and George F. Butterick, eds., *The Postmoderns: The New American Poetry Revised* (New York: Grove Press, 1982): 290-296. See "Phi Upsilon Kappa" and "Revolt" in Donald Allen and Warren Tallman, eds., *The Poetics of the New American Poetry* (New York: Grove Press, 1973): 416-444. William R. King, "Michael McClure," in *The Beats: Literary Bohemians in Postwar America*, ed. Ann Charters (Detroit: Gale Research, 1983): 382-400 provides background and numerous references. David Kherdian, ed., *Six San Francisco Poets* (Fresno, CA: Giligia, 1965): 37-40 provides an impression of McClure. David Meltzer, ed., *Golden Gate* (San Francisco: Wingbow, 1976): 195-228 is a valuable interview. See also Steven Watson, "Michael McClure," in *The Birth of the Beat Generation* (New York: Pantheon, 1995): 209-212, Gregory Stephenson, "From the Substrate: Notes on the Work of Michael McClure," in *The Daybreak Boys* (Carbondale: University of Southern Illinois Press, 1990): 105-130, Geoffrey Thurley, "The Development of the New Language: Michael McClure, Philip Whalen, and Gregory Corso," in *The Beats: Essays in Criticism* (Jefferson, NC: McFarland, 1981): 165-180, and Ann Charters, *Beats and Company* (Garden City, NY: Doubleday, 1986): 61, 68, 153. McClure reads "Grahhh! Michael in the Lion's Den," from "Dark Brown," and from "Ghost Tantras" on *Howls, Raps, and Roars: Recordings from the San Francisco Poetry Renaissance* (Berkeley, CA: Fantasy Records, 1993).

Norman Mailer (1923-   )

Norman Mailer is a prolific writer whose work has earned him much recognition, including the National Book Award and the Pulitzer Prize, and has made him one of the most controversial writers of the twentieth century. Since the publication of *The Naked and the Dead* (New York: Rinehart, 1948), he has written dozens of works of fiction and nonfiction. Mailer's connection to the Beats is principally revealed in his essay "The White Negro," which originally appeared in *Dissent* in the summer of 1957 but subsequently appeared in *Advertisements for Myself* (New York: Putnam's, 1959). One finds the essay also in Ann Charters, ed., *The Portable Beat Reader* (New York: Viking, 1992): 582-605 and in *Legacy of "Dissent"* (New York: Simon and Schuster, 1994). The significance of the essay is also reflected in Lawrence Ferlinghetti's publication of *The White Negro* as a separate pamphlet (San Francisco: City Lights, 1957). Some readers find that Marion Faye of *The Deer Park* (New York: Putnam's, 1955) is representative of Beat values. Selections from *The Deer Park* appear in Seymour Krim, ed., *The Beats* (Greenwich, CT: Fawcett, 1960). In *Why Are We in Vietnam?* (New York: Putnam's, 1967) Mailer adopts a style that compares to the work of William S. Burroughs in *Naked Lunch* (1959). *The Gospel According to the Son* (New York: Random House, 1997) makes Jesus Himself the narrator of His life. "Superman Comes to the Supermarket" is included in *The Sixties: Art, Politics, and Media of Our Most Explosive Decade* (New York: Marlowe, 1995). For bibliographical information, see Laura Adams, *Norman Mailer: A Comprehensive Bibliography* (Metuchen, NJ: Scarecrow, 1974). Joseph Wenke, "Norman Mailer," in *The Beats: Literary Bohemians in Postwar America*, ed. Ann Charters (Detroit: Gale Research, 1983): 361-371 offers background and a useful list of references. Hilary Mills, *Norman Mailer, a Biography* (New York: Empire Books, 1982) tells Mailer's life, but one may want to compare Adele Mailer, *The Last Party: My Life with Norman Mailer* (New York: Barricade Books, 1997) and Carl E. Rollyson, *The Lives of Norman Mailer* (New York: Paragon House, 1991). Robert Merrill, *Norman Mailer Revisited* (New York: Twayne, 1992) is criticism and interpretation in book format; a potentially useful complement is Merrill, *Norman Mailer* (New York: Twayne, 1991), a computer-optical disk about Mailer. Michael K. Glenday, *Norman Mailer* (London: Macmillan, 1995)

offers criticism, interpretation, and bibliographical information. See
a chapter on Mailer in *Aquarius Revisited* (New York: Citadel,
1991); Nigel Leigh, *Radical Fictions and the Novels of Norman
Mailer* (New York: St. Martin's, 1990) offers further insight. A video
Norman Mailer Talking with David Frost (Alexandria, VA: PBS,
1992) features a wide-ranging discussion.

Edward Marshall (1932-   )

Though not a prolific poet, Edward Marshall has had a profound
influence on the Beat Generation because of his poem "Leave the
Word Alone," *Black Mountain Review* 7 (Autumn 1957): 38-51. Allen
Ginsberg acknowledges the influence of this poem on the composi-
tion of "Kaddish" (1959), and Donald Allen includes Marshall's
lengthy poem in *The New American Poetry* (New York: Grove Press,
1960). Marshall's "Poem" appeared in John Wieners' *Measure* 1
(Summer 1957): 11. Three poems are in Ira Cohen and Richard
Richkin, eds., *The Great Society* (New York: Heddaona, 1967): 25-
28. Seven poems are in *Mulch* 2 (October 1971): 74-96. See George
F. Butterick, "Edward Marshall," in *The Beats: Literary Bohemians in
Postwar America*, ed. Ann Charters (Detroit: Gale Research, 1983):
371-375.

Taylor Mead (date of birth not publicly known)

Taylor Mead is the author of various explicit diaries, including
Excerpts from the Anonymous Diary of a New York Youth (Venice,
CA: Taylor Mead, 1961), *Excerpts from the Anonymous Diary of a
New York Youth, Volume 2* (New York: Taylor Mead, 1962), and *On
Amphetamine and in Europe: Excerpts from the Anonymous Diary of
a New York Youth, Volume 3* (New York: Boss Books, 1968). *Son of
Andy Warhol* (Madras, NY: Hanuman Books, 1986) continues the
publication of excerpts from a diary. Mead is known as an actor in
films and plays associated with the Beats. In film, Mead has been in
Adolfas Mekas, *Halleluja the Hills* (1962), Ron Rice, *The Queen of
Sheba Meets the Atom Man* (1963), Bob Downey, *Babo 73* (1964),
Win Chamberlain, *Brand X* (1969), and Andy Warhol, *Lonesome*

Cowboys (1968). The 1963 version of *The Queen of Sheba Meets the Atom Man* has been put into a final form by Mead himself (New York: Arthouse, 1996). On the stage, Mead has played in dramas by Michael McClure and LeRoi Jones/Amiri Baraka, in *Le Désir Attrapé par la Queue* by Picasso, and in *The General Returns from One Place to Another* by Frank O'Hara. See Gordon Ball, "Taylor Mead," in *The Beats: Literary Bohemians in Postwar America*, ed. Ann Charters (Detroit: Gale Research, 1983): 400-404.

David Meltzer (1937-   )

Meltzer refers to himself as a second-generation Beat writer. He served as co-editor of *Journal for the Protection of All Beings* (1961). His work has been included in Donald Allen, ed., *The New American Poetry: 1945-1960* (New York: Grove Press, 1960); Donald Allen and George F. Butterick, eds., *The Postmoderns: The New American Poetry Revised* (New York: Grove Press, 1982); and David Kherdian, *Beat Voices* (New York: Henry Holt, 1995). Meltzer's "From the Rabbi's Dream Book" is in *The Book: Spiritual Instrument* (New York: Granary Books, 1996). Meltzer's work has appeared in *Yugen*, *Big Table*, *Beatitude*, *White Dove Review*, *Coyote's Journal*, *Floating Bear*, and *Caterpillar*. Meltzer is noteworthy for his interviews with Rexroth, Everson, Ferlinghetti, Welch, McClure, and Brautigan in Meltzer, ed., *The San Francisco Poets* (New York: Ballantine, 1971), which was revised as *Golden Gate* (Berkeley, CA: Wingbow Press, 1976). *Arrows: Selected Poetry 1957-1992* (Santa Rosa, CA: Black Sparrow Press, 1994) offers a wide variety of Meltzer's writing. See Robert Hawley and Ann Charters, "David Meltzer," in *The Beats: Literary Bohemians in Postwar America*, ed. Ann Charters (Detroit: Gale Research, 1983): 405-410. David Kherdian devotes a chapter to Meltzer in *Six San Francisco Poets* (Fresno, CA: Giligia Press, 1965): 33-34. See also Ann Charters, *Beats and Company* (Garden City, NY: Doubleday, 1986): 62. Meltzer's papers, including his correspondence with Ferlinghetti, Welch, and others, are housed at Washington University. Meltzer reads "Baby's Hands," "Rain Poems," "Nerve Root Poem," "Two Poems to My Wife," and "Poem for Lew Welch" on *Howls, Raps, and Roars: Recordings from the San Francisco Poetry Renaissance* (Berkeley, CA: Fantasy Records, 1993).

Jack Micheline (Harvey Martin Silver, 1929-   )

Jack Micheline is the author of *River of Red Wine* (New York: Troubador Press, 1958), which features introductory remarks by Jack Kerouac and received a favorable review from Dorothy Parker. In 1967, Micheline's play *East Bleeker: A Drama with Music* was staged at Cafe LaMama as an Ellen Stewart Production. According to Gerald Nicosia, "Kuboya" (1972) is Micheline's masterpiece. A valuable collection is *North of Manhattan: Collected Poems, Ballads, and Songs* (South San Francisco: Manroot, 1976). Other books include *Primer to Self-Liberation* (Kansas City, MO: Howling Dog Press, 1985) and *Acapella Rabbi* (Pueblo, CO: Quick Books, 1986). "Poet of the Streets" is in Ann Charters, ed., *The Portable Beat Reader* (New York: Viking, 1992): 395-398. His work is also included in Elias Wilentz, ed., *The Beat Scene* (New York: Corinth Books, 1960) and Seymour Krim, ed., *The Beats* (Greenwich, CT: Fawcett, 1960). See Gerald Nicosia, "Jack Micheline," in *The Beats: Literary Bohemians in Postwar America*, ed. Ann Charters (Detroit: Gale Research, 1983): 410-415. See also Ann Charters, *Beats and Company* (Garden City, NY: Doubleday, 1986): 152. A cassette tape of Micheline reading with Carl Solomon at Naropa at the Jack Kerouac Conference in 1982 is available from Naropa, at the Chicago Public Library, and at the University of California, Berkeley. See and hear Micheline reading "Imaginary Conversation with Jack Kerouac" on *The Beat Generation: Volume One: Another Lost Generation: The Origin of the Beats* (New York: Thin Air Video, 1995). *Recent Readings/NY: Volume 14: Micheline-Clausen* (New York: Thin Air Video, 1996) divides a cassette between Micheline and Andy Clausen.

John Montgomery (1919-1993)

John Montgomery corresponds to Henry Morley in Jack Kerouac's *The Dharma Bums* (1958) and Alex Fairbrother in Kerouac's *Desolation Angels* (1965). In Kerouac's *Satori in Paris* (1966), Montgomery is referred to as the "greatest librarian in America." Montgomery's poems are scattered in small magazines across the country, but "Beat Generation without Haloes," "Tom

Clark's Academic Antidote," "The San Francisco Blues," "Seeing It Is Like Falling in Love," and "Collected Ginsberg" are in Rudi Horemans, ed., *Beat Indeed!* (Antwerp, Belgium: EXA, 1985). Montgomery might be more well known for works that counterpoint the views in popular media and academic circles: *Jack Kerouac: A Memoir in Which Is Revealed Secret Lives and West Coast Whispers, Being the Confessions of Henry Morley, Alex Fairbrother, and John Montgomery, Tribune Madman of "The Dharma Bums," "Desolation Angels," and Other Trips* (Fresno, CA: Giligia Press, 1970), *Kerouac West Coast* (Palo Alto: Fels and Firn, 1970), and *The Kerouac We Knew: Unposed Portraits, Action Shots Compiled by John Montgomery Honoring the Kerouac Conference at Naropa Institute* (Kentfield, CA: Fels and Firn, 1982).

Harold Norse (1916-   )

Norse is the author of *Carnivorous Saint: Gay Poems, 1941-1946* (San Francisco: Gay Sunshine Press, 1977). *Beat Hotel*, translated into German by Carl Weissner (Augsberg: Maro Verlag, 1975) is a set of cut-ups written during a stay at a Paris hotel frequented by Burroughs, Corso, Ginsberg, Orlovsky, and Gysin. See also *Hotel Nirvana: Selected Poems 1953-1973* (San Francisco: City Lights Books, 1974). Norse was the editor of *Bastard Angel*. The first of three issues was published in San Francisco in the spring of 1972; the magazine included Burroughs, Kerouac, Kaufman, Lipton, McClure, DiPrima, Bowles, Plymell, Ferlinghetti, Ginsberg, Malanga, Nin, Orlovsky, Genet, Bukowski, Snyder, Whalen, Meltzer, Cohen, Everson, and Rexroth. Norse is especially proud of G. G. Belli, *The Roman Sonnets*, trans. Harold Norse, with an introduction by William Carlos Williams (Highlands, NC: J. Williams, 1960). In 1956, the printer for the *Hudson Review* refused to set the type for an extended selection of the sonnets that the editors wanted to publish. The publication of the sonnets went forward after contractual agreements with the uncooperative printer expired. Harold Norse, *The Love Poems, 1940-1985* (Trumans Crossing Press, 1986) and Norse, *Memoirs of a* (London: Bloomsbury, 1990). The corresponde William Carlos Williams is found in *T* *Correspondence* (San Francisco: Bri

Charles Bukowski, *Charles Bukowski, Philip Lamantia, and Harold Norse* (London: Penguin, 1969) and Neeli Cherkovski, *Whitman's Wild Children* (Venice, CA: Lapis Press, 1988). Kit Knight, "Harold Norse," in *The Beats: Literary Bohemians in Postwar America*, ed. Ann Charters (Detroit: Gale Research, 1983): 419-422 provides essential background.

Frank O'Hara (1926-1966)

The Collected Poems of Frank O'Hara, ed. Donald Allen (Berkeley: University of California Press, 1995) updates *The Collected Poems of Frank O'Hara*, ed. Donald Allen (New York: Knopf, 1971) and features a bibliography. *The Selected Poems of Frank O'Hara*, ed. Donald Allen (Manchester, England: Carcanet, 1991) is an alternative to *The Selected Poems of Frank O'Hara*, ed. Donald Allen (New York: Knopf, 1974). Individual books include *A City Winter and Other Poems* (New York: Tibor de Nagy Gallery, 1952), *Meditations in an Emergency* (New York: Grove Press, 1957), *Odes* (New York: Tiber Press, 1960), *Second Avenue* (New York: Totem Press/Corinth Books, 1960), *Lunch Poems* (San Francisco: City Lights, 1964), and *Love Poems (Tentative Title)* (New York: Tiber de Nagy Editions, 1965). Essays are in *Standing Still and Walking in New York*, ed. Donald Allen (Bolinas, CA: Grey Fox, 1975) and plays are in *Selected Plays* (New York: Full Court Press, 1978). Four poems are included in Ann Charters, ed., *The Portable Beat Reader* (New York: Viking, 1992): 399-403; see photos and two poems in Elias Wilentz, ed., *The Beat Scene* (New York: Corinth Books, 1960): 46-51. A selection of poems is part of Donald Allen, ed., *The New American Poetry* (New York: Grove Press, 1960): 239-270 and Donald Allen and George F. Butterick, eds., *The Postmoderns: The New American Poetry Revised* (New York: Grove Press, 1982): 192-205. See "Personism: A Manifesto," "About ̇ivago and His Poems," and "Larry Rivers; A Memoir" in Donald ̇d Warren Tallman, eds., *The Poetics of the New American* ̇York: Grove Press, 1973): 353-372. Alexander Smith, ̇ra: A Comprehensive Bibliography* (New York: ̇eful resource despite its date of publication.

See Marjorie Perloff, *Frank O'Hara: Poet Among Painters* (New York: Braziller, 1977), Charles Molesworth, "'The Clear Architecture of the Nerves': The Poetry of Frank O'Hara," in *The Fierce Embrace: A Study of Contemporary American Poetry* (Columbia: University of Missouri Press, 1979): 85-97, Richard Howard, "Frank O'Hara," in *Alone with America* (New York: Atheneum, 1969): 396-412, Bill Berkson, "Frank O'Hara," in *The Beats: Literary Bohemians in Postwar America*, ed. Ann Charters (Detroit: Gale Research, 1983): 423-427, Eric Mottram, "Frank O'Hara," in *American Poetry: The Modernist Ideal* (New York: St. Martin's, 1995), Brad Gooch, *City Poet: The Life and Times of Frank O'Hara* (New York: Knopf, 1993), Geoff Ward, *Statues of Liberty: The New York School of Poets* (New York: St. Martin's, 1993), and Mutlu Konik Blasing, *Politics and Form in Postmodern Poetry: O'Hara, Bishop, Ashbery, and Merrill* (New York: Cambridge University Press, 1995). A thirty-three-minute video of Frank O'Hara "reading selections and talking at an informal interview" is at the American Poetry Archive, the Poetry Center, San Francisco State University.

Charles Olson (1910-1970)

Olson's manifesto in *Poetry New York* (1950) strongly influenced the Beats and other writers. Olson advocated a prosody based on breathing and thinking, not on counts of syllables or stresses. He believed that sound should have a priority over sense; that is, sound is not the servant of sense for emphasis and embellishment. Finally, the poet is part of the landscape, not separate from nature and the outside world. Olson's poetic theories mark the beginnings of post-modernism (1945-1960). *Montevallo Review* (1950) includes "The Kingfisher," which Olson offers as a poem in correspondence to the theory of projective verse. Paul Christensen argues that "The Kingfisher" is as influential as Lowell's "Skunk Hour" or Ginsberg's "Howl." *Call Me Ishmael: A Study of Melville* (New York: Reynal and Hitchcock, 1947) represents Olson's literary criticism. Olson's first book of poetry, *Y and X* (Washington, DC: Black Sun Press, 1948) is followed by an issue of Cid Corman's *Origin* (1953) devoted entirely to Olson's work and designed and edited by Robert Creeley. Olson was associated with Black Mountain College (1947-1956) and eventually assumed the role of Rector. Olson is noteworthy for *The Maximus Poems*, a series published over two decades and appearing in a series of separate books (Stuttgart: Jonathan Williams, 1953; Stuttgart: Jonathan Williams, 1956; New York: Jargon Corinth Books, 1960; London: Cape Goliard, 1968; New York: Grossman, 1975). Other books include *Archeologist of the Morning* (London: Cape Goliard, 1970) and *Human Universe and Other Essays*, ed. Donald Allen (San Francisco: Auerhahn Society, 1965). *Selected Writings*, ed. Robert Creeley (New York: New Directions, 1966) is augmented by *The Collected Poems of Charles Olson*, ed. George F. Butterick (Berkeley: University of California Press, 1987) and *Selected Poems*, ed. Robert Creeley (Berkeley: University of California Press, 1993). See "Projective Verse," "Letter to Elaine Feinstein," "Human Universe," "The Resistance," "Equal, That Is, to the Real Itself," and "Proprioception" in Donald Allen and Warren Tallman, eds., *The Poetics of the New American Poetry* (New York: Grove Press, 1973): 147-184. In this edition, see Ed Dorn's "What I See in The Maximus Poems": 147-184. See also Paul Christensen, "Charles Olson," *The Beats: Literary Bohemians in Postwar America*, ed. Ann Charters (Detroit: Gale Research, 1983): 427-433, Edward Halsey Foster, "Charles Olson: Poetry as Politics," in *Understanding the Black Mountain Poets* (Columbia: University of South Carolina Press, 1995): 25-80, which features a bibliography, James Dickey, "Charles Olson," in *Babel to Byzantium* (New York: Farrar, Straus, and Giroux, 1968): 136-139, Ann Charters, *Beats and Company* (Garden City, NY: Doubleday, 1986): 17, 104-111, Joseph N. Riddel, *The Turning Word: American Literary Modernism and Continental Theory* (Philadelphia: University of Pennsylvania Press, 1996), Gavin Selerie, "Charles Olson," in *American Poetry: The Modernist Ideal* (New York: St. Martin's, 1995), and Stephen Fredman, *The Grounding of American Poetry: Charles Olson and the Emersonian Tradition* (New York: Cambridge University Press, 1993). A general study is Eniko Bollobas, *Charles Olson* (New York: Twayne, 1992); biographical works include Ralph Maud, *Charles Olson's Reading: A Biography* (Carbondale: University of Southern Illinois Press, 1996), Charles Boer, *Charles Olson in Connecticut* (Rocky Mount: North Carolina Wesleyan College Press, 1991), and Tom Clark, *Charles Olson: The Allegory of a Poet's Life* (New York: Norton, 1991).

Peter Orlovsky (1933-   )

Peter Orlovsky may be best known as the lover of Allen Ginsberg, but his literary output is noteworthy in several respects. With Allen Ginsberg, Orlovsky is the co-author of *Straight Hearts' Delight: Love Poems and Selected Letters* (San Francisco: Gay Sunshine Press, 1980). In 1958, Orlovsky's work was published in *Beatitude*, and in 1960 his material was included in *Beatitude Anthology* (San Francisco: City Lights, 1960). Donald Allen included him in *The New American Poetry* (New York: Grove Press, 1960). One poem by Orlovsky appears in Elias Wilentz, ed., *The Beat Scene* (New York: Corinth Books, 1960). Five of Orlovsky's poems are in Anne Waldman, ed., *The Beat Book: Poems and Fictions from the Beat Generation* (Boston: Shambhala, 1996). Two poems are in David Kherdian, ed., *Beat Voices: An Anthology of Beat Poetry* (New York: Henry Holt, 1995). See "Lepers Cry" in Ann Charters, ed., *The Portable Beat Reader* (New York: Viking Penguin, 1992). Ann Charters gives background in "Peter Orlovsky," in *The Beats: Literary Bohemians in Postwar America*, ed. Ann Charters (Detroit: Gale Research, 1983): 433-439. See Peter Orlovsky in the video *Fried Shoes Cooked Diamonds* (New York: Mystic Fire Video, 1978); Orlovsky reads "A Rainbow" and "Morning Again" on *Howls, Raps, and Roars: Recordings from the San Francisco Poetry Renaissance* (Berkeley, CA: Fantasy Records, 1993).

Kenneth Patchen (1911-1972)

Though Kenneth Patchen was bedridden for much of his life, he was an important and prolific poet who influenced many Beat writers, especially on the West Coast. Kenneth and Miriam Patchen were editors and distributors for James Laughlin's New Directions publishing house in the 1930's and 1940's. Patchen's first book, *Before the Brave* (New York: Random House, 1936), was followed by *The Journal of Albion Moonlight* (New York: Kenneth Patchen, 1941). *Poems of Humor and Protest* (San Francisco: City Lights, 1955) was one of the first books Ferlinghetti published. *Awash with Roses: The Collected Love Poems of Kenneth Patchen* (Huron, OH: Bottom Dog Press, 1991) is an interesting contrast to the City Lights book. Patchen is famous for combining poetry and jazz and made the recordings *Kenneth Patchen Reads with the Chamber Jazz Sextet* (1958) and *Kenneth Patchen Reads with Jazz in Canada* (1959). His jazz play *Don't Look Now* (1959) was performed off Broadway in New York. See Larry Smith, *Kenneth Patchen: The Search for Wonder and Joy* (Boston: Twayne, 1978) and Richard Morgan, ed., *Kenneth Patchen: A Collection of Essays* (New York: AMS Press, 1977). Smith's "Kenneth Patchen" in *The Beats: Literary Bohemians in Postwar America*, ed. Ann Charters (Detroit: Gale Research, 1983): 440-445 gives a concise background and offers valuable references. Other useful studies include Kenneth Rexroth, "Kenneth Patchen: Naturalist of the Public Nightmare" in *Bird in the Bush: Obvious Essays* (New York: New Directions, 1959): 94-105, Raymond Nelson, *Kenneth Patchen and American Mysticism* (Chapel Hill: University of North Carolina Press, 1984), and Henry Miller, *Patchen: Man of Anger and Light* (New York: Padell, 1946), which is included in Henry Miller, *Stand Still Like a Hummingbird: Collected Essays* (New York: New Directions, 1967): 27-37. See James Dickey, "Kenneth Patchen," in *Babel to Byzantium* (New York: Farrar, Straus and Giroux, 1968): 71-72. Patchen reads to jazz accompaniment on "The Murder of Two Men by a Young Kid Wearing Lemon Colored Gloves" on *The Beat Generation* (Santa Monica, CA: Rhino Records, 1992).

Stuart Z. Perkoff (1930-1974)

Some of Perkoff's books are *Suicide Room* (Karlsruhe: Jonathan Williams, 1956), *Kowboy Poems* (Golden, CO: Croupier Press, 1973), *Eat the Earth* (Denver: Black Ace/Bovery Press, 1971), and *Alphabet* (Los Angeles: Red Hill Press, 1973). "Three Prayers" appears in David Kherdian, ed., *Beat Voices* (New York: Henry Holt, 1995): 36-37. See John Arthur Maynard, *Venice West: The Beat Generation in Southern California* (New Brunswick, NJ: Rutgers University Press, 1991). Maynard recommends *Love Is the Silence*, ed. Paul Vangelisti (Los Angeles: The Red Hill Press, 1975) and *How It Is, Doing What I DO: Poems and Drawings, Bowery #21*, ed. Tony Scibella (Denver: Black Ace, 1976). One may see Perkoff's appearance with Groucho Marx on *You Bet Your Life* on the video

The Beats: An Existential Comedy (New York: Cinema Guild/Raven Productions, no date).

Charles Plymell (1935-)

The Trashing of America (New York: Kulchur Foundation, 1975) collects previous work, including *Neon Poems* (Syracuse, NY: Atom Mind Publications, 1970), *The Last Moccasins* (San Francisco: City Lights, 1973), and *Over the State of Kansas* (New York: Telephone Books, 1973), as well as some new works. *Are You a Kid?* (Cherry Valley, NY: Cherry Valley Editions, 1977) reveals Plymell's work with younger writers. See also *In Memory of My Father* (Cherry Valley, NY: Cherry Valley Editions, 1977). Plymell edited various literary magazines: *Poets' Corner, Mikrokosmos, Dreams of Straw, Now, Bulletin from Nothing, The Last Times, Zap Comix, Grist Magazine*, and *Coldspring Journal*. Plymell also served as editor for Cherry Valley Editions, a press that published Ginsberg, Burroughs, Mary Beach, and Janine Pommy Vega. For Plymell's commentary about his distrust of the Beats, the Language School, the St. Mark's group, and the Naropa Institute, see *San Francisco Review of Books* 6.4 (1980) and *Northeast Rising Sun* 4.19 (1980). The poem "Ten Years After the Blast," which is in *The Trashing of America*, offers some of Plymell's insights about Ginsberg. See Brown Miller, "Charles Plymell," in *The Beats: Literary Bohemians in Postwar America* (Detroit: Gale Research, 1983): 448-452. An interview with Plymell appears in *The Harder They Come* (Santa Barbara, CA: Am Here Books, 1985). On *Disconnected* (New York: Giorno Poetry Systems, 1974), Plymell reads. At www.buchenroth.com/cplymell.html, one finds biographical and bibliographical information on Plymell.

Dan Propper (1937-)

"Afternoon" appears in Elias Wilentz, ed. *The Beat Scene* (New York: Corinth Books, 1960) and Park Honan, ed., *The Beats: An Anthology of Beat Writing* (London: J. M. Dent, 1987). *The Fable of the Final Hour* (New York: Energy Press, 1958) is included in

Seymour Krim, ed., *The Beats* (Greenwich, CT: Fawcett, 1960).
Propper was book editor for *Nugget* and *Swank*. Some books include
The Tale of the Amazing Tramp (Cherry Valley, NY: Cherry Valley
Editions, 1977), *For Kerouac in Heaven* (New York: Energy Press,
1980), and *Pablo Neruda, 23 Poems*, trans. Dan Propper (Albion,
CA: Wilderness Poetry Press, 1979). "Looking for a Stranger" is on a
sound cassette *Nature: Man's Obsession in Transit* (Dayton, OH:
Nexus Magazine, 1990). See Hugh Fox, "Dan Propper," in *The Beats:
Literary Bohemians in Postwar America*, ed. Ann Charters (Detroit:
Gale Research, 1983): 453-455.

Kenneth Rexroth (1905-1982)

Though sometimes described as a father figure for the writers of
the Beat Generation, Rexroth also expressed strong criticism of Beat
authors. Rexroth's early life is unfolded in *An Autobiographical
Novel* (Garden City, NY: Doubleday, 1966); his first book, *In What
Hour* (New York: Macmillan, 1940), delivers direct, polemical
poems; and long poems in avant-garde style appear in *The
Homestead Called Damascus* (New York: New Directions, 1963) and
The Art of Worldly Wisdom (Prairie City, IL: Decker Press, 1949).
Anarchopacifist beliefs emerge in *The Phoenix and the Tortoise*
(Norfolk, CT: New Directions, 1944), and love poems are in *The
Signature of All Things* (New York: New Directions, 1950). A general
source for material by Rexroth is *Selected Poems* (New York: New
Directions, 1984). Rexroth aided in the founding of the Pacifica
Foundation, which created listener-sponsored radio; he also was
associated in the founding of the Poetry Center at San Francisco
State College. Though listed as one of six authors for the famous
reading at the Six Gallery in San Francisco on October 7, 1955,
Rexroth actually served as moderator for that important event. At
the obscenity trial of Ginsberg's *Howl and Other Poems*, Rexroth
was a witness for the defense. *In Defense of the Earth* (New York:
New Directions, 1956) includes "Thou Shalt Not Kill," the tribute to
Dylan Thomas that is perhaps Rexroth's most famous poem.
Rexroth's commentaries on the Beat literary scene appeared in
Nation, the *New York Times*, *Evergreen Review*, *New World Writing
Anthology*, and the *San Francisco Chronicle*. See also "The
Commercialization of the Image of Revolt," *The Beats: Literary*

Bohemians in Postwar America, ed. Ann Charters (Detroit: Gale Research, 1983): 643-650. His collections of essays, including *Bird in the Bush: Obvious Essays* (New York: New Directions, 1959) and *American Poetry in the Twentieth Century* (New York: Herder and Herder, 1971), reveal a changing perception of the Beats. Rexroth is depicted as Rheinhold Cocoethes in Jack Kerouac's *The Dharma Bums* (1958), though Rexroth did not appreciate the characterization. "Poems from the Japanese" and "Thou Shalt Not Kill" are in Ann Charters, ed., *The Portable Beat Reader* (New York: Viking, 1992). See a selection of materials by Rexroth, including an excerpt of an interview with David Meltzer, in Carole Tonkinson, ed., *Big Sky Mind: Buddhism and the Beat Generation* (New York: Riverhead Books, 1995). The full interview with David Meltzer is "Rexroth" in *Golden Gate* (San Francisco: Wingbow, 1976): 19-65. See material by Rexroth in Stephen Berg and Robert Mezey, eds., *Naked Poetry: Recent American Poetry in Open Forms* (Indianapolis: Bobbs-Merrill, 1969). "Disengagement: The Art of the Beat Generation" is in Park Honan, ed., *The Beats: An Anthology of Beat Writing* (London: J. M. Dent, 1987), 199-215. Some of the correspondence is available in *Kenneth Rexroth and James Laughlin: Selected Letters*, ed. Lee Bartlett (New York: Norton, 1991). See Morgan Gibson, *Kenneth Rexroth* (New York: Twayne, 1972) and Thomas Parkinson, "Kenneth Rexroth: Poet" *Ohio Review* 17 (Winter 1976). Brown Miller and Ann Charters, "Kenneth Rexroth," in *The Beats: Literary Bohemians in Postwar America*, ed. Ann Charters (Detroit: Gale Research, 1983): 456-464 gives detailed background on Rexroth and lists valuable sources. Rexroth's role in the San Francisco Poetry Renaissance is covered in various texts: John Arthur Maynard, *Venice West: The Beat Generation in Southern California* (New Brunswick, NJ: Rutgers University Press, 1991), Warren French, *The San Francisco Poetry Renaissance, 1955-1960* (Boston: G. K. Hall, 1991), and Michael Davidson, *The San Francisco Poetry Renaissance: Poetics and Community at Mid-century* (New York: Cambridge University Press, 1989). Other studies include Thomas Evans, "Kenneth Rexroth," in *American Poetry: The Modernist Ideal* (New York: St. Martin's, 1995), Donald Gutierrez, *Breaking Through to the Other Side: Essays on Realization in Modern Literature* (Troy, NY: Whitson Publishing, 1994), which includes "The Holiness of the Real: The Short Poems of Kenneth Rexroth," Linda Hamalian, *A Life of Kenneth Rexroth* (New York: Norton, 1992), and Lee Bartlett, *Kenneth Rexroth* (Boise, ID: Boise State

University Western Writers Series, 1988). See references to Rexroth
in Bruce Cook, *The Beat Generation: The Tumultuous 50's
Movement and Its Impact on Today* (New York: Quill, 1994); Steven
Watson, "Kenneth Rexroth," in *The Birth of the Beat Generation*
(New York: Pantheon, 1995): 197-200 gives a brief perspective. See a
photo in Ann Charters, *Beats and Company* (Garden City, NY:
Doubleday, 1986): 57. A recording of Rexroth reading "Thou Shalt
Not Kill" is on *Howls, Raps, and Roars: Recordings from the San
Francisco Poetry Renaissance* (Berkeley, CA: Fantasy Records,
1993). "Married Blues" is done by Kenneth Rexroth on *The Beat
Generation* (Santa Monica, CA: Rhino Records, 1992).

Michael Rumaker (1932-)

Rumaker, a graduate of Black Mountain College, is the author of
a collection of stories originally published as *Exit 3 and Other Stories*
(Harmondsworth, England: Penguin, 1966) but later republished as
Gringos and Other Stories (New York: Grove Press, 1967). His
stories have appeared in *Black Mountain Review, Evergreen Review,
Redbook, Seventeen, Nation*, and *Cosmopolitan*. "The Teddy Bear" is
in *The Moderns: An Anthology of New Writing in America*, ed. LeRoi
Jones (New York: Corinth Books, 1963): 159-168, and "Pizza" is in
City Lights Anthology, ed. Lawrence Ferlinghetti (San Francisco: City
Lights, 1974): 71-74. Rumaker is noteworthy for his early review
"Allen Ginsberg's 'Howl,'" *Black Mountain Review* 7 (Autumn 1957):
228-237, which is reprinted in Lewis Hyde, ed., *On the Poetry of
Allen Ginsberg* (Ann Arbor: University of Michigan Press, 1984): 36-
40. Rumaker's theoretical essay "The Use of the Unconscious in
Writing" is in *Measure* 2 (Winter 1958): 2-4. Rumaker's *The Butterfly*
(New York: Scribner's, 1962) is a novel reviewed by Charles Poore
in the *New York Times* 7 Apr. 1962: 23. Rumaker's discovery of his
gay identity is unfolded in *A Day and a Night at the Baths* (Bolinas,
CA: Grey Fox Press, 1979) and *My First Satyrnalia* (Bolinas, CA:
Grey Fox Press, 1981). "The Bar" is in *Prose 1: Edward Dorn,
Michael Rumaker, Warren Tallman* (San Francisco: City Lights,
1964); "From Pagan Days" appears in *3 X 3* (Rocky Mount, NC:
North Carolina Wesleyan College Press, 1989); and "The Pipe"
appears in John Chesley Taylor, compiler, *The Short Story: Fiction in
Transition* (New York: Scribner's, 1969). See also Rumaker, *Robert

Duncan in San Francisco (San Francisco: Grey Fox Press, 1996). For bibliographical data, see George F. Butterick, "Michael Rumaker: A Checklist," *Athanos* 6 (Spring 1975): 45-49, and for background, see Butterick, "Michael Rumaker," in *The Beats: Literary Bohemians in Postwar America*, ed. Ann Charters (Detroit: Gale Research, 1983): 465-472. See also Martin Duberman, *Black Mountain: An Exploration in Community* (New York: Dutton, 1972).

Ed Sanders (1939-   )

Sanders has written "The Legacy of the Beats" in *Beat Culture and the New America* (New York: Whitney Museum of American Art/Flammarion, 1995): 244-247, a poem in which he captures the spirit of the Beats. *Poem from Jail* (San Francisco: City Lights, 1963) was his first published poem. Sanders is noteworthy for his editing of *Fuck You: A Magazine of the Arts*, which ran for thirteen issues and featured Blackburn, Burroughs, Corso, Creeley, DiPrima, Ferlinghetti, Ginsberg, McClure, Mailer, Marshall, O'Hara, Olson, Oppenheimer, Snyder, Whalen, Wieners, and Sanders. The publication faced charges of obscenity. Sanders expanded his work as an editor, establishing Fuck You Press and producing *Bugger: An Anthology of Buttuckry* (New York: Fuck You Press, 1964), which is now reproduced as *Bugger: An Anthology* (Minneapolis: Baby Split Bowling News, 1993), *Despair: Poems to Come Down By* (New York: Fuck You Press, 1964), *Poems for Marilyn* (New York: Fuck You Press, 1962), and *A Valorium Edition of the Entire Extant Work of Thales* (New York: Fuck You Press, 1964). Fuck You Press also produced William S. Burroughs, *Roosevelt After Inauguration*, Carol Bergé, *The Vancouver Report*, and Marguerite Harris, ed., *Maxims and Aphorisms from the Lettters of D. H. Lawrence*. Sanders' Peace Eye Bookstore, where Fuck You Press was housed, was raided in 1966. Obscenity charges were set aside with the help of the ACLU. Sanders is also famous for his participation in The Fugs, a musical group with whom Sanders recorded six albums during the period 1965-1969. He also recorded one solo album; the lyrics for many of the songs recorded on albums are in *The Fugs' Songbook!*, ed. Ed Sanders, Ken Weaver, and Betsy Klein, with notes by Ed Sanders (New York: Peace Eye Bookstore, 1965). As the 1960's progressed, Sanders revealed his diversity: he wrote a collection of poems *Peace*

Eye (Buffalo: Frontier Press, 1965); relating events leading up to the Democratic National Convention of 1968, Sanders wrote *Shards of God* (New York: Grove Press, 1970); about the Manson murders he wrote *The Family: The Story of Charles Manson's Dune Buggy Attack Battalion* (New York: Dutton, 1971); *Tales of Beatnik Glory* (New York: Stonehill, 1973) is a recounting of the activities of a legendary group; another book of poems that Sanders wrote is *20,000 A.D.* (Plainfield, VT: North Atlantic Books, 1976); *Investigative Poetry* (San Francisco: City Lights, 1976) is a theoretical essay; and a satirical novel is *Fame and Love in New York* (Berkeley, CA: Turtle Island Foundation, 1980). *The Party* (Woodstock, NY: Poetry, Crime, and Culture Press, 1977) is the product of Sanders' class at the Naropa Institute, in which students investigated the forced disrobing of W. S. Merwin and his companion at the order of Chogyam Trungpa. Selections appear in Ann Charters, ed., *The Portable Beat Reader* (New York: Viking, 1992), and "The Cutting Prow" is in David Kherdian, ed., *Beat Voices* (New York: Henry Holt, 1995). Selections appear in Donald Allen and George F. Butterick, eds., *The Postmoderns: The New American Poetry Revised* (New York: Grove Press, 1982). See George F. Butterick, "Ed Sanders," in *The Beats: Literary Bohemians in Postwar America*, ed. Ann Charters (Detroit: Gale Research, 1983): 473-486, which includes a list of helpful references. See Ann Charters, *Beats and Company* (Garden City, NY: Doubleday, 1986): 87. Sanders' papers are at the University of Connecticut. Sanders appeared on the William F. Buckley show *Firing Line* with Jack Kerouac, and a clip of this appearance can be seen on *What Happened to Kerouac?*, a video directed by Richard Lerner and Lewis MacAdams in 1985 (Vidmark, 1987). See Ed Sanders in *The Beat Generation: Volume One: Another Lost Generation: The Origin of the Beats* (New York: Thin Air Video, 1995) and in Maria Beatty, *Gang of Souls* (New York: Mystic Fire Video, 1988). *An Evening with Ed Sanders and the Fugs: Words and Music* (New York: Thin Air Video, 1996) features Sanders on his "talking necktie" and "light organ."

Gary Snyder (1930-   )

Though Gary Snyder is depicted as Japhy Ryder in Jack Kerouac's *The Dharma Bums* and although Snyder performed as part of the famous reading at the Six Gallery on October 7, 1955 (along with Ginsberg, Lamantia, Whalen, and McClure, with Rexroth as moderator), Snyder disassociates himself from the Beats. Whitman's long line and the prophetic voices of Blake and Shelley, which mark Ginsberg and other Beats, are not found in Snyder. Nevertheless, Snyder's perspectives on nature and the environment, his interpretation of native culture and myths, and his investigation of Asian culture and religion have continued to establish a connection between him and Beat writers, whose work also reaches into these areas. Snyder's B. A. thesis done at Reed College is available as *He Who Hunted Birds in His Father's Village: The Dimensions of a Haida Myth* (Bolinas, CA: Grey Fox Press, 1979). See Lew Welch, *I Remain: The Letters of Lew Welch and the Correspondence of His Friends 1949-1971*, 2 volumes (Bolinas, CA: Grey Fox Press, 1980) for some insight about attitudes of Snyder in the 1950's and 1960's. Books of poetry by Gary Snyder include *Riprap* (Ashland, MA: Origin Press, 1959), *Myths & Texts* (New York: Totem Press/Corinth Books, 1960), which was republished in New York by New Directions in 1978, *Riprap & Cold Mountain Poems* (San Francisco: Four Seasons Foundation, 1965), which was later republished in San Francisco by North Point Press in 1990, *Six Sections from Mountains & Rivers Without End* (San Francisco: Four Seasons Foundation, 1965), which was later republished in an enlarged edition by the same publisher in 1970, *A Range of Poems* (London: Fulcrum Press, 1970), *Cold Mountain Poems: Twenty-four Poems by Han Shan Translated by Gary Snyder* (Portland, OR: Press 22, 1970), *Manzanita* (Bolinas, CA: Four Seasons Foundation, 1972), *The Fudo Trilogy* (Berkeley, CA: Shaman Drum, 1973), *Turtle Island* (New York: New Directions, 1974), *Little Songs for Gaia* (Port Townshend, WA: Copper Canyon Press, 1979), *Axe Handles* (San Francisco: North Point Press, 1983), and *Left Out in the Rain: New Poems 1947-1985* (San Francisco: North Point Press, 1986). Works in prose include *Earth House Hold: Technical Notes & Queries to Fellow Dharma Revolutionaries* (New York: New Directions, 1969), *The Old Ways: Six Essays* (San Francisco: City Lights Books, 1977), *He Who Hunted Birds in His Father's Village* (Bolinas, CA: Grey Fox Press, 1979), *Passage Through India* (San Francisco: Grey Fox Press, 1983), and *The Practice of the Wild: Essays by Gary Snyder* (San Francisco: North Point Press, 1990). *Mountains and Rivers Without End* (Washington, DC: Counterpoint, 1996) is the complete version of an epic poem begun in the 1950's. *Gary Snyder Papers: Finding*

Aid are available at the University of California, Davis. A non-circulating copy is available at the Bancroft Library at Berkeley. Available interviews include Donald Allen, ed., *On Bread and Poetry: A Panel Discussion with Gary Snyder, Lew Welch & Philip Whalen* (Bolinas, CA: Grey Fox Press, 1977), Ekbert Faas, "Gary Snyder," in *Towards a New American Poetics: Essays and Interviews* (Santa Barbara, CA: Black Sparrow Press, 1979): 90-142, James McKenzie, "Moving the World a Millionth of an Inch: Gary Snyder," in *The Beat Vision*, eds. Arthur Winfield Knight and Kit Knight (New York: Paragon, 1987): 1-27, and William Scott McLean, ed., *The Real Work: Interviews and Talks, 1964-1979* (New York: New Directions, 1980). An interview and question-and-answer session held at the Unterberg Poetry Center at the 92nd Street YMHA in New York City on October 26, 1992, is printed in *The Paris Review* 141 (Winter 1996): 89-118. Katherine McNeill, *Gary Snyder: A Bibliography* (New York: Phoenix Book Shop, 1983) identifies and comments on important sources. Snyder's importance is reflected in his inclusion in almost all anthologies related to the Beats: Donald Allen, ed., *The New American Poetry* (New York: Grove Press, 1960), Donald Allen and George F. Butterick, eds., *The Postmoderns: The New American Poetry Revised* (New York: Grove Press, 1982), Carole Tonkinson, ed., *Big Sky Mind* (New York: Riverhead Books, 1995), Anne Waldman, ed., *The Beat Book* (Boston: Shambhala, 1996), Stephen Berg and Robert Mezey, eds., *Naked Poetry* (Indianapolis: Bobbs-Merrill, 1969), Stephen Berg and Robert Mezey, eds., *The New Naked Poetry* (Indianapolis: Bobbs-Merrill, 1976), David Kherdian, ed., *Beat Voices* (New York: Henry Holt, 1995), Park Honan, ed., *The Beats* (London: J. M. Dent, 1987), and Ann Charters, ed., *The Portable Beat Reader* (New York: Viking, 1992). See "Buddhism and the Coming Revolution," "Poetry and the Primitive," and "Passage to More than India" in Donald Allen and Warren Tallman, eds., *The Poetics of the New American Poetry* (New York: Grove Press, 1973): 392-415. Books about Gary Snyder include Bert Almon, *Gary Snyder* (Boise, ID: Boise State University, 1979), Tim Dean, *Gary Snyder and the American Unconscious: Inhabiting the Ground* (New York: St. Martin's, 1991), Jon Halper, *Gary Snyder: Dimensions of a Life* (San Francisco: Sierra Club Books, 1991), Howard McCord, *Some Notes on Gary Snyder's Myths & Texts* (Berkeley, CA: Sand Dollar, 1971), Charles Molesworth, *Gary Snyder's Vision: Poetry and the Real Work* (Columbia: University of Missouri Press, 1983), Patrick D. Murphy, ed., *Critical Essays on Gary Snyder* (Boston: G. K. Hall,

1990), Robert Jordan Schuler, *Journeys Toward the Original Mind: The Long Poems of Gary Snyder* (New York: Peter Lang, 1994), and Bob Steuding, *Gary Snyder* (Boston: Twayne, 1976). Book chapters or sections about Gary Snyder include Patrick D. Murphy, "Penance or Perception: Spirituality and Land in the Poetry of Gary Snyder and Wendell Berry," in *Earthly Words: Essays on Contemporary American Nature and Environmental Writers* (Ann Arbor: University of Michigan Press, 1994), Bruce Cook, *The Beat Generation* (New York: Quill, 1994): 28-36, David Kherdian, ed., "Gary Snyder," in *Six San Francisco Poets* (Fresno, CA: Giligia Press, 1965): 21-26, Steven Watson, "Gary Snyder," in *The Birth of the Beat Generation* (New York: Pantheon, 1995): 212-215, Richard Howard, "Gary Snyder," in *Alone with America* (New York: Atheneum, 1969): 485-498, Thomas Parkinson, "The Poetry of Gary Snyder," in *The Beats: Essays in Criticism* (Jefferson, NC: McFarland, 1981): 133-146, Robert Kern, "Clearing the Ground: Gary Snyder and the Modernist Imperative," in *The Beats: Essays in Criticism* (Jefferson, NC: McFarland, 1981): 147-164, James Wright, "The Work of Gary Snyder," in *Collected Prose*, ed. Anne Wright (Ann Arbor: University of Michigan Press, 1983): 105-119, Michael McClure, "Pastures New: Gary Snyder," in Michael McClure, *Lighting the Corners* (Albuquerque: University of New Mexico College of Arts and Sciences, 1993): 178-180, and James I. McClintock, *Nature's Kindred Spirits: Aldo Leopold, Joseph Wood Krutch, Edward Abbey, Annie Dillard, and Gary Snyder* (Madison: University of Wisconsin Press, 1994). For a list of articles in journals and reviews, see Patrick Murphy, *Understanding Gary Snyder* (Columbia: University of South Carolina Press, 1994): 174-176. To get a personal impression of Snyder, see *Gary Snyder: Literary Video* (Los Angeles: Lannan Foundation, 1989), which includes two VHS cassettes. The presentation by Snyder took place on December 12, 1988, and the tape includes an interview conducted by Lewis MacAdams. *This Is Our Body* (1989) is an audio recording prepared by Watershed Tapes on which Snyder reads. *Turtle Island* (1990) is an audio recording prepared by Chelsea Green and features Snyder and the Paul Winter Consort. *Gary Snyder Reads Poems from Riprap and Essays from the Practice of the Wild* (1993) is available from the American Audio Prose Library. *Here in the Mind* (New York: Northbridge Communications, 1995) features Snyder and Daisy Zamora on a PBS program hosted by Bill Moyers. Ann Charters features a series of photos of Snyder in *Beats and Company* (Garden City, NY: Doubleday, 1986): 63, 64, 67, 68, 69. On the internet, one can find poems, a short biography, and bibliographical data at **http://www.wnet.org/lol/snyder.html**.

Carl Solomon (1928-   )

Solomon, who met Allen Ginsberg at the New York State Psychiatric Institute in Rockland, New York, where they were both patients, is famous among readers of Beat literature because Ginsberg's "Howl" is dedicated to Solomon and an extended portion of the poem refers repeatedly to Solomon. In addition, a personal event related by Solomon to Ginsberg is incorporated into the text of "Howl": the throwing of potato salad at a lecture on Stéphane Mallarmé. Though this event did actually occur, Solomon also related other tall tales and exaggerated stories to Ginsberg, who went on to present them as real events or episodes in "Howl." Ginsberg got the phrases "pubic beards" and "lunatic saint" from Solomon as he uttered the phrases when he emerged from shock treatments at Rockland, where both Solomon and Ginsberg were being treated for mental problems. Solomon, through his uncle, A. A. Wyn, the publisher of Wyn Books and Ace Paperbacks, became an intermediary in the process that led to the publication of William S. Burroughs' *Junkie* (written under the pen name William Lee). When Kerouac submitted *On the Road* for publication, Solomon agreed with others at Ace on a rejection of the book, which had been submitted not as a neatly boxed manuscript, but as a cumbersome roll of continuously attached sheets of paper. Solomon's writings include various memoirs and anecdotes about the Beats. *Mishaps, Perhaps*, ed. Mary Beach (San Francisco: Beach Books Texts and Documents/City Lights Books, 1966) includes "Report from the Asylum: Afterthoughts of a Shock Patient," and *More Mishaps*, ed. Mary Beach (San Francisco: Beach Books Texts and Documents/City Lights, 1968) expands upon recollections of the Beat experience. Carl Solomon, *Emergency Messages: An Autobiographical Miscellany* (New York: Paragon House, 1989) further expands on the memoirs related to the the Beats. One can also see "Report from the Asylum" in Gene Feldman and Max Gartenberg, eds., *The Beat Generation and the Angry Young Men* (New York: Citadel Books, 1958). Material by Solomon is included in *The Beat Book*, eds. Arthur Winfield Knight and Glee Knight

(California, PA: unspeakable visions of the individual, 1974) and *The Beat Diary*, eds. Arthur Winfield Knight and Kit Knight (California, PA: unspeakable visions of the individual, 1977). See material by Solomon in Ann Charters, ed., *The Portable Beat Reader* (New York: Viking Penguin, 1992). Interviews include "John Tytell Talks with Carl Solomon" in *The Beat Vision*, eds. Arthur Winfield Knight and Kit Knight (New York: Paragon, 1987): 241-257. Tytell's "An Interview with Carl Solomon" is in *The Beat Book*, eds. Arthur and Glee Knight (California, PA: unspeakable visions of the individual, 1974). See also Tom Collins, "Carl Solomon," in *The Beats: Literary Bohemians in Postwar America*, ed. Ann Charters (Detroit: Gale Research, 1983): 501-510. See also Steven Watson, "Carl Solomon," in *The Birth of the Beat Generation* (New York: Pantheon, 1995): 76-78, and Ann Charters, *Beats and Company* (Garden City, NY: Doubleday, 1986): 153.

Jack Spicer (1925-1965)

The posthumous *The Collected Books of Jack Spicer*, ed. Robin Blaser (Los Angeles: Black Sparrow Press, 1975) was subsequently republished (Santa Rosa, CA: Black Sparrow Press, 1989). Some of the books are *After Lorca* (San Francisco: White Rabbit Press, 1957), *Billy the Kid* (Stinson Beach, CA: Enkidu Surrogate, 1959), *Lament for the Makers* (Oakland: White Rabbit Press, 1962), *The Heads of the Town up to the Aether* (San Francisco: Auerhahn Society, 1962), *The Holy Grail* (San Francisco: White Rabbit Press, 1964), *Language* (San Francisco: White Rabbit Press, 1965), *Book of Magazine Verse* (San Francisco: White Rabbit Press, 1966), *A Book of Music* (San Francisco: White Rabbit Press, 1969), *The Red Wheelbarrow* (Berkeley, CA: Arif Press, 1971), *15 False Propositions About God* (no city named: Man/Root Books, 1974), *Admonitions* (New York: Adventures in Poetry, 1974), and *One Night Stand and Other Poems* (San Francisco: Grey Fox Press, 1980). Alastair Johnston, *A Bibliography of White Rabbit Press* (Berkeley, CA: Poltroon Press, 1985) offers data on Spicer. Michael Davidson describes Spicer's theory that poetry is "a foreign agent, a parasite that invades the poet's language and expresses what 'it' wants to say." In this belief, Spicer contrasts with the Beats, but he shares with the Beats an interest in public performance and served as a leader in the flowering of artistic work associated with the San Francisco Renaissance. In 1953, he helped form the Six Gallery, the site of the famous reading on October 7, 1955. Spicer's work is included in Donald Allen, ed., *The New American Poetry* (New York: Grove Press, 1960) and is retained in Donald Allen and George F. Butterick, eds., *The Postmoderns: The New American Poetry Revised* (New York: Grove Press, 1982). "Jack Spicer to Federico Garcia Lorca" and "Excerpts from the Vancouver Lectures" are in Donald Allen and Warren Tallman, eds., *The Poetics of the New American Poetry* (New York: Grove Press, 1973): 226-234. Special issues of *Manroot*, *Boundary*, and *Caterpillar* are devoted to Spicer. See Michael Davidson, "Jack Spicer," in *The Beats: Literary Bohemians in Postwar America*, ed. Ann Charters (Detroit: Gale Research, 1983): 511-517, and Davidson, *The San Francisco Renaissance* (New York: Cambridge University Press, 1989), which has a chapter on Spicer and other references to him. Edward Halsey Foster, *Jack Spicer* (Boise, ID: Boise State University, 1991), and Norman Finkelstein, *The Utopian Moment in Contemporary American Poetry* (Lewisburg, PA: Bucknell University Press, 1988), offer additional interpretation. See also Michael McClure, "An Empire of Signs: Jack Spicer," in Michael McClure, *Lighting the Corners* (Albuquerque: University of New Mexico College of Arts and Sciences, 1993): 113-127. Spicer's papers are in the Bancroft Poetry Archive at the University of California, Berkeley.

Charles Upton (1948-   )

Although he was born several years after the beginnings of the Beat literary movement, Charles Upton is linked to the Beats because of his writing style, which recalls the long line used by Whitman and Ginsberg, and his principal publisher, City Lights. *Panic Grass* (San Francisco: City Lights, 1968) combines travel and spirituality, creating a gloomy effect; *Time Raid* (San Francisco: Four Seasons Foundation, 1969) is visionary. "Some Back Talk for Ma Kali" is included in *City Lights Anthology* (San Francisco: City Lights, 1974). Upton's work has also appeared in *Floating Island*, *Beatitude*, and *Invisible City*. He has edited *Because You Talk* (San Francisco: Other Voices Literary Society, 1976). See Pat Nolan,

"Charles Upton," in *The Beats: Literary Bohemians in Postwar America*, ed. Ann Charters (Detroit: Gale Research, 1983): 517-520.

Janine Pommy Vega (1942-)

Vega was the friend and associate of numerous Beat writers, especially Herbert Huncke. Her life is very much affected by tragic death. *Poems to Fernando* (San Francisco: City Lights, 1968) chronicles the phases in the author's response to the death of her husband, Peruvian painter Fernando Vega. *Journal of a Hermit* (Cherry Valley, NY: Cherry Valley Editions, 1974) was later revised as *Journal of a Hermit* + (Cherry Valley, NY: Cherry Valley Editions, 1979). This collection, like *Morning Passage* (New York: Telephone Books, 1976), draws from her experience in traveling to Peru and Colombia. *Here at the Door* (New York: Zonepress, 1978) is written in response to the death of her father. *The Bard Owl* (New York: Kulchur Foundation, 1980) collects poems from previous volumes and from various literary magazines. See R'lene H. Dahlberg, "Janine Pommy Vega," in *The Beats: Literary Bohemians in Postwar America*, ed. Ann Charters (Detroit: Gale Research, 1983): 520-527. See also "Janine Pommy Vega: Lyric Adventurer," in Brenda Knight, ed., *The Women of the Beat Generation* (Berkeley, CA: Conari Press, 1996): 223-240. On the companion cassette tapes to *The Women of the Beat Generation* (San Bruno, CA: Audio Literature, 1996), Janine Pommy Vega reads several pieces.

Anne Waldman (1945-)

Waldman is younger than most Beat poets, yet she is closely connected to many Beat writers because of her work as editor, administrator, and writer. As editor, she has produced *The Beat Book* (Boston: Shambhala, 1996), which presents extended selections from fourteen writers and offers background and bibliographical information, *Out of This World: An Anthology of Writing from the Saint Mark's Poetry Project 1966-1991* (New York: Crown, 1992), *The World Anthology* (Indianapolis: Bobbs-Merrill, 1970), and *Another World* (New York: Bobbs-Merrill, 1971). In addition (with Andrew

Schelling) Waldman has edited *Disembodied Poetics, Annals of the Jack Kerouac School* (Albuquerque: University of New Mexico Press, 1994) and (with Marilyn Webb) *Talking Poetics from Naropa Institute*, 2 volumes (Boulder: Shambhala, 1978). With Ron Padgett, she has led Full Court Press, and with Lewis Warsh, she has edited *Angel Hair* and Angel Hair Books. As administrator, she is co-founder and co-director of the Jack Kerouac School of Disembodied Poetics, where she co-organized the 1982 conference on the occasion of the twenty-fifth anniversary of the publication of *On the Road*. Tapes of the events and readings at the 1982 conference are available from the Naropa Institute. Copies of some of the tapes are part of the Charters Collection, held at the Berg Collection at the New York Public Library. Some tapes are also held at the Bancroft Library at the University of California, Berkeley. For ten years at the Poetry Project at St. Mark's Church in New York City, Waldman organized readings that often featured Beat artists, and at the twenty-fifth anniversary reading of "Howl" at Columbia University, Waldman introduced Allen Ginsberg. She has written more than thirty pamphlets and books of poems, including *Kill or Cure* (New York: Penguin Books, 1994), *Iovis: All Is Full of Jove* (Minneapolis: Coffee House Press, 1993), and *Helping the Dreamer: New and Selected Poems 1966-1988* (Minneapolis: Coffee House Press, 1989). Waldman's work is included in Donald Allen and George F. Butterick, eds., *The Postmoderns: The New American Poetry Revised* (New York: Grove Press, 1982), Carole Tonkinson, ed., *Big Sky Mind* (New York: Riverhead Books, 1995), David Kherdian, ed., *Beat Voices* (New York: Henry Holt, 1995), and Ann Charters, ed., *The Portable Beat Reader* (New York: Viking, 1992). See Ann Charters, "Anne Waldman," in *The Beats: Literary Bohemians in Postwar America*, ed. Ann Charters (Detroit: Gale Research, 1983): 528-533, which provides helpful references. See "Anne Waldman: Fast-Speaking Woman," in Brenda Knight, ed., *The Women of the Beat Generation* (Berkeley, CA: Conari, 1996): 286-307. On the companion cassette tapes to *The Women of the Beat Generation* (San Bruno, CA: Audio Literature, 1996), Waldman reads from "Fast Speaking Woman" and "I Am the Guard!" A video *Anne Waldman* (Los Angeles: Lannan Foundation, 1991) captures her reading on 11 Mar. 1991 and offers an interview with Lewis MacAdams. One can also see Waldman on *The New York Beat Generation Show: Volume Two: Women and the Beats* (New York: Thin Air Video, 1995) and *The Beat Generation: Volume One: Another Lost Generation: The*

Origin of the Beats (New York: Thin Air Video, 1995). On Maria Beatty, *Gang of Souls* (New York: Mystic Fire Video, 1988), Waldman also appears, and she may be seen on *Fried Shoes Cooked Diamonds* (New York: Mystic Fire Video, 1995). *Recent Readings/NY, Volume 2: Waldman-Vicuña* (New York: Thin Air Video, 1996) pairs Waldman with Cecilia Vicuña on a single tape.

Alan Watts (1915-1973)

Watts helped popularize Buddhism in the United States, especially among the young. The Beats admired his writings and attended his presentations. Watts wrote prolifically, but his article "Beat Zen Square Zen and Zen" had the greatest influence on the Beats. The esssay appeared originally in *Chicago Review* (Summer 1958) and was published subsequently by City Lights (1959). The essay is reprinted in Ann Charters, ed., *The Portable Beat Reader* (New York: Viking Penguin, 1992). *The Way of Zen* (New York: Pantheon, 1957) extended Watts' influence over the perception and understanding of Buddhism in the West. Dan McLeod, "Alan Watts," in *The Beats: Literary Bohemians in Postwar America* (Detroit: Gale Research, 1983): 534-539 unfolds Watts' connection to the Beats well and provides valuable references. See Theodore Roszak, *The Making of a Counter Culture* (Garden City, NY: Doubleday, 1969): 124-154; see also Robert S. Ellwood, Jr., *Alternative Altars: Unconventional and Eastern Spirituality in America* (Chicago: University of Chicago Press, 1979): 136-166.

Lew Welch (1926-1971)

Welch's life was plagued by mental breakdowns and alcoholism. He was torn between two worlds, one the workaday world that could provide the money to live, the other an expressive and creative existence that could provide artistic satisfaction. In Jack Kerouac's *Big Sur*, Welch is depicted as Dave Wain. *Trip Trap: Haiku Along the Road from San Francisco to New York, 1959* (Bolinas, CA: Grey Fox Press, 1973) is a collection of haiku by Welch, Kerouac, and Albert Saijo written during a trip from San Francisco to New York in the fall of 1959. *I Remain: The Letters of Lew Welch and the Correspondence of His Friends*, 2 volumes (Bolinas, CA: Grey Fox Press, 1980) chronicles Welch's ongoing struggle. The collection includes Welch's letters and letters by Gary Snyder, Welch's mother, and Philip Whalen. Welch is mostly the author of poetry, but there is also *I, Leo, An Unfinished Novel* (Bolinas, CA: Grey Fox Press, 1977), and a biography of Gertrude Stein, *How I Read Gertrude Stein* (Bolinas, CA: Grey Fox Press, 1996), a product of his senior thesis from Reed College. An excellent source is Donald Allen, ed., *Ring of Bone: Collected Poems 1950-1971* (Bolinas, CA: Grey Fox Press, 1973). Welch's work is included in Donald Allen, ed., *The New American Poetry* (New York: Grove Press, 1960), Donald Allen and George F. Butterick, eds., *The Postmoderns: The New American Poetry Revised* (New York: Grove Press, 1982), Carole Tonkinson, ed., *Big Sky Mind* (New York: Riverhead Books, 1995), Ann Charters, ed., *The Portable Beat Reader* (New York: Viking Penguin, 1992), Elias Wilentz, ed., *The Beat Scene* (New York: Corinth Books, 1960), and Anne Waldman, ed., *The Beat Book* (Boston: Shambhala, 1996). Interviews with Welch are in David Meltzer, ed., *The San Francisco Poets* (New York: Ballantine Books, 1971), which was later published as *Golden Gate* (San Francisco: Wingbow, 1976): 155-193; and Donald Allen, ed., *On Bread and Poetry, a Panel Discussion with Gary Snyder, Lew Welch, and Philip Whalen* (Bolinas, CA: Grey Fox Press, 1977). A stylized narrative that nevertheless serves well as a biography of Welch and provides an impression of his milieu and the circumstances that led to Welch's apparent suicide is Aram Saroyan, *Genesis Angels: The Saga of Lew Welch and the Beat Generation* (New York: William Morrow, 1979). See Sam Charters, "Lew Welch," in *The Beats: Literary Bohemians in Postwar America*, ed. Ann Charters (Detroit: Gale Research, 1983): 539-553, which includes valuable references and photos. Welch reads from "Hermit Poems" on *Howls, Raps, and Roars: Recordings from the San Francisco Poetry Renaissance* (Berkeley, CA: Fantasy Records, 1993).

Philip Whalen (1923-   )

Whalen, Gary Snyder, and Lew Welch were friends at Reed College and their interrelationships persisted as their literary careers developed. See some of Whalen's letters in *I Remain: The Letters of Lew Welch and the Correspondence of His Friends*, 2 volumes (Bolinas, CA: Grey Fox Press, 1980). Whalen was one of five readers at the Six Gallery reading hosted by Kenneth Rexroth on October 7, 1955 in San Francisco. In Jack Kerouac's *The Dharma Bums* (1958), Whalen is depicted as Warren Coughlin. Whalen's first full-length book *Like I Say* (New York: Totem Press/Corinth Books, 1960) refers directly to many figures associated with the Beats, including Wieners, Olson, Creeley, McClure, Ginsberg, and Kerouac. While Whalen's work embodies the open forms, the quest for identity, and the necessity of naked honesty found in many Beat writers, he is not political or polemical in the manner of Snyder or Ginsberg. Most of his works are collections of poems, but he has written two novels: *You Didn't Even Try* (New York: Coyote, 1967) and *Imaginary Speeches for a Brazen Head* (Los Angeles: Black Sparrow Press, 1972). Some of Whalen's books of poetry are *On Bear's Head: Selected Poems* (New York: Harcourt, Brace & World/Coyote, 1969), *Severance Pay: Poems 1967-1969* (San Francisco: Four Seasons Foundation, 1970), *The Kindness of Strangers: Poems, 1969-1974* (Bolinas, CA: Four Seasons Foundation, 1976), *Decompressions: Selected Poems* (Bolinas, CA: Grey Fox Press, 1977), and *Enough Said: Fluctat Nec Mergitur: Poems 1974-1979* (San Francisco: Grey Fox Press, 1980). See Whalen's work in Donald Allen, ed., *The New American Poetry* (New York: Grove Press, 1960), Donald Allen and George F. Butterick, eds., *The Postmoderns: The New American Poetry Revised* (New York: Grove Press, 1982), Carole Tonkinson, ed., *Big Sky Mind* (New York: Riverhead Books, 1995), Ann Charters, ed., *The Portable Beat Reader* (New York: Viking, 1992), Elias Wilentz, ed., *The Beat Scene* (New York: Corinth Books, 1960), David Kherdian, ed., *Beat Voices* (New York: Henry Holt, 1995), and Anne Waldman, ed., *The Beat Book* (Boston: Shambhala, 1996). See also Whalen, "'Goldberg Is Waiting'; or, P. W.; His Magic Education as a Poet," in Donald Allen and Warren Tallman, eds., *The Poetics of the New American Poetry* (New York: Grove Press, 1973): 453-460. Interviews with Whalen may be found in Donald Allen, ed., *On Bread and Poetry: A Panel Discussion with Gary Snyder, Lew Welch, and Philip Whalen* (Bolinas, CA: Grey Fox Press, 1977) and Donald Allen, ed., *Off the Wall: Interviews with Philip Whalen* (Bolinas, CA: Four Seasons Foundation, 1978). Some books offering commentary and interpretation are Michael Davidson, *The San Francisco Renaissance* (New

York: Cambridge University Press, 1989): 95-124, Warren French, *The San Francisco Poetry Renaissance, 1955-1960* (Boston: Twayne, 1991): 71-73, Paul Christensen, "Philip Whalen," in *The Beats: Literary Bohemians in Postwar America*, ed. Ann Charters (Detroit: Gale Research, 1983): 554-572, David Kherdian, ed., *Six San Francisco Poets* (Fresno, CA: Giligia Press, 1965): 29-30, Steven Watson, "Philip Whalen," in *The Birth of the Beat Generation* (New York: Pantheon, 1995): 217-219, and Geoffrey Thurley, "The Development of the New Language: Michael McClure, Philip Whalen, and Gregory Corso," in *The Beats: Essays in Criticism* (Jefferson, NC: McFarland, 1981): 165-180. Whalen reads from "The Art of Literature" on *Howls, Raps, and Roars: Recordings from the San Francisco Poetry Renaissance* (Berkeley, CA: Fantasy Records, 1993). See a photo of Whalen in Ann Charters, *Beats and Company* (Garden City, NY: Doubleday, 1986): 70. *Recent Readings/NY: Volume 13 Whalen-Godfrey* (New York: Thin Air Video, 1996) combines presentations by Whalen and John Godfrey.

John Wieners (1934-   )

Wieners was the editor of *Measure*, a journal which published mostly Black Mountain poets. Wieners is noteworthy for *The Hotel Wentley Poems* (San Francisco: Auerhahn Press, 1958); a revised edition was later released (San Francisco: Dave Haselwood, 1965). These poems are despairing and confessional as they describe the sordid underworld. *Pressed Wafer* (Buffalo, NY: Gallery Upstairs Press, 1967) is homoerotic; *Nerves* (New York: Cape Goliard/Grossman, 1970) may be his finest work; some readers appreciate the notebook style of *Behind the State Capitol, or Cincinnati Pike* (Boston: Good Gay Poets, 1975). See George F. Butterick, "John Wieners: A Checklist," *Athanor* (Summer/Fall 1973): 53-63 for bibliographical data. See Wieners' writing in Donald Allen, ed., *The New American Poetry* (New York: Grove Press, 1960), Donald Allen and George F. Butterick, eds., *The Postmoderns: The New American Poetry Revised* (New York: Grove Press, 1982), Ann Charters, ed., *The Portable Beat Reader* (New York: Viking, 1992), and Anne Waldman, ed., *The Beat Book* (Boston: Shambhala, 1996). See Wieners, "The Address of the Watchman to the Night," in Donald Allen and Warren Tallman, eds.,

The Poetics of the New American Poetry (New York: Grove Press, 1973): 351-352. Chapters on Wieners are in Neeli Cherkovski, *Whitman's Wild Children* (Venice, CA: Lapis Press, 1988) and Lita Hornick, *Night Flight* (New York: The Kulchur Foundation, 1982). Wieners reads "A Poem for Cocksuckers" and "A Poem for the Old Man" on *Howls, Raps, and Roars: Recordings from the San Francisco Poetry Renaissance* (Berkeley, CA: Fantasy Records, 1993).

William Carlos Williams (1883-1963)

Like Charles Olson, Ezra Pound, Kenneth Rexroth, and Robert Duncan, William Carlos Williams was a predecessor of the Beats. Williams helped shape the alternative poetics that the Beats used as a springboard for innovations. *In the American Grain* (New York: Boni, 1925) is a collection of essays revealing Williams' pursuit of a new tradition for American poetry free of European models. Williams had early success with *Poems* (1909), *Al Que Quiere* (1917), *Kora in Hell* (1920), *Sour Grapes* (1921), and *Spring and All* (1923), but he suffered some loss of public attention with *Go Go* (1923). *Collected Poems: 1921-1931* appeared in 1934. *White Mule* (1937), *In the Money* (1940), and *The Build-Up* (1952) are about Williams' wife. A comprehensive edition *The Complete Collected Poems of William Carlos Williams* (New York: New Directions, 1938) gathers together Williams' prolific poetic production. In the following years, Williams continued to produce, writing *The Wedge* (1944), *The Desert Music and Other Poems* (1954), *Journey to Love* (1955), and *Pictures from Brueghel and Other Poems* (1962). His later years were devoted to *Paterson* (1946-1958). Collections of stories include *The Knife of the Times and Other Stories* (1932) and *Life along the Passaic River* (1938). The essays "The Poem as a Field of Action" and "On Measure – Statement for Cid Corman" are included in *The Selected Essays of William Carlos Williams* (1954). Williams and Ginsberg had a special friendship. Williams wrote introductions for *Howl and Other Poems* (1956) and *Empty Mirror* (1961). In *Paterson*, Williams includes letters from Ginsberg, and through the friendship with Ginsberg, Williams had occasion to meet Kerouac, Corso, and Orlovsky. In Jack Kerouac's *Desolation Angels*, Williams appears as himself in chapter 43 of the section "Passing through New York." Ginsberg dedicates a poem "To W. C. W." in *Indian Journals* to

Williams and comments on Williams on the *Voices and Visions* video about Williams, which is now available from Mystic Fire Video. For correspondence, see *The Selected Letters of William Carlos Williams*, ed. John C. Thirwall (New York: McDowell Obolensky, 1957); for bibliographical data, see Emily Mitchell Wallace, *A Bibliography of William Carlos Williams* (Middletown, CT: Wesleyan University Press, 1968). See Paul Christensen, "William Carlos Williams," in *The Beats: Literary Bohemians in Postwar America*, ed. Ann Charters (Detroit: Gale Research, 1983): 583-590. J. Hillis Miller, ed., *William Carlos Williams: A Collection of Critical Essays* (Englewood Cliffs, NJ: Prentice-Hall, 1966) is useful for students.

Chapter 7

TOPICS
FOR INVESTIGATION
AND WRITING

*There are no barriers to poetry or prophecy; by their
nature they are barrier-breakers, bursts of perception,
lines into infinity.*
— Lenore Kandel

The topics provided here are intentionally very broad and meant
to be suggestive. The narrowing or limiting of topics is the
responsibility of writers, who must evaluate the length of their
assignments and the requirements for the depth of research. If the
question asks how the works of Kerouac, Ginsberg, Burroughs, and
others represent innovations in form, then one might narrow a
written response to a consideration of only Burroughs, perhaps also
limiting consideration to *Naked Lunch*, or a particular section in
Naked Lunch. In addition, the range of topics here is by no means
exhaustive, and hundreds more might be added. Perhaps the variety
in this list will stimulate writers to invent their own approaches.

321

The Problem of Censorship

1. How has the fight for literary freedom been led by artists associated with the Beat Generation? Consider publishers, editors, and writers like Lawrence Ferlinghetti, Allen Ginsberg, William S. Burroughs, Michael McClure, Ed Sanders, Lenore Kandel, Paul Carroll, and others.

2. In attacking the work of Beat artists, to what have the censors objected? To what extent are their objections valid? What goals and designs do the censors have for their communities? If the objections of the censors are put into effect, what consequences may follow for artists and the societies in which they create?

3. How have the efforts of Beat artists created change in terms of what is permissible? What was permissible when the Beats first started to publish their material? What is permissible now that fifty years of Beat expression have passed? What remains prohibited?

The Problem of Marginalization

4. What forces have kept the Beats as a whole out of the mainstream of literary publication? What have literary critics done to ostracize the Beats? To what degree have the Beats, with the passage of time, been able to win a place among mainstream publishers and critics?

5. Within the Beats, which artists have been inadequately acknowledged for their contributions? What factors account for the marginalization of artists within the Beat group? How have the editors of anthologies created the problem of marginalization, and to what extent have they fought against it?

6. To what degree is the Beat artist in need of being an outsider? How does the reaction of publishers, editors, and critics against Beats provide strength for the existence, survival, and creativity of the Beats?

The Quest for Innovation

7. How do the works of Kerouac, Ginsberg, Burroughs, and others represent innovations in theme? Which works reveal the introduction of new ideas rarely associated with American literature previously?

8. How do the works of Kerouac, Ginsberg, Burroughs, and others represent innovations in form? Which works reveal techniques such as spontaneous composition, jazz composition, non-narrative novels, cut-ups, and other literary innovations?

9. To what degree are the literary innovations of the Beats a success? To what degree are these innovations failures?

Drugs and Alcohol

10. What variety of opinions and behaviors exists in the Beat community with respect to drugs and alcohol? How do the lives of figures like Ginsberg, Burroughs, Kerouac, Leary, Cassady, Welch, and Corso reflect on the advantages and disadvantages of drugs and alcohol?

11. In Beat literature, how is the user of drugs and alcohol depicted? Does Beat literature present a well-rounded view of the use of drugs and alcohol, or is the view narrow and limited?

12. How do Beat artists use the idea of drug and alcohol consumption and dependency as a metaphor? What is the message behind the metaphor?

Travel

13. How do the writers of the Beat Generation contribute to the literature of the road? What works are based on journeys along the

road, and what do literary characters hope to find at the end of the road?

14. To what extent does Beat literature create a global perspective? What works go beyond the United States to give impressions of Latin America, Europe, Africa, the Far East, and other locations? Consider the travels of Ferlinghetti, Ginsberg, Burroughs, Snyder, and others.

15. How does the road in Beat literature reflect inspiration and freedom on one hand and desperation and loneliness on the other?

Cats and Chicks

16. What standards for male behavior are exemplified by Beat writers? Consider, among other ideas, a man's place in a family, his love relationships, and his sources of satisfaction. How do writers like Corso, Snyder, Ferlinghetti, Ginsberg, Kerouac, Burroughs, and others exemplify male behavior?

17. A principal objection to the Beat movement has been that women were not treated as equals. How do the lives and literature of the Beat Generation reveal that women were treated unfairly?

18. How do artists like Carolyn Cassady, Joyce Johnson, Hettie Jones, Jan Kerouac, Anne Waldman, Joanne Kyger, Bobbie Louise Hawkins, Diane DiPrima, and other women suffer from being seen first as women and second as individual artists?

Celebrating America

19. Although the Beats are often remembered for their challenging of the establishment in America and the world, the Beats often celebrated the richness of the American experience. How do the writings of Kerouac, Snyder, Johnson, and others demonstrate the enthusiasm of the Beat artists for their land and people?

20. Who are the heroes of the Beats? What are the achievements of these heroes? How are the heroes honored in Beat literature?

21. What geographical locations are sources of inspiration and pleasure for the Beats? How is this satisfaction revealed in the works of Beat artists?

Questioning and Challenging Authority

22. Which leaders and authority figures are attacked in Beat literature? For example, how do Ginsberg and Burroughs attack drug enforcement officials? How does Ferlinghetti attack particular politicians?

23. How do writers like Allen Ginsberg and Kenneth Rexroth use topical allusions in order to call attention to the abuses carried out by authority figures?

24. How do Beat writers challenge the practices of authorities with respect to the environment, nuclear weapons, violations of human rights, invasions of privacy, and other issues?

Predecessors and Influences

25. Which writers have had the greatest influence on the Beats? Consider the influences not only of Wolfe, Olson, Williams, Rexroth, and Duncan, but also of Dostoyevsky, Whitman, Melville, Rimbaud, Shakespeare, and others.

26. What contemporary artists have a debt to the Beats? For example, who are the members of the so-called second generation of Beats, and how do they represent the Beat tradition?

27. How have visual and musical artists influenced the writers of the Beat generation? How have artists like Joans, Ferlinghetti, and Ginsberg shown strengths as both literary and visual artists? How

have writers like Kerouac, Ferlinghetti, Patchen, and Rexroth combined music with their work?

The Literary Tradition

28. Though often known as rebels, to what degree are the Beats part
of literary tradition? What do the Beats have in common with
previous movements of nonconformity and rebellion in literature
and art? To what degree is Beat rebellion a predictable response to
the literary movements that immediately preceded the Beats?

29. How do the works of William Burroughs represent an extension
and furthering of the ideas of Joyce and Proust?

30. How do the Beats reveal a carrying on of the tradition of the
Romantics? For example, what is Corso's debt to Shelley? What is
Ginsberg's debt to Blake?

Perceptions of the Future

31. What is William Burroughs' vision of the future? To what degree
is his vision accurate, and to what degree is it flawed?

32. In fifty years, will the Beats still be read? How will they be seen
by historians and literary historians?

33. If the Beats have taken literature forward in terms of form and
theme, what innovations are likely to follow and who will be the
artists to bring about such innovations?

A Literature of Music

34. Take a passage or section from a work by Kerouac and explicate
it as a musical composition.

35. What musical artists (real or fictional) are paid tribute in Beat literature? What makes these musicians especially beautiful and meaningful?

36. How well do the recordings of Beat literary artists in combination with musical artists reveal interdisciplinary performance? How successful are artists like Rexroth, Patchen, Ferlinghetti, Ginsberg, and Kerouac when they combine music with the written word?

The Intensity of Experience

37. In Jack Kerouac's *On the Road*, Sal says, "[T]he only people for me are the mad ones, the ones who are mad to live, mad to talk, mad to be saved, desirous of everything at the same time, the ones who never yawn or say a commonplace thing, but burn, burn, burn like fabulous yellow roman candles exploding like spiders across the stars and in the middle you see the blue centerlight pop and everybody goes 'Awww!'" Which characters in *On the Road* live up to Sal's description?

38. In "Howl," Allen Ginsberg refers to "angelheaded hipsters burning for the ancient heavenly connection to the starry dynamo in the machinery of night." How do the details of "Howl" by Allen Ginsberg reveal lives of frantic intensity?

39. In "Dog," Lawrence Ferlinghetti refers to "touching and tasting and testing everything/ investigating everything." How is the dog an example of this intensity in life?

Sympathy and Tenderness

40. When Steve Allen asked Jack Kerouac to explain what it means to be Beat, Kerouac answered, "Sympathetic." How does this word apply to examples of Beat literature you know?

41. How does the term "tenderness" apply to the lives and literature of the Beat Generation?

42. How do the Beats and the people in their literature fail to be sympathetic and tender?

Food and Eating

43. Who are the big eaters among the Beats? What descriptions of food and eating are especially impressive?

44. Who among the Beats abstains from eating? What passages refer to the minimalization, absence, or avoidance of food?

45. What makes a restaurant, diner, or other food service Beat? Which descriptions of Beat restaurants are especially impressive?

The Critical Reception and the Literary Reputation

46. Which literary critics were antagonistic to the Beats in the 1950's and 1960's? What comments were made by writers like Norman Podhoretz, Diana Trilling, John Ciardi, and others?

47. Which literary critics were receptive to the Beats in the 1950's and 1960's? What comments were made by Mary McCarthy, Marshall McLuhan, M. L. Rosenthal, and others?

48. How has appreciation of the Beats changed over the course of fifty years? What is the literary reputation of the Beats today?

Valiant Editors

49. How are the Beats indebted to Donald Allen for his role as editor and publisher?

50. What risks were taken by editors and publishers like Lawrence Ferlinghetti, Ed Sanders, Paul Carroll, Irving Rosenthal, LeRoi

Jones, Diane DiPrima, and others? How well did these individuals overcome the obstacles that faced them?

51. Who are the Beat editors today? What decisions characterize the work of Ann Charters, Anne Waldman, David Kherdian, and others?

Beat Theater

52. What is the history of the production of Michael McClure's *The Beard*?

53. Who were the directors and producers who made Beat theater possible through their support and cooperation? For example, how did Jay and Fran Landesman contribute? What were the roles of Diane DiPrima and LeRoi Jones?

54. What plays dramatize the life and times of the Beats?

Environmental Awareness

55. How have writers like Allen Ginsberg, Gary Snyder, and Michael McClure incorporated environmental awareness into their writings?

56. How do the Beats reveal their awareness of the sea, mountains, and forests? What descriptions are especially impressive?

57. What is the role of weather conditions in Beat literature? Are descriptions of weather metaphoric? If so, how?

The Geography of the Beats

58. What areas of New York were the territories of the Beats? How do places like Greenwich Village, Times Square, the upper West Side, and other areas play roles in Beat literature?

59. How does the poetry of the San Francisco Renaissance present a literary tour of San Francisco, North Beach, and other West Coast Beat sites?

60. How do places like New Orleans, Mexico City, and Tangier fit into the experience of William Burroughs and other Beats?

Beats in Film, in Photos, and on Video

61. How do photographers like Ann Charters, Allen Ginsberg, Chris Felver, Fred McDarrah, and others characterize the Beats?

62. What are some of the Hollywood characterizations of the Beats? How have the characterizations changed as decades have passed?

63. What roles have Beats William S. Burroughs, Allen Ginsberg, Gregory Corso, and others played in film and video productions?

Performance Art

64. Who were the readers at the Six Gallery on October 7, 1955, and how did their work represent performance art?

65. Choose several of the routines typically done live by William S. Burroughs, and review them as performance pieces.

66. What are the contributions of Anne Waldman to the art of performance?

Separating Legend from Fact

67. How did *Life*, *Time*, and other sources create popular views of the Beats?

68. In *Memoirs of a Beatnik*, how does Diane DiPrima reveal the contrast between misconceptions and realities about the Beats?

69. How was it painful for Kerouac and other Beats to steer a course between the legend of the Beats and the reality of their serious dedication to literary art?

NAME AND AUTHOR INDEX

333

ABOUT THE AUTHOR

William Lawlor is Professor of English at the University of Wisconsin – Stevens Point, where he has taught since 1978. He has written various articles about the Beats for reference texts and encyclopedias. The National Endowment for the Humanities awarded him a Summer Study Grant to further his work on the Beats, and during the 1997-1998 academic year, he was a Visiting Fellow at the Institute for Research in the Humanities at the University of Wisconsin – Madison.